SUICIDE RESEARCH:
SELECTED READINGS
Volume 11

November 2013 – April 2014

A. Novic, E. Barker, K. Kõlves, D. De Leo

Australian Institute for Suicide Research and Prevention

Griffith
UNIVERSITY

WHO Collaborating Centre for
Research and Training in Suicide Prevention

National Centre of Excellence in Suicide Prevention

First published in 2014
Australian Academic Press
18 Victor Russell Drive,
Samford QLD 4520, Australia
Australia
www.australianacademicpress.com.au

ISBN: 9781922117311

Book and cover design by Maria Biaggini — The Letter Tree.

Contents

Foreword

This volume contains quotations from internationally peer-reviewed suicide research published during the semester November 2013 – April 2014; it is the eleventh of a series produced biannually by our Institute with the aim of assisting the Commonwealth Department of Health in being constantly updated on new evidences from the scientific community.

As usual, the initial section of the volume collects a number of publications that could have particular relevance for the Australian people in terms of potential applicability. These publications are accompanied by a short comment from us, and an explanation of the motives that justify why we have considered of interest the implementation of studies' findings in the Australian context. An introductory part provides the rationale and the methodology followed in the identification of papers.

The central part of the volume represents a selection of research articles of particular significance; their abstracts are reported *in extenso*, underlining our invitation at reading those papers in full text: they represent a remarkable advancement of suicide research knowledge.

The last section reports all items retrievable from major electronic databases. We have catalogued them on the basis of their prevailing reference to fatal and non-fatal suicidal behaviours, with various sub-headings (e.g. epidemiology, risk factors, etc). The deriving list guarantees a level of completeness superior to any individual system; it can constitute a useful tool for all those interested in a quick update of what is most recently published on the topic.

Our intent was to make suicide research more approachable to non-specialists, and in the meantime provide an opportunity for a *vademecum* of quotations credible also at the professional level. A compilation such as the one that we provide here is not easily obtainable from usual sources and can save a considerable amount of time to readers. We believe that our effort in this direction may be an appropriate interpretation of one of the technical support roles to the Government that the new status of National Centre of Excellence in Suicide Prevention — which has deeply honoured our commitment —entails for us.

The significant growth of our centre, the Australian Institute for Suicide Research and Prevention, and its influential function, both nationally and internationally, in the fight against suicide, could not happen without the constant support of Queensland Health and Griffith University. We hope that our passionate dedication to the cause of suicide prevention may compensate their continuing trust in our work.

Diego De Leo, DSc
Director, Australian Institute for Suicide Research and Prevention

Acknowledgments

This report has been produced by the Australian Institute for Suicide Research and Prevention, WHO Collaborating Centre for Research and Training in Suicide Prevention and National Centre of Excellence in Suicide Prevention. The assistance of the Commonwealth Department of Health in the funding of this report is gratefully acknowledged.

Introduction

Context

Suicide places a substantial burden on individuals, communities and society in terms of emotional, economic and health care costs. In Australia, about 2000 people die from suicide every year, a death rate well in excess of transport-related mortality. At the time of preparing this volume, the latest available statistics released by the Australian Bureau of Statistics1 indicated that, in 2012, 2,535 deaths by suicide were registered in Australia, representing an age-standardized rate of 11.2 per 100,000.

Further, a study on mortality in Australia for the years 1997–2001 found that suicide was the leading cause of avoidable mortality in the 25–44 year age group, for both males (29.5%) and females (16.7%), while in the age group 15–24 suicide accounted for almost a third of deaths due to avoidable mortality[2]. In 2003, self-inflicted injuries were responsible for 27% of the total injury burden in Australia, leading to an estimated 49,379 years of life lost (YLL) due to premature mortality, with the greatest burdens observed in men aged 25–64[3].

Despite the estimated mortality, the prevalence of suicide and self-harming behaviour in particular remains difficult to gauge due to the often secretive nature of these acts. Indeed, ABS has acknowledged the difficulties in obtaining reliable data for suicides in the past few years[4, 5]. Without a clear understanding of the scope of suicidal behaviours and the range of interventions available, the opportunity to implement effective initiatives is reduced. Further, it is important that suicide prevention policies are developed on the foundation of evidence-based empirical research, especially as the quality and validity of the available information may be misleading or inaccurate. Additionally, the social and economic impact of suicide underlines the importance of appropriate research-based prevention strategies, addressing not only significant direct costs on health system and lost productivity, but also the emotional suffering for families and communities.

The Australian Institute for Suicide Research and Prevention (AISRAP) has, through the years, gained an international reputation as one of the leading research institutions in the field of suicide prevention. The most important recognition came via the designation as a World Health Organization (WHO) Collaborating Centre in 2005. In 2008, the Commonwealth Department of Health appointed AISRAP as the National Centre of Excellence in Suicide Prevention. This latter recognition awards not only many years of high-quality research, but also of fruitful cooperation between the Institute and several different governmental agencies. The new role given to AISRAP will translate into an even deeper commitment to the cause of suicide prevention amongst community members of Australia.

As part of this initiative, AISRAP is committed to the creation of a databank of the recent scientific literature documenting the nature and extent of suicidal and self-harming behaviour and recommended practices in preventing and responding to these behaviours. The key output for the project is a critical bi-annual review of the national and international literature outlining recent advances and promising developments in research in suicide prevention, particularly where this can help to inform national activities. This task is not aimed at providing a critique of new researches, but rather at drawing attention to investigations that may have particular relevance to the Australian context. In doing so, we are committed to a user-friendly language, in order to render research outcomes and their interpretation accessible also to a non-expert audience.

In summary, these reviews serve three primary purposes:

1. To inform future State and Commonwealth suicide prevention policies;
2. To assist in the improvement of existing initiatives, and the development of new and innovative Australian projects for the prevention of suicidal and self-harming behaviours within the context of the Living is for Everyone (LIFE) Framework (2008);
3. To provide directions for Australian research priorities in suicidology.

The review is presented in three sections. The first contains a selection of the best articles published in the last six months internationally. For each article identified by us (see the method of chosing articles described below), the original abstract is accompanied by a brief comment explaining why we thought the study was providing an important contribution to research and why we considered its possible applicability to Australia. The second section presents the abstracts of the most relevant literature — following our criteria — collected between November 2013 and April 2014; while the final section presents a list of citations of all literature published over this time-period.

Methodology

The literature search was conducted in four phases.

Phase 1

Phase 1 consisted of weekly searches of the academic literature performed from November 2013 to April 2014. To ensure thorough coverage of the available published research, the literature was sourced using several scientific electronic databases including: Pubmed, Proquest, Scopus, Safetylit and Web of Science, using the following key words: *suicide OR suicidal OR self-harm OR self-injury OR parasuicide.*

Results from the weekly searches were downloaded and combined into one database (deleting duplicates).

Specific inclusion criteria for Phase 1 included:

- Timeliness: the article was published (either electronically or in hard-copy) between November 2013 and April 2014;
- Relevance: the article explicitly referred to fatal and/or non-fatal suicidal behaviour and related issues and/or interventions directly targeted at preventing/treating these behaviours.

- The article was written in English.

Articles about euthanasia, assisted suicide, suicide terrorist attacks, and/or book reviews, abstracts and conference presentations were excluded.

Also, articles that have been published in electronic versions (ahead of print) and therefore included in the previous volume (Volumes 1 to 10 of *Suicide Research: Selected Readings*) were excluded to avoid duplication.

Phase 2

Following an initial reading of the abstracts (retrieved in Phase 1), the list of articles was refined down to the most relevant literature. In Phase 2 articles were only included if they were published in an international, peer-reviewed journal.

In Phase 2, articles were excluded when they:

- were not particularly instructive or original
- were of a descriptive nature (e.g. a case-report)
- consisted of historical/philosophical content
- were a description of surgical reconstruction/treatment of self-inflicted injuries
- concerned biological and/or genetic interpretations of suicidal behaviour, the results of which could not be easily adoptable in the context of the LIFE Framework.

In order to minimise the potential for biased evaluations, two researchers working independently read through the full text of all articles selected to create a list of most relevant papers. This process was then duplicated by a third researcher for any articles on which consensus could not be reached.

The strength and quality of the research evidence was evaluated, based on the *Critical Appraisal Skills Programme (CASP) Appraisal Tools* published by the Public Health Resource Unit, England (2006). These tools, publically available online, consist of checklists for critically appraising systematic reviews, randomized controlled trials (RCT), qualitative research, economic evaluation studies, cohort studies, diagnostic test studies and case control studies.

Phase 3

One of the aims of this review was to identify research that is both evidence-based and of potential relevance to the Australian context. Thus, the final stage of applied methodology focused on research conducted in countries with populations or health systems sufficiently comparable to Australia. Only articles in which the full-text was available were considered. It is important to note that failure of an article to be selected for inclusion in Phase 3 does not entail any negative judgment on its 'objective' quality.

Specific inclusion criteria for Phase 3 included:

- applicability to Australia
- the paper met all criteria for scientificity (i.e., the methodology was considered sound)
- the paper represented a particularly compelling addition to the literature, which would be likely to stimulate suicide prevention initiatives and research

- inevitably, an important aspect was the importance of the journal in which the paper was published (because of the high standards that have to be met in order to obtain publication in that specific journal); priority was given to papers published in high impact factor journals
- particular attention has been paid to widen the literature horizon to include socio-logical and anthropological research that may have particular relevance to the Australian context.

After a thorough reading of these articles ('Key articles' for the considered timeframe), a written comment was produced for each article detailing:

- methodological strengths and weaknesses (e.g., sample size, validity of measurement instruments, appropriateness of analysis performed)
- practical implications of the research results to the Australian context
- suggestions for integrating research findings within the domains of the LIFE framework suicide prevention activities.

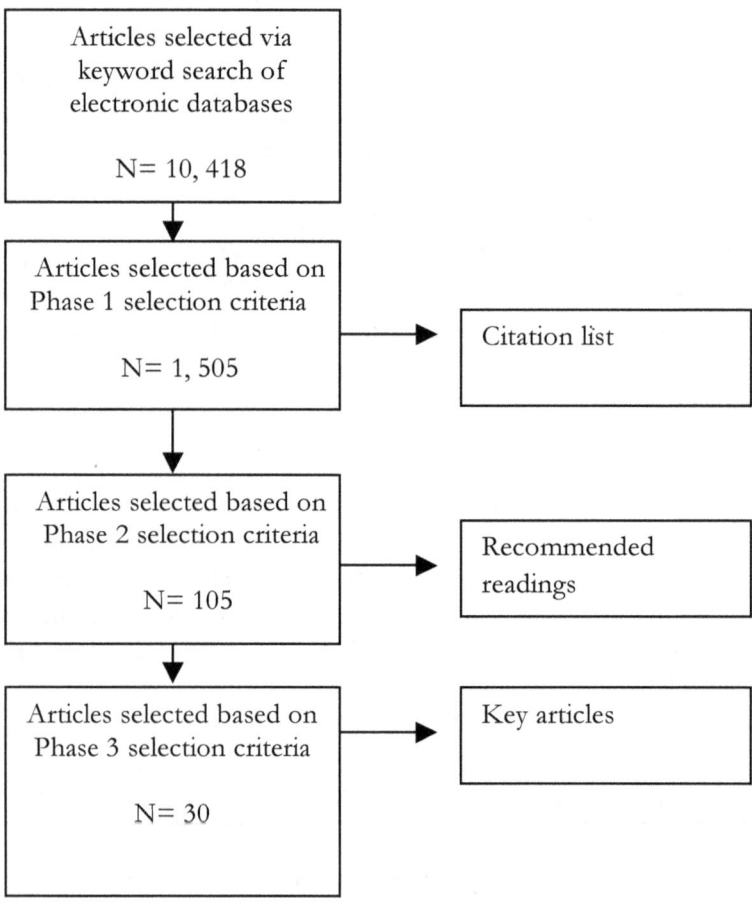

```
┌──────────────────────────┐
│   Articles selected via  │
│    keyword search of     │
│   electronic databases   │
│                          │
│       N= 10, 418         │
└──────────────────────────┘
            │
            ▼
┌──────────────────────────┐
│ Articles selected based on│      ┌─────────────────────┐
│ Phase 1 selection criteria│─────▶│    Citation list    │
│                          │      │                     │
│       N= 1, 505          │      └─────────────────────┘
└──────────────────────────┘
            │
            ▼
┌──────────────────────────┐
│ Articles selected based on│      ┌─────────────────────┐
│ Phase 2 selection criteria│─────▶│    Recommended      │
│                          │      │    readings         │
│        N= 105            │      └─────────────────────┘
└──────────────────────────┘
            │
            ▼
┌──────────────────────────┐
│ Articles selected based on│      ┌─────────────────────┐
│ Phase 3 selection criteria│─────▶│    Key articles     │
│                          │      │                     │
│        N= 30             │      └─────────────────────┘
└──────────────────────────┘
```

Figure 1

Phase 4

In the final phase of the search procedure all articles were divided into the following classifications:

- *Fatal suicidal behaviour* (epidemiology, risk and protective factors, prevention, postvention and bereavement)
- *Non-fatal suicidal/self-harming behaviours* (epidemiology, risk and protective factors, prevention, care and support)
- *Case reports* include reports of fatal and non-fatal suicidal behaviours
- *Miscellaneous* includes all research articles that could not be classified into any other category.

Allocation to these categories was not always straightforward, and where papers spanned more than one area, consensus of the research team determined which domain the article would be placed in. Within each section of the report (i.e., Key articles, Recommended readings, Citation list) articles are presented in alphabetical order by author.

Endnotes

1   Australian Bureau of Statistics (2014). *Causes of Death, Australia, 2012, Suicides.* Cat. No. 3303.0. ABS: Canberra.

2   Page A, Tobias M, Glover J, Wright C, Hetzel D, Fisher E (2006). *Australian and New Zealand Atlas of avoidable mortality.* Public Health Information Development Unit, University of Adelaide: Adelaide.

3   Begg S, Vos T, Barker B, Stevenson C, Stanley L, Lopez A (2007). *The burden of disease and injury in Australia 2003.* Australian Institute for Health and Welfare, Canberra.

4   Australian Bureau of Statistics (2009). *Causes of Death, Australia, 2007*, Technical Note 1, Cat. No. 3303.0. ABS: Canberra.

5   Australian Bureau of Statistics (2009c). *Causes of Death, Australia, 2007, Explanatory Notes.* Cat. No. 3303.0. ABS: Canberra.

Key Articles

A regional approach to understanding farmer suicide rates in Queensland

Arnautovska U, McPhedran S, De Leo D (Australia)

Social Psychiatry and Psychiatric Epidemiology 2013.

Purpose: Elevated suicide rates among farmers have been observed across a number of countries, including Australia. However, studies on farmer suicide have typically treated farmers as a homogenous group, and have predominately been focussed at a national level. This overlooks potential variability in suicide rates (and, by extension, contributory factors) within different groups of farmers (for example, different age groups), as well as across different geographical locations.

Methods: Using a unique data source, the Queensland Suicide Register, the current study examined variation in farmer suicide rates by age, sex, and location within Queensland.

Results: Although farmer suicide rates varied substantially across different regions of Queensland, no significant associations were found between rates of farmer and non-farmer suicide, or between the proportion of farmers in a region and farmer suicide rates.

Conclusions: This suggests that farmer suicide may be characterised by unique combinations of occupational and location-related effects that are likely to vary substantially within and between different regions, and provides caution against treating farmer suicide as a homogenous phenomenon. The highest rates of farmer suicide were observed among younger farmers (aged 18-34 years), highlighting a need for targeted suicide prevention initiatives for this group.

Comment

Main Findings: Elevated suicide rates among farmers are evident in various countries around the world, including Australia[1,2]. With a lack of sufficient evidence to indicate an influence of psychiatric disorders on farmer suicides, the authors have considered the compositional (e.g. demographic) and social (e.g. social norms) factors–that exist in the Australian setting–from a more community-based perspective. This approach led to the examination of farmer suicide (during the period 2000-2009) across age groups, gender, and geographic regions in Queensland (13 statistical divisions[3]) using data from the Queensland Suicide Register (QSR) and National Coronial Information System (NCIS). Farmers accounted for 2.6% of all suicides during the study period with an overall suicide rate of 28.9/100,000. Compared to the suicide rates of the non-farmer group, the overall farmer suicide rate was twice as high and significantly higher in younger (up to 34 years) and older (55+ years) farmer age groups; highest among younger males. Furthermore, farmer suicide rates across seven regions (Central West, Darling Downs, Far North, Mackay, Northern, West Moreton, and Wide Bay-Burnett) were significantly higher than rates of non-farmer suicides. There was no evidence of an association between the proportion of farmers in a region and farmer suicides in that region. There was also no observed association between farmer and non-farmer suicide rates (i.e. no 'location effect').

Implications: Incidence and rates of suicide vary across different regions of Queensland; there is no association between farmer and non-farmer suicide rates within regions (i.e. a pattern of suicide rates between farmers and non-farmers). This overshadows the assumptions that suicide among farmers should be treated collectively within a given jurisdiction. Rather, the study supports theories regarding the role of specific compositional factors in farmer suicide. Specific risk and protective factors (e.g. the impact of weather conditions on produce and belonging to a broader farming community) may apply differently to farmers depending on their location. High suicide rates among farmers should be viewed as a combination of both location and occupation effects, which vary considerably between regions. Furthermore, prevention strategies for younger males are advocated – with high rates of suicide among younger farmers suggested to be a reflection of their job position (e.g. farm labourers) and its vulnerabilities (e.g. job insecurity during times of hardship). Differences in the level of income and debt between farming and other non-farming occupations (farmers generally have a lower yearly income and greater household debt[4]) support the notion of potential vulnerabilities arising during time of financial hardship. Young people may yet be attempting to establish themselves within the agricultural industry, with less experience in dealing with the region-specific adversities that may arise during their employment.

Endnotes

1. Page AN, Frager LJ (2002). Suicide in Australian farming, 1988-1997. *Australasian Psychiatry* 36, 81-85.

2. Andersen K, Hawgood J, Klieve H, Kõlves K, De Leo D (2010). Suicide in selected occupations in Queensland: evidence from the state suicide register. *Australian and New Zealand Journal of Psychiatry* 44, 243-249.

3. Australian Bureau of Statistics (2006). *Statistical Geography volume 1–Australian Standard Geographical Classification (ASGC)* (Cat. No. 1216.0). Australian Bureau of Statistics, Canberra.

4. McPhedran S, De Leo D (2013). Risk factors for suicide among rural men: are farmers more socially isolated? *International Journal of Sociology and Social Policy* 33, 762-772.

What differentiates homeless persons who died by suicide from other suicides in Australia? A comparative analysis using a unique mortality register

Arnautovska U, Sveticic J, De Leo D (Australia)

Social Psychiatry and Psychiatric Epidemiology. Published online: 08 October 2013. doi: 10.1007/s00127-013-0774-z, 2013

Purpose: To study the incidence of suicide by homeless persons over a 20-year period, and identify demographic and clinical characteristics that distinguish these cases from those in non-homeless persons.

Methods: A comparative analysis of homeless and non-homeless persons who died by suicide between 1990 and 2009 in Queensland, Australia. Ninety-two persons (82 males and 10 females) were identified from the Queensland Suicide Register as being homeless at the time of death. Suicide rates were calculated for the second decade only due to the lack of population numbers of homeless persons in the first decade.

Results: Homeless persons had almost twice higher suicide rate than non-homeless counterparts. They were more often male, of young age, single/never married, non-Indigenous, unemployed, had at least one physical illness or other stressful life event prior to death, had drug and alcohol abuse problems, and also were more likely to have evidence for an untreated mental illness. Regression analysis showed that being unemployed, having a history of legal problems and not being diagnosed with mental illness were strongly associated with suicide among homeless persons.

Conclusions: This study is the first in Australia, and the second study internationally, to examine the characteristics of homeless people who died by suicide. Although based on a relatively small sample, the present work nonetheless carries practical implications for the development of targeted suicide prevention strategies in this peculiar population of individuals.

Comment

Main findings: A high prevalence of mental illnesses[1] and non-fatal self-harm has been reported within homeless populations, with a recent UK paper reporting that more than half (68%) of the homeless sample analysed had engaged in self-harming behaviour in the past[2]. In line with this finding, limited research has also suggested an increased risk of suicide mortality within this population[3], although little is known about the individual demographic and social factors contributing to this risk. The current paper used the Queensland Suicide Register (QSR), a comprehensive database holding records of all suicides in Queensland from 1990 onwards, to compare the rates and characteristics of 92 homeless people who had died by suicide to 11,091 non-homeless Queensland suicides. During 2000-2009, homeless persons had an overall suicide rate of 27.6 deaths per 100,000. The rate was higher in homeless males (40.9 per 100,000) than homeless females (8.9 per

100,000) and among those in the age groups 35-44 years (107.1 per 100,000) and 25-34 years (89.7 per 100,000). Homeless suicides differed significantly from non-homeless suicides on a number of variables; they were more likely to be young, unmarried, non-Indigenous, unemployed, and suffering from a physical illness, substance abuse problems or untreated mental illness. Homeless individuals were also more likely to have experienced a number of negative life events including financial, legal or child custody problems. No significant differences were found with regards to relationship issues, interpersonal/familial conflict or bereavement/loss of a loved one before death. Consistent with the distribution of overall suicide methods in Queensland[4], hanging was the most common method of suicide by homeless persons but these individuals were less likely to die by firearm, and more likely to die in an outside location.

Implications: In an area which is greatly lacking in current research[5], this paper was the first to compare homeless and non-homeless suicides in Queensland, Australia. The findings supported and expanded on previous studies[3] by not only identifying increased risk, but also particular characteristics which may contribute to death by suicide within this vulnerable group. These results may prove useful when developing screening tools specifically for the identification of at-risk homeless individuals.

Higher prevalence of untreated mental illnesses identified in homeless suicides may indicate that mental health support services are not able to reach these individuals or just that limited services are available for this group. This may be particularly true for male homeless persons, as the disparity between male and female suicide rates identified in this group was greater than is usually observed in the general population. There is a need for the development of new approaches which will allow and encourage access to targeted health care and suicide prevention services for homeless individuals.

Endnotes

1. Fazel S, Khosla V, Doll H, Geddes J (2008). The prevalence of mental disorders among the homeless in Western countries: Systematic review and meta-regression analysis. *PLoS Medicine* 5, e225.

2. Pluck G, Lee K-H, Parks RW (2013). Self-harm and homeless adults. *Crisis* 34, 363-366.

3. Haw C, Hawton K, Casey D (2006). Deliberate self-harm patients of no fixed abode: A study of characteristics and subsequent deaths in patients presenting to a general hospital. *Social Psychiatry and Psychiatric Epidemiology* 41, 918-925.

4. De Leo D, Sveticic J, Kumpula E-K (2013). *Suicide in Queensland 2008-2010: Mortality rates and related data.* Australian Institute for Suicide Research and Prevention: Brisbane.

5. Christensen RC (2013). Commentary on suicide and homelessness: What differentiates homeless persons who died by suicide from other suicides in Australia? A comparative analysis using a unique mortality registry. *Social Psychiatry and Psychiatric Epidemiology*. Published online: 9 November 2013. doi: 10.1007/s00127-013-0790-z

Suicide around public holidays

Barker E, O'Gorman J, De Leo D (Australia)

Australasian Psychiatry. Published online: 4 February 2014. doi: 10.1177/1039856213519293, 2014

Objective: To examine the frequency of suicides on holidays and special days of the year, specifically in Queensland, Australia.

Methods: We analysed data from the Queensland Suicide Register between 1990 and 2009. The days examined were: Easter, Christmas, New Year, Valentine's Day and Anzac Day. We compared suicide cases on these days with the average counts for periods before and after the days.

Results: There was a statistically significant increase in suicides on Christmas Eve and on New Year's Day. Our results are discussed in light of trends reported in the literature.

Conclusion: The beginning and end of the festive season are times when special attention is warranted for those with a heightened risk of suicide.

Comment

Main findings: Rates of suicide in Australia have been shown to fluctuate depending on the season[1] or the day of the week[2]. Previous international research has also shown differences in the prevalence of suicide around public holidays, including increases in suicide in the days following Christmas, around New Years, and during the Easter period[3]. This Australian study used data from the Queensland Suicide Register (QSR) from 1990-2009 to analyse the occurrence of suicide mortality around major public holidays and significant days including Easter, Christmas Day, New Year's Day, Anzac Day and Valentine's Day. The sample included 10,511 cases of suicide which had an accurate date of death available for analysis. The average number of suicides occurring on significant days was compared to those occurring in comparison periods in the weeks before and after the significant day to avoid any confounding effects of seasonality. Results showed a significant increase in suicides on Christmas Eve and New Years day. The high point during the Easter period was the Tuesday after Easter Monday, however the increase on this day was not statistically significant. Similarly, there were no significant differences in numbers of suicide on Anzac Day or Valentine's Day.

Implications: This paper adds to the previous international literature by analysing the risk of suicide on public holidays in Queensland, Australia. The importance of this research in the Australian context is evident when considering the different emphasis placed on certain holidays and significant days between different countries. From the perspective of suicide prevention, the findings suggest the need for family/friends and mental health workers to be aware of the potential for increased suicide risk around New Year's Day and the beginning of the Christmas period in Australia.

Endnotes

1. Cantor CH, Hickey PA, De Leo D (2000). Seasonal variation in suicide in a predominantly Caucasian tropical/subtropical region of Australia. *Psychopathology* 33, 303-306.

2. Law CK, De Leo D (2013). Seasonal differences in the day-of-the-week pattern of suicide in Queensland, Australia. *International Journal of Environmental Research and Public Health* 10, 2825-2833.

3. Jessen G, Jensen BF (1999). Postponed suicide death? Suicides around birthdays and major public holidays. *Suicide and Life-Threatening Behavior* 29, 272-283.

Are hospital services for self-harm getting better? An observational study examining management, service provision and temporal trends in England

Cooper J, Steeg S, Bennewith O, Lowe M, Gunnell D, House A, Hawton K, Kapur N (UK)

British Medical Journal Open 3, e003444, 2013

Objectives: To describe the characteristics and management of individuals attending hospital with self-harm and assess changes in management and service quality since an earlier study in 2001, a period in which national guidance has been available.

Design: Observational study.

Setting: A stratified random sample of 32 hospitals in England, UK.

Participants: 6442 individuals presenting with 7689 episodes of self-harm during a 3-month audit period between 2010 and 2011.

Outcome: Self-harm episodes, key aspects of individual management relating to psychosocial assessment and follow-up, and a 21-item measure of service quality.

Results: Overall, 56% (3583/6442) of individuals were women and 51% (3274/6442) were aged under 35 years. Hospitals varied markedly in their management. The proportion of episodes that received a psychosocial assessment by a mental health professional ranged from 22% to 88% (median 58%, IQR 48-70%); the proportion of episodes resulting in admission to general hospitals varied from 22% to 85% (median 54%, IQR 41-63%); a referral for specialist mental health follow-up was made in 11-64% of episodes (median 28%, IQR 22-38%); a referral to non-statutory services was made in 4-62% of episodes (median 15%, IQR 8-23%); 0-21% of episodes resulted in psychiatric admission (median 7%, QR 4-12%). The specialist assessment rate varied by method of harm; the median rate for self-cutting was 45% (IQR 28-63%) vs 58% (IQR 48-73%) for self-poisoning. Compared with the 2001 study, there was little difference in the proportion of episodes receiving specialist assessment; there was a significant increase in general hospital admission but a decrease in referrals for specialist mental health follow-up. However, scores on the service quality scale had increased from a median of 11.5-14.5 (a 26% increase).

Conclusions: Services for the hospital management of self-harm remain variable despite national guidelines and policy initiatives. We found no evidence for increasing levels of assessment over time but markers of service quality may have improved. This paper forms part of the study 'Variations in self-harm service delivery: an observational study examining outcomes and temporal trends'.

Comment

Main findings: Deliberate self-harm is one of the greatest predictors of eventual death by suicide[1], however, patients presenting to hospital emergency departments with self-harm are often discharged without psychosocial assessment or hospital treatment[2]. This large observational study described the characteristics and hospital management of individuals with self-harm presenting to 32 hospitals across England. These results were then compared to a previous study by Bennewith and colleagues[3] to see if hospital management of people with self-harm had improved over the last 10 years. Data was collected from each hospital on all episodes of self-harm in adults aged 18 and over occurring during a 3-month period between May 2010 and June 2011. Overall, a total of 6,442 individuals presented to hospital during the study period with 7,689 episodes of self-harm. The majority of self-harm episodes involved poisoning with drugs (79%), followed by self-cutting (14%) and other methods (6%), and 53% of cases involved alcohol consumption within the past 6 hours. Half of the patients presenting during the study period had previous episodes of self-harm (51%) and one-third (32%) of cases were currently receiving some psychiatric treatment. At presentation to hospital, psychological assessment was conducted 58% of the time and the median waiting time for these assessments was 11 hours (5 hours for those not admitted to a medical bed and 14 hours for those who were admitted). Assessment was more common in patients presenting with self-poisoning (58% of cases) than those who engaged in self-cutting (45% of cases). When compared to the earlier study in 2001-2002, self-harm episodes increased overall by 24%. There was no significant difference in the number of episodes resulting in psychosocial assessment (55% compared to 58% in present study) and the median proportion of episodes receiving specialist mental health follow-up significantly decreased by 13%. However, admissions to medical wards significantly increased from 39% to 54%. As with the previous study, the quality of service still varied considerably between individual hospitals.

Implications: Effective hospital treatment for deliberate self-harm is an important factor in the prevention of suicide[2]. The results of this large-scale study suggest that the quality of hospital service for individuals presenting with self-harm in England still varies depending on hospital, and that close to half of all presentations will not lead to psychiatric assessment. In particular, the study found that cases of self-cutting are less likely to receive psychiatric assessment, despite research showing that individuals who engage in self-cutting are at an increased risk of repeating this behaviour[4]. This finding is consistent with Australian research, finding that individuals presenting to emergency departments with drug overdose had the greatest odds of receiving immediate medical care, while self-cutters were given lower priority, and were more likely to wait 60-120 minutes for medical treatment[5]. Results suggest that it is important to continue to consider ways in which the hospital management of individuals presenting with self-harm (particularly self-cutting) may be improved.

Endnotes

1. Hawton K, Zahl D, Weatherall R (2003). Suicide following deliberate self-harm: Long-term follow-up of patients who presented to a general hospital. *British Journal of Psychiatry* 182, 537-542.

2. Gunnell D, Bennewith O, Peters TJ, House A, Hawton K (2005). The epidemiology and management of self-harm amongst adults in England. *Journal of Public Health* 27, 67-73.

3. Bennewith O, Gunnell D, Peters TJ, Hawton K, House A (2004). Variations in the hospital management of self-harm in adults in England: An observational study. *British Medical Journal* 328, 1108-1109.

4. Lilley R, Owens D, Horrocks J, House A, Noble R, Bergen H..., Kapur N (2008). Hospital care and repetition following self-harm: A multicentre comparison of self-poisoning and self-injury. *British Journal of Psychiatry* 192, 440-445.

5. Milner A, Kõlves K, Kõlves K, Gladman B, De Leo D (2013). Treatment priority for suicide ideation and behaviours at an Australian emergency department. *World Journal of Psychiatry* 3, 34-40.

Longitudinal trajectories of suicidal ideation and subsequent suicide attempts among adolescent inpatients

Czyz EK, King CA (USA)

Journal of Clinical Child and Adolescent Psychology. Published online: 30 September 2013. doi: 10.1080/15374416.2013.836454, 2013

A period of particularly high risk for suicide attempts among adolescent inpatients is within 12 months after discharge. However, little is known about longitudinal trajectories of suicidal ideation in this high-risk group and how these relate to posthospitalization suicide attempts and rehospitalizations. Our objectives were to identify these trajectories and examine their relationships with posthospitalization psychiatric crises. We also examined predictors of trajectory group membership. Participants (N = 376; ages 13-17; 72% female) were assessed at hospitalization and 3, 6, and 12 months later. Trajectory groups, and their predictors, were identified with latent class growth modeling. We used logistic regression to examine associations between trajectory groups and likelihood of suicide attempts and rehospitalization, controlling for attempt history. Three trajectory groups were identified: (a) subclinical ideators (31.6%), (b) elevated ideators with rapidly declining ideation (57.4%), and (c) chronically elevated ideators (10.9%). Adolescents in the chronically elevated ideation group had 2.29, confidence interval (CI) [1.08, 4.85], p = .03, and 4.15, CI [1.65, 10.44], p < .01, greater odds of attempting suicide and 3.23, CI [1.37, 7.69], p = .01, and 11.20, CI [4.33, 29.01], p < .001, greater odds of rehospitalization relative to rapidly declining and subclinical groups, respectively. Higher baseline hopelessness was associated with persisting suicidal ideation. Results suggest that suicidal ideation severity at hospitalization may not be an adequate marker for subsequent suicidal crises. It is important to identify adolescents vulnerable to persisting suicidal ideation, as they are at highest risk of psychiatric crises. Addressing hopelessness may facilitate faster declines in ideation after hospitalization. Results also highlight a need for consistent monitoring of these adolescents' suicidal ideation after discharge.

Comment

Main findings: The transitional period to adolescence is a sensitive developmental period with the potential for suicidal ideation and attempts. The prevalence of suicide ideation increases promptly between the ages of 12 and 17 years, while plans and attempts are shown to increase between ages of 12 and 15[1]. Psychiatrically hospitalised adolescents are particularly vulnerable as they are at high risk of repeated suicide attempts[2]. This study from US aimed to develop a better understanding of the course of suicidal ideation and the most at-risk group (for suicide attempt and psychiatric rehospitalisation) of psychiatrically hospitalised adolescents. A total of 376 adolescents were followed for a 1-year period post discharge; assessments at index hospitalisation, 3 months, 6 months, and 12 months. Three distinct groups/trajectories emerged following discharge: a subclinical suicidal ideation group (SC), an elevated and then fast declining suicidal ideation group

(E-FD), and an elevated suicidal ideation group (E). More severe baseline (index psychiatric hospitalisation) depressive symptoms, externalizing problems, and hopelessness predicted an E trajectory. Only more severe hopelessness at baseline differentiated E from E-FD. The E trajectory was also associated with a four-fold increase in the likelihood of a suicide attempt when compared with SC and were also two times more likely to make an attempt than E-FD. Similar patterns were noted for psychiatric rehospitalisation, barring an increased likelihood for E-FD when compared to SC.

Implications: Australian adolescent's (aged 12 to 17 years) presenting for mental health care show comparable proportions of suicidal ideation to older individuals (aged 18 to 30 years) attending the same service[3]. Suicidal ideation at the time of psychiatric hospitalisation may not be sufficient in highlighting suicide attempt risk. This approach might overlook potential subgroups of adolescents who may be most vulnerable to a suicidal crisis. There is a need to closely monitor persisting suicidal ideation among recently discharged psychiatric inpatients. The impact of persistent suicidal ideation may interfere with important developmental opportunities (e.g. social, emotional, and cognitive) fundamental during the adolescence period. One pathway for addressing persistent suicidal thinking in adolescents could be to reduce their sense of hopelessness. Addressing key vulnerability factors that predict the course of suicidal ideation may shorten the duration of such thoughts after hospitalisation and thus prevent continued suicidal crises.

Endnotes

1. Nock MK, Green JG, Hwang I, McLaughlin KA, Sampson NA, Zaslavsky AM, Kessler RC (2013). Prevalence, correlates, and treatment of lifetime suicidal behaviour among adolescents: Results from the National Comorbidity Survey Replication Adolescent Supplement. *JAMA Psychiatry* 70, 300-310.
2. Goldston DB, Daniel SS, Reboussin BA, Reboussin DM, Frazier PH, Harris AE (2001). Cognitive risk factors and suicide attempts among formerly hospitalised adolescents: A prospective naturalistic study. *Journal of the American Academy of Child & Adolescent Psychiatry* 40, 91-99.
3. Scott EM, Hermens DF, Naismith SL, White D, Whitwell B, Guastella AJ…, Hickie IB (2012). Thoughts of death or suicidal ideation are common in young people aged 12 to 30 years presenting for mental health care. *BMC Psychiatry* 12, 234.

Gender-specific suicide risk factors: A case-control study of individuals with major depressive disorder

Dalca IM, McGirr A, Renaud J, Turecki G (Canada)
Journal of Clinical Psychiatry 74, 1209-1216, 2013

Objective: Available information on risk for suicide completion in females is limited and often extrapolated from studies conducted in males. However, the validity of extending to females risk factors identified among male suicide cases is unclear. In this study, we aimed to investigate clinical and behavioural risk factors for suicide among female depressed patients and compare them to similar factors among male depressed patients.

Method: We identified 201 suicide completers (160 male and 41 female) who died during an episode of major depressive disorder (MDD). Cases were compared to 127 living patients with MDD (88 male and 39 female). All subjects were characterized for Axis I and II diagnoses using the Structured Clinical Interview for DSM-IV Axis I Disorders and Structured Clinical Interview for DSM-IV Axis II Personality Disorders according to the DSM-IV, as well as behavioural and temperament dimensions using proxy-based interviews. The primary outcome was measures of impulsive and impulsive-aggressive behaviours.

Results: Compared to controls, male, but not female suicide cases had higher levels of impulsive aggression (P < .05). Non-impulsive aggression differentiated both female (P < .05) and male (P < .01) suicide cases from controls. However, non-impulsive aggression and impulsive aggression were correlated constructs in males (r = 0.297; P < .001), yet uncorrelated among females (r = 0.121; P = .390). Established risk factors for suicide, such as alcohol and substance dependence, cluster B disorders, and elevated hostility and aggression, were replicated in the pooled-sex analyses, and, though not statistically significant in discriminating between suicide cases and controls by gender, maintained strong group differences.

Conclusions: Males and females share many risk factors for suicide in MDD, yet alcohol dependence is much more specific though less sensitive among depressed females. Non-impulsive aggression is part of a diathesis for suicide in females, which is distinct from the well-characterized impulsive aggression that is consistently reported in a portion of male suicide cases.

Comment

Main findings: Death due to suicide is much more prominent among males than females[1]. However, attempts of suicide occur more frequently among females[2], potentially resulting in more visits to a relevant clinic for an assessment of further risk. In order to examine gender differences in clinical vulnerability to suicide, the current Canadian study compared depressed male and female suicide cases (201 suicide cases with clinical depression) to depressed male and female never-suicidal control group (127 individuals with clinical depression and no history of non-fatal suicidal behaviour). Clinical vulnerabilities for suicide included psychological disorders and specific behavioural characteristics. Holistically, the suicide cases were more likely than the never-suicidal group with MDD to have received a diagnosis of substance abuse, met criteria for a personality disorder, and had greater histories of aggression and higher levels of hostility. Characterisation as being 'highly impulsive' was more likely in the male suicide cases compared to controls, but not for the female suicide cases. The behavioural component of impulsive-aggression distinguished male suicide attempters from never-suicidal comparison groups while non-impulsive aggression distinguished female suicide cases from female never-suicidal controls.

Implications: Risk factors for suicide between males and females have commonalities and differences. Alcohol and drug dependence appears more likely in cases of suicide for both genders, revealing a clinical feature that may warrant further attention and assessment for suicidal behaviour. Individually, males presenting with clinically harmful behaviour characterised as dramatic, emotional or erratic may also encourage clinical assessment for suicidality. Further vulnerability in this group also emerges with behaviour that is both impulsive and aggressive. The risk for suicide among females, however, is not strongly related to impulsivity. Rather, females with greater suicide risk were characterised by aggression and low levels of impulsivity (i.e. non-impulsive aggression). This may provide a key personality characteristic that could potentially help to clinically identify those at greater risk of suicidal behaviours.

Endnotes

1. Australian Bureau of Statistics (2014). *Causes of Death, Australia, 2012.* Cat. no. 3303.0, Canberra: Australian Bureau of Statitstics.
2. Milner A, Kõlves K, Kõlves KE, Gladman B, De Leo D (2013). Treatment priority for suicide ideation and behaviours at an Australian emergency department. *World Journal of Psychiatry* 3, 34-40.

Course of bereavement over 8-10 years in first degree relatives and spouses of people who committed suicide: Longitudinal community based cohort study

de Groot M, Kollen BJ (The Netherlands)
British Medical Journal 347, f5519, 2013

Objective: To identify factors predicting the long term course of complicated grief, depression, and suicide ideation in a community based sample of relatives bereaved through suicide.

Design: Longitudinal cohort study. Included in the multilevel regression models were sociodemographic and personality features, mental health history, records of received help, long term complicated grief, depression, and suicide ideation.

Setting: Community based sample located in the northern part of the Netherlands.

Participants: 153 first degree relatives and spouses of 74 people who had committed suicide.

Main Outcome Measures: Complicated grief, depression, and suicide ideation assessed at 2.5 months, 13 months and 96-120 months (8-10 years) by means of self report questionnaires.

Results: Complicated grief, depression, and suicide ideation were mutually associated in relatives and spouses of people who had committed suicide. A history of attempted suicide was associated with long term suicide ideation (odds ratio 5.5, 95% confidence interval 1.8 to 16.7; P=0.003). Depression was more likely to be predicted by female sex and low mastery, whereas complicated grief was more likely to be predicted by the trauma of losing a child. The risk of both complicated grief and depression decreased over time; for complicated grief the change corresponded with a Cohen's d effect size of 0.36 at 13 months and 0.89 at 96-120 months; for depression these figures were 0.28 at 13 months and 0.94 at 96-120 months. The long term course of bereavement was not affected by family based cognitive behavioural therapy, support from a general practitioner, and/or mental healthcare. Mutual support was associated with an increased risk of complicated grief: B regression coefficient=6.4 (95% confidence interval 1.8 to 11.0; P=0.006). Throughout this long term study, selection bias might have affected some outcomes.

Conclusion: In relatives bereaved by suicide, suicide ideation is associated with an increased risk of long term complicated grief and depression. The risk of complicated grief and depression decreases over time. Although mutual support is associated with an increased risk of complicated grief, we could not draw conclusions about a causal relation.

Comment

Main Findings: Suicidal behaviour among family members is associated with an increased risk of suicide for relatives directly (genetically) and indirectly (non-genetically) connected to the individual[1]. The risk of suicide is also higher in people who have experienced the death of a first-degree relative further exacerbated after bereavement by suicide[2]. In this study the authors aimed to uncover the long term causes of complicated grief (characterised by a preoccupation with the deceased, avoidance, detachment, and irritability[3]), depression, and suicidal ideation by exploring sociodemogrpahic factors of the deceased first-degree relative, personality features of the bereaved, and symptoms following suicide bereavement (inclusive of suicidal ideation). Measures were taken at 2.5 months, 13 months, and 8-10 years following suicide. The majority of suicides were by men (76%) with an average age of 44 years. Bereaved individuals (aged over 15 years) were first degree relatives and spouses of those who had died by suicide. At 2.5 months following suicide, 26% of the bereaved suffered from suicidal ideation. Over the course of bereavement, 8-10 years after suicide, the presence of suicidal ideation decreased to 9%, which was higher than the Dutch national average at the time (3%). Bereaved persons with higher levels of neuroticism were at a greater risk of suicidal ideation, while greater levels of self-esteem were associated with a lower risk. Suicidal ideation was also found to be strongly associated with long-term complicated grief and depression, both of which were shown to decrease over time. Previously attempted suicide among the participants was also associated with long term suicide ideation. Parents of the deceased were most likely to be at risk of complicated grief. Mutual support (i.e. support from an individual with similar experiences) was noted to be associated with an increased risk of complicated grief.

Implications: There appears to be a greater risk of suicidality in bereaved relatives of suicide. However, relatives bereaved following a suicide seem to recover over the course of time. The initial 13 months following the suicide of a relative do not appear to greatly change the level of depression and complicated grief. It is important to assess the history and characteristics of individuals bereaved by suicide in order to determine their risk of long-term grief and depression. Engaging protective personality characteristics may be beneficial in deterring suicidal ideation. Healthcare providers should be cautious when offering mutual support opportunities to individuals bereaved by suicide as an increased risk of complicated grief may arise, dependent on the characteristics of the bereaved.

However, there are community-based programs offering support to those bereaved by suicide. In Australia, the Standby Response Service[4] provides 24-hour crisis response to those who have lost someone through suicide. The aim of this service is to reduce potential adverse health outcomes while addressing further suicidal behaviour.

Endnotes

1. Qin P, Agerbo E, Mortensen PB (2002). Suicide risk in relation to family history of completed suicide and psychiatric disorders: a nested case-control study based on longitudinal registers. *Lancet* 360, 1126-1130.

2. Kõlves K, De Leo D (2013). Is Suicide Grief Different? Data from Empirical Studies. In: D. De Leo, A. Cimitan, K. Dyregrov, O. Grad, & K. Andriessen (Eds.), *Bereavement After Traumatic Death: Helping the Survivors* (pp. 161-173). Göttingen: Hogrefe.

3. Prigerson HG, Horowitz MJ, Jacobs SC, Parkes C, Goodkin A, Raphael B (2009). Prolonged grief disorder: psychometric validation of criteria proposed for DSM-V and ICD-11. *PLoS Med* 6, e1000121.

4. United Synergies. Standby Response Service. Retrieved 28 April 2014 from http://www.unitedsynergies.com.au/index.php?option=com_content&view=article&id=40&Itemid=40

Suicide by cop: Clinical risks and subtypes

Dewey L, Allwood M, Fava J, Arias E, Pinizzotto A, Schlesinger L (USA)
Archives of Suicide Research 17, 448-461, 2013

This study examines whether clinical classification schemes from general suicide research are applicable for cases of suicide by cop (SbC) and whether there are indicators as to why the police might be engaged in the suicide. Using archival law enforcement data, 13 clinical risks were examined among 68 cases of SbC using exploratory factor analysis and k-means cluster analysis. Three subtypes of SbC cases emerged: Mental Illness, Criminality, and Not Otherwise Specified. The subtypes varied significantly on their levels of mental illness, substance use, and criminal activity. Findings suggest that reducing fragmentation between law enforcement and mental health service providers might be a crucial goal for suicide intervention and prevention, at least among cases of SbC.

Comment

Main findings: Suicide by cop (SbC) occurs when a suicidal person attempts to purposely provoke the police into shooting him/her with the intention of ending their life[1]. While the overall prevalence of SbC is currently unknown; a recent study has shown that 41% of officer-involved shooting incidents involved some aspect of suicidality (the person either prompted police to shoot them or took their own life while communicating with police)[2]. This U.S. study sought to build on previous research by assessing the clinical risk factors of SbC in comparison with suicides in general, and to evaluate why police come to be involved in suicide attempts. Eighty-five cases of police officer involved shootings that occurred between 1979 and 2005 were collected from law enforcement agencies across 55 jurisdictions. Cases of SbC were identified through the consensus of an FBI agent and clinical psychologist, a clinical-forensic psychologist, and three clinical-forensic psychologist students. Of the 68 cases identified as SbC, 62 (91%) were males and 6 (9%) were females with an average age of 35.9 years. Three subtypes of suicide were apparent after analysis, namely, mental illness (96% in this group had depression, 80% had a diagnosed mental illness and 88% had prior suicidal ideation), criminality (100% had history of arrest, 83.3% were facing the prospect of jail time and 75% had recently experienced legal problems) and not otherwise specified (no distinguishing risk factors). Results suggested that individuals who decide to engage police in their suicide attempt may do so due to familiarity with police, with a large number of suicide attempters in the current sample having either a prior history of contact with police through criminal activity or emergency mental health care, previous attempts by SbC or former employment as a police officer.

Implications: Little is currently known about the risk factors for SbC and the best way to prevent these incidents from occurring. This study plays an important role in expanding the current knowledge; however, further research (particularly in Australia) is necessary. An important finding from this study is that these incidents often appear to involve similar risk factors to suicide by other methods (e.g. high prevalence of mental illness). Therefore, past involvement and familiarity with police may be an important factor in determining who is at risk of attempting suicide by this particular method. The potential for suicide prevention within this group may lie largely in improved education of law enforcement personnel around the best screening and prevention procedures to implement in these situations. The authors suggest that the development of interventions would be most effective through a joint effort between police and mental health workers.

Endnotes

1. Mohandie K, Meloy JR (2000). Clinical and forensic indicators of "suicide by cop". *Journal of Forensic Sciences* 45, 384-389.
2. Mohandie K, Meloy JR, Collins PI (2009). Suicide by cop among officer-involved shooting cases. *Journal of Forensic Sciences* 54, 456-462.

Deaths by suicide and their relationship with general and psychiatric hospital discharge: 30-year record linkage study

Dougall N, Lambert P, Maxwell M, Dawson A, Sinnott R, McCafferty S, Morris C, Clark D, Springbett A (UK, Australia)

British Journal of Psychiatry. Published online: 30 January 2014. doi: 10.1192/bjp.bp.112.122374, 2014

Background: Studies have rarely explored suicides completed following discharge from both general and psychiatric hospital settings. Such research might identify additional opportunities for intervention.

Aims: To identify and summarise Scottish psychiatric and general hospital records for individuals who have died by suicide.

Method: A linked data study of deaths by suicide, aged >/=15 years from 1981 to 2010.

Results: This study reports on a UK data-set of individuals who died by suicide (n = 16 411), of whom 66% (n = 10 907) had linkable previous hospital records. Those who died by suicide were 3.1 times more frequently last discharged from general than from psychiatric hospitals; 24% of deaths occurred within 3 months of hospital discharge (58% of these from a general hospital). Only 14% of those discharged from a general hospital had a recorded psychiatric diagnosis at last visit; an additional 19% were found to have a previous lifetime psychiatric diagnosis. Median time between last discharge and death was fourfold greater in those without a psychiatric history. Diagnoses also revealed that less than half of those last discharged from general hospital had had a main diagnosis of 'injury or poisoning'.

Conclusions: Suicide prevention activity, including a better psychiatric evaluation of patients within general hospital settings deserves more attention. Improved information flow between secondary and primary care could be facilitated by exploiting electronic records of previous psychiatric diagnoses.

Comment

Main findings: Research has suggested that a large percentage of individuals who die by suicide make contact with either a general or mental health service in the year prior to their death[1]. An Australian study found that 76.9% of suicide cases had seen a GP within the three months before death[2]. This study analysed factors relating to the last discharge from a general or psychiatric hospital before death by suicide in Scotland. The study extracted records of 16,411 suicide deaths from the National Records of Scotland (NRS) deaths register over a 30-year period (1981-2010). Of these 16,411 individuals, 5275 had no linked hospital records, and 229 died in hospital with no previous admission, leaving 10,907 individuals who met the criteria for inclusion in the study. Seventy-six percent of individuals in the study had been last treated by a general hospital, while 21% had been last treated in a psychiatric hospital, and the remaining 3% had both general and psychiatric care in the last period of hospitalisation. Around one quarter of individuals who died by suicide had been discharged from hospital within the three months prior to their death. Due to the large number of patients dying by suicide after general hospital discharge, the authors provided more detailed analyses on these cases. Within this group, only 14% of patients had a co-morbid psychiatric diagnosis at last visit, while 19% had a history of psychiatric diagnosis during the lifetime (not diagnosed at last visit). The time to death after general hospital discharge differed depending on psychiatric diagnosis, with results showing that individuals with a psychiatric diagnosis at last presentation had the shortest median time until death (7 months), follow by patients with a past diagnosis of psychiatric illness (9 months) and those without any diagnosis of a psychiatric condition (33 months).

Implications: A large number of individuals are in contact with health services prior to death by suicide[1,2], creating the opportunity to work towards suicide prevention in this group. Unlike previous papers focussing solely on general[3] or mental health services[4], this study was able to compare differences in suicide after the last discharge from a general or psychiatric service. The finding that more people who die by suicide are in contact with a general health service than a psychiatric service is not overly surprising (due to the fact that admissions to general hospitals are much more common than psychiatric hospitals). However, the results do highlight the importance that staff members treating patients in the general setting are aware of the potential suicide risk and can implement risk screening and follow-up procedures when necessary.

Endnotes

1. Luoma JB, Martin CE, Pearson JL (2002). Contact with mental health and primary care providers before suicide: A review of the evidence. *American Journal of Psychiatry* 159, 909-916.

2. De Leo D, Draper B, Snowdon J, Kõlves K (2013). Contacts with health professionals before suicide: Missed opportunities for prevention? *Comprehensive Psychiatry* 54, 1117-1123.

3. Chang CM, Liao SC, Chiang HC, Chen YY, Tseng KC, Chau YL..., Lee MB (2009). Gender differences in healthcare service utilization 1 year before suicide: National record linkage study. *British Journal of Psychiatry* 195, 459-460.

4. Appleby L, Shaw J, Amos T, McDonnell R, Harris C, McCann K..., Parsons R (1999). Suicide within 12 months of contact with mental health services: National Clinical Survey. *British Medical Journal* 318, 1235.

Lesbian, gay, bisexual, and transgender hate crimes and suicidality among a population-based sample of sexual-minority adolescents in Boston

Duncan DT, Hatzenbuehler ML (USA)

American Journal of Public Health 104, 272-278, 2014

Objectives: We examined whether past-year suicidality among sexual-minority adolescents was more common in neighborhoods with a higher prevalence of hate crimes targeting lesbian, gay, bisexual, and transgender (LGBT) individuals.

Methods: Participants' data came from a racially/ethnically diverse population-based sample of 9th- through 12th-grade public school students in Boston, Massachusetts (n = 1292). Of these, 108 (8.36%) reported a minority sexual orientation. We obtained data on LGBT hate crimes involving assaults or assaults with battery between 2005 and 2008 from the Boston Police Department and linked the data to the adolescent's residential address.

Results: Sexual-minority youths residing in neighborhoods with higher rates of LGBT assault hate crimes were significantly more likely to report suicidal ideation (P = .013) and suicide attempts (P = .006), than were those residing in neighborhoods with lower LGBT assault hate crime rates. We observed no relationships between overall neighborhood-level violent and property crimes and suicidality among sexual-minority adolescents (P > .05), providing evidence for specificity of the results to LGBT assault hate crimes.

Conclusions: Neighborhood context (i.e., LGBT hate crimes) may contribute to sexual-orientation disparities in adolescent suicidality, highlighting potential targets for community-level suicide-prevention programs.

Comment

Main findings: Research has shown that sexual minority adolescents are significantly more likely to experience sexual abuse, parental physical abuse, assault at school, to miss school due to fear of victimisation[1], and to report suicidal thoughts and behaviours[2]. This study from Boston in the U.S. analysed whether sexual minority adolescents (9th to 12th grade) living in neighbourhoods with a higher prevalence of sexuality-related hate crimes were more likely to report suicidal ideation and attempts within the past year. Of 1,292 students who completed the survey, 108 identified as part of a minority sexual orientation as; mostly heterosexual, bisexual, mostly homosexual, gay, lesbian or unsure. Thirty-two percent of sexual-minority adolescents reported suicidal ideation in the previous year and 16.7% reported suicide attempts, compared to 9.4% and 2.4% of heterosexual peers respectively. The addresses of adolescents were matched with assault hate crime data obtained from Boston Police Department. Results showed that the sexual-minority adolescents reporting suicidal behaviour were more likely to reside in neighbourhoods which had higher numbers of assault hate crimes against LGBT individuals. Conversely, there was no significant relationship between LGBT assault hate crimes and suicidal ideation or attempts in adolescents identifying as heterosexual or between non-LGBT crimes and increased suicidal behaviour in sexual-minority adolescents.

Implications: Recent research in Australia has analysed the risk of suicide mortality in LGBTI individuals with regards to individual, familial and school/work factors[3]. This US study is one of the few to use an ecological design to examine this risk from a broader social perspective, with results suggesting that suicide prevention efforts could benefit from measures to reduce hate crimes directed at sexual-minority individuals. Further Australian research using a larger sample size and including a wider range of minority sexualities (ie. Transgender individuals) could build on these findings and be useful in determining how similar prevention efforts could be implemented in the Australian community.

Endnotes

1. Friedman MS, Marshal MP, Guadamuz TE, Wei C, Wong CF, Saewyc EM, Stall R (2011). A meta-analysis of disparities in childhood sexual abuse, parental physical abuse, and peer victimization among sexual minority and sexual nonminority individuals. *American Journal of Public Health* 101, 1481-1494.

2. Russell S, Joyner K (2001). Adolescent sexual orientation and suicide risk: Evidence from a national study. *American Journal of Public Health* 91, 1276-1281.

3. Skerrett DM, Kõlves K, De Leo D (2014). Suicides among lesbian, gay, bisexual, and transgender populations in Australia: An analysis of the Queensland suicide register. *Asia-Pacific Psychiatry.* Published online: 2 April 2014. doi: 10.1111/appy.12128.

Suicide attempt in young people: A signal for long-term health care and social needs

Goldman-Mellor SJ, Caspi A, Harrington H, Hogan S, Nada-Raja S, Poulton R, Moffitt TE (USA, UK, New Zealand)

JAMA Psychiatry 71, 119-127, 2013

Importance: Suicidal behavior has increased since the onset of the global recession, a trend that may have long-term health and social implications.

Objective: To test whether suicide attempts among young people signal increased risk for later poor health and social functioning above and beyond a preexisting psychiatric disorder.

Design: We followed up a cohort of young people and assessed multiple aspects of their health and social functioning as they approached midlife. Outcomes among individuals who had self-reported a suicide attempt up through age 24 years (young suicide attempters) were compared with those who reported no attempt through age 24 years (nonattempters). Psychiatric history and social class were controlled for.

Setting and participants: The population-representative Dunedin Multidisciplinary Health and Development Study, which involved 1037 birth cohort members comprising 91 young suicide attempters and 946 nonattempters, 95% of whom were followed up to age 38 years.

Main outcomes and measures: Outcomes were selected to represent significant individual and societal costs: mental health, physical health, harm toward others, and need for support.

Results: As adults approaching midlife, young suicide attempters were significantly more likely to have persistent mental health problems (eg, depression, substance dependence, and additional suicide attempts) compared with nonattempters. They were also more likely to have physical health problems (eg, metabolic syndrome and elevated inflammation). They engaged in more violence (eg, violent crime and intimate partner abuse) and needed more social support (eg, long-term welfare receipt and unemployment). Furthermore, they reported being lonelier and less satisfied with their lives. These associations remained after adjustment for youth psychiatric diagnoses and social class.

Conclusions and relevance: Many young suicide attempters remain vulnerable to costly health and social problems into midlife. As rates of suicidal behavior rise with the continuing global recession, additional suicide prevention efforts and long-term monitoring and after-care services are needed.

Comment

Main Findings: Hospital treatment for deliberate self-harm, including attempted suicide, is highest among young Australians aged between their teenage years and middle age[1]. While it has been established that suicidal attempts are one of the biggest predictors of suicidal behaviour and death by suicide later on in life[2], few studies have examined the potential for other negative outcomes following these events. This New Zealand paper explored the notion that suicide attempts in young people aged 24 and under, may act as potential predictors for future vulnerability to psychiatric and physical health problems, criminal justice problems, significant costs to the welfare system and poor social well-being throughout the lifetime. Participants were sourced from the Dunedin Multidisciplinary Health and Development Study, which measured the health and behaviour of 1,037 New Zealand residents born between April 1972 and March 1973, with assessments carried out longitudinally at birth, and ages 3, 5, 7, 9, 11, 13, 15, 18, 21, 26, 32 and 38 years. Ninety-one participants of the original sample reported a suicide attempt before the age of 24 years and 86 of these people were successfully followed-up until the age of 38 years. Five of the suicide attempters had died before the final follow-up was conducted. During middle-age, young attempters were found to have more mental health problems; they were twice as likely to have ongoing problems with depression and substance abuse. In addition, suicide attempters were significantly more likely to suffer from poor physical health, to inflict harm upon others or to be victimised by their intimate partners, need more support due to histories of unemployment and dependence on welfare benefits, suffer from loneliness and to report less overall satisfaction with their lives. In line with previous findings[2] young suicide attempters were more likely than non-attempters to continue engaging in suicidal behaviours after the first attempt (more than 20% engaged in additional suicide attempts from 26-38 years of age).

Implications: The findings of the current study have a number of important practical implications. An Australian study by SANE showed that a large number of Australians presenting to medical centres for self-harm were not referred for ongoing mental health treatment, or provided with a crisis plan to implement when feeling suicidal in the future[3]. This paper lends support to the notion that follow-up treatment is imperative for the prevention of suicidal behaviours, but also emphasises the importance of follow-up treatment to avoid a number of other adverse psycho-social and somatic outcomes. In particular, the findings of poor physical health in individuals who attempt suicide may suggest that overall lifestyle changes may be needed to prevent patterns of self-neglect, while on a wider scale, the fact that suicidal individuals are more likely to be lonely and dissatisfied with their life may suggest the ongoing need to break down the societal stigma relating to suicide and suicidal behaviour.

Endnotes

1. Milner A, Kõlves K, Kõlves K, Gladman B, De Leo D (2013). Treatment priority for suicide ideation and behaviours at an Australian emergency department. *World Journal of Psychiatry* 3, 34-40

2. Suominen K, Isometsa E, Suokas J, Haukka J, Achte K, Lonnqvist J (2004). Completed suicide after a suicide attempt: A 37-year follow-up study. *The American Journal of Psychiatry* 161, 562-563

3. SANE research (2010). *Suicide, self-harm and mental illness.* SANE Research Bulletin 11. Retrieved from http://www.sane.org/images/stories/information/research/1001_info_rb11.pdf

Living beyond Aboriginal suicide: Developing a culturally appropriate and accessible suicide postvention service for Aboriginal communities in South Australia

Goodwin-Smith I, Hicks N, Hawke M, Alver G, Raftery P (Australia)

Advances in Mental Health 11, 238-245, 2013

Anglicare SA's Living Beyond Suicide program (LBS) is a postvention service which partners with crisis services such as the police and ambulance who attend each suicide in South Australia and who provide families with an immediate link to the service. LBS workers visit in the hours and days after the suicide, companion survivors through post-suicide processes, and provide a vital link between families and the community. The support given is practical and based on a family's needs. It is also based on evidence which suggests that postvention services are important in mitigating the negative effects of grief and suicide contagion. Despite the overrepresentation of Aboriginal people in suicide statistics, LBS is significantly underutilised by Aboriginal people. The aim of this research is to investigate how programmes such as LBS can be made more accessible and appropriate for Aboriginal people so that all people in the community have the opportunity to access the service should they experience bereavement through suicide. The project constitutes the beginning of a 'both ways', asset-based dialogue, and seeks to enhance the service's capacity through dialogue with Aboriginal stakeholders, whilst investigating the potential of the service to augment the capacity of Aboriginal people and communities to live beyond suicide. To this end, the research here gathers information from a number of Aboriginal people who have been bereaved by suicide, and Aboriginal service providers who work with people who have been in this situation. It asks whether or not there is a need for a service such as LBS for Aboriginal families and communities and, if so, how the current programme could be modified to make it more accessible and/or appropriate for Aboriginal people. Overarching those service specific questions, the project investigates the potential utility of predicating social service provision on a process of 'walking together'.

Comment

Main findings: Aboriginal and Torres Strait Islander Australians die by suicide at higher rates than non-Indigenous Australians[1,2]. This study aimed to test the successfulness and cultural appropriateness of Anglicare SA's postvention service "Living Beyond Suicide" (LBS), in providing support to Aboriginal Australians bereaved by suicide. The main research question addressed in the study was "is there a role for a service such as LBS, in partnership with Aboriginal people, communities and service providers, to enhance a sustainable capacity for resilience in relation to the negative health and wellbeing impacts of Aboriginal suicide?" Data was collected during 2011 through four focus groups with Aboriginal service providers and health workers and 15 semi-structured interviews with Aboriginal people who had lost a loved one to suicide. Participants felt that the use of postvention services by Aboriginal people bereaved by suicide would depend largely on the accessibility and appeal of the program. Many of the participants had never heard of the LBS program, despite being personally affected by suicide, suggesting the need for improved promotion and dissemination of material relating to the service. The composition of staff teams was raised as a significant issue, with participants noting the importance of having a choice between male and female workers, and Aboriginal or non-Aboriginal workers, as well as workers from different Aboriginal groups. Other important factors for inclusion were information on financial assistance to help with the cost of funeral services and other increased bills, information on how long processes can take after the death of a loved one (for example length of time taken to prepare coroner's reports) and the need for services to be outreach-based so that bereaved individuals do not have to worry about travelling to access the service. The findings of the study suggest that LBS has the potential to provide important support to Aboriginal survivors of suicide, particularly if the program is enhanced to directly address the unique cultural needs of Aboriginal Australians.

Implications: Bereavement by suicide can result in a number of negative outcomes including an increased risk of suicidal ideation[3]. Postvention services providing support to those bereaved by suicide have been identified as a priority within Aboriginal communities due to the high rates of suicide and lack of support available in these communities[4]. The current study emphasises the importance of working in partnership with these communities to ensure that these support services are culturally appropriate and are able to provide adequate assistance to Aboriginal Australians who have lost a loved one to suicide.

Endnotes

1. Australian Bureau of Statistics (2014). *Causes of death, Australia, 2012.* Canberra: ABS.
2. De Leo D, Sveticic J, Milner A (2011). Suicide in indigenous people in Queensland, Australia: Trends and methods, 1994-2007. *Australian and New Zealand Journal of Psychiatry* 45, 532-538.
3. Mitchell AM, Kim Y, Prigerson HG, Mortimer MK (2011). Complicated grief and suicidal ideation in adult survivors of suicide. *Suicide and Life-Threatening Behavior* 35, 498-506.
4. Mitchell P (2000). *Valuing young lives: Evaluation of the national youth suicide prevention strategy.* Melbourne: Australian Institute of Family Studies.

Self-harm in prisons in England and Wales: An epidemiological study of prevalence, risk factors, clustering, and subsequent suicide

Hawton K, Linsell L, Adeniji T, Sariaslan A, Fazel S (UK, Sweden)

The Lancet. Published online: 16 December 2013. doi: 10.1016/S0140-6736(13)62118-2, 2013

Background: Self-harm and suicide are common in prisoners, yet robust information on the full extent and characteristics of people at risk of self-harm is scant. Furthermore, understanding how frequently self-harm is followed by suicide, and in which prisoners this progression is most likely to happen, is important. We did a case-control study of all prisoners in England and Wales to ascertain the prevalence of self-harm in this population, associated risk factors, clustering effects, and risk of subsequent suicide after self-harm.

Methods: Records of self-harm incidents in all prisons in England and Wales were gathered routinely between January, 2004, and December, 2009. We did a case-control comparison of prisoners who self-harmed and those who did not between January, 2006, and December, 2009. We also used a Bayesian approach to look at clustering of people who self-harmed. Prisoners who self-harmed and subsequently died by suicide in prison were compared with other inmates who self-harmed.

Findings: 139 195 self-harm incidents were recorded in 26 510 individual prisoners between 2004 and 2009; 5-6% of male prisoners and 20-24% of female inmates self-harmed every year. Self-harm rates were more than ten times higher in female prisoners than in male inmates. Repetition of self-harm was common, particularly in women and teenage girls, in whom a subgroup of 102 prisoners accounted for 17 307 episodes. In both sexes, self-harm was associated with younger age, white ethnic origin, prison type, and a life sentence or being unsentenced; in female inmates, committing a violent offence against an individual was also a factor. Substantial evidence was noted of clustering in time and location of prisoners who self-harmed (adjusted intra-class correlation 0·15, 95% CI 0·11-0·18). 109 subsequent suicides in prison were reported in individuals who self-harmed; the risk was higher in those who self-harmed than in the general prison population, and more than half the deaths occurred within a month of self-harm. Risk factors for suicide after self-harm in male prisoners were older age and a previous self-harm incident of high or moderate lethality; in female inmates, a history of more than five self-harm incidents within a year was associated with subsequent suicide.

Interpretation: The burden of self-harm in prisoners is substantial, particularly in women. Self-harm in prison is associated with subsequent suicide in this setting. Prevention and treatment of self-harm in prisoners is an essential component of suicide prevention in prisons.

Funding: Wellcome Trust, National Institute for Health Research, National Offender Management Service, and Department of Health.

Comment

Main findings: Prisoners in a number of countries, including Australia, have been shown to be at an increased risk of suicide compared to the general population[1]. A major risk factor for death by suicide in custody is previous self harm, with past research on 141 prisoners who died by suicide showing that more than half (78 prisoners) had previously engaged in self-harming behaviour[2]. In this large-scale study using data from prisons in England and Wales between 2004-2009, Hawton and colleagues analysed the prevalence, risk factors, and clustering effects of self-harm, as well as the risk of suicide after engagement in self-harm. During the study period, 139,195 self-harm incidents involving 26,510 prisoners were recorded. Despite making up a small percentage of the overall prison population (5-6% each year), female inmates were involved in around half of the incidents of self-harm (20-24% of female prisoners self harmed each year compared to 5-6% of male prisoners). For both males and females, self-harm was most common in younger inmates aged below 20 years (23% of males who self-harmed and 21% of females who self-harmed). Other risk factors included being Caucasian (males and females), prison type (males and females), having a life sentence or being unsentenced (males and females) and having committed a violent offence against another person (females only). Among the 26,510 individuals who had self-harmed, 109 prisoners eventually died by suicide in custody (95 males and 14 females). The mean annual rate of male inmates who self-harmed and died by suicide was close to double the rate in females (334 per 100,000 compared to 149 per 100,000) and was higher than the suicide rate in individuals who did not engage in self-harm before death (79 per 100,000 in males and 98 per 100,000 in females). Bivariate analysis showed that male prisoners aged 30-49 years were at a high risk for death by suicide, particularly those who had a history of self-harm with moderate or high lethality. In multivariate analysis, a life sentence and more than five self-harm incidents per year were significant risk factors for suicide.

Implications: Research has shown that suicide prevention programs can have the ability to reduce self-harm and suicide in prisons, and the identification of risk factors is imperative to the successful development and implementation of these programs[3]. The current paper provides important findings regarding at-risk prisoners, building on previous studies by using a large sample size and analysing risk factors in offenders of all ages, genders and in different types of correctional facilities. Risk of suicide appears to differ, depending on the characteristics of the correctional institution, suggesting that similar research in Australia may be necessary.

An important finding from the current study is the high rate of self-harm in female and young prisoners, despite the smaller proportion of these individuals in prison. This finding supports those of previous studies that female and young prisoners may have distinct health needs from the majority prison population[4], and suggests the need for programs specially designed to address self-harm in these specific sub-groups.

Endnotes

1. Fazel S, Grann M, Kling B, Hawton K (2011). Prison suicides in 12 countries: An ecological study of 861 suicides during 2003-2007. *Social Psychiatry and Psychiatric Epidemiology* 46, 191-195.

2. Shaw J, Baker D, Hunt IM, Moloney A, Appleby L (2004). Suicide by prisoners: National clinical survey. *The British Journal of Psychiatry* 184, 263-267.

3. Barker E, Kõlves K, De Leo D (2014). Management of suicidal and self-harming behaviors in prison: Systematic literature review of evidence-based activities. *Archives of Suicide Research.* Published online: 11 May 2014. doi: 10.1080/13811118.2013.824830

4. Harris F, Hek G, Condon L (2006). Health needs of prisoners in England and Wales: The implications for prison healthcare of gender, age and ethnicity. *Health and Social Care in the Community* 15, 56-66.

Risk of suicide according to level of psychiatric treatment: A nationwide nested case-control study

Hjorthoj CR, Madsen T, Agerbo E, Nordentoft M (Denmark)

Social Psychiatry and Psychiatric Epidemiology. Published online: 18 March 2014. doi: 10.1007/s00127-014-0860-x, 2014

Purpose: Knowledge of the epidemiology of suicide is a necessary prerequisite of suicide prevention. We aimed to conduct a nationwide study investigating suicide risk in relation to level of psychiatric treatment.

Methods: Nationwide nested case-control study comparing individuals who died from suicide between 1996 and 2009 to age-, sex-, and year-matched controls. Psychiatric treatment in the previous year was graded as "no treatment," "medicated," "outpatient contact," "psychiatric emergency room contact," or "admitted to psychiatric hospital."

Results: There were 2,429 cases and 50,323 controls. Compared with people who had not received any psychiatric treatment in the preceding year, the adjusted rate ratio (95 % confidence interval) for suicide was 5.8 (5.2-6.6) for people receiving only psychiatric medication, 8.2 (6.1-11.0) for people with at most psychiatric outpatient contact, 27.9 (19.5-40.0) for people with at most psychiatric emergency room contacts, and 44.3 (36.1-54.4) for people who had been admitted to a psychiatric hospital. The gradient was steeper for married or cohabiting people, those with higher socioeconomic position, and possibly those without a history of attempted suicide.

Conclusions: Psychiatric admission in the preceding year was highly associated with risk of dying from suicide. Furthermore, even individuals who have been in contact with psychiatric treatment but who have not been admitted are at highly increased risk of suicide.

Comment

Main findings: Understanding the epidemiology of suicide is a key step in suicide prevention. Increased risks have been related to various psychiatric diagnoses, further amplified by specific demographic characteristics[1]. An investigation into the various types of contact with the psychiatric system (inpatients, outpatients, emergency room (ER), psychiatric hospital, and medication) and the degree of contact provides the foundation of this study. From 1995 to 2009, a total of 2,429 suicide cases (71.8% men) were compared with 50,320 matched controls. Fifty-three percent had received some form of psychiatric treatment in the preceding year of their death. A significant association was observed between dying by suicide and level of contact with the psychiatric system. Compared to those suicide cases not receiving psychiatric treatment, those receiving psychiatric medication, psychiatric outpatient contact, psychiatric ER contact, and cases receiving psychiatric hospitalisation were all more likely to die by suicide. For those receiving outpatient treatment, the risk of suicide was elevated by nearly 30 times for those diagnosed with a psychotic or affective disorder, compared to 12 times for other psychiatric disorders.

Implications: Australian research has shown that people who die by suicide have more frequent contacts with mental health professionals than those who die by sudden death[2]. In the current study, increased rates of suicide were seen with increasing levels of psychiatric treatment (medication, psychiatric outpatients, psychiatric ER, and psychiatric hospitalisation). This particular pattern may indicate the ability of psychiatric treatment systems to correctly identify people in need of treatment. However, a specific focus is needed on suicidal behaviour within outpatient clinics and general practices. Greater monitoring of individuals accessing these resources for treatment should be encouraged. Furthermore, all diagnostic groups (psychotic, affective, etc.) should be assessed for risk of suicide.

Endnotes

1. Qin P, Nordentoft M (2005). Suicide risk in relation to psychiatric hospitalization: evidence based on longitudinal registers. *Archives of General Psychiatry* 62, 427-432.
2. De Leo D, Draper BM, Snowdon J, Kõlves K (2013). Contacts with health professionals before suicide: Missed opportunities for prevention? *Comprehensive Psychiatry* 54, 1117-1123.

Tracking suicide risk factors through twitter in the U.S.

Jashinsky J, Burton SH, Hanson CL, West J, Giraud-Carrier C, Barnes MD, Argyle T (USA)
Crisis 35, 51-59, 2014

Background: Suicide is a leading cause of death in the United States. Social media such as Twitter is an emerging surveillance tool that may assist researchers in tracking suicide risk factors in real time.

Aims: To identify suicide-related risk factors through Twitter conversations by matching on geographic suicide rates from vital statistics data.

Method: At-risk tweets were filtered from the Twitter stream using keywords and phrases created from suicide risk factors. Tweets were grouped by state and departures from expectation were calculated. The values for suicide tweeters were compared against national data of actual suicide rates from the Centers for Disease Control and Prevention.

Results: A total of 1,659,274 tweets were analyzed over a 3-month period with 37,717 identified as at-risk for suicide. Midwestern and western states had a higher proportion of suicide-related tweeters than expected, while the reverse was true for southern and eastern states. A strong correlation was observed between state Twitter-derived data and actual state age-adjusted suicide data.

Conclusion: Twitter may be a viable tool for real-time monitoring of suicide risk factors on a large scale. This study demonstrates that individuals who are at risk for suicide may be detected through social media.

Comment

Main findings: The majority of Twitter users post material about themselves[1] and readily share information of a personal nature[2]. Social media platforms possess the possibility for surveying and influencing large groups of individuals through the collection of real time data. This data may provide an opportunity for an analysis of suicidal behaviours and relevant interventions. The authors sought to determine whether the numbers of suicide-related Twitter posts are related to actual suicide rates of US states and the District of Columbia. Following criteria used to retrieve only at-risk suicide 'tweets' (Twitter posts), there were a total of 733,011 tweets from 594,776 unique users over a four month period in 2012. A specific US state could be identified in 37,717 tweets from 28,088 unique users. The most at-risk (i.e. higher proportion of suicide related users than expected) states tended to be Alaska, midwestern and western states. The lowest at-risk states tended to be the southern and eastern states. The geographical distribution of actual suicide rates was significantly associated with the rates of tweets by Twitter users at risk of suicide.

Implications: Twitter (and other social media platforms) is regularly used in Australia[3] and may be a useful tool for future suicide research and public health interventions. This American study provides preliminary acceptability of the value of this data source in monitoring and understanding suicide risks. However, the ecological nature of the study prevents concrete conclusions being drawn. Nevertheless, the use of this type of information sharing opens up avenues for detecting and responding to suicidality on social media. Individuals flagged as at risk of suicide may be engaged in social media conversations with trained practitioners offering relevant information and direction to relevant resources. The real-time data that is provided allows for a more prompt and thorough response to users that are identified as potentially vulnerable.

Endnotes

1. Humphreys L, Gill P, Krishnamurthy B (2010, June). *How much is too much? Privacy issues on Twitter.* Paper presented at the 60th Annual Conference of the International Communication Association, Singapore. Retrieved from http://www.citeulike.org/user/lukehutton/article/10571629

2. West JH, Hall PC, Prier K, Hanson CL, Giraud-Carrier C, Neeley ES, Barnes MD (2012). Temporal variability of problem drinking on Twitter. *Open Journal of Preventative Medicine* 2, 43-48.

3. Sensis (2013). *Yellow Pages Social Media Report.* Retrieved 21 May, 2014, from http://about.sensis.com.au/News/Media-Releases/?ItemID=1225

Prospective prediction of suicide in a nationally representative sample: Religious service attendance as a protective factor

Kleiman EM, Liu RT (USA)

British Journal of Psychiatry. Published online: 10 October 2013. doi: 10.1192/bjp.bp.113.128900

Background: Previous research into religious service attendance as a protective factor against suicide has been conducted only retrospectively, with psychological autopsy studies using proxy informants of completed suicide, rather than prospectively, with completed suicide as a dependent variable.

Aims: To determine whether individuals who frequently attended religious services were less likely to die by suicide than those who did not attend so frequently.

Method: We analysed data from a nationally representative sample (n = 20 014), collected in the USA between 1988 and 1994, and follow-up mortality data from baseline to the end of 2006.

Results: Cox proportional hazard regression analysis indicated that those who frequently attended religious services were less likely to die by suicide than those who did not attend, after accounting for the effects of other relevant risk factors.

Conclusions: Frequent religious service attendance is a long-term protective factor against suicide.

Comment

Main findings: Religious affiliation has been associated with decreased levels of suicidal ideation and suicide attempts[1]. Two main theories exist for the link between religion and suicidality; that religious service attendance increases social support and integration and therefore decreases suicidality[2], and that commitment to core religious beliefs, values and practices may deter suicidal behaviour[3]. This longitudinal prospective study analysed the frequency of religious service attendance in U.S. adults who died by suicide to further explore the role of religiosity as a potential protective factor for suicide. Data was collected from the nationally representative Third National Health and Nutrition Examination Survey (NHANES III in 1988-1994) and included information on demographic and social variables, socioeconomic status, alcohol and drug use, lifetime psychiatric diagnosis, and suicidal ideation and attempts. This information was linked with mortality files from the National Death Index (NDI) of the U.S. Government Centers for Disease Control and Prevention (CDC) until 31 December 2006. Univariate Cox proportional hazard regression analysis was used to compare time to suicide in those who frequently attended religious services (at least 24 times per year or twice per month) to those who did not attend frequently. Results showed that male gender, older age, frequent marijuana use and infrequent religious service attendance all predicted death by suicide. When controlling for other factors, only male gender and infrequent religious service attendance remained significant in the final model. In conclusion, people who attended religious services frequently were 67% less likely to die by suicide by the end of the study period (more specifically, only 8 out of 25 suicides reported frequent engagement in religious services).

Implications: Although previous studies have identified a link between religiosity and suicidality, the vast majority of this research has focused on non-fatal suicidal behaviour. This paper was the first to make use of longitudinal prospective methodology to examine the relationship between suicide mortality and religious service attendance. The use of prospective methodology reduced the potential for reporting biases which may occur when retrospective study designs are used.

The association between suicidal behaviours and religiosity is yet to be examined in Australia. Due to differences in religious practices between countries, it is important that research is carried out in the Australian context. While theories exist as to why religious attendance may act as a protective factor against suicidality, further research exploring the reasons for this association is warranted and may contribute to suicide prevention efforts.

Endnotes

1. Dervic K, Oquendo MA, Grunebaum MF, Ellis S, Burke AK, Mann J (2004). Religious affiliation and suicide attempt. *American Journal of Psychiatry* 161, 2303-2308.
2. Durkheim E (1951). *Suicide.* Translated by Spaulding JA, Simpson G. New York: Free Press.
3. Stack S (1983). The effect of religious commitment on suicide: A cross-national analysis. *Journal of Health and Social Behavior* 24, 362–374.

Suicide in medical doctors and nurses: An analysis of the Queensland suicide register.

Kõlves K, De Leo D

Journal of Nervous and Mental Disease 201, 987-990, 2013.

This study aimed to estimate the risk for suicide among medical doctors and nurses compared with the education professions and the general population and to describe the characteristics of their suicides. Suicide cases and rates in the age group of 25 to 64 years were analyzed using the Queensland Suicide Register (QSR) during 1990 to 2007. The male medical doctors had lower suicide rates than those of the male education professionals and significantly lower rates than those of the general population. The female medical doctors had significantly higher rates than those of the education professionals, but the rates were similar to those of the general population. Among the nurses, both sexes had significantly higher rates than those of the education professionals; however, their rates were similar to those of the general population. Poisoning was used significantly more often by the medical professionals (59.3%) and the nurses (44.1%) than by the education professionals (23.5%) and others (18.8%). Depression was more common in suicide of the medical doctors than the nurses, the education professionals, and others. Work-related problems were most prevalent for the medical doctors (18.5%) followed by the education professionals (16.5%).

Comment

Main Findings: Like all individuals, medical professionals may experience work-related stress, depression, negative life events, and isolation. Considering their profession, they may feel uncomfortable approaching colleagues and other health professionals to seek assistance[1], potentially due to of the belief that it will harm their careers along with the ease in self-diagnosis and self-medicating. An increased suicide rate has been acknowledged for those involved in medical occupations when compared with the general population[2] and other academic professionals[3]. However, inconsistent findings of suicidality among medical professionals have prompted the authors to investigate the prevalence of the risk for suicide among these professionals (aged 25 to 64), while also describing the characteristics of these suicides using data from the Queensland Suicide Register (QSR) and Australian Bureau of Statistics (ABS).

There were 27 suicides by medical doctors, 59 by nursing professionals, and 85 by teaching professionals for the period 1990 to 2007. Male nursing professionals had a significantly greater suicide rate when compared with male education professionals. This significance did not remain when compared with the rates of the total male population. Female medical doctors and nursing professionals both had significantly greater suicide rates when compared to female education professionals. However, like that of males, this significance did not remain when compared to the rates of total female population. Of these suicide cases, poisoning methods occurred in 59.3% of medical doctors and 44.1% of nursing professionals, significantly more than in education professionals (23.5%) and others (18.8%). There were no marked differences in somatic conditions at the time of death between the groups. However, psychiatric disorders were more prevalent among medical doctors (59.3%) and nurses (55.9%) compared to education professionals (44.7%) and others (40.1%), and were or had been more frequently receiving psychiatric treatment. Of the lifestyle factors, work-related problems were the most prevalent for medical doctors (18.5%).

Implications: Contrary to previous findings, individuals working in the medical and nursing professions do not appear to be at greater risk of suicide when compared to the total population of suicide cases. This inconsistency with previous findings may be embedded in the social nuances that distinguish one culture from the next. In Queensland, the conditions of employment for these health professionals may represent a standard that is both comfortable and prestigious, emerging from an increasing demand of these professionals. However, there is still evidence suggestive that these professionals are not immune to risks of suicide. The male suicide rate in Queensland (2007 to 2009) was 3.5 times higher than the female rate[4], much more than the difference observed between male and female medical doctor suicides (i.e. 1.5 times greater for men) in this study. This convergence may signify an importance of the factors that surround these types of professions. Self-poisoning was found to be the most frequent suicide method for medical doctors and nurses, a relationship tied to their knowledge of and ease of access to potentially lethal drugs. Work-related problems were also identified as a potential risk and are considered an important aspect of suicide in medical doctors. However, there appears to be no lack of treatment seeking among medical and nursing professionals, as many cases were found to have engaged another professional, particularly for psychiatric conditions.

Endnotes

1. Center C, Davis M, Detre T, Ford DE, Hansbrough W, Hendin H..., Silverman MM (2003). Confronting depression and suicide in physicians: A consensus statement. *JAMA* 289, 3161-3166.

2. Schernhammer ES, Colditz GA (2004). Suicide rates among physicians: A quantitative and gender assessment (meta-analysis). *American Journal of Psychiatry* 161, 2295-2302.

3. Aasland OG, Ekeberg O, Schweder T (2001). Suicide rates from 1960 tom1989 in Norwegian physicians compared with other educational groups. *Social Science and Medicine* 52, 259-265.

4. De Leo D, Sveticic J (2012). *Suicide in Queensland, 2005-2007. Mortality rates and related data.* Brisbane, Australia: Australian Institute for Suicide Research and Prevention.

Longitudinal follow-up study of adolescents who report a suicide attempt: Aspects of suicidal behavior that increase risk of a future attempt

Miranda R, De Jaegere E, Restifo K, Shaffer D (USA, Belgium, The Netherlands)
Depression and Anxiety 31, 19-26, 2013

Background: Previous studies have noted that a past suicide attempt (SA) predicts a future SA, but few studies have reported whether previous SAs that predict a future attempt differ from those that do not. Knowing which characteristics of previous SAs predict future attempts would assist in evaluating adolescents at risk of attempt repetition. This longitudinal study of an unreferred sample examined which characteristics of adolescent SAs increased risk for repeat attempts.

Methods: Fifty-four adolescents who had attempted suicide were identified through a two-stage screening of 1,729 high school students. Adolescents reported details of their past SA on the Adolescent Suicide Interview and were reassessed 4-6 years later by telephone.

Results: Eighteen of the 54 teens (33%) reported that they had made another SA since baseline, and 17 of these reported characteristics of their later attempt. The odds of a further attempt were significantly increased by being alone (OR = 6.1, 95% CI = 1.1-34.8), retrospectively reporting a serious wish to die (OR = 5.2, 95% CI = 1.2-22.7), and planning the attempt for an hour or more (OR = 5.1, 95% CI = 1.1-25.0). The method of attempt remained consistent from baseline to follow-up attempt (= .67).

Conclusions: Screening high school students to identify those who are at risk for making future SAs should include questions about number of previous SAs and such indicators of risk as isolation, wish to die, and extent of planning prior to a SA.

Comment

Main findings: The period of adolescence can be one of increased psychosocial stressors that may further increase risk for suicidal behaviour[1]. Understanding the factors involved in repetitions of suicide attempt among this group could help direct clinical examination to improve identification of those at risk of another suicide attempt. The purpose of this US study was to examine the features of an adolescent suicide attempt that increase the risk for future attempts. A further examination of changes in suicide attempt method with repetition was also carried out. The study involved follow-up of 54 adolescents (aged 12 to 18 years) with a history of suicide attempt. At the initial assessment, overdose (61%) and cutting (26%) were the most predominant suicide methods. Over half of the adolescents reported that they thought (or were uncertain) that the method of attempt would kill them. A second attempt, occurring within the 4 to 6 year follow-up period, was made by one third of adolescents (16 females and 2 males). Those reporting that they wanted to die had over five times higher odds of making a subsequent suicide attempt compared to those who did not wish to die or were uncertain. All adolescents making an additional attempt had reported a definite or uncertain wish to die during their initial attempt. The majority (87%) of these repeat attempts were planned for less than an hour and involved no warnings or threats. Planning, isolation, and wish to die were features of a suicide attempt that enhanced risk of repeat attempts.

Implications: In order to determine risk for repetition of a suicide attempt, assessment of adolescents who attempt suicide might benefit from questions regarding planning, isolation, and wish to die. Clinicians working with adolescents who attempt suicide should particularly focus on reducing the seriousness of the adolescent's desire to die (e.g. thoughts of burdensomeness). Treatment of this group should also seek to build problem-solving capacity when encountering circumstances that lead to consideration of suicide. This may be encouraged in areas of Australian schooling where there may be opportunities to help engage adolescents in problem-solving skills relevant in the community.

Endnote

1. Bridge JA, Goldstein TR, Brent DA (2006). Adolescent suicide and suicidal behaviour. *Journal of Child Psychology and Psychiatry* 47, 372-394.

Mental pain as a mediator of suicidal tendency: A path analysis

Nahaliel S, Sommerfeld E, Orbach I, Weller A, Apter A, Zalsman G (Israel)
Comprehensive Psychiatry 55, 944-951, 2014

Background: This study used path-analysis to examine the assumption that the presence of mental pain in adults mediates the relationship between self-destruction, number of losses experienced in one's life, and suicidal tendency.

Methods: Fifty suicidal inpatients, 50 non-suicidal inpatients and 50 healthy volunteers were assessed for self-destruction, losses experienced, depression, suicidal tendency, and mental pain.

Results: Self-destruction was found to have both a direct effect on suicidal tendency as well as one mediated by the presence of mental pain. Number of losses effected suicidal tendency only indirectly, mediated by the presence of mental pain. Overall, self-destruction was a more significant determinant of suicidal tendency than were the number of losses experienced during one's life. A competing model, with depression replacing mental pain as the mediator, was also found to fit the data.

Discussion: These findings provide evidence that the presence of mental pain is a mediator in the relationships between both self-destruction and number of losses experienced, and between suicidal tendencies. More studies are needed in order to further differentiate between mental pain and depression as mediators in suicidal tendency.

Comment

Main findings: Consideration of the various processes and interactions between predictive factors could contribute to a greater understanding of suicidality. The current study from Israel investigated combinations of three predictors (self-destruction processes, losses over one's life, and mental pain) drawn from a model of known factors involved in suicidal behaviour[1]. The predicted outcome of suicidal tendency is derived from attitudes toward life and death (e.g. repulsion to life and attraction to death)[2]. Suicidal inpatients, non-suicidal inpatients, and healthy participants formed the groups analysed in the study, with each participant completing relevant measures (questionnaires) on all factors. Overall, suicidal inpatients reported higher levels of suicidal tendency compared to the other groups; this group also scored higher in measures of self-destruction processes (internal modes of self-abuse). Collectively the inpatients reported higher levels of loss (material, mental, physical, social) than healthy participants. Suicidal inpatients also reported higher levels of mental pain in comparison to the other groups. The model developed for the predictors of suicidal tendency shows that self-destruction has a direct and indirect effect on suicidal tendency. However, number of losses had only an indirect effect on suicidal tendency that was mediated by the presence of mental pain. The mediating role of mental pain was similar to that of depression.

Implications: Self-destruction processes appear to be a more important determinant of suicidal tendency than lifetime number of losses. An individual experiencing a number of losses seems to be at risk of suicidal tendencies when in the presence of intense psychological pain. This mental pain provides a connection between life circumstances and suicidality. Furthermore, mental pain and depression may both play a similar role in mediating the relationship between losses and self-destruction with suicidal tendencies. These two factors are highly associated yet distinct from one another. Not every depressed person is suicidal and not every suicide attempt occurs during a depressive episode[3]. Thus, mental pain may prove to be a useful predictor of suicide.

Endnotes

1. Orbach I (1997). A Taxonomy of factors related to suicidal behaviour. *Clinical Psychology: Science and Practice* 4, 208-224.
2. Orbach I, Milstein I, Har-Even D, Apter A, Tiano S, Elizur A (1991). A multi-attitude suicide tendency scale for adolescents. *Psychological Assessment* 3, 398-404.
3. Harkavy-Friedman JM, Nelson EA, Venarde DF, Mann JJ (2004). Suicidal behaviour in schizophrenia and schizoaffective disorder: examining the role of depression. *Suicide and Life-Threatening Behavior* 34, 66-76.

Suicide in young adults: Psychiatric and socio-economic factors from a case-control study

Page A, Morrell S, Hobbs C, Carter G, Dudley M, Duflou J, Taylor R (Australia)

BMC Psychiatry 14, 68, 2014

Background: Suicide in young adults remains an important public health issue in Australia. The attributable risks associated with broader socioeconomic factors, compared to more proximal psychiatric disorders, have not been considered previously in individual-level studies of young adults. This study compared the relative contributions of psychiatric disorder and socio-economic disadvantage associated with suicide in terms of relative and attributable risk in young adults.

Method: A population-based case-control study of young adults (18-34 years) compared cases of suicide (n = 84) with randomly selected controls (n = 250) from population catchments in New South Wales (Australia), with exposure information collected from key informant interviews (for both cases and controls). The relative and attributable risk of suicide associated with ICD-10 defined substance use, affective, and anxiety disorder was compared with educational achievement and household income, adjusting for key confounders. Prevalence of exposures from the control group was used to estimate population attributable fractions (PAF).

Results: Strong associations were evident between mental disorders and suicide for both males and females (ORs 3.1 to 18.7). The strongest association was for anxiety disorders (both males and females), followed by affective disorders and substance use disorders. Associations for socio-economic status were smaller in magnitude than for mental disorders for both males and females (ORs 1.1 to 4.8 for lower compared to high SES groups). The combined PAF% for all mental disorders (48% for males and 52% for females) was similar in magnitude to socio-economic status (46% for males and 58% for females).

Conclusion: Socio-economic status had a similar magnitude of population attributable risk for suicide as mental disorders. Public health interventions to reduce suicide should incorporate socio-economic disadvantage in addition to mental illness as a potential target for intervention.

Comment

Main findings: Suicide is the leading cause of death in the young Australians[1]. Although this rate has been declining (18.1/100,000 persons in 2003), the most recent finalised data for 2010 from the Australian Bureau of statistics shows that Australian young adults aged 25-34 years still died by suicide at a rate of 13.3/100,000 persons (higher than the national average of 11.3/100,000 persons)[1]. This study analysed prevalent psychiatric disorders and socio-economic disadvantage as potential risk factors for suicide in young adult Australians aged 18-34, living in New South Wales. Information collected from interviews with the next of kin of eighty-four suicide cases, was compared to information recorded from interviews with a nominated informant (parent, relative, friend) of 250 randomly selected living controls. For both males and females, psychiatric disorders were strongly associated with suicide risk, particularly anxiety disorders, even when adjusting for marital status, family history and socio-economic status. The association between socio-economic status and suicide risk was less prominent, particularly when controlling for marital status and family history of mental disorder. Despite this, suicide risk was higher in the lowest and middle socio-economic status groups in both males and females when compared to the highset socio-economic group. The adjusted population attributable fractions (PAF%) were highest for substance use disorder in males, and anxiety disorders for females. When combined, the PAF% for all psychiatric disorders was similar in magnitude to socio-economic status in both males and females.

Implications: There are a wide range of suicide prevention efforts worldwide, with programs focussing on increasing public awareness of suicide risk and mental illness, improving responses by mental health professionals, the responsible media reporting of suicides and removing access to means[2]. While research has suggested that increased physician education on treatment and identification of depression and the restriction of access to lethal means have the ability to reduce suicide rates, other interventions are in need of further research to determine their efficacy[2]. The need for further research is also evident when looking specifically at youth suicide prevention, the Australian National Youth Prevention Strategy (NYSPS), introduced in 1995, was not associated with any significant decrease in suicide rates, however research evaluating this program included a number of limitations which would be important to address[3].

The results of this study on suicide mortality support those of previous studies focussing on suicide attempts in Australia[4], which suggest the importance of the introduction of suicide prevention initiatives which target the effects of socio-economic deprivation on young adults in the Australian community.

Endnotes

1. Australian Bureau of Statistics (2014). *Causes of death, Australia, 2012.* Canberra: ABS.
2. Mann J, Apter A, Bertolote J, Beautrais A, Currier D, Haas A..., Hendin H (2005). Suicide prevention strategies: A systematic review. *JAMA* 294, 2064-2074.
3. Page A, Taylor R, Gunnell D, Carter G, Morrell S, Martin G (2011). Effectiveness of Australian youth suicide prevention initiatives. *British Journal of Psychiatry* 199, 423-429.
4. Page A, Taylor R, Hall W, Carter G (2009). Mental disorders and socio-economic status: Impact on population risk of attempted suicide in Australia. *Suicide and Life-Threatening Behavior* 39, 471-481.

Willingness to disclose a mental disorder and knowledge of disorders in others: Changes in Australia over 16 years

Reavley NJ, Jorm AF (Australia)

Australian and New Zealand Journal of Psychiatry 48, 162-168, 2014

Objective: To assess whether willingness to disclose experience of a mental disorder and treatment, and awareness of others' experiences have changed over a 16-year period.

Methods: In 2011, telephone interviews were carried out with 6019 Australians aged 15+. The survey interview used the same questions as those of the 1995 and 2003/4 national mental health literacy surveys, in which participants were presented with a case vignette describing either depression, depression with suicidal thoughts (2003/4 only), early schizophrenia or chronic schizophrenia (2003/4 only). Participants were asked whether they had a close friend or family member who had experienced a problem similar to that described in the vignette and whether the person received professional help. They were also asked whether they had experienced such a problem and whether they received professional help.

Results: The numbers of those disclosing experiences of depression and early schizophrenia, and of having received professional help for depression, have increased since 1995. Awareness of a family member or close friend with experiences of depression and early schizophrenia also increased between these years, as did awareness that the person received professional help.

Conclusions: The numbers of those disclosing experiences of and treatment for mental disorders has increased in the last 16 years. This is likely to be due to increased willingness to disclose rather than increased prevalence of disorders or increased rates of help-seeking.

Comment

Main findings: People suffering from a mental illness may face stigmatising attitudes from the general community, leading to social isolation, distress and difficulties in gaining employment[1]. Research has shown that Australians may perceive stigmatising attitudes in the community to be more prevalent than they actually are[2], meaning that even when these attitudes are not present, individuals may still be reluctant to disclose their mental illness or seek professional help over fears of discrimination[2]. This paper assessed whether the willingness to disclose a mental disorder has changed over the past 16 years, using data collected through telephone interviews with 6,019 Australians aged 15 and over. Change over time was analysed by comparing the results of the current 2011 interview to data collected from the 1995 and 2003/2004 National Mental Health Literacy surveys. Results showed a significant increase since 1995 of individuals disclosing depression and early schizophrenia, as well as an increase in awareness of a family member or close friend with depression or early schizophrenia. Between 2003/4 and 2011 there was a significant increase in the number of respondents seeking professional help for depression. Between 2003/4 and 2011 the change in females receiving professional help for depression was significantly greater than the change for males and individuals born outside of Australia were significantly more likely to disclose depression with suicidal thoughts than those born in Australia.

Implications: Mental illness is a major risk factor for both non-fatal and fatal suicidal behaviour[3]. The reduction of stigma may help to prevent suicide by ensuring that people with mental illness are more inclined to access support from the community or from mental health professionals. This paper shows that Australians who have been diagnosed with a mental disorder are more inclined to disclose this information or to access help than they were in 1995. These results may reflect the efforts of services such as the *beyondblue: The national depression initiative*[4] and suggest the importance of continuing efforts to improve the mental health literacy of Australians.

Endnotes

1. Crisp AH, Gelder MG, Rix S, Meltzer HI, Rowlands OJ (2000). Stigmatisation of people with mental illness. *British Journal of Psychiatry* 177, 4-7.

2. Griffiths KM, Nakane Y, Christensen H, Yoshioka K, Jorm AF, Nakane H (2006). Stigma in response to mental disorders: A comparison of Australia and Japan. *BMC Psychiatry* 6, 21.

3. Beautrais AL (2000). Risk factors for suicide and attempted suicide among young people. *Australian and New Zealand Journal of Psychiatry* 34, 420-436.

4. Website of *Beyondblue: The National Depression Initiative* (2014). Retrieved from http://www.beyondblue.org.au/about-us

What do the bereaved by suicide communicate in online support groups?

Schotanus-Dijkstra M, Havinga P, van Ballegooijen W, Delfosse L, Mokkenstorm J, Boon B (The Netherlands, Belgium)

Crisis 35, 27-35, 2013

Background: Every year, more than six million people lose a loved one through suicide. These bereaved by suicide are at relatively high risk for mental illnesses including suicide. The social stigma attached to suicide often makes it difficult to talk about grief. Participating in online forums may be beneficial for the bereaved by suicide, but it is unknown what they communicate in these forums.

Aims: What do the bereaved by suicide communicate in online forums? We examined which self-help mechanisms, grief reactions, and experiences with health-care services they shared online.

Method: We conducted a content analysis of 1,250 messages from 165 members of two Dutch language forums for the bereaved by suicide.

Results: We found that sharing personal experiences featured most prominently in the messages, often with emotional expressions of grief. Other frequently used self-help mechanisms were expressions of support or empathy, providing advice, and universality (recognition), while experiences with health-care services featured only occasionally. Compared with previous studies about online forums for somatic illnesses, the bereaved by suicide communicated more personal experiences and engaged much less in chitchat.

Conclusion: Online forums appear to have relevant additional value as a platform for talking about grief and finding support.

Comment

Main findings: Bereavement support groups encourage individuals to recognise and share feelings and experiences relating to the death of a loved one. A relatively new form of bereavement support is the use of online support groups, which allow individuals to share these feelings without the need for face-to-face interactions. This study aimed to determine which self-help mechanisms, grief reactions, and experiences with health care services are communicated by individuals in an online support group for people bereaved by suicide. The authors conducted a content analysis of messages in two online forums in Belgium (958 forum members and 5,281 messages on the forum) and the Netherlands (1,064 forum members and 1,039 messages on the forum). The study included 1,250 messages that were posted by 165 members between September 2010 and May 2011 (messages from moderators, double-posted messages and suicidal messages were excluded). The majority of participants were women (70%) and the mean age was 32 years of age. Five percent of participants had lost more than one loved one to suicide. Results indicated that participants shared personal experiences in 77% of the messages including information on their loved one, the method of suicide and the circumstances of the day that the suicide happened, and their current and past feelings about the loss. Forty percent of messages on the forums contained messages of support or empathy for other bereaved individuals, while around one quarter of messages contained some message of information or advice. Negative grief reactions were noted in 45% of messages, while only 14% contained positive grief reactions. Only 7% of posts contained any positive mention of health-care services and participants reported greater satisfaction with online support groups, specialised psychologists and spiritual support providers rather than general psychologists or practitioners. On the other hand, five percent of messages expressed negative feelings towards health care services.

Implications: Research on bereavement support groups has so far returned mixed results regarding the effectiveness of these groups[1]. This study adds to the current knowledge about the effectiveness of these services, particularly online support services for those bereaved by suicide. Studies including such services are important considering previous suggestions that the experiences of individuals bereaved by suicide may differ from bereavement through other causes of death, and that stigma may result in increased isolation and the need for increased social support in these individuals[2].

Participants appeared to be satisfied with their experience of online support forums which suggests that services such as "Support after Suicide"[3] in Australia may offer low-cost and easily accessible alternatives to conventional health-care services.

Endnotes

1. Jordan JR, Neimeyer RA (2003). Does grief counseling work? *Death Studies* 27, 765-786.
2. Jordan JR (2001). Is suicide bereavement different? A reassessment of the literature. *Suicide and Life-Threatening Behavior* 31, 91-102.
3. Website of Support after Suicide (2014). Retrieved from http://www.supportaftersuicide.org.au/

High impact child abuse may predict risk of elevated suicidality during antidepressant initiation

Singh AB, Bousman CA, Ng CH, Berk M (Australia)

Australian and New Zealand Journal of Psychiatry 47, 1191-1195, 2013

Background: Concerns have emerged that initiation of an antidepressant can lead to or exacerbate suicidality. If those more at risk could be identified prior to treatment, treatment risk benefit analysis and patient risk management could be assisted.

Aims: This study investigated the role of child abuse and ongoing emotional impact from abuse on the risk of suicidality during the first week of treatment with an antidepressant. The patient sample for this study was drawn from one site of a larger pharmacogenetic study. The hypothesis was that subjects with high impact child abuse would have greater elevation of suicidality during the first week of antidepressant treatment.

Methods: Fifty-one subjects were initiated on either venlafaxine (VEN) or escitalopram (ESC) for major depressive disorder (MDD) and had pre-treatment suicidality assayed with the reasons for living scale (RFLS), which was repeated after one week of treatment. Several clinical, demographic and genotype variables were controlled for. The 15-item Impact of Event Scale (IES-15) was administered to subjects reporting abuse to dichotomise the abuse group into low and high (IES-15 $\geq$ 26) impact groups for sub-analysis as per the scales validated rating guidelines.

Results: Subjects reporting no child abuse exposure were less likely to have increased suicidality during the first week of antidepressant treatment (7.6%) compared to subjects with low impact abuse (38.5%, p = 0.041) and high impact abuse (58.3%, p = 0.009). Only high impact abuse predicted increased suicidality after adjustment for potential confounders such as depression severity (OR = 31.5, 95% CI = 1.3 to 748.7, p = 0.03).

Conclusions: If these findings are replicated in larger samples, child abuse history could become an important element of assessing risk benefit balance when initiating antidepressants and may help guide the level of patient review needed during antidepressant initiation.

Comment

Main findings: Child abuse and neglect may potentially influence the development of psychological disorders and suicidality later in life. However, the Food and Drug Administration in the US have previously issued warnings concerning antidepressant initiation and suicidality in younger populations[1]. In order to establish those more at risk, this Australian study investigated the role of child abuse on risk of suicidality during antidepressant initiation of patients (18 years and over) with a principle diagnosis of Major Depressive Disorder (MDD). Compared to those with childhood abuse exposure, those with no childhood abuse exposure were less likely to have increased suicidality from pre-treatment to one week of antidepressant treatment. However, there was no difference in suicidality at this time between those with low and high impact child abuse exposure. During the first week of antidepressant treatment, patients with high impact of child abuse exposure had significantly higher risk of suicidal ideation after controlling for other clinical factors (e.g. depression severity) compared to those reporting no child abuse exposure.

Implications: From this Australian study it appears that those with MDD and significant ongoing emotional impact from child abuse are at greater risk of developing suicidality. However, further investigation into this relationship is needed due to the small size of the sample in the current study. The emotional impact from child abuse risk factor may assist those prescribing antidepressant medications to carefully monitor and conduct more frequent clinical reviews for individuals at greater risk. It may also help prescribers to weigh-up potential risks and benefits of antidepressant treatment, allowing for a more informed treatment plan. The use of other mental health resources (e.g. community supports) may be encouraged or strengthened during the initial stages of antidepressant treatment among the at-risk group (high impact child abuse).

Endnote

1. Khan A, Khan S, Kolts R, Brown WA (2003). Suicide rates in clinical trials of SSRIs, other antidepressants, and placebo: analysis of FDA reports. *American Journal of Psychiatry* 160, 790-792.

Effectiveness of online self-help for suicidal thoughts: Results of a randomised controlled trial

Spijker AJ, Straten Av, Kerkhof JF (The Netherlands)

PLoS ONE. Published online: 27 February 2014. doi: 10.1371/journal.pone.0090118, 2014

Background: Many people with suicidal thoughts do not receive treatment. The Internet can be used to reach more people in need of support.

Objective: To test the effectiveness of unguided online self-help to reduce suicidal thoughts.

Method: 236 adults with mild to moderate suicidal thoughts were randomised to the intervention (n = 116) or a waitlist control group (n = 120). Assessments took place at baseline, and 2, 4 and 6 weeks later. Primary outcome was suicidal thoughts. Secondary outcomes were depressive symptoms, anxiety, hopelessness, worry, and health status.

Results: The intervention group showed a small significant effect in reducing suicidal thoughts (d = 0.28). Effects were more pronounced for those with a history of repeated suicide attempts. There was also a significant reduction in worry (d = 0.33). All other secondary outcomes showed small but non-significant improvements.

Conclusions: Although effect sizes were small, the reach of the internet could enable this intervention to help many people reduce their suicidal thoughts.

Comment

Main findings: Many people experiencing suicidal ideation encounter intrapersonal barriers to help seeking[1]. Web-based interventions provide an avenue for additional support collaborated with regular treatment. In order to investigate the effectiveness of such interventions in reducing the frequency and intensity of suicidal thoughts, this randomised intervention trial compared an unguided web-based self-help online tool with a waitlist control group in Netherlands. The self-help intervention is based on cognitive behavioural therapy (CBT), as well as components of dialectic behavioural therapy (DBT), problem solving therapy (PST), and mindfulness based cognitive therapy (MBCT). Participants in the waitlist group received general information about suicidality. Suicidal thoughts, depression, hopelessness, anxiety, worry, and health status were substantial at baseline measures among the sample. There was significantly greater improvement in suicidal thoughts over time in the online self-help group compared to the waitlist group. Measures of worry also revealed a significant difference in improvement for the online self-help group compared to controls. Overall, the average reduction in suicidal thoughts was twice as much per two-week period in the intervention group compared to the waitlist group. Those with a history of suicide attempt also benefited from the online self-help intervention.

Implications: The advent of new technologies is an opportunity for innovative methods in healthcare, such as the use of social media in understanding suicide[2].

Web-based self-help interventions can be an effective means to reduce suicidal thoughts. This online method offers a valid way of reaching people who might not be actively seeking help. As there were participants in the sample who had already been receiving care, this online intervention may be employed in conjunction with regular care. Those who are reluctant to engage in help seeking, due to intrapersonal barriers, may benefit from the anonymity of online intervention tools. Integrating additional preventative strategies (e.g. email referrals to more intensive supports) on the online platform provides an immediate response to at-risk individuals.

Endnotes

1. Bruffaerts R, Demytenaere K, Hwang I, Chiu WT, Sampson N, Kessler RC…, Nock MK (2011). Treatment of suicidal people around the world. *British Journal of Psychiatry* 199, 64-70.
2. Jashinsky J, Burton SH, Hanson CL, West J, Giraud-Carrier C, Barnes MD, Argyle T (2014). Tracking suicide risk factors through Twitter in the US. *Crisis* 35, 51-59.

Self-harm in young adolescents (12-16 years): Onset and short-term continuation in a community sample

Stallard P, Spears M, Montgomery AA, Phillips R, Sayal K (UK)

BMC Psychiatry 13, 328, 2013

Background: To investigate the prevalence of self-harm in young adolescents and factors associated with onset and continuity over a one year period.

Method: Prospective longitudinal study. Participants were young adolescents (n = 3964) aged 12-16 years attending 8 secondary schools in the Midlands and South West of England.

Results: Over a one year period 27% of young adolescents reported thoughts of self-harm and 15% reported at least one act of self-harm. Of those who self-harmed, less than one in five (18%) had sought help for psychological problems of anxiety or depression. Compared with boys, girls were at increased risk of developing thoughts (OR 1.61, 95% CI 1.26-2.06) and acts (OR 1.40, 95% CI 1.06-1.84) of self-harm, particularly amongst those girls in school year 9 (aged 13/14, thoughts adjusted Odds Ratio (aOR) 1.97, 95% CI 1.27-3.04; acts aOR 2.59, 95% CI 1.52-4.41). Of those reporting thoughts of self-harm at baseline, 60% also reported these thoughts at follow-up. Similarly 55% of those who reported an act of self-harm at baseline also reported that they had self-harmed at follow-up. Insecure peer relationships increased the likelihood that boys and girls would develop self-harming behaviours, as did being bullied for boys. Low mood was associated with the development of self-harming thoughts and behaviours for boys and girls, whilst a strong sense of school membership was associated with a reduced risk of developing thoughts of self-harm for boys and increased the likelihood of self-harming thoughts and behaviours ceasing for girls.

Conclusion: Self-harm in young adolescents is common, with one in four reporting self-harming thoughts and one in six engaging in self-harming behaviour over a one year period. Self-harm is already established by 12/13 years of age and for over half of our sample, self-harming thoughts and behaviour persisted over the year. Secure peer and strong school relationships were associated with less self-harm. Few seek help for psychological problems, suggesting a need to increase awareness amongst all professionals who work with young adolescents about self-harm and associated risk factors.

Comment

Main findings: Self-harming thoughts and behaviours in adolescence are a notable problem. Of the adolescents who do self-harm, approximately half will do so more than once[1]. Thoughts of self-harm are also associated with non-fatal suicidal behaviour in adolescents within the community[2]. In order to understand the factors associated with short-term continuation or cessation of self-harm in young adolescents, the authors examined pupils from 8 schools in the UK over a time period of 12-months (assessed twice for suicide ideation in the preceding 6 months). Of the participants, 27% experienced thoughts of self-harm and 15% reported acts of self-harm at some stage over the time-period. Of those not reporting thoughts of self-harm initially, 9.1% reported experiencing thoughts of self-harm over the 6-month period; more girls (11%) than boys (7%). Of those not reporting any self-harm behaviour initially, 6.0% had self-harmed by the second assessment; more acts by girls (7%) than boys (5%). Continuation of self-harming thoughts were reported by 59.5% of those initially thinking of self-harm, while 55.1% of those initially self-harming reported continued acts of self-harm. Cannabis use and symptoms of low mood increased the risk of developing self-harming thoughts and behaviours. Boys who were being regularly bullied were twice as likely to report thoughts of self-harm continuation. Adolescents reporting initial self-harm thoughts were more likely to develop self-harming behaviour than those who did not initially report self-harm thoughts or behaviours.

Implications: Adolescents as young as 12 years of age are known to experience self-harming thoughts and behaviours; these experiences can persist over time. Self-harming prevention activities should incorporate a focus on young adolescents, before these experiences become firmly established later on in life. Improving general mental health and developing positive cognitive skills is likely to help reduce the numbers of self-harming events. This may be achieved with an increased awareness of these behaviours and their associated risk factors. Training addressing the nature of self-harm and its risk factors may be provided to those who are in regular contact with young adolescents to improve identification of such behaviours. Schools offer an opportune location for delivering programs to improve mental wellbeing and prevent suicide such as the MindMatters project in Australia[3].

Endnotes

1. Morey C, Corcoran P, Arensman E, Perry IJ (2008). The prevalence of self-reported deliberate self-harm in Irish adolescents. *BMC Public Health* 8, 79. doi: 10.1186/1471-2458-8-79.
2. Kokkevi A, Rotsika V, Arapaki A, Richardson C (2012). Adolescent's self-reported suicide attempts, self-harm, thoughts and their correlates across 17 European countries. *Journal of Child Psychology and Psychiatry* 53, 381-389.
3. MindMatters (2014). *What is MindMatters.* Retrieved 22 May, 2014, from http://www.mindmatters.edu.au/about-mindmatters/what-is-mindmatters

Criminality and suicide: A longitudinal Swedish cohort study

Stenbacka M, Romelsjo A, Jokinen J (Sweden)

British Medical Journal Open 4, e003497, 2014

Objectives: This study aimed to investigate whether violent and non-violent offending were related to elevated risk of suicide. We also investigated whether the risk was higher among those with repeated offences and how experiences of substance misuse and suicide attempt modified the relationship.

Design: A nationwide prospective cohort study.

Setting: A register study of 48 834 conscripted men in 1969/1970 in Sweden followed up during a 35-year period in official registers.

Participants: A birth cohort of 48 834 men who were mandatory conscripted for military service in 1969/70 at the age of 18-20 years. Possible confounders were retrieved from psychological assessments at conscription and the cohort was linked to mortality and hospitalisation and crime records from 1970 onwards. Estimates of suicide risks were calculated as HR with 95% CIs using Cox proportional regression analyses with adjustment for potential confounding by family, psychological and behavioural factors including substance use and psychiatric disorders.

Results: Of the total cohort, 2671 (5.5%) persons died during the follow-up period. Of these, 615 (23%) persons died due to suicide. Non-violent criminality was evident for 29% and violent criminality for 4.7% of all the participants. In the crude model, the violent offenders had nearly five times higher risk (HR=4.69, 3.56 to 6.19) to die from suicide and non-violent criminals had about two times higher risk (HR=2.08, 1.72 to 2.52). In the fully adjusted model, the HRs were still significant for suicide in the non-violent group.

Conclusions: Experiences of violent or non-violent criminality were associated with increased risk of suicide. Comorbidity with alcohol and substance use and psychiatric disorders modified the risk, but the suicide risk remained significantly elevated for non-violent criminals. It is crucial to identify offenders and especially repeated offenders who also suffer from alcohol or substance misuse and psychiatric illness in clinical settings in order to prevent suicide.

Comment

Main findings: Prison inmates and offenders recently released from prison are at an increased risk of suicide compared to the general population[1]. Limited studies have assessed the risk of suicide in offenders who have not been incarcerated, despite research showing that as many people are in contact with a police officer (either as victim or offender) in the three weeks before death by suicide, than are in contact with a mental health professional[2]. This longitudinal Swedish study followed 48,834 adult males aged 18-20 over 35 years to examine the relationship between offending and risk of completed suicide. Participants initially completed two questionnaires and a structured interview including factors relating to their family and psychosocial background and health, and their alcohol and drug use behaviours. Follow-up involved the use of data from the National Crime Register and the Cause of Death Register. Overall, 2,671 participants died during the 35 year follow-up period, 615 of whom died by suicide. Suicide was the cause of death in close to one-third of individuals who had committed a violent offence before death and one quarter of those who committed a non-violent offence before death. When a number of confounding factors were controlled for (including fathers occupation, medication for nervous problems among family members, conduct problems at school, prior contact with police, medication for a psychiatric disorder, emotional control, intellectual capacity, psychiatric diagnosis, contact with police and juvenile authorities) both violent and non-violent offenders had significantly higher risks of suicide when compared to non-offenders. However, when alcohol and substance misuse and past attempted suicide were controlled for in the fully adjusted model, only non-violent offending remained a significant predictor of increased risk of suicide.

Implications: In an area which has been largely neglected in research to date, this paper provides important findings; strengthened by the large national cohort, longitudinal study design and the inclusion of a number of potential confounding variables. The results suggest the need for research in Australia which includes non-incarcerated violent and non-violent offenders rather than focussing solely on current or recently released inmates. Suicide prevention efforts directed at offenders should also attempt to target these individuals.

Endnotes

1. Kariminia A, Butler TG, Corben SP, Levy MH, Grant L, Kaldor JM, Law MG (2007). Extreme cause-specific mortality in a cohort of adult prisoners – 1988 to 2002: A data-linkage study. *The International Journal of Epidemiology* 36, 310-316.

2. Linsley KR, Johnson N, Martin J (2007). Police contact within 3 months of suicide and associated health service contact. *British Journal of Psychiatry* 190, 170-171.

Influence of violent video gaming on determinants of the acquired capability for suicide

Teismann T, Förtsch EMAD, Baumgart P, Het S, Michalak J (Germany)
Psychiatry Research 215, 217-222, 2013

The interpersonal theory of suicidal behavior proposes that fearlessness of death and physical pain insensitivity is a necessary requisite for self-inflicted lethal self-harm. Repeated experiences with painful and provocative events are supposed to cause an incremental increase in acquired capability. The present study examined whether playing a first-person shooter-game in contrast to a first-person racing game increases pain tolerance, a dimension of the acquired capability construct, and risk-taking behavior, a risk factor for developing acquired capability. N=81 male participants were randomly assigned to either play an action-shooter or a racing game before engaging in a game on risk-taking behavior and performing a cold pressor task (CPT). Participants exhibited higher pain tolerance after playing an action shooter game than after playing a racing game. Furthermore, playing an action shooter was generally associated with heightened risk-taking behavior. Group-differences were not attributable to the effects of the different types of games on self-reported mood and arousal. Overall these results indicate that action-shooter gaming alters pain tolerance and risk-taking behavior. Therefore, it may well be that long-term consumption of violent video games increases a person's capability to enact lethal self-harm.

Comment

Main findings: Violent video games have been associated with an increased propensity for violent and aggressive behaviour in children and young adults, as well as increases in psychological arousal and aggressive thoughts and feelings, and a decrease in prosocial behaviour[1]. This study was the first of its kind in analysing the effect of these games on the potential for suicidal behaviour, based on Thomas Joiner's Interpersonal Psychological Theory of Suicidal Behaviour[2]. The theory purports that three factors must be present for someone to die by suicide: A sense of thwarted belongingness, perceived burdensomeness and an acquired capability for suicide, stemming from recurring exposure to painful and or/ fear inducing experiences[2]. Teismann and colleagues tested the effect of violent video games on the acquired capability for suicide by examining whether a first person shooting game (Counter Strike: Source) increased levels of pain tolerance (measured through a cold pressor task) and impulsivity (measured through a risk taking game) more than a non-violent racing game (Need for Speed: Shift). The sample included 81 males aged 18-39 years who were recruited through face-to-face interaction or by responding to posted flyers. After playing both of the games, participants felt more animated and slightly less positive than before they played. Differences emerged between the two games, with participants playing Counter Strike having higher levels of pain tolerance and risk-taking behaviour compared to those playing Need for Speed.

Implications: While violent video games have been linked to violent behaviour against others in the past[1] this study provides the first step in analysing whether these games may have an effect on the propensity for self-directed violence through suicidal behaviour. As noted by the authors, further research that takes into account the relationship between these games and fear of dying may be a valuable addition to the findings reported in this study. From a practical sense, the results may suggest that the restriction of access to these video games or the time spent playing these games may play a role in the prevention of suicidality in vulnerable individuals.

Endnotes

1. Anderson CA, Bushman BJ (2001). Effects of violent video games on aggressive behavior, aggressive cognition, aggressive affect, physiological arousal, and prosocial behavior. *A Meta-analytic Review of the Scientific Literature* 12, 353.
2. Joiner T (2005). *Why people die by suicide.* Cambridge, MA: Harvard University Press.

Anxiety disorders are independently associated with suicide ideation and attempts: Propensity score matching in two epidemiological samples

Thibodeau MA, Welch PG, Sareen J, Asmundson GJG (Canada)

Depression and Anxiety 30, 947-954, 2013

Background: Research suggests that suicidal behavior in individuals with anxiety disorders is attributable to cooccurring risk factors, such as depression. We argue that these conclusions are founded primarily in statistical adjustments that may obscure independent associations. We explored independent associations between specific anxiety disorders and suicide attempts and ideation by means of propensity score matching, a process that simulates a case-control study by creating matched groups that differ in group status (e.g., diagnosis of a specific anxiety disorder) but that are statistically equivalent on observed covariates.

Methods: We made use of the National Comorbidity Survey Replication (NCS-R) and the National Epidemiologic Survey on Alcohol and Related Conditions (NESARC), which include a total of 43,935 adults. Diagnoses included agoraphobia without panic disorder, generalized anxiety disorder, panic disorder with or without agoraphobia, posttraumatic stress disorder, social anxiety disorder, and specific phobia.

Results: Each anxiety disorder was (95% confidence intervals) associated with increased odds of lifetime suicide attempts (odds ratios 3.57-6.64 [NCS-R], 3.03-7.00 [NESARC]) and suicidal ideation (odds ratios 2.62-4.87 [NCS-R], 3.34-10.57 [NESARC]). Odds ratios for each disorder remained statistically significant after matching on diagnostic status of dysthymia, major depressive disorder, alcohol abuse/dependence, substance abuse/dependence, bipolar disorder I, bipolar disorder II, all other anxiety disorders, and on sociodemographic variables.

Conclusions: This is the first report to present evidence that each anxiety disorder is associated with suicide ideation and suicide attempts beyond the effects of cooccurring mental disorders. These findings warrant consideration in assessment, intervention, and related policies.

Comment

Main findings: Anxiety disorders are an exceedingly common mental disorder[1] with 14.4% of Australians aged 16 to 85 years reporting an anxiety disorder within a 12-month period[2]. However, investigations into anxiety disorders and suicide have not been as thorough as current methods allow. In an effort to estimate causal effects, the authors have adopted a statistical technique (propensity score matching) to explore independent associations between specific anxiety disorders (agoraphobia without panic disorder, generalised anxiety disorder, panic disorder, posttraumatic stress disorder, social anxiety disorder, and specific phobia) and suicide ideation and suicide attempts. Two separate US national surveys were used and involved matching people who experienced suicide ideation and suicide attempt to those without. The odds of each specific anxiety disorder were significantly greater in people with suicide ideation – compared to those without – in both national surveys. Similar results were found for attempted suicide, but only in one of the surveys used (agoraphobia without panic disorder did not increase odds of suicide attempt in the second survey).

Implications: Individuals with anxiety disorders have higher risk of suicide ideation and attempts, independent of common co-occurring mental disorders. Australians with any anxiety disorder also experience suicidal ideation (8.9%) and suicide attempts (2.1%)[3]. However, no Australian research has investigated suicidality in specific anxiety disorders. The established relationship between anxiety disorders and suicidality might suggest similar causal pathways as other disorders, such as depression. The impact of anxiety disorders on the multifaceted nature of suicidality should be reflected in health policies, training opportunities for healthcare providers, and the development of interventions for this type of mental disorder. Patients with anxiety disorders not reporting symptoms of depression might benefit from screening and monitoring practices for suicidality. Adequate identification of suicide risk in individuals with an anxiety disorder supersedes the risks inherent in overlooking this vulnerability for suicide.

Endnotes

1. Kessler RC, Berglund P, Demler O, Jin R, Merikangas KR, Walters EE (2005). Lifetime prevalence and age-of-onset distributions of DSM-IV disorders in the national Comorbidity Survey Replication. *Archives of General Psychiatry* 62, 593-602.

2. Australian Bureau of Statistics (2008). *National Survey of Mental Health and Wellbeing: Summary of Results, 2007.* Cat. no. 4326.0, Canberra: Australian Bureau of Statistics.

3. Johnston AK, Pirkis JE, Burgess PM (2009). Suicidal thoughts and behaviours among Australian adults: Findings from the 2007 National Survey of Mental Health and Wellbeing. *Australian and New Zealand Journal of Psychiatry* 43, 635-643.

Suicide-related events in young people following prescription of SSRIs and other antidepressants: A self-controlled case series analysis

Wijlaars LPMM, Nazareth I, Whitaker HJ, Evans SJW, Petersen I (UK)

British Medical Journal Open 3, e003247, 2013

Objectives: We aimed to examine the temporal association between selective serotonin reuptake inhibitors (SSRI) and tricyclic antidepressant (TCA) prescriptions and suicide-related events in children and adolescents.

Design: Self-controlled case series.

Setting: Electronic health records were used from 479 general practices in The Health Improvement Network (THIN) UK primary care database from 1995 to 2009.

Participants: 81 young people aged 10-18 years with a record of completed suicide, 1496 who attempted suicide, 1178 with suicidal ideation and 2361 with intentional self-harm.

Main Outcome Measures: Incidence Rate Ratios (IRRs) for completed and attempted suicide, suicidal ideation and intentional self-harm.

Results: For non-fatal suicide-related behaviour, IRRs were similar for the time the person was prescribed either SSRIs or TCAs: IRRs increased during pre-exposure, peaked on prescription day, were stable up to the fourth prescription-week, and decreased after the prescriptions were stopped. For both types of antidepressants, IRRs were lower or similar to pre-exposure levels during the period of prescription. For SSRIs, there was an increase in the IRR for completed suicide on the day of prescription (N=5; IRR=42.5, 95% CI 4.5 to 403.4), and during the fourth week of SSRI prescription (N=2; IRR=11.3, 95% CI 1.1 to 115.6).

Conclusions: We found that a very small number of young people were prescribed antidepressants and that there was an absence of a sustained increase in rates of suicide-related events in this group. There were no systematic differences between the association of TCAs and SSRIs and the incidence risk ratios for attempted suicide, suicidal ideation or intentional self-harm and, apart from the day of prescription, rates did not exceed pre-exposure levels. The pattern of IRR for suicide for SSRIs was similar to that found in non-fatal suicide-related events. Our results warrant a re-evaluation of the current prescription of SSRIs in young people. We recommend the creation of a pragmatic registry for active pharmacovigilance.

Comment

Main findings: Vulnerability to major depression and suicidality emerges particularly at the time of adolescence. There exists concern that selective serotonin reuptake inhibitors (SSRI's) may increase the rate of suicide-related events and self-harm. This potential susceptibility has prompted the authors to investigate the time-based association between pharmaceutical treatments, i.e., SSRI and tricyclic antidepressant (TCA) prescriptions, and risk of suicidality and self-harm in young people in the UK. Prospectively recorded primary care data of young people (aged 10 to 18 years) was taken from the Health Improvement Network between the start of 1995 to end of 2009. This sample contained information regarding a suicide-related event (suicide: 81 cases, suicide attempt: 1,496 cases, suicide ideation: 1,178 cases, and self-harm: 2,361 cases) along with prescribed antidepressant medication. The risk period of interest included a baseline measure, four 1-month pre-exposure periods, the day of prescription, four 1-week early exposure periods, remainder period of antidepressant exposure, and three 1-month periods after the end of the antidepressant episode.

The non-fatal suicidal behaviours of young people prescribed SSRI or TCA showed similar patterns of the behaviour over the risk period (i.e. upward trend during pre-exposure; peak on the day of exposure; stable/slight increase during first weeks of prescription, decrease to the end of antidepressant episode). The greatest increase on the day of prescription was for young people with a record of suicidal ideation. Of those that had died by suicide and were taking SSRIs, 14% had died within the risk period with the highest incidence on the day of prescription. Apart from the day of prescription, there were no significant increases in risk from pre-exposure levels.

Implications: Some suicide-related events are expected to occur within a young population experiencing symptoms of depression, irrespective of SSRI prescription[1]. A failure to relieve suicide-related events during the first month of prescription may possibly be due to a lag in the antidepressant effect or treatment-resistant depression. Furthermore, novel suicidal emotions and experiences may arise as a result of the antidepressant treatment, whereby early improvements in clinical depression may lead to individuals acting on existing suicidal feelings (activation syndrome[2]). However, the increase in suicide-related events on the day of prescription could also be explained by GP recording behaviour and the severity of the symptoms/condition. The findings suggest that risk posed by untreated depression may be greater than any potential temporary increase in suicide-related events due to the use of SSRI's.

Endnotes

1. Bridge JA, Goldstein TR, Brent DA (2006). Adolescent suicide and suicidal behaviour. *Journal of Child Psychology and Psychiatry* 47,372-394.
2. Sinclair LI, Christmas DM, Hood SD, Potokar JP, Robertson A, Isaac A..., Davies SJ (2009). Antidepressant-induced jitteriness/anxiety syndrome: systematic review. *British Journal of Psychiatry* 194, 483-490.

Distinctive emotional responses of clinicians to suicide-attempting patients — a comparative study

Yaseen ZS, Briggs J, Kopeykina I, Orchard KM, Silberlicht J, Bhingradia H, Galynker II (USA)
BMC Psychiatry 13, 230, 2013

Background: Clinician responses to patients have been recognized as an important factor in treatment outcome. Clinician responses to suicidal patients have received little attention in the literature however, and no quantitative studies have been published. Further, although patients with high versus low lethality suicidal behaviors have been speculated to represent two distinct populations, clinicians' emotional responses to them have not been examined.

Methods: Clinicians' responses to their patients when last seeing them prior to patients' suicide attempt or death were assessed retrospectively with the Therapist Response/Countertransference Questionnaire, administered anonymously via an Internet survey service. Scores on individual items and subscale scores were compared between groups, and linear discriminant analysis was applied to determine the combination of items that best discriminated between groups.

Results: Clinicians reported on patients who completed suicide, made high-lethality attempts, low-lethality attempts, or died unexpectedly non-suicidal deaths in a total of 82 cases. We found that clinicians treating imminently suicidal patients had less positive feelings towards these patients than for non-suicidal patients, but had higher hopes for their treatment, while finding themselves notably more overwhelmed, distressed by, and to some degree avoidant of them. Further, we found that the specific paradoxical combination of hopefulness and distress/avoidance was a significant discriminator between suicidal patients and those who died unexpectedly non-suicidal deaths with 90% sensitivity and 56% specificity. In addition, we identified one questionnaire item that discriminated significantly between high- and low-lethality suicide patients.

Conclusions: Clinicians' emotional responses to patients at risk versus not at risk for imminent suicide attempt may be distinct in ways consistent with responses theorized by Maltsberger and Buie in 1974. Prospective replication is needed to confirm these results, however. Our findings demonstrate the feasibility of using quantitative self-report methodologies for investigation of the relationship between clinicians' emotional responses to suicidal patients and suicide risk.

Comment

Main findings: When treating patients for suicide, clinicians may sometimes struggle to identify signs and symptoms that could provide an opportunity for appropriate intervention. Furthermore, the way in which a clinician responds emotionally to their patients is an important factor related to treatment outcome[1]. This online survey compared emotional responses of clinicians in the encounter preceding a suicide-related event (i.e. death by suicide, high-lethality attempters, and low-lethality attempters) and non-suicide death. Half of the sample was medical doctors (50%) followed by clinicians with a PhD qualification (17.5%). Clinicians treating suicidal patients recalled moderately positive feelings towards these patients (although significantly less than clinicians recalling non-suicidal patients). These clinicians had higher hopes for treatment but experienced more distress and avoidance of the patient. A combination of feelings of hopefulness and distress/avoidance distinguished between clinicians treating suicidal patients and those treating non-suicide patients. There was no clear distinction between clinicians experiences of patients that made high-lethality attempts (or died by suicide) and low-lethality attempts. However, clinicians treating patients in the group that had died or made highly lethal attempts experienced more sadness in their encounter.

Implications: Problems in the management of emotional reactions to patients may interfere with the effectiveness of treatment. One Australian study has identified poor staff-patient relationships as a key factor in clinical suicide prevention[2]. Quantitative self-assessment of emotional responses in the treatment of suicidal patients may provide a foundation for treatment efficacy. This type of self-assessment may reveal patterns generated by the clinician's unconscious processes, bringing greater awareness of the clinician's interpersonal experience with the patient and a greater opportunity to appropriately assess suicide-risk.

Endnotes

1. Bruck E, Winston A, Aderholt S, Muran JC (2006). Predictive validity of patient and therapist attachment and introject styles. *American Journal of Psychotherapy* 60, 393-406.
2. Burgess P, Pirkis J, Morton J, Corke E (2000). Lessons from a comprehensive clinical audit of users of psychiatric services who committed suicide. *Psychiatric Services* 51, 1555-1560.

Recommended Readings

Severe bereavement stress during the prenatal and childhood periods and risk of psychosis in later life: Population based cohort study

Abel KM, Heuvelman HP, Jorgensen L, Magnusson C, Wicks S, Susser E, Hallkvist J, Dalman C
(UK, Sweden, USA)

British Medical Journal 348, f7679, 2014

Objective: To examine the risk of psychosis associated with severe bereavement stress during the antenatal and postnatal period, between conception to adolescence, and with different causes of death.

Design: Population based cohort study.

Setting: Swedish national registers including births between 1973 and 1985 and followed-up to 2006.

Participants: In a cohort of 1 045 336 Swedish births (1973-85), offspring born to mothers exposed to severe maternal bereavement stress six months before conception or during pregnancy, or exposed to loss of a close family member subsequently from birth to 13 years of age were followed until 2006. Admissions were identified by linkage to national patient registers.

Main Outcome Measures: Crude and adjusted odds ratios for all psychosis, non-affective psychosis, and affective psychosis.

Results: Maternal bereavement stress occurring preconception or during the prenatal period was not associated with a significant excess risk of psychosis in offspring (adjusted odds ratio, preconception 1.24, 95% confidence interval 0.96 to 1.62; first trimester 0.95, 0.58 to1.56; second trimester 0.79, 0.46 to 1.33; third trimester 1.14, 0.78 to 1.66). Risks increased modestly after exposure to the loss of a close family member from birth to adolescence for all psychoses (adjusted odds ratio 1.17, 1.04 to 1.32). The pattern of risk was generally similar for non-affective and affective psychosis. Thus estimates were higher after death in the nuclear compared with extended family but remained non-significant for prenatal exposure; the earlier the exposure to death in the nuclear family occurred in childhood (all psychoses: adjusted odds ratio, birth to 2.9 years 1.84, 1.41 to 2.41; 3-6.9 years 1.47, 1.16 to 1.85; 7-12.9 years 1.32, 1.10 to 1.58) and after suicide. Following suicide, risks were especially higher for affective psychosis (birth to 2.9 years 3.33, 2.00 to 5.56; 6.9 years 1.84, 1.04 to 3.25; 7-12.9 years 2.68, 1.84 to 3.92). Adjustment for key confounders attenuated but did not explain associations with risk.

Conclusions: Postnatal but not prenatal bereavement stress in mothers is associated with an increased risk of psychosis in offspring. Risks are especially high for affective psychosis after suicide in the nuclear family, an effect that is not explained by family psychiatric history. Future studies are needed to understand possible sources of risk and resilience so that structures can be put in place to support vulnerable children and their families.

Health care contacts in the year before suicide death

Ahmedani BK, Simon GE, Stewart C, Beck A, Waitzfelder BE, Rossom R, Lynch F, Owen-Smith A, Hunkeler EM, Whiteside U, Operskalski BH, Coffey MJ, Solberg LI (USA)

Journal of General Internal Medicine. Published online: 25 February 2014. doi: 10.1007/s11606-014-2767-3, 2014

Background: Suicide prevention is a public health priority, but no data on the health care individuals receive prior to death are available from large representative United States population samples.

Objective: To investigate variation in the types and timing of health services received in the year prior to suicide, and determine whether a mental health condition was diagnosed.

Design: Longitudinal study from 2000 to 2010 within eight Mental Health Research Network health care systems serving eight states.

Participants: In all, 5,894 individuals who died by suicide, and were health plan members in the year before death.

Main Measures: Health system contacts in the year before death. Medical record, insurance claim, and mortality records were linked via the Virtual Data Warehouse, a federated data system at each site.

Key Results: Nearly all individuals received health care in the year prior to death (83 %), but half did not have a mental health diagnosis. Only 24 % had a mental health diagnosis in the 4-week period prior to death. Medical specialty and primary care visits without a mental health diagnosis were the most common visit types. The individuals more likely to make a visit in the year prior to death (p < 0.05) tended to be women, individuals of older age (65+ years), those where the neighborhood income was over \$40,000 and 25 % were college graduates, and those who died by non-violent means.

Conclusions: This study indicates that opportunities for suicide prevention exist in primary care and medical settings, where most individuals receive services prior to death. Efforts may target improved identification of mental illness and suicidal ideation, as a large proportion may remain undiagnosed at death.

Using structured telephone follow-up assessments to improve suicide-related adverse event detection

Arias SA, Zhang Z, Hillerns C, Sullivan AF, Boudreaux ED, Miller I, Camargo CA (USA)

Suicide and Life-Threatening Behavior. Published online: 3 March 2014. doi: 10.1111/sltb.12088, 2014

Adverse event (AE) detection and reporting practices were compared during the first phase of the Emergency Department Safety Assessment and Follow-up Evaluation (ED-SAFE), a suicide intervention study. Data were collected using a combination of chart reviews and structured telephone follow-up assessments postenrollment. Beyond chart reviews, structured telephone follow-up assessments identified 45% of the total AEs in our study. Notably, detection of suicide attempts significantly varied by approach with 53 (18%) detected by chart review, 173 (59%) by structured telephone follow-up assessments, and 69 (23%) marked as duplicates. Findings provide support for utilizing multiple methods for more robust AE detection in suicide research.

Cholesterol and the "cycle of violence" in attempted suicide

Asellus P, Nordström P, Nordström AL, Jokinen J (Sweden)

Psychiatry Research 215, 646-650, 2014

An association between low levels of serum cholesterol and violent or suicidal behaviour has frequently been reported. However the role of serum cholesterol in the cycle of violence (Widom, 1989) has not been studied. The aim of this study was to investigate association between exposure to violence during childhood and used adult violence in suicide attempters with low and high serum cholesterol levels. 81 suicide attempters were assessed with the Karolinska Interpersonal Violence Scale (KIVS) measuring exposure to violence and expressed violent behaviour in childhood (between 6 and 14 years of age) and during adult life (15 years or older). We used median split to dichotomise groups below and above median serum cholesterol. In patients with serum cholesterol below median, the correlation between exposure to violence as a child and used adult violence was significant (rho=0.52, p=0.002), while in patients with serum cholesterol above median, the correlation between exposure to violence as a child and expressed violent behaviour as an adult was not significant (rho=0.25, p=0.2). Comorbid substance abuse predicted violent behaviour as an adult only in patients with serum cholesterol above median. Serum cholesterol may modify the effect of the "Cycle of Violence".

Prison suicides in South Australia: 1996-2010

Austin AE, van den Heuvel C, Byard RW (Australia)

Journal of Forensic Sciences. Published online: 18 March 2014. doi: 10.1111/1556-4029.12454, 2014

Forty-eight deaths occurring in prisons in South Australia were identified between January 1996 and December 2010, including 25 cases of suicide (mean age = 37 years; median age = 34 years; age range = 24-70 years). Most suicides were due to hanging (23/25; 92.0%) with victims using bedding, belts, or shoelaces attached to cell shelves, air vents, doors, or other accessible projections. There were no suicides attributed to drug overdose or sharp force injury. Over a third of all suicides (39.1%) occurred during the first month of confinement, with 26.1% of cases occurring within the first week. There was one suicide reported after 2 years of imprisonment. Given that suicide in state prisons currently occurs at a rate approximately eight times that of the general South Australian community, it appears that the subset of incarcerated individuals represents a group in need of effective preventive strategies to enable more appropriate provisions of existing prisoner resources.

Depressive symptoms and suicide risk in older adults: Value placed on autonomy as a moderator for men but not women

Bamonti PM, Price EC, Fiske A (USA)

Suicide and Life-Threatening Behavior. Published online: 13 November 2013. doi: 10.1111/sltb.12062, 2013

Risk for suicide is elevated among older men. We examined whether value placed on autonomy amplifies the relation between depressive symptoms and suicide risk differently for older men and women. Participants were 98 community-dwelling older adults, M age 73.6 (SD = 8.6), 65.1% female, 93.1% White. Questionnaires measured suicide risk (SBQ-R), depressive symptoms (CESD), and value placed on autonomy (PSI-II autonomy). Among men, depressive symptoms were associated with suicide risk only when PSI-II autonomy was elevated. Among women, greater depressive symptoms were associated with suicide risk at all levels of PSI-II autonomy. Further research on attitudes toward autonomy is warranted.

Management of suicidal and self-harming behaviors in prisons: Systematic literature review of evidence-based activities

Barker E, Kõlves K, De Leo D (Australia)

Archives of Suicide Research. Published online: 10 March 2014. doi: 10.1080/13811118.2013.824830, 2014

Objectives: Systematically analyse existing literature testing the effectiveness of programs involving the management of suicidal and self-harming behaviours in prisons.

Methods: 545 English-language articles published in peer reviewed journals were retrieved using the terms "suicid*", "prevent*" "prison", or "correctional facility" in SCOPUS, MEDLINE, PROQUEST and Web of Knowledge.

Results: Twelve articles were relevant, six involving multi-factored suicide prevention programs, and two involving peer focused programs. Others included changes to the referral and care of suicidal inmates, staff training, legislation changes and a suicide prevention program for inmates with Borderline Personality Disorder.

Conclusions: Multi-factored suicide prevention programs appear most effective in the prison environment. Using trained inmates to provide social support to suicidal inmates is promising. Staff attitudes towards training programs were generally positive.

Rapid treatment response of suicidal symptoms to lithium, sleep deprivation, and light therapy (chronotherapeutics) in drug-resistant bipolar depression

Benedetti F, Riccaboni R, Locatelli C, Poletti S, Dallaspezia S, Colombo C (Italy)

Journal of Clinical Psychiatry 75, 133-140, 2014

Background: One third of patients with bipolar disorder attempt suicide. Depression in bipolar disorder is associated with drug resistance. The efficacy of antidepressants on suicidality has been questioned. Total sleep deprivation and light therapy prompt a rapid and stable antidepressant response in bipolar disorder.

Method: We studied 143 consecutively admitted inpatients (December 2006-August 2012) with a major depressive episode in the course of bipolar disorder (DSM-IV criteria). Among the 141 study completers, 23% had a positive history of attempted suicide and 83% had a positive history of drug resistance. During 1 week, patients were administered 3 consecutive total sleep deprivation cycles (each composed of a period of 36 hours awake followed by recovery sleep) combined with bright light therapy in the morning for 2 weeks. At admission, patients who had been taking lithium continued it, and those who had not been taking lithium started it. Severity of depression was rated according to the Hamilton Depression Rating Scale (HDRS) (primary outcome measure) and Beck Depression Inventory (BDI).

Results: Two patients switched polarity. Among the 141 who completed the treatment, 70% achieved a 50% reduction in HDRS score in 1 week, which persisted 1 month after in 55%. The amelioration involved an immediate and persistent decrease in suicide scores soon after the first total sleep deprivation cycle (F3,411 = 42.78, P < .00001). A positive history of suicide attempts was associated with worse early life stress and with worse suicide scores at baseline, but it did not influence response. Patients with current suicidal thinking or planning responded equally well (F 3,42 = 20.70, P < .000001). Remarkably, however, nonresponders achieved a benefit, with significantly decreased final scores also including suicidality ratings (F3,120 = 6.55, P =.0004). Self-ratings showed the same pattern of change. Previous history of drug resistance did not hamper response. During the following month, 78 of 99 responders continued to stay well and were discharged from the hospital on lithium therapy alone.

Conclusions: The combination of total sleep deprivation, light therapy, and lithium is able to rapidly decrease depressive suicidality and prompt antidepressant response in drug-resistant major depression in the course of bipolar disorder.

Suicidal behaviors among adolescents in juvenile detention: Role of adverse life experiences

Bhatta MP, Jefferis E, Kavadas A, Alemagno SA, Shaffer-King P (USA)
PLoS ONE. Published online: 24 February 2014. doi: 10.1371/journal.pone.0089408, 2014

Purpose: The purpose of this study was to assess the influence of multiple adverse life experiences (sexual abuse, homelessness, running away, and substance abuse in the family) on suicide ideation and suicide attempt among adolescents at an urban juvenile detention facility in the United States.

Materials and Methods: The study sample included a total of 3,156 adolescents processed at a juvenile detention facility in an urban area in Ohio between 2003 and 2007. The participants, interacting anonymously with a voice enabled computer, self-administered a questionnaire with 100 items related to health risk behaviors.

Results: Overall 19.0% reported ever having thought about suicide (suicide ideation) and 11.9% reported ever having attempted suicide (suicide attempt). In the multivariable logistic regression analysis those reporting sexual abuse (Odds Ratio = 2.75; 95% confidence interval = 2.08-3.63) and homelessness (1.51; 1.17-1.94) were associated with increased odds of suicide ideation, while sexual abuse (3.01; 2.22-4.08), homelessness (1.49; 1.12-1.98), and running away from home (1.38; 1.06-1.81) were associated with increased odds of a suicide attempt. Those experiencing all four adverse events were 7.81 times more likely (2.41-25.37) to report having ever attempted suicide than those who experienced none of the adverse events.

Conclusions: Considering the high prevalence of adverse life experiences and their association with suicidal behaviors in detained adolescents, these factors should not only be included in the suicide screening tools at the intake and during detention, but should also be used for the intervention programming for suicide prevention.

Predicting suicidal ideations in sexually abused female adolescents: A 12-month prospective study

Brabant M-E, Hébert M, Chagnon F (Canada)

Journal of Child Sexual Abuse. Published online: 18 March 2014. doi: 10.1080/10538712.2014.896842, 2014

This study investigates the contribution of post-traumatic stress symptoms to the prediction of suicidality among female adolescent survivors of sexual abuse. A one-year prospective study of 52 female survivors aged 12 to 18 years was conducted. A negative binomial regression analysis revealed that depressive symptoms as well as post-traumatic stress symptoms associated with the sexual trauma were significant predictors of suicidal ideations a year later. Post-traumatic stress symptoms remained a significant predictor of suicidal ideations even when controlling for depressive symptomatology and the presence of a past suicide attempt, thus emphasizing the relevance of post-traumatic stress symptoms in regard to suicidality in sexually abused youths. Results are discussed within the context of therapeutic modalities for survivors of a sexual trauma.

Last suicide attempt before completed suicide in severe depression: An extended suicidal process may be found in men rather than women

Bradvik L (Sweden)

Archives of Suicide Research 17, 426-433, 2013

The objective of this study was to compare the time from last suicide attempt to suicide in men and women with major depressive disorder with melancholic and/or psychotic features. The case records of 100 suicide victims with severe depression were evaluated. All suicide attempts during the course of depression were noted. The time from last suicide attempt to suicide was compared as well as the occurrence of suicide attempt during the last depressive episode, by gender. Male suicide attempters made fewer suicide attempts than women during their last depressive episode before suicide (8% versus 37%). Men appeared to have a more extended suicidal process from suicide attempt to completed suicide, which ought to be considered in the after-care.

Suicide ideation and associated mortality in adult survivors of childhood cancer

Brinkman TM, Zhang N, Recklitis CJ, Kimberg C, Zeltzer LK, Muriel AC, Stovall M, Srivastava DK, Sklar CA, Robison LL, Krull KR (USA)

Cancer 120, 271-277, 2013

Background: Adult survivors of childhood cancer are at risk for suicide ideation, although longitudinal patterns and rates of recurrent suicide ideation are unknown. This study investigated the prevalence of late report (ie, after initial assessment) and recurrent suicide ideation in adult survivors of childhood cancer, identified predictors of suicide ideation, and examined associations among suicide ideation and mortality.

Methods: Participants included 9128 adult survivors of childhood cancer and 3082 sibling controls enrolled in the Childhood Cancer Survivor Study who completed a survey question assessing suicide ideation on one or more occasions between 1994 and 2010. Suicide ideation was assessed using the Brief Symptom Inventory-18 instrument. Mortality data was ascertained from the National Death Index.

Results: Survivors were more likely to report late (odds ratio [OR]=1.9, 95% confidence interval [CI]=1.5-2.5) and recurrent suicide ideation (OR=2.6, 95% CI=1.8-3.8) compared to siblings. Poor physical health status was associated with increased risk of suicide ideation in survivors (late report: OR=1.9, 95% CI=1.3-2.7; recurrent: OR=1.9, 95% CI=1.2-2.9). Suicide ideation was associated with increased risk for all-cause mortality (hazard ratio=1.3, 95% CI=1.03-1.6) and death by external causes (hazard ratio=2.4, 95% CI=1.4-4.1).

Conclusions: Adult survivors of childhood cancer are at risk for late-report and recurrent suicide ideation, which is associated with increased risk of mortality. Routine screening for psychological distress in adult survivors appears warranted, especially for survivors who develop chronic physical health conditions.

Life-time prevalence and psychosocial correlates of adolescent direct self-injurious behavior: A comparative study of findings in 11 European countries

Brunner R, Kaess M, Parzer P, Fischer G, Carli V, Hoven CW, Wasserman C, Sarchiapone M, Resch F, Apter A, Balazs J, Barzilay S, Bobes J, Corcoran P, Cosmanm D, Haring C, Iosuec M, Kahn JP, Keeley H, Meszaros G, Nemes B, Podlogar T, Postuvan V, Saiz PA, Sisask M, Tubiana A, Varnik A, Wasserman D (Germany, Australia, Sweden, USA, Italy, Israel, Hungary, Spain Ireland, Romania, Austria, France, Slovenia, Estonia)

Journal of Child Psychology and Psychiatry. Published online: 12 November 2013. doi: 10.1111/jcpp.12166, 2013

Objectives: To investigate the prevalence and associated psychosocial factors of occasional and repetitive direct self-injurious behavior (D-SIB), such as self-cutting, -burning, -biting, -hitting, and skin damage by other methods, in representative adolescent samples from 11 European countries.

Methods: Cross-sectional assessment of adolescents was performed within the European Union funded project, Saving and Empowering Young Lives in Europe (SEYLE), which was conducted in 11 European countries. The representative sample comprised 12,068 adolescents (F/M: 6,717/5,351; mean age: 14.9 +/- 0.89) recruited from randomly selected schools. Frequency of D-SIB was assessed by a modified 6-item questionnaire based on previously used versions of the Deliberate Self-Harm Inventory (DSHI). In addition, a broad range of demographic, social, and psychological factors was assessed.

Results: Overall lifetime prevalence of D-SIB was 27.6%; 19.7% reported occasional D-SIB and 7.8% repetitive D-SIB. Lifetime prevalence ranged from 17.1% to 38.6% across countries. Estonia, France, Germany, and Israel had the highest lifetime rates of D-SIB, while students from Hungary, Ireland, and Italy reported low rates. Suicidality as well as anxiety and depressive symptoms had the highest odds ratios for both occasional and repetitive D-SIB. There was a strong association of D-SIB with both psychopathology and risk-behaviors, including family related neglect and peer-related rejection/victimization. Associations between psychosocial variables and D-SIB were strongly influenced by both gender and country. Only a minor proportion of the adolescents who reported D-SIB ever received medical treatment.

Conclusion: These results suggest high lifetime prevalence of D-SIB in European adolescents. Prevalence as well as psychosocial correlates seems to be significantly influenced by both gender and country. These results support the need for a multidimensional approach to better understand the development of SIB and facilitate culturally adapted prevention/intervention.

The fallen hero: Masculinity, shame and farmer suicide in Australia

Bryant L, Garnham B (Australia)
Gender, Place and Culture. Published online: 7 February 2014. doi: 10.1080/0966369X.2013.855628, 2014

The drought-stricken Australian rural landscape, cultures of farming masculinity and an economy of value, moral worth and pride form a complex matrix of discourses that shape subjective dynamics that render suicide a possibility for distressed farmers. However, the centrality of a 'mental health' perspective and reified notions of 'stoicism' within this discursive field operate to exclude consideration of the ways in which cultural identity is linked to emotions. To illuminate and explore complex connections between subjectivity, moral worth and affect in relation to understanding farmer suicide, this article draws on theory and literature on agrarian discourses of masculine subjectivity and shame to analyze empirical data from interviews with farmers during times of environmental, social and economic crisis. The idealized notion of the farming man as 'Aussie battler' emerges from romantic agrarian mythology in which pride and self-worth are vested in traditional values of hard work, struggle and self-sacrifice. However, the structural context of agriculture, as it is shaped by the political economy of neoliberalism, threatens farm economic viability and is eroding the pride, self-worth and masculine identity of farmers. The article suggests that the notion of the 'fallen hero' captures a discursive shift of a masculinity 'undone', a regress from the powerful position of masculine subjectivity imbued with pride to one of shame that is of central importance to understanding how suicide emerges as a possibility for farmers.

The effect of successful and unsuccessful smoking cessation on short-term anxiety, depression, and suicidality

Capron DW, Allan NP, Norr AM, Zvolensky MJ, Schmidt NB (USA)
Addictive Behaviors 39, 782-788, 2014

Research on the mental health effects of quitting smoking is limited. Smokers with mental illness appear to be at a higher risk of unsuccessful smoking cessation. Recent work suggests they are at elevated risk for post-cessation increases in anxiety, depression and suicidal ideation. The current study tested the effects of successful and unsuccessful smoking cessation on short-term psychopathology in 192 community participants. Smoking cessation outcomes were classified using expired carbon monoxide levels that were taken at quit week, 1 and 2. week follow-up and 1. month follow-up. We found no psychopathology increases in participants who successfully quit smoking. For individuals struggling to quit our results partially supported a recently proposed struggling quitters hypothesis. However, the vast majority of individuals posited to be vulnerable by the struggling quitters hypothesis did not experience clinically significant increases in psychopathology. These findings have implications for clinicians whose clients are interested in smoking cessation.

A newly identified group of adolescents at "invisible" risk for psychopathology and suicidal behavior: Findings from the SEYLE study

Carli V, Hoven CW, Wasserman C, Chiesa F, Guffanti G, Sarchiapone M, Apter A, Balazs J, Brunner R, Corcoran P, Cosman D, Haring C, Iosue M, Kaess M, Kahn JP, Keeley H, Postuvan V, Saiz P, Varnik A, Wasserman D (Sweden, USA, Italy, Israel, Hungary, Germany, Ireland, Romania, Austria, France, Slovenia, Spain, Estonia)

World Psychiatry 13, 78-86, 2014

This study explored the prevalence of risk behaviors (excessive alcohol use, illegal drug use, heavy smoking, reduced sleep, overweight, underweight, sedentary behavior, high use of Internet/TV/videogames for reasons not related to school or work, and truancy), and their association with psychopathology and self-destructive behaviors, in a sample of 12,395 adolescents recruited in randomly selected schools across 11 European countries. Latent class analysis identified three groups of adolescents: a low-risk group (57.8%) including pupils with low or very low frequency of risk behaviors; a high-risk group (13.2%) including pupils who scored high on all risk behaviors, and a third group ("invisible" risk, 29%) including pupils who were positive for high use of Internet/TV/videogames for reasons not related to school or work, sedentary behavior and reduced sleep. Pupils in the "invisible" risk group, compared with the high-risk group, had a similar prevalence of suicidal thoughts (42.2% vs. 44%), anxiety (8% vs. 9.2%), subthreshold depression (33.2% vs. 34%) and depression (13.4% vs. 14.7%). The prevalence of suicide attempts was 5.9% in the "invisible" group, 10.1% in the high-risk group and 1.7% in the low-risk group. The prevalence of all risk behaviors increased with age and most of them were significantly more frequent among boys. Girls were significantly more likely to experience internalizing (emotional) psychiatric symptoms. The "invisible" group may represent an important new intervention target group for potentially reducing psychopathology and other untoward outcomes in adolescence, including suicidal behavior.

Medication nonadherence and psychiatry

Chapman SCE, Horne R (UK)

Current Opinion in Psychiatry 26, 446, 2013

Nonadherence to appropriately prescribed medication for psychiatric disorders prevents patients from realizing the full benefits of their treatment and negatively impacts on individuals, their families and the healthcare system. Understanding and reducing nonadherence is therefore a key challenge to quality care for patients with psychiatric disorders. This review highlights findings regarding the prevalence and consequence of nonadherence, barriers to adherence and new intervention methods from 2012 onwards. Recent research has highlighted that nonadherence is a global challenge for psychiatry and has linked nonadherence to poorer outcomes, including hospital admissions, suicide and mortality. Optimizing medication regimens can reduce nonadherence; however, often a complex interplay of factors affects individuals' motivation and ability to follow their prescription. Psychiatrists can enable patients to develop an accurate model of their illness and treatment and facilitate adherence. However, nonadherence is often a hidden issue within consultations. Novel interventions using new technologies and tailoring techniques may have the potential to reduce nonadherence. Nonadherence remains a significant challenge for patients with psychiatric disorders, physicians and healthcare systems. New developments demonstrate the importance of developing tailored interventions to enable patients to overcome perceptual and practical barriers to adherence.

Risk of adolescent offspring's completed suicide increases with prior history of their same-sex parents' death by suicide

Cheng Ccj, Yen Wj, Chang Wt, Wu Kc-c, Ko Mc, Li Cy (Taiwan)
Psychological Medicine. Published online: 24 September 2013. doi: 10.1017/S0033291713002298, 2013

Background: To investigate the risk of completed suicide in offspring during adolescence in relation to prior history of the same-sex parent's death by suicide and other causes.

Method: A total of 500 adolescents who died by suicide at age 15-19 years between 1997 and 2007 were identified from the Taiwan Mortality Registration (TMR). For each case, 30 age- and time-matched controls were selected randomly from all adolescents registered in the Taiwan Birth Registry (TBR). A multivariate conditional logistic regression model was used to assess the risk of adolescent completed suicide in relation to their same-sex parent.

Results: Adolescent suicide risk was positively associated with both paternal [odds ratio (OR) 5.38, 95% confidence interval (CI) 2.17-13.33] and maternal suicide (OR 6.59, 95% CI 1.82-23.91). The corresponding risk estimates associated with paternal and maternal deaths from non-suicidal causes were much lower, at 1.88 and 1.94 respectively. The risk of suicide in male adolescents was significantly associated with prior history of paternal death by suicide (OR 8.23, 95% CI 2.96-22.90) but not of maternal death by suicide (OR 3.50, 95% CI 0.41-30.13). On the other contrary, the risk of suicidal death in female adolescents was significantly associated with prior history of maternal suicide (OR 9.71, 95% CI 1.89-49.94) but not of paternal suicide (OR 2.42, 95% CI 0.30-19.57). However, these differences did not reach statistical significance.

Conclusions: Although limited by sample size, our study indicates that adolescent offspring suicidal death is associated with prior history of their same-sex parent's death by suicide.

The relationship between prior suicidal behavior and mortality among individuals in community corrections

Clark CB, Waesche MC, Hendricks PS, McCullumsmith CB, Redmond N, Katiyar N, Lawler RM, Cropsey KL (USA)

Crisis 34, 428-433, 2013

Background: Individuals under community corrections have multiple risk factors for mortality including exposure to a criminal environment, drug use, social stress, and a lack of medical care that predispose them to accidents, homicides, medical morbidities, and suicide. The literature suggests that prior suicidal behavior may be a particularly potent risk factor for mortality among individuals in the criminal justice system.

Aims: This study looked to extend the link between history of a suicide attempt and future mortality in a community corrections population.

Method: Using an archival dataset (N = 18,260) collected from 2002 to 2007 of individuals being monitored under community corrections supervision for an average of 217 days (SD = 268), we examined the association between past history of a suicide attempt and mortality.

Results: A Cox Proportional Hazard Model controlling for age, race, gender, and substance dependence indicated that past history of a suicide attempt was independently associated with time to mortality, and demonstrated the second greatest effect after gender.

Conclusion: These data suggest the need for a greater focus on screening and preventive services, particularly for individuals with a history of suicidal behavior, so as to reduce the risk of mortality in community corrections populations.

The health and well-being of transgender high school students: Results from the New Zealand adolescent health survey (youth'12)

Clark TC, Lucassen MFG, Bullen P, Denny SJ, Fleming TM, Robinson EM, Rossen FV (New Zealand)

Journal of Adolescent Health. Published online: 15 January 2014. doi:10.1016/j.jadohealth.2013.11.008, 2014

Purpose: To report the prevalence of students according to four gender groups (i.e., those who reported being non-transgender, transgender, or not sure about their gender, and those who did not understand the transgender question), and to describe their health and well-being.

Methods: Logistic regressions were used to examine the associations between gender groups and selected outcomes in a nationally representative high school health and well-being survey, undertaken in 2012.

Results: Of the students (n = 8,166), 94.7% reported being non-transgender, 1.2% reported being transgender, 2.5% reported being not sure about their gender, and 1.7% did not understand the question. Students who reported being transgender or not sure about their gender or did not understand the question had compromised health and well-being relative to their non-transgender peers; in particular, for transgender students perceiving that a parent cared about them (odds ratio [OR], .3; 95% confidence interval [CI], .2-.4), depressive symptoms (OR, 5.7; 95% CI, 3.6-9.2), suicide attempts (OR, 5.0; 95% CI, 2.9-8.8), and school bullying (OR, 4.5; 95% CI, 2.4-8.2).

Conclusions: This is the first nationally representative survey to report the health and well-being of students who report being transgender. We found that transgender students and those reporting not being sure are a numerically small but important group. Transgender students are diverse and are represented across demographic variables, including their sexual attractions. Transgender youth face considerable health and well-being disparities. It is important to address the challenging environments these students face and to increase access to responsive services for transgender youth

Antidepressants and suicide attempts in children

Cooper WO, Callahan ST, Shintani A, Fuchs DC, Shelton RC, Dudley JA, Graves AJ, Ray WA (USA)
Pediatrics. Published online: 6 January 2014. doi: 10.1542/peds.2013-0923, 2014

Objectives: Recent data showing possible increased risk for suicidal behavior among children and adolescents treated with selective serotonin reuptake inhibitors (SSRIs) and serotonin-norepinephrine reuptake inhibitors (SNRIs) antidepressants have created significant concern among patients, families, and providers, including concerns about the risk of individual antidepressants. This study was designed to compare the risk for medically treated suicide attempts among new users of sertraline, paroxetine, citalopram, escitalopram, and venlafaxine to risk for new users of fluoxetine.

Methods: A retrospective cohort study included 36 842 children aged 6 to 18 years enrolled in Tennessee Medicaid between 1995 and 2006 who were new users of 1 of the antidepressant medications of interest (defined as filling no prescriptions for antidepressants in the preceding 365 days). Medically treated suicide attempts were identified from Medicaid files and vital records and confirmed with medical record review.

Results: Four hundred nineteen cohort members had a medically treated suicide attempt with explicit or inferred attempt to die confirmed through medical record review, including 4 who completed suicide. The rate of confirmed suicide attempts for the study drugs ranged from 24.0 per 1000 person-years to 29.1 per 1000 person-years. The adjusted rate of suicide attempts did not differ significantly among current users of SSRI and SNRI antidepressants compared with current users of fluoxetine. Users of multiple antidepressants concomitantly had increased risk for suicide attempt.

Conclusions: In this population-based study of children recently initiating an antidepressant, there was no evidence that risk of suicide attempts differed for commonly prescribed SSRI and SNRI antidepressants.

Comfort from suicidal cognition in recurrently depressed patients

Crane C, Barnhofer T, Duggan DS, Eames C, Hepburn S, Shah D, Williams JMG (UK)

Journal of Affective Disorders 155, 241-246, 2013

Background: Previous research has suggested that some individuals may obtain comfort from their suicidal cognitions.

Method: This study explored clinical variables associated with comfort from suicidal cognition using a newly developed 5 item measure in 217 patients with a history of recurrent depression and suicidality, of whom 98 were followed up to at least one relapse to depression and reported data on suicidal ideation during the follow-up phase.

Results: Results indicated that a minority of patients, around 15%, reported experiencing comfort from suicidal cognitions and that comfort was associated with several markers of a more severe clinical profile including both worst ever prior suicidal ideation and worst suicidal ideation over a 12 month follow-up period.

Limitations: Few patients self-harmed during the follow-up period preventing an examination of associations between comfort and repetition of self-harm.

Conclusions: These results, although preliminary, suggest that future theoretical and clinical research would benefit from further consideration of the concept of comfort from suicidal thinking.

The power of the web: A systematic review of studies of the influence of the internet on self-harm and suicide in young people

Daine K, Hawton K, Singaravelu V, Stewart A, Simkin S, Montgomery P (UK)

PLoS ONE. Published online: 30 October 2013. doi: 10.1371/journal.pone.0077555, 2013

Background: There is concern that the internet is playing an increasing role in self-harm and suicide. In this study we systematically review and analyse research literature to determine whether there is evidence that the internet influences the risk of self-harm or suicide in young people.

Methods: An electronic literature search was conducted using the PsycINFO, MEDLINE, EMBASE, Scopus, and CINAHL databases. Articles of interest were those that included empirical data on the internet, self-harm or suicide, and young people. The articles were initially screened based on titles and abstracts, then by review of the full publications, after which those included in the review were subjected to data extraction, thematic analysis and quality rating.

Results: Youth who self-harm or are suicidal often make use of the internet. It is most commonly used for constructive reasons such as seeking support and coping strategies, but may exert a negative influence, normalising self-harm and potentially discouraging disclosure or professional help-seeking. The internet has created channels of communication that can be misused to 'cyber-bully' peers; both cyber-bullying and general internet use have been found to correlate with increased risk of self-harm, suicidal ideation, and depression. Correlations have also been found between internet exposure and violent methods of self-harm.

Conclusions: Internet use may exert both positive and negative effects on young people at risk of self-harm or suicide. Careful high quality research is needed to better understand how internet media may exert negative influences and should also focus on how the internet might be utilised to intervene with vulnerable young people.

A retrospective study of murder-suicide at the forensic institute of Ghent University, Belgium: 1935-2010

De Koning E, Piette MH (Belgium)
Medicine, Science and the Law 54, 88-98, 2014

Murder followed by suicide (M-S) is a rare phenomenon that has been studied in several countries. Previous studies show that offenders of M-S are predominately men who live in an intimate relationship. Amorous jealousy is often the trigger to commit M-S. Shooting is the most common way to kill a partner and/or children. In general, women are likely to become victims. The aim of this study was to identify M-S and detect patterns of M-S in the district of Ghent and the surrounding areas, since no research on this event was conducted in Belgium. Over a period of 75 years, a total of 80 M-S incidents was recorded involving 176 individuals. Eighty-six percent of the offenders were males and 14% were females. Murder-suicides were mostly completed with firearms. The main motive for offenders to execute M-S is amorous jealousy (56%), followed by familial, financial, or social stressors (27%). In addition, three types of M-S were selected (e.g., spousal murder-suicides, filicide-suicides, and familicides-suicides). Our results suggest differences in these types of M-S in which younger couples' intentions were amorous jealousy; as for older couples the prominent motive was mercy killing; most likely women killed their children and only men committed familicides. Finally a study of the evolution during this period was carried out.

Preterm birth and mortality and morbidity: A population-based quasi-experimental study

D'Onofrio BM, Class QA, Rickert ME, Larsson H, Langstrom N, Lichtenstein P (USA, Sweden)

JAMA Psychiatry 70, 1231-1240, 2013

Importance: Preterm birth is associated with increased mortality and morbidity. However, previous studies have been unable to rigorously examine whether confounding factors cause these associations rather than the harmful effects of being born preterm.

Objective: To estimate the extent to which the associations between early gestational age and offspring mortality and morbidity are the result of confounding factors by using a quasi-experimental design, the sibling-comparison approach, and by controlling for statistical covariates that varied within families.

Design, Setting and Participants: A population-based cohort study, combining Swedish registries to identify all individuals born in Sweden from 1973 to 2008 (3 300 708 offspring of 1 736 735 mothers) and link them with multiple outcomes.

Main Outcomes and Measures: Offspring mortality (during infancy and throughout young adulthood) and psychiatric (psychotic or bipolar disorder, autism, attention-deficit/hyperactivity disorder, suicide attempts, substance use, and criminality), academic (failing grades and educational attainment), and social (partnering, parenthood, low income, and social welfare benefits) outcomes through 2009.

Results: In the population, there was a dose-response relationship between early gestation and the outcome measures. For example, extreme preterm birth (23-27 weeks of gestation) was associated with infant mortality (odds ratio, 288.1; 95% CI, 271.7-305.5), autism (hazard ratio [HR], 3.2; 95% CI, 2.6-4.0), low educational attainment (HR, 1.7; 1.5-2.0), and social welfare benefits (HR, 1.3; 1.2-1.5) compared with offspring born at term. The associations between early gestation and mortality and psychiatric morbidity generally were robust when comparing differentially exposed siblings and controlling for statistical covariates, whereas the associations with academic and some social problems were greatly or completely attenuated in the fixed-effects models.

Conclusions and Relevance: The mechanisms responsible for the associations between preterm birth and mortality and morbidity are outcome-specific. Associations between preterm birth and mortality and psychiatric morbidity are largely independent of shared familial confounds and measured covariates, consistent with a causal inference. However, some associations, particularly predicting suicide attempt, educational attainment, and social welfare benefits, are the result of confounding factors. The findings emphasize the importance of both reducing preterm birth and providing wraparound services to all siblings in families with an offspring born preterm.

Paternal age at childbearing and offspring psychiatric and academic morbidity

D'Onofrio BM, Rickert ME, Frans E, Kuja-Halkola R, Almqvist C, Sjolander A, Larsson H, Lichtenstein P (USA, Sweden)

JAMA Psychiatry 71, 432-438, 2014

Importance: Advancing paternal age is associated with increased genetic mutations during spermatogenesis, which research suggests may cause psychiatric morbidity in the offspring. The effects of advancing paternal age at childbearing on offspring morbidity remain unclear, however, because of inconsistent epidemiologic findings and the inability of previous studies to rigorously rule out confounding factors.

Objective: To examine the associations between advancing paternal age at childbearing and numerous indexes of offspring morbidity.

Design, Setting, and Participants: We performed a population-based cohort study of all individuals born in Sweden in 1973-2001 (N = 2 615 081), with subsets of the data used to predict childhood or adolescent morbidity. We estimated the risk of psychiatric and academic morbidity associated with advancing paternal age using several quasi-experimental designs, including the comparison of differentially exposed siblings, cousins, and first-born cousins.

Exposure: Paternal age at childbearing.

Main Outcomes and Measures: Psychiatric (autism, attention-deficit/hyperactivity disorder, psychosis, bipolar disorder, suicide attempt, and substance use problem) and academic (failing grades and low educational attainment) morbidity.

Results: In the study population, advancing paternal age was associated with increased risk of some psychiatric disorders (eg, autism, psychosis, and bipolar disorders) but decreased risk of the other indexes of morbidity. In contrast, the sibling-comparison analyses indicated that advancing paternal age had a dose-response relationship with every index of morbidity, with the magnitude of the associations being as large or larger than the estimates in the entire population. Compared with offspring born to fathers 20 to 24 years old, offspring of fathers 45 years and older were at heightened risk of autism (hazard ratio [HR] = 3.45; 95% CI, 1.62-7.33), attention-deficit/hyperactivity disorder (HR = 13.13; 95% CI, 6.85-25.16), psychosis (HR = 2.07; 95% CI, 1.35-3.20), bipolar disorder (HR = 24.70; 95% CI, 12.12-50.31), suicide attempts (HR = 2.72; 95% CI, 2.08-3.56), substance use problems (HR = 2.44; 95% CI, 1.98-2.99), failing a grade (odds ratio [OR] = 1.59; 95% CI, 1.37-1.85), and low educational attainment (OR = 1.70; 95% CI, 1.50-1.93) in within-sibling comparisons. Additional analyses using several quasi-experimental designs obtained commensurate results, further strengthening the internal and external validity of the findings.

Conclusions and Relevance: Advancing paternal age is associated with increased risk of psychiatric and academic morbidity, with the magnitude of the risks being as large or larger than previous estimates. These findings are consistent with the hypothesis that new genetic mutations that occur during spermatogenesis are causally related to offspring morbidity.

The effects of suicide ideation assessments on urges to self-harm and suicide

Eynan R, Bergmans Y, Antony J, Cutcliffe JR, Harder HG, Ambreen M, Balderson K, Links PS (Canada)

Crisis 35, 123-131, 2013

Background: Participants' safety is the primary concern when conducting research with suicidal or potentially suicidal participants. The presence of suicide risk is often an exclusion criterion for research participants. Subsequently, few studies have examined the effects of research assessments on study participants' suicidality.

Aims: The purpose of this research was to examine the patterns of postassessment changes in self-harm and suicide urges of study participants who were recently discharged from an inpatient psychiatric service.

Method: Study participants (N = 120) were recruited from patients with a lifetime history of suicidal behavior admitted with current suicidal ideation or suicide attempt to an inpatient psychiatric service and/or a crisis stabilization unit. Participants were assessed for suicidal ideation with the Suicide Ideation Scale at 1, 3, and 6 months following their discharge from hospital. The risk assessment protocol was administered at the start and at the end of each of the study follow-up assessments.

Results: Changes in self-harm and suicide urges following study assessments were small, infrequent, and were most likely to reflect a decrease in suicidality. Similarly, participants rarely reported worsening self-control over suicidal urges, and when they did, the effect was minimal. By the end of the 6-month follow-up period, increases in self-harm and suicidal urges postassessment were not seen.

Conclusion: The inclusion of suicidal participants in research interviews rarely increased suicide risk. Research involving suicidal individuals is possible when study protocols are well planned and executed by trained assessors and clinicians who are able to identify participants at risk and provide intervention if necessary. The few participants that required intervention had high levels of suicide ideation and behavior at baseline and almost all reported symptoms of posttraumatic stress disorder. Further study is needed to better characterize this subgroup of participants.

Suicidality among older male veterans in the United States: Results from the national health and resilience in veterans study

Fanning JR, Pietrzak RH (USA)

Journal of Psychiatric Research 47, 1766-1775, 2013

Older men have a higher rate of suicide than the general population, but little is known about the prevalence and correlates of suicidality among older male veterans. In this study, we evaluated the prevalence, and risk and protective factors associated with current suicidal ideation (SI) and past suicide attempt (SA) in a contemporary, nationally representative sample of older male veterans. We analyzed data from 1962 male veterans aged 60 or older who participated in the National Health and Resilience Veterans Survey (NHRVS) between October and December 2011. Bivariate analyses and multivariate logistic regression were used to evaluate risk and protective factors associated with current SI and past SA in the full sample, and separately among combat and non-combat veterans. Six percent of the sample reported past 2-week SI, and combat veterans were more likely to contemplate suicide (9.2%) than non-combat (4.0%) veterans. Lifetime SA was reported by 2.6% of respondents. Major depression and physical health difficulties were the strongest risk factors for SI in combat veterans, while generalized anxiety disorder (GAD) was the strongest risk factor for SI in non-combat veterans. Posttraumatic stress disorder (PTSD) was independently associated with SI in both groups of veterans, and social connectedness was negatively related to SI in both groups. These results suggest that a significant proportion of older male veterans in the United States contemplates suicide, with higher rates of SI among combat than non-combat veterans. Interventions designed to mitigate psychological distress and physical difficulties, and to promote social connectedness may help mitigate suicidality risk in this population.

Higher perceived stress but lower cortisol levels found among young Greek adults living in a stressful social environment in comparison with Swedish young adults

Faresjo A, Theodorsson E, Chatziarzenis M, Sapouna V, Claesson H-P, Koppner J, Faresjo T
(Sweden, Greece)

PLoS ONE. Published online: 16 September 2013. doi: 10.1371/journal.pone.0073828, 2013

The worldwide financial crisis during recent years has raised concerns of negative public health effects. This is notably evident in southern Europe. In Greece, where the financial austerity has been especially pronounced, the prevalence of mental health problems including depression and suicide has increased, and outbreaks of infectious diseases have risen. The main objective in this study was to investigate whether different indicators of health and stress levels measured by a new bio-marker based on cortisol in human hair were different amongst comparable Greek and Swedish young adults, considering that Sweden has been much less affected by the recent economic crises. In this cross-sectional comparative study, young adults from the city of Athens in Greece (n = 124) and from the city of Linkoping in Sweden (n = 112) participated. The data collection comprised answering a questionnaire with different health indicators and hair samples being analyzed for the stress hormone cortisol, a biomarker with the ability to retro-spectively measure long-term cortisol exposure. The Greek young adults reported significantly higher perceived stress (p < 0.0001), had experienced more serious life events (p = 0.002), had lower hope for the future (p < 0.0001), and had sig-nificantly more widespread symptoms of depression (p < 0.0001) and anxiety (p < 0.0001) than the Swedes. But, the Greeks were found to have significantly lower cortisol levels (p < 0.0001) than the Swedes, and this difference was still significant in a multivariate regression (p < 0.0001), after adjustments for potential inter-vening variables. A variety of factors related to differences in the physical or soci-ocultural environment between the two sites, might possibly explain this finding. However, a potential biological mechanism is that long-term stress exposure could lead to a lowering of the cortisol levels. This study points out a possible hypothesis that the cortisol levels of the Greek young adults might have been sup-pressed and their HPA-axis down-regulated after living in a stressful environment with economic and social pressure.

Suicide, fatal injuries, and other causes of premature mortality in patients with traumatic brain injury: A 41-year Swedish population study

Fazel S, Wolf A, Pillas D, Lichtenstein P, Långström N (UK, Sweden)
JAMA Psychiatry 71, 326-333, 2014

Importance: Longer-term mortality in individuals who have survived a traumatic brain injury (TBI) is not known.

Objectives: To examine the relationship between TBI and premature mortality, particularly by external causes, and determine the role of psychiatric comorbidity.

Design, Setting and Patients: We studied all persons born in 1954 or later in Sweden who received inpatient and outpatient International Classification of Diseases-based diagnoses of TBI from 1969 to 2009 (n = 218 300). We compared mortality rates 6 months or more after TBI to general population controls matched on age and sex (n = 2 163 190) and to unaffected siblings of patients with TBI (n = 150 513). Furthermore, we specifically examined external causes of death (suicide, injury, or assault). We conducted sensitivity analyses to investigate whether mortality rates differed by sex, age at death, severity (including concussion), and different follow-up times after diagnosis.

Main Outcomes and Measures: Adjusted odds ratios (AORs) of premature death by external causes in patients with TBI compared with general population controls.

Results: Among those who survived 6 months after TBI, we found a 3-fold increased odds of mortality (AOR, 3.2; 95% CI, 3.0-3.4) compared with general population controls and an adjusted increased odds of mortality of 2.6 (95% CI, 2.3-2.8) compared with unaffected siblings. Risks of mortality from external causes were elevated, including for suicide (AOR, 3.3; 95% CI, 2.9-3.7), injuries (AOR, 4.3; 95% CI, 3.8-4.8), and assault (AOR, 3.9; 95% CI, 2.7-5.7). Among those with TBI, absolute rates of death were high in those with any psychiatric or substance abuse comorbidity (3.8% died prematurely) and those with solely substance abuse (6.2%) compared with those without comorbidity (0.5%).

Conclusions and Relevance: Traumatic brain injury is associated with substantially elevated risks of premature mortality, particularly for suicide, injuries, and assaults, even after adjustment for sociodemographic and familial factors. Current clinical guidelines may need revision to reduce mortality risks beyond the first few months after injury and address high rates of psychiatric comorbidity and substance abuse.

Control strategies and suicidal ideation in older primary care patients with functional limitations

Fiske A, Bamonti P, Nadorff M, Petts R, Sperry J (USA)

International Journal of Psychiatry in Medicine 46, 271-289, 2013

Objectives: Failure to adapt to limitations in control may place older adults at risk for suicidal behavior. The present study examined the relation between control strategies, depressive symptoms, and suicidal ideation in older adults with health-related limitations.

Methods: Cross-sectional study of 50 older adult (aged 65-94) primary care patients with health-related limitations.

Results: Compensatory primary control strategies characterized by seeking help from others were associated with lower levels of suicidal ideation, independent of depressive symptoms. Selective primary control strategies (e.g., persistence) were also associated with reduced suicidal ideation independent of depressive symptoms, but only when a low level of compensatory primary control strategies was endorsed. Selective secondary control strategies were associated with higher suicidal ideation, whereas compensatory secondary control strategies (e.g., goal disengagement) were unrelated in this sample after controlling for covariates.

Conclusions: Findings demonstrate that primary care patients with functional limitations who are not striving to meet their goals, either through persistence or by seeking help from others, are at elevated risk of suicidal thinking.

Aggression-impulsivity, mental pain, and communication difficulties in medically serious and medically non-serious suicide attempters

Gvion Y, Horresh N, Levi-Belz Y, Fischel T, Treves I, Weiser M, David HS, Stein-Reizer O, Apter A (Israel)

Comprehensive Psychiatry 55, 40-50, 2014

Background: Unbearable mental pain, depression, and hopelessness have been associated with suicidal behavior in general, while difficulties with social communication and loneliness have been associated with highly lethal suicide attempts in particular. The literature also links aggression and impulsivity with suicidal behavior but raises questions about their influence on the lethality and outcome of the suicide attempt.

Objectives: To evaluate the relative effects of aggression and impulsivity on the lethality of suicide attempts we hypothesized that impulsivity and aggression differentiate between suicide attempters and non-attempters and between medically serious and medically non-serious suicide attempters.

Method: The study group included 196 participants divided into four groups: 43 medically serious suicide attempters; 49 medically non-serious suicide attempters, 47 psychiatric patients who had never attempted suicide; and 57 healthy control subjects. Data on sociodemographic parameters, clinical history, and details of the suicide attempts were collected. Participants completed a battery of instruments for assessment of aggression-impulsivity, mental pain, and communication difficulties. *Results:* The medically serious and medically non-serious suicide attempters scored significantly higher than both control groups on mental pain, depression, and hopelessness (p <.001 for all) and on anger-in, anger-out, violence, and impulsivity (p <.05 for all), with no significant difference between the two suicide attempter groups. Medically serious suicide attempters had significantly lower self-disclosure (p <.05) and more schizoid tendencies (p <.001) than the other three groups and significantly more feelings of loneliness than the medically non-serious suicide attempters and nonsuicidal psychiatric patients (p <.05). Analysis of aggression-impulsivity, mental pain, and communication variables with suicide lethality yielded significant correlations for self-disclosure, schizoid tendency, and loneliness. The interaction between mental pain and schizoid traits explained some of the variance in suicide lethality, over and above the contribution of each component alone.

Conclusions: Aggression-impulsivity and mental pain are risk factors for suicide attempts. However, only difficulties in communication differentiate medically serious from medically non-serious suicide attempters. The combination of unbearable mental pain and difficulties in communication has a magnifying effect on the risk of lethal suicidal behavior.

Suicidal ideation, mental health problems and social function in adolescents with eczema: A population-based study

Halvorsen JA, Lien L, Dalgard F, Bjertness E, Stern RS (Norway, China, USA)
Journal of Investigative Dermatology. Published online: 4 February 2014. doi: 10.1038/jid.2014.70, 2014

There are few studies of psycho-social problems in adolescents with eczema. We performed a cross-sectional, questionnaire-based study to explore the relationship of suicidal ideation, mental health problems, and social functioning with eczema. A total of 4,744 adolescents (18-19 years) were invited and 3,775 (80%) participated. The overall prevalence of current eczema was 9.7%. Among those with current eczema, 15.5% reported suicidal ideation compared to 9.1% among those without eczema, significantly associated in a multivariate model (odds ratio 1.87, 95% confidence interval 1.31-2.68). In a subgroup analyses the prevalence of suicidal ideation in those with both eczema and itch was 23.8%, and was significantly associated compared to those witout eczema (3.57, 2.46-5.67). Eczema was associated with mental health problems assessed by Strength and Difficulties Questionnaire (1.72, 1.21-2.45) and Hopkins Symptom Checklist 10 (1.63, 1.23-2.16). Five questions assessed social function: feeling attached to family and friends, thriving at school, experiencing bullying, and romantic relationship. Boys with current eczema were less likely to have had romantic relationship (1.93, 1.21-3.08). Eczema in late adolescence is associated with suicidal ideation and mental health problems, but rarely with social problems. Our findings point to the importance of addressing mental health issues in adolescents with eczema.

Other- and self-directed forms of violence and their relationships to DSM-IV substance use and other psychiatric disorders in a national survey of adults

Harford TC, Yi H-y, Grant BF (USA)

Comprehensive Psychiatry 54, 731-739, 2013

Objective: To examine associations between DSM-IV psychiatric disorders and other- and self-directed violence in the general population.

Methods: Data were obtained from the National Epidemiologic Survey on Alcohol and Related Conditions (NESARC) Waves 1 & 2 (n = 34,653). Four violence categories were derived from a latent class analysis (LCA) of 5 other-directed and 4 self-directed violent behavior indicators. Multinomial logistic regression examined class associations for gender, race ethnicity, age and DSM-IV substance use, mood, anxiety, and personality disorders.

Results: Approximately 16% of adults reported some form of violent behavior distributed as follows: other-directed only, 4.6%; self-directed only, 9.3%; combined self- and other-directed, 2.0%; and no violence, 84.1%. The majority of the DSM-IV disorders included in this study were significantly and independently related to each form of violence. Generally, other-directed violence was more strongly associated with any substance use disorders (81%) and any personality disorders (42%), while self-directed violence was more strongly associated with mood (41%) and anxiety disorders (57%). Compared with these two forms of violence, the smaller group with combined self- and other-directed violence was more strongly associated with any substance use disorders (88%), mood disorders (63%), and personality disorders (76%).

Conclusion: Findings from this study are consistent with recent conceptualizations of disorders as reflecting externalizing disorders and internalizing disorders. The identification of the small category with combined forms of violence further extends numerous clinical studies which established associations between self- and other-directed violent behaviors. The extent to which the combined violence category represents a meaningful and reliable category of violence requires further detailed studies.

Exploring the use and effects of deliberate self-harm websites: An internet-based study

Harris IM, Roberts LM (UK)

Journal of Medical Internet Research 15, e285, 2013

Background: In the United Kingdom, rates of deliberate self-harm (DSH) are rising. Alongside this, there has been an increase in the number of websites available with DSH content, and the Internet is known as a valuable resource for those who feel isolated by their condition(s). However, there is little and contradictory evidence available on the effects of using such websites. Further research is therefore required to examine the use and effects of DSH websites.

Objective: Our objectives were to explore (1) the reasons people engage in the use of self-harm forums/websites, (2) the beliefs of users of self-harm forums regarding the role of such websites, (3) how the use of self-harm forums/websites modulates self-harm behaviors, and (4) other ways that self-harm forums affect the lives of individuals who use them.

Methods: Data were collected by a questionnaire hosted on 20 websites with self-harm content. Participants were self-selected from users of these sites. Results were analyzed using descriptive statistics and simple thematic analysis.

Results: In total, 329 responses were received with 91.8% (302/329) from female site users. The majority of participants (65.6%, 187/285) visited these sites at least twice per week, and most participants used the sites to find information (78.2%, 223/285) or participate in the forums (68.4%, 195/285). Positive effects of website use such as gaining help and support, isolation reduction, and a reduction in self-harm behaviors were reported by a large number of participants. However, smaller but important numbers reported negative effects including worsened self-harm, being triggered to self-harm, and additional negative physical and psychological effects.

Conclusions: This is the first multisite study to explore DSH website use in depth. There are clear and important benefits to engaging in website use for many individuals; however, these are not experienced by all website users. Negative effects were experienced by moderate numbers following website use, and clinicians should consider the impact of a patient's website use when consulting.

Psychiatric disorders in patients presenting to hospital following self-harm: A systematic review

Hawton K, Saunders K, Topiwala A, Haw C (UK)

Journal of Affective Disorders 151, 821-830, 2013

Background: Psychiatric disorders occur in approximately 90% of individuals dying by suicide. The prevalence of psychiatric disorders in people who engage in non-fatal self-harm has received less attention.

Method: Systematic review using electronic databases (Embase, PsychINFO and Medline) for English language publications of studies in which psychiatric disorders have been assessed using research or clinical diagnostic schedules in self-harm patients of all ages presenting to general hospitals, followed by meta-analyses using random effects methods.

Results: A total of 50 studies from 24 countries were identified. Psychiatric (Axis I) disorders were identified in 83.9% (95% CI 74.7-91.3%) of adults and 81.2% (95% CI 60.9-95.5%) of adolescents and young persons. The most frequent disorders were depression, anxiety and alcohol misuse, and additionally attention deficit hyperactivity disorder (ADHD) and conduct disorder in younger patients. Personality (Axis II) disorders were found in 27.5% (95% CI 17.6-38.7%) of adult patients. Psychiatric disorders were somewhat more common in patients in Western (89.6%, 95% CI 83.0-94.7%) than non-Western countries (70.6%, 95% CI 50.1-87.6%).

Limitations: Heterogeneity between study results was generally high. There were differences between studies in identification of study participants and diagnostic procedures.

Conclusions: Most self-harm patients have psychiatric disorders, as found in people dying by suicide. Depression and anxiety disorders are particularly common, together with ADHD and conduct disorder in adolescents. Psychosocial assessment and aftercare of self-harm patients should include careful screening for such disorders and appropriate therapeutic interventions. Longitudinal studies of the progress of these disorders are required.

Differences in incidence of suicide attempts between bipolar I and II disorders and major depressive disorder

Holma KM, Haukka J, Suominen K, Valtonen HM, Mantere O, Melartin TK, Sokero TP, Oquendo MA, Isometsä ET (Finland, USA)

Bipolar Disorders. Published online: 17 March 2014. doi: 10.1111/bdi.12195, 2014

Objectives: Whether risk of suicide attempts (SAs) differs between patients with bipolar disorder (BD) and patients with major depressive disorder (MDD) is unclear. We investigated whether cumulative risk differences are due to dissimilarities in time spent in high-risk states, incidence per unit time in high-risk states, or both.

Methods: Incidence rates for SAs during various illness phases, based on prospective life charts, were compared between patients from the Jorvi Bipolar Study (n = 176; 18 months) and the Vantaa Depression Study (n = 249; five years). Risk factors and their interactions with diagnosis were investigated with Cox proportional hazards models.

Results: By 18 months, 19.9% of patients with BD versus 9.5% of patients with MDD had attempted suicide. However, patients with BD spent 4.6% of the time in mixed episodes, and more time in major depressive episodes (MDEs) (35% versus 21%, respectively) and in subthreshold depression (39% versus 31%, respectively) than those with MDD. Compared with full remission, the combined incidence rates of SAs were 5-, 25-, and 65-fold in subthreshold depression, MDEs, and BD mixed states, respectively. Between cohorts, incidence of attempts was not different during comparable symptom states. In Cox models, hazard was elevated during MDEs and subthreshold depression, and among patients with preceding SAs, female patients, those with poor social support, and those aged < 40 years, but was unrelated to BD diagnosis.

Conclusions: The observed higher cumulative incidence of SAs among patients with BD than among those with MDD is mostly due to patients with BD spending more time in high-risk illness phases, not to differences in incidence during these phases, or to bipolarity itself. BD mixed phases contribute to differences involving very high incidence, but short duration. Diminishing the time spent in high-risk phases is crucial for prevention.

School effects on risk of non-fatal suicidal behaviour: A national multilevel cohort study

Jablonska B, Ostberg V, Hjern A, Lindberg L, Rasmussen F, Modin B (Sweden)

Social Psychiatry and Psychiatric Epidemiology. Published online: 26 October 2013. doi: 10.1007/s00127-013-0782-z, 2013

Objective: Research has demonstrated school effects on health, over and above the effects of students' individual characteristics. This approach has however been uncommon in mental health research. The aim of the study was to assess whether there are any school-contextual effects related to socioeconomic characteristics and academic performance, on the risk of hospitalization from non-fatal suicidal behaviour (NFSB).

Methods: A Swedish national cohort of 447,929 subjects was followed prospectively in the National Patient Discharge Register from the completion of compulsory school in 1989-93 (approximately 16 years) until 2001. Multilevel logistic regression was used to assess the association between school-level characteristics and NFSB.

Results: A small but significant share of variation in NFSB was accounted for by the school context (variance partition coefficient <1 %, median odds ratio = 1.26). The risk of NFSB was positively associated with the school's proportion of students from low socioeconomic status (SES), single parent household, and the school's average academic performance. School effects varied, in part, by school location.

Conclusion: NFSB seems to be explained mainly by individual-level characteristics. Nevertheless, a concentration of children from disadvantaged backgrounds in schools appears to negatively affect mental health, regardless of whether or not they are exposed to such problems themselves. Thus, school SES should be considered when planning prevention of mental health problems in children and adolescents.

Predictors of suicidal ideation in a community sample: Roles of anger, self-esteem, and depression

Jang JM, Park JI, Oh KY, Lee KH, Kim MS, Yoon MS, Ko SH, Cho HC, Chung YC (Korea)

Psychiatry Research 216, 74-81, 2014

The objective of this cross-sectional study was to investigate the relationships of anger, self-esteem, and depression with suicidal ideation. A survey was conducted in a wide range of community areas across Jeollabuk-do Province, Korea. A total of 2964 subjects (mean age=44.4 yr) participated in this study. Hierarchical regression was used to investigate predictors of suicidal ideation in terms of their sociodemographic characteristics, depression, self-esteem, and anger. Hierarchical regression analyses revealed that anger and self-esteem were significantly associated with suicidal ideation regardless of age and after controlling for depression. Moderation analysis showed that the impact of anger on suicidal ideation was significantly greater among females than males in adolescents, but not in other age groups. Additionally, there were some differences in sociodemographic predictors of suicidal ideation among age groups. Predictors included gender and family harmony in adolescents, marital status and family harmony in middle-aged individuals, and economic status and family harmony in elderly individuals. Our results revealed that anger and self-esteem play important roles in suicidal ideation beyond the effect of depression. Development and implementation of preventive strategies, including management of anger and self-esteem, could possibly reduce suicidal ideation and subsequent suicide attempts.

A pocket of very high suicide rates in a non-violent, egalitarian and cooperative population of south-east Asia

Jollant F, Malafosse A, Docto R, Macdonald C (Canada, Switzerland, Philippines, France)
Psychological Medicine. Published online: 17 January 2014. doi: 10.1017/S0033291713003176, 2014

Background: Extremely high rates of suicide localized within subgroups of populations where suicide is rare have been reported. We investigated this intriguing observation in a population of South-East Asia, where local culture should theoretically be preventative of suicide.

Method: A team including an anthropologist and a psychiatrist surveyed all cases of suicide that had occurred over 10 years in four isolated regions. A psychological autopsy was carried out comparing each suicide case with two matched control cases.

Results: In a region of 1192 inhabitants, 16 suicides occurred, leading to an annual suicide rate of 134/1 000 00 which is 10 times the rate in the USA or Canada. By contrast, three ethnically similar distant communities showed low to null rates. The gender ratio was three males to one female and two-thirds of cases were aged below 35 years. Methods of suicide were poisoning and hanging and motives mainly included interpersonal discord. The pattern of developmental and clinical risk factors was somewhat different from Western countries, showing no childhood maltreatment, only one case of alcohol/substance abuse and impulsive-aggressive personality but elevated rates of social anxiety. Suicide cases had very high frequencies of second-degree biological relatives who committed suicide.

Conclusions: Our study confirms a persistent phenomenon of high suicide rates restricted to a subgroup of a pre-industrialized population. We hypothesized this might be explained by isolation and endogamy, which may have promoted the selection/amplification of genetic vulnerability factors, or a contagion effect. These findings shed light on suicide from both a singular and a universal perspective, suggesting that particular local conditions may significantly modulate the rate of this complex behavior.

The impact of indiscriminate media coverage of a celebrity suicide on a society with a high suicide rate: Epidemiological findings on copycat suicides from South Korea

Ju Ji N, Young Lee W, Seok Noh M, Yip PSF (Korea, Hong Kong)

Journal of Affective Disorders 156, 56-61, 2013

Background: This study examines the extent to which the indiscriminate media coverage of the famous young actress Lee Eun-ju's suicide in 2005 affected suicides overall and in specific subgroups (by age, gender, and suicide method) in a suicide-prone society, South Korea.

Methods: South Korea's 2003-2005 suicide data (n=34,237) were obtained from death certificate records of the National Statistical Office (NSO). Data was analyzed with Poisson time series auto-regression models.

Results: After adjusting for confounding factors (such as seasonal variation, calendar year, temperature, humidity, and unemployment rate), there was a significant increase in suicide (RR=1.40, 95%, CI=1.30-1.51, no. of excess mortalities=331; 95% CI=267-391) during the 4 weeks after Lee's suicide. This increase was more prominent in subgroups with similar characteristics to the celebrity. In particular, the relative risk of suicide during this period was the largest (5.24; 95% CI=3.31-8.29) in young women who used the same suicide method as the celebrity. Moreover, the incidence of these copycat suicides during the same time significantly increased in both genders and in all age subgroups among those who committed suicide using the same method as the celebrity (hanging).

Limitations: It is difficult to prove conclusively that the real motivation of the suicides was Lee's death.

Conclusions: The findings from this study imply that, if the media indiscreetly reports the suicide of a celebrity in a suicide-prone society, the copycat effect can be far-reaching and very strong, particularly for vulnerable people.

Railway suicide attempts are associated with amount of sunlight in recent days

Kadotani H, Nagai Y, Sozu T (Japan)

Journal of Affective Disorders 152-154, 162-168, 2013

Background: To assess the relationship between hours of sunlight and railway suicide attempts, 3-7 days before these attempts.

Methods: All railway suicide attempts causing railway suspensions or delays of 30 min or more between 2002 and 2006. We used a linear probability model to assess this relationship. This study was conducted at Tokyo, Kanagawa, and Osaka prefectures in Japan. Data were collected from the railway delay incident database of the Japanese Railway Technical Research Institute and public weather database of the Japan Meteorological Agency.

Results: About 971 railway suicides attempts occurred between 2002 and 2006 in

Tokyo, Kanagawa, and Osaka. Less sunlight in the 7 days leading up to the railway suicide attempts was associated with a higher proportion of attempts (p=0.0243). Sunlight over the 3 days before an attempt had a similar trend (p=0.0888). No difference was found in sunlight hours between the days with (median: 5.6 [IQR: 1.1-8.8]) and without (median: 5.7 [IQR: 1.0-8.9]) railway suicide attempts in the evening. Finally, there was no apparent correlation between the railway suicide attempts and the monthly average sunlight hours of the attempted month or those of a month before.

Limitations: Railway suicides were not the main suicidal methods in Japan,.

Conclusions: We observed an increased proportion of railway suicide attempts after several days without sunlight. Light exposure (blue light or bright white light) in trains may be useful in reducing railway suicides, especially when consecutive days without sunshine are forecasted.

Association between antidepressant prescribing and suicide rates in OECD countries: An ecological study

Kamat MA, Edgar L, Niblock P, McDowell C, Kelly CB (UK)
Pharmacopsychiatry 47, 18-21, 2013

We have conducted an ecological study to assess the association between antidepressant prescribing and suicide rates using the Organisation for Economic Cooperation and Development (OECD) health data, making this the largest ecological study in recent times.Data were derived for the years 1995-2008 from the OECD health data set. The residuals for all variables were adjusted for country and year within each country. These were then analysed to identify predictors of suicide rate. Pearson's rank correlation coefficient and linear regression model were employed to assess associations and identify significant predictors of suicide rate.Suicide rate has significant positive correlations with antidepressant rates (p=0.031) and unemployment (p=0.028). It also has a significant negative correlation with inpatient psychiatric beds (p=0.039). The actual coefficients are less than +/-0.16, indicating weak relationships. After adjusting for other variables, the only variable that is a statistically significant predictor of suicide rate is antidepressant prescribing (p=0.005, r(2)=0.09).Our analysis using this large data set suggests a statistically significant, albeit weak positive, association between antidepressant prescribing and suicide rates.

Long-term depression and suicidal ideation outcomes subsequent to emancipation from foster care: Pathways to psychiatric risk in the métis population

Kaspar V (Canada)

Psychiatry Research 215, 347-354, 2013

Major depressive episode (MDE) and suicidal ideation (SI) associated with history of foster care placement (HxFCP), and mediating effects of psychosocial and socioeconomic factors through which placement may confer psychiatric risks in the years subsequent to emancipation were examined in a national sample of 7534 Métis. More than one third of emancipated respondents reported past year MDE, a prevalence rate nearly 50% higher than the rate of MDE among Métis respondents without a history of placement in foster care. The 25% lifetime prevalence rate of SI in the emancipated group was more than twice the rate observed in the non-fostered group. Direct effects of HxFCP on post placement MDE and SI were significant in multivariate logistic regression analyses, even when effects of childhood predispositional risk factors were controlled statistically. Emancipated individuals were unduly affected by psychosocial and socioeconomic disadvantages signifying pathways that linked foster care placement history and psychiatric status. Main mediators of the effects demonstrated using effect decomposition procedures were self-esteem, income, and community adversity. The findings warrant consideration of foster care history in clarifying the complex etiologies of suicidal ideation and major depressive episode in the Métis population and risk factors ensuing in the intervening years as integral to the process linking placement to long-term psychiatric outcomes.

Social support and positive events as suicide resiliency factors: Examination of synergistic buffering effects

Kleiman EM, Riskind JH, Schaefer KE (USA)

Archives of Suicide Research. Published online: 12 March 2014. doi: 10.1080/13811118.2013.826155, 2014

Objectives: We present a study on the role of social support and positive events as protective factors in suicide.

Methods: Participants (n = 379) were administered measures of social support, life events, depressive symptoms and suicide ideation.

Results: Results indicated that (a) social support had a direct protective effect on suicide ideation (b) social support and positive events acted as individual buffers in the relationship between negative events and suicide ideation, and (c) social support and positive events synergistically buffered the relationship between negative events and suicide ideation.

Conclusion: Our results provide evidence that positive events and social support act as protective factors against suicide individually and synergistically when they co-occur.

Suicide risk among individuals with sleep disturbances in Japan: A case-control psychological autopsy study

Kodaka M, Matsumoto T, Katsumata Y, Akazawa M, Tachimori H, Kawakami N, Eguchi N, Shirakawa N, Takeshima T (Japan)
Sleep Medicine 15, 430-435, 2014

Objective: This case-control psychological autopsy study aimed to explore a relationship between sleep disturbances and suicide among Japanese, as well as determine the importance and usability of screening for sleep disturbances in suicide prevention.

Methods: A semi-structured interview was conducted with the close family members of 49 adult suicide completers and 145 gender-, age-, and residential municipality-matched living controls. The survey included sections on demographics, sleep disturbances, and mental disorders. Conditional logistic regression analyses were performed to compare sleep disturbance prevalence between the two groups.

Results: A significantly higher prevalence of sleep disturbances was found among the suicide group (75.5%) compared to the controls (11.0%) (odds ratio [OR]=21.6, p < 0.001). The association remained significant after adjusting for mental disorders (OR = 12.7, p < 0.001). The population attributable risk percent of suicide associated with sleep disturbances and mental disorders was estimated to be 56.4% and 35.3%, respectively.

Conclusions: The study confirmed that sleep disturbances are an important risk factor of suicide, independent of mental disorders. Sleep disturbances accounted for a greater proportion of suicide cases than did mental disorders in the Japanese population given the higher prevalence, and could thus be considered an important target in suicide prevention in Japan.

Improving communication and practical skills in working with inpatients who self-harm: A pre-test/post-test study of the effects of a training programme

Kool N, van Meijel B, Koekkoek B, van der Bijl J, Kerkhof A (The Netherlands)
BMC Psychiatry 14, 64, 2014

Background: Differing perspectives of self-harm may result in a struggle between patients and treatment staff. As a consequence, both sides have difficulty communicating effectively about the underlying problems and feelings surrounding self-harm. Between 2009 and 2011, a programme was developed and implemented to train mental health care staff (nurses, social workers, psychologists, psychiatrists, and occupational therapists) in how to communicate effectively with and care for patients who self-harm. An art exhibition focusing on self-harm supported the programme. Lay experts in self-harm, i.e. people who currently harm themselves, or who have harmed themselves in the past and have the skills to disseminate their knowledge and experience, played an important role throughout the programme.

Methods: Paired sample t-tests were conducted to measure the effects of the training programme using the Attitude Towards Deliberate Self-Harm Questionnaire, the Self-Perceived Efficacy in Dealing with Self-Harm Questionnaire, and the Patient Contact Questionnaire. Effect sizes were calculated using r. Participants evaluated the training programme with the help of a survey. The questionnaires used in the survey were analysed descriptively.

Results: Of the 281 persons who followed the training programme, 178 completed the questionnaires. The results show a significant increase in the total scores of the three questionnaires, with large to moderate effect sizes. Respondents were positive about the training, especially about the role of the lay expert.

Conclusion: A specialised training programme in how to care for patients who self-harm can result in a more positive attitude towards self-harm patients, an improved self-efficacy in caring for patients who self-harm, and a greater closeness with the patients. The deployment of lay experts is essential here.

Feasibility of a web-based gatekeeper training: Implications for suicide prevention

Lancaster PG, Moore JT, Putter SE, Chen PY, Cigularov KP, Baker A, Quinnett P (USA, Australia)
Suicide and Life-Threatening Behavior. Published online: 27 February 2014. doi: 10.1111/sltb.12086, 2014

Web-based training programs have advantages such as increased scheduling flexibility and decreased training costs. Yet the feasibility of applying them to injury prevention programs such as suicide prevention gatekeeper training has not been empirically verified. Two studies were conducted to assess the feasibility and effectiveness of a web-based version of the Question, Persuade, and Refer (QPR) gatekeeper training program. Results of Study 1 revealed that participants in a web-based training demonstrated significant gains in knowledge of suicide prevention, self-efficacy for suicide prevention, and behavioral intentions to engage in suicide prevention, as compared to those in a control group. Results of Study 2 further showed that the web-based training may be as effective as the face-to-face QPR training across pre- (T1) and post training (T2); however, knowledge, self-efficacy, and behavioral intentions in both groups generally declined from T2 to 6-months after the training. Overall, these results provide initial evidence to support the feasibility of adopting web-based media to deliver gatekeeper training. Moreover, the present findings suggest the need to understand how to maintain gatekeepers' knowledge, confidence, motivation, and skills after training.

Risk factors for repetition of self-harm: A systematic review of prospective hospital-based studies

Larkin C, Blasi ZD, Arensman E (Ireland)

PLoS ONE. Published online: 20 January 2014. doi: 10.1371/journal.pone.0084282, 2014

Background: Self-harm entails high costs to individuals and society in terms of suicide risk, morbidity and healthcare expenditure. Repetition of self-harm confers yet higher risk of suicide and risk assessment of self-harm patients forms a key component of the health care management of self-harm patients. To date, there has been no systematic review published which synthesises the extensive evidence on risk factors for repetition.

Objective: This review is intended to identify risk factors for prospective repetition of self-harm after an index self-harm presentation, irrespective of suicidal intent.

Data Sources: PubMed, PsychInfo and Scirus were used to search for relevant publications. We included cohort studies which examining factors associated with prospective repetition among those presenting with self-harm to emergency departments. Journal articles, abstracts, letters and theses in any language published up to June 2012 were considered. Studies were quality-assessed and synthesised in narrative form.

Results: A total of 129 studies, including 329,001 participants, met our inclusion criteria. Some factors were studied extensively and were found to have a consistent association with repetition. These included previous self-harm, personality disorder, hopelessness, history of psychiatric treatment, schizophrenia, alcohol abuse/dependence, drug abuse/dependence, and living alone. However, the sensitivity values of these measures varied greatly across studies. Psychological risk factors and protective factors have been relatively under-researched but show emerging associations with repetition. Composite risk scales tended to have high sensitivity but poor specificity.

Conclusions: Many risk factors for repetition of self-harm match risk factors for initiation of self-harm, but the most consistent evidence for increased risk of repetition comes from long-standing psychosocial vulnerabilities, rather than characteristics of an index episode. The current review will enhance prediction of self-harm and assist in the efficient allocation of intervention resources.

Clinical and sociodemographic correlates of suicidality in patients with major depressive disorder from six Asian countries

Lim AY, Lee AR, Hatim A, Tian-Mei S, Liu CY, Jeon HJ, Udomratn P, Bautista D, Chan E, Liu SI, Chua HC, Hong JP (South Korea, Malaysia, China, Taiwan, Thailand, Singapore)

BMC Psychiatry 14, 37, 2014

Background: East Asian countries have high suicide rates. However, little is known about clinical and sociodemographic factors associated with suicidality in Asian populations. The aim of this study was to evaluate the factors associated with suicidality in patients with major depressive disorder (MDD) from six Asian countries.

Methods: The study cohort consisted of 547 outpatients with MDD. Patients presented to study sites in China (n = 114), South Korea (n = 101), Malaysia (n = 90), Singapore (n = 40), Thailand (n = 103), and Taiwan (n = 99). All patients completed the Mini-International Neuropsychiatric Interview (MINI), the Montgomery-Asberg Depression Rating Scale (MADRS), the Global Severity Index(SCL-90R), the Fatigue Severity Scale, the 36-item short-form health survey, the Sheehan Disability Scale, and the Multidimensional Scale of Perceived Social Support (MSPSS). Patients were classified as showing high suicidality if they scored >=6 on the MINI suicidality module. Multivariate logistic regression analysis was used to examine sociodemographic and clinical factors related to high suicidality.

Results: One hundred and twenty-five patients were classed as high suicidality. Unemployed status (adjusted odds ratio [OR] 2.43, p < 0.01), MADRS score (adjusted OR 1.08), p < 0.001, and GSI (SCL-90R) score (adjusted OR 1.06, p < 0.01) were positively related to high suicidality. Hindu (adjusted OR 0.09, p < 0.05) or Muslim (adjusted OR 0.21, p < 0.001) religion and MSPSS score (adjusted OR 0.82, p < 0.05) were protective against high suicidality.

Conclusions: A variety of sociodemographic and clinical factors were associated with high suicidality in Asian patients with MDD. These factors may facilitate the identification of MDD patients at risk of suicide.

The association between suicidality and internet addiction and activities in Taiwanese adolescents

Lin IH, Ko CH, Chang YP, Liu TL, Wang PW, Lin HC, Huang MF, Yeh YC, Chou WJ, Yen CF (Taiwan, USA)

Comprehensive Psychiatry 55, 504-510, 2014

Objective: The aims of this cross-sectional study were to examine the associations of suicidal ideation and attempt with Internet addiction and Internet activities in a large representative Taiwanese adolescent population.

Methods: 9510 adolescent students aged 12-18 years were selected using a stratified random sampling strategy in southern Taiwan and completed the questionnaires. The five questions from the Kiddie Schedule for Affective Disorders and Schizophrenia were used to inquire as to the participants' suicidal ideation and attempt in the past one month. The Chen Internet Addiction Scale was used to assess participants' Internet addiction. The kinds of Internet activities that the adolescents participated in were also recorded. The associations of suicidal ideation and attempt with Internet addiction and Internet activities were examined using logistic regression analysis to control for the effects of demographic characteristics, depression, family support and self-esteem.

Results: After controlling for the effects of demographic characteristics, depression, family support and self-esteem, Internet addiction was significantly associated with suicidal ideation and suicidal attempt. Online gaming, MSN, online searching for information, and online studying were associated with an increased risk of suicidal ideation. While online gaming, chatting, watching movies, shopping, and gambling were associated with an increased risk of suicidal attempt, watching online news was associated with a reduced risk of suicidal attempt.

Conclusions: The results of this study indicated that adolescents with Internet addiction have higher risks of suicidal ideation and attempt than those without. Meanwhile, different kinds of Internet activities have various associations with the risks of suicidal ideation and attempt.

Offspring death and subsequent psychiatric morbidity in bereaved parents: Addressing mechanisms in a total population cohort

Ljung T, Sandin S, Langstrom N, Runeson B, Lichtenstein P, Larsson H (Sweden)
Psychological Medicine. Published online: 01 November 2013. doi: 10.1017/S0033291713002572, 2013

Background: It is unclear if psychiatric morbidity among parents bereaved of a child is related to major loss in general or if the cause of death matters. Whether such a link is consistent with a causal explanation also remains uncertain.

Method: We identified 3 114 564 parents through linkage of Swedish nationwide registers. Risk of psychiatric hospitalization was assessed with log-linear Poisson regression and family-based analyses were used to explore familial confounding.

Results: A total of 3284 suicides and 14 095 any-cause deaths were identified in offspring between 12 and 25 years of age. Parents exposed to offspring suicide had considerably higher risk of subsequent psychiatric hospitalization than unexposed parents [relative risk (RR) 1.90, 95% confidence interval (CI) 1.72-2.09], higher than parents exposed to offspring non-suicide death relative to controls (RR 1.18, 95% CI 1.11-1.26). We found no risk increase among stepfathers differentially exposed to biologically unrelated stepchildren's death or suicide, and the relative risk was notably lower among full siblings differentially exposed to offspring death or suicide.

Conclusions: Parental psychiatric hospitalization following offspring death was primarily found in offspring suicide. Familial (e.g. shared genetic) effects seemed important, judging from both lack of psychiatric hospitalization in bereaved stepfathers and attenuated risk when bereaved parents were contrasted to their non-bereaved siblings. We conclude that offspring suicide does not 'cause' psychiatric hospitalization in bereaved parents.

Preventing suicide at suicide hotspots: A case study from Australia

Lockley A, Cheung YTD, Cox G, Robinson J, Williamson M, Harris M, Machlin A, Moffat C, Pirkis J (Australia)

Suicide and Life-Threatening Behavior. Published online: 15 February 2014. doi: 10.1111/sltb.12080, 2014

The Gap Park Self-Harm Minimisation Masterplan project is a collaborative attempt to address jumping suicides at Sydney's Gap Park through means restriction, encouraging help-seeking, and increasing the likelihood of third-party intervention. We used various data sources to describe the Masterplan project's processes, impacts, and outcomes. There have been reductions in reported jumps and confirmed suicides, although the trends are not statistically significant. There has been a significant increase in police call-outs to intervene with suicidal people who have not yet reached the cliff's edge. The collaborative nature of the Masterplan project and its multifaceted approach appear to be reaping benefits.

Stable time patterns of railway suicides in Germany: Comparative analysis of 7,187 cases across two observation periods (1995-1998; 2005-2008)

Lukaschek K, Baumert J, Erazo N, Ladwig KH (Germany)

BMC Public Health 14, 124, 2014

Background: The majority of fatalities on the European Union (EU) railways are suicides, representing about 60% of all railway fatalities. The aim of this study was to compare time patterns of suicidal behaviour on railway tracks in Germany between two observation periods (1995-1998 and 2005-2008) in order to investigate their stability and value in railway suicide prevention.

Methods: Cases were derived from the National Central Registry of person accidents on the German railway network (STABAG). The association of daytime, weekday and month with the mean number of suicides was analysed applying linear regression. Potential differences by observation period were assessed by adding observation period and the respective interaction terms into the linear regression. A 95% confidence interval for the mean number of suicides was computed using the t distribution.

Results: A total of 7,187 railway suicides were recorded within both periods: 4,102 (57%) in the first period (1995-1998) and 3,085 (43%) in the second (2005-2008). The number of railway suicides was highest on Mondays and Tuesdays in the first period with an average of 3.2 and 3.5 events and of 2.6 events on both days in the second period. In both periods, railway suicides were more common between 6:00 am and noon, and between 6:00 am and midnight. Seasonality was only prominent in the period 1995-1998.

Conclusions: Over the course of two observation periods, the weekday and circadian patterns of railway suicides remained stable. Therefore, these patterns should be an integral part of railway suicide preventive measures, e.g. gatekeeper training courses.

Acute influence of alcohol, thc or central stimulants on violent suicide: A Swedish population study

Lundholm L, Thiblin I, Runeson B, Leifman A, Fugelstad A (Sweden)

Journal of Forensic Sciences 59, 436-440, 2013

Alcohol and substance abuse in general is a risk factor for suicide, but very little is known about the acute effect in relation to suicide method. Based on information from 18,894 medico-legal death investigations, including toxicological findings and manner of death, did the present study investigate whether acute influence of alcohol, tetrahydrocannabinol (THC), or central stimulants (amphetamine and cocaine) was related to the use of a violent suicide method, in comparison with the nonviolent method self-poisoning and alcohol-/illicit drug-negative suicide decedents. Multivariate analysis was conducted, and the results revealed that acute influence of THC was related to using the violent suicide method— jumping from a height (RR 1.62; 95% CI 1.01-2.41). Alcohol intoxication was not related to any violent method, while the central stimulant-positive suicide decedent had a higher, albeit not significant, risk of several violent methods. The study contributes with elucidating suicide methods in relation to acute intoxication.

A mixed method study to determine the attitude of Australian emergency health professionals towards patients who present with deliberate self-poisoning

Martin C, Chapman R (Australia)

International Emergency Nursing 22, 98-104, 2013

Introduction: Deliberate self-poisoning is one of the frequent presentation types to emergency departments. It has been reported that attitudes of emergency staff may have negative consequences for the wellbeing of the self-poisoning patient.
Aim: Determine the attitude of nursing and medical staff towards patients who present with deliberate self-poisoning and to identify if differences exist between the two groups.
Design: Mixed-method.
Methodology: The "Attitudes towards Deliberate Self-Harm Questionnaire" was distributed to all nursing and medical staff who had direct patient contact at three emergency departments (N = 410). Total and factor scores were generated and analysed against variables age, gender, length of experience working in the emergency department, level of education and by profession. Two open ended questions asked staff to write their perceptions and stories about patients who deliberate self-poison and were analysed using qualitative data analysis.
Results: Forty-five percent of staff returned the questionnaire. The attitude of emergency nurses and doctors was positive towards patients who deliberately self-poison. Doctors had significantly higher total and Factor 2 'dealing effectively with the deliberate self-poisoning patient' scores than nurses. After adjusting for length of time working in the emergency department only Factor 2 'dealing effectively

with the deliberate self-poisoning patient' remained statistically significant. Staff reported high levels of frustration, in particular to patients who represent.

Conclusion/Relevance to practice: This information may be used to develop and implement educational strategies for staff to improve the experiences of and better support patients presenting to the emergency department who deliberately self-poison.

The effect of public awareness campaigns on suicides: Evidence from Nagoya, Japan

Matsubayashi T, Ueda M, Sawada Y (Japan)

Journal of Affective Disorders 152-154, 526-529, 2013

Background: Public awareness campaigns about depression and suicide have been viewed as highly effective strategies in preventing suicide, yet their effectiveness has not been established in previous studies. This study evaluates the effectiveness of a public-awareness campaign by comparing suicide counts before and after a city-wide campaign in Nagoya, Japan, where the city government distributed promotional materials that were aimed to stimulate public awareness of depression and promote care-seeking behavior during the period of 2010-2012.

Methods: In each of the sixteen wards of the city of Nagoya, we count the number of times that the promotional materials were distributed per month and then examine the association between the suicide counts and the frequency of distributions in the months following such distributions. We run a Poisson regression model that controls for the effects of ward-specific observed and unobserved heterogeneities and temporal shocks.

Findings: Our analysis indicates that more frequent distribution of the campaign material is associated with a decrease in the number of suicides in the subsequent months. The campaign was estimated to have been especially effective for the male residents of the city.

Limitation: The underlying mechanism of how the campaign reduced suicides remains to be unclear.

Conclusion: Public awareness campaigns can be an effective strategy in preventing suicide.

Group problem-solving skills training for self-harm: Randomised controlled trial

McAuliffe C, McLeavey BC, Fitzgerald T, Corcoran P, Carroll B, Ryan L, O'Keeffe B, Fitzgerald E, Hickey P, O'Regan M, Mulqueen J, Arensman E (Ireland)

British Journal of Psychiatry. Published online: 16 January 2014. doi: 10.1192/bjp.bp.111.101816, 2014

Background: Rates of self-harm are high and have recently increased. This trend and the repetitive nature of self-harm pose a significant challenge to mental health services.

Aims: To determine the efficacy of a structured group problem-solving skills training (PST) programme as an intervention approach for self-harm in addition to treatment as usual (TAU) as offered by mental health services.

Method: A total of 433 participants (aged 18-64 years) were randomly assigned to TAU plus PST or TAU alone. Assessments were carried out at baseline and at 6-week and 6-month follow-up and repeated hospital-treated self-harm was ascertained at 12-month follow-up.

Results: The treatment groups did not differ in rates of repeated self-harm at 6-week, 6-month and 12-month follow-up. Both treatment groups showed significant improvements in psychological and social functioning at follow-up. Only one measure (needing and receiving practical help from those closest to them) showed a positive treatment effect at 6-week ($P = 0.004$) and 6-month ($P = 0.01$) follow-up. Repetition was not associated with waiting time in the PST group.

Conclusions: This brief intervention for self-harm is no more effective than treatment as usual. Further work is required to establish whether a modified, more intensive programme delivered sooner after the index episode would be effective.

Risk factors for suicide among rural men: Are farmers more socially isolated?

McPhedran S, De Leo D (Australia)

The International Journal of Sociology and Social Policy 33, 762-772, 2013

Purpose: International evidence demonstrates elevated suicide rates among farming occupations, relative to other occupations. A psychosocial factor commonly argued to contribute to farmer suicide is social isolation and lack of social support, which in turn may indicate a need for policies and programs to support farmers' social participation and connectedness with others. However, there has been very little empirical investigation of perceived levels of social connectedness and social participation among farmers. The paper aims to discuss these issues.

Design/methodology/approach: This study used a cross-section of a nationally representative dataset, the Household, Income, and Labour Dynamics in Australia survey. This enabled quantification of Australian farmers' self-reported levels of social connectedness and social participation, relative to rural adult males in other occupations.

Findings: Levels of perceived social support and social participation among farmers were approximately equivalent to social support and social participation among rural men in other occupations.

Research Limitations/Implications: Possible mediating variables, such as influences of social support on mental health, were not examined in this study. However, these findings nonetheless suggest the assumption that social isolation is higher among farmers requires careful consideration.

Originality/value: This is the first study that quantifies social support and social participation among farmers, using a comparative approach.

Functional disability and death wishes in older Europeans: Results from the eurodep concerted action

Mellqvist Fassberg M, Ostling S, Braam AW, Backman K, Copeland JR, Fichter M, Kivela SL, Lawlor BA, Lobo A, Magnusson H, Prince MJ, Reischies FM, Turrina C, Wilson K, Skoog I, Waern M (Sweden)

Social Psychiatry and Psychiatric Epidemiology. Published online: 20 February 2014. doi: 10.1007/s00127-014-0840-1, 2014

Purpose: Physical illness has been shown to be a risk factor for suicidal behaviour in older adults. The association between functional disability and suicidal behaviour in older adults is less clear. The aim of this study was to examine the relationship between functional disability and death wishes in late life.

Methods: Data from 11 population studies on depression in persons aged 65 and above were pooled, yielding a total of 15,890 respondents. Level of functional disability was trichotomised (no, intermediate, high). A person was considered to have death wishes if the death wish/suicidal ideation item of the EURO-D scale was endorsed. Odds ratios for death wishes associated with functional disability were calculated in a multilevel logistic regression model.

Results: In total, 5 % of the men and 7 % of the women reported death wishes. Both intermediate (OR 1.89, 95 % CI 1.42; 2.52) and high functional disability (OR 3.22, 95 % CI 2.34; 4.42) were associated with death wishes. No sex differences could be shown. Results remained after adding depressive symptoms to the model.

Conclusions: Functional disability was independently associated with death wishes in older adults. Results can help inform clinicians who care for older persons with functional impairment.

Suicide reattempters: A systematic review

Mendez-Bustos P, de Leon-Martinez V, Miret M, Baca-Garcia E, Lopez-Castroman J (Chile, Spain, France)

Harvard Review of Psychiatry 21, 281-295, 2013

Learning Objectives: After participating in this educational activity, the psychiatrist should be better able to 1. Identify the characteristic features of suicide reattempters. 2. Evaluate the limitations of the literature. 3. Compare the characteristic features of single attempters and suicide reattempters. The aim of this study is to identify the characteristic features of suicide reattempters. The recognition of the suicide reattempters population as a distinct clinical population may encourage future preventive and clinical work with this high-risk subgroup and thus reduce deaths. A systematic literature review was carried out in order to identify the key demographic, psychological, and clinical variables associated with the repetition of suicide attempts. In addition, we wished to analyze the operational definitions of the repetition of suicide attempts proposed in the scientific literature. Studies published from 2000 to 2012 were identified in PubMed, PsycINFO, and Web of Science databases and were selected according to predetermined criteria. We examined a total of 1480 articles and selected 86 that matched our search criteria. The literature is heterogeneous, with no consensus regarding the operational definitions of suicide reattempters. Comparison groups in the literature have also been inconsistent and include subjects making a single lifetime attempt and subjects who did not reattempt during a defined study period. Suicide reattempters were associated with higher rates of the following characteristics: unemployment, unmarried status, diagnosis of mental disorders, suicidal ideation, stressful life events, and family history of suicidal behavior. Additional research is needed to establish adequate differentiation and effective treatment plans for this population.

Antidepressant class, age, and the risk of deliberate self-harm: A propensity score matched cohort study of SSRI and SNRI users in the USA

Miller M, Pate V, Swanson Sa, Azrael D, White A, Stürmer T (USA)
CNS Drugs 28, 79-88, 2013

Background: The US Food and Drug Administration's meta-analyses of placebo-controlled antidepressant trials found approximately twice the rate of suicidal behaviors among children and adults aged 24 years and younger who were randomized to receive antidepressant medication than among those who were randomized to placebo. Rates of suicidal behavior were similar for subjects aged 25-64 years whether they received antidepressants or placebo, and subjects aged 65 years or older randomized to antidepressants were found to have lower rates of suicidal behavior. The age-stratified FDA meta-analyses did not have adequate power to investigate rates of suicidal behaviors by antidepressant drug class.

Objective: Our objective was to assess the risk of deliberate self-harm associated with the two most commonly prescribed classes of antidepressant agents.

Design: Propensity score matched cohort study of incident users of antidepressant agents.

Setting: Population-based healthcare utilization data of US residents.

Patients: US residents aged 10-64 years with a recorded diagnosis of depression who initiated use of selective serotonin reuptake inhibitors (SSRIs) or serotonin norepinephrine reuptake inhibitors (SNRIs) between 1 January 1998 and 31 December 2010.

Main Outcome Measures: ICD-9 external cause of injury codes E950.x-E958.x (deliberate self-harm).

Results: A total of 102,647 patients aged between 10 and 24 years, and 338,021 aged between 25 and 64 years, initiated therapy with antidepressants. Among 10-24 year olds, prior to propensity score matching, 75,675 initiated therapy with SSRIs and 5,344 initiated SNRIs. After matching, there were 5,344 SNRI users and 10,688 SSRI users. Among the older cohort, 36,037 SNRI users were matched to 72,028 SSRI users (from an unmatched cohort of 225,952 SSRI initiators).

Regardless of age cohort, patients initiating SSRIs and patients initiating SNRIs had similar rates of deliberate self-harm. Restriction to patients with no antidepressant use in the past 3 years did not alter our findings.

Conclusions: Our findings of similar rates of deliberate self-harm for depressed patients who initiate treatment with either an SSRI or an SNRI suggests that physicians who have decided that their patients would benefit from initiating antidepressant therapy need not weigh differential suicide risk when deciding which class of antidepressant to prescribe.

The effects of involuntary job loss on suicide and suicide attempts among young adults: Evidence from a matched case-control study

Milner A, Page A, Morrell S, Hobbs C, Carter G, Dudley M, Duflou J, Taylor R (Australia)
Australian and New Zealand Journal of Psychiatry 48, 333-340, 2014

Objective: To assess the influence of involuntary job loss on suicide and attempted suicide in young adults.

Method: A population-based case-control study of young adults (18-34 years) was conducted in New South Wales, Australia. Cases included both suicides (n=84) and attempts (n=101). A structured interview was conducted with next of kin (for suicide cases) and suicide attempters admitted to hospital. Controls selected from the general population were matched to cases by age and sex. Job dismissal or redundancy (involuntary job loss) in the 12 months before suicide or attempt was the main study variable of interest. Suicide and attempts were modelled separately and in combination as outcomes using conditional logistic regression modelling. The analysis was also adjusted for marital status, socio-economic status and diagnosis of an affective or anxiety disorder.

Results: Following adjustment for other variables, involuntary job loss was associated with an odds ratio of 1.82 for suicide and attempted suicide (combined) (95% CI 0.98 to 3.37; p=0.058). Low socio-economic status was associated with an odds ratio of 3.80 for suicide and attempted suicide (95% CI 2.16 to 6.67; p<0.001) compared to high socio-economic status (after adjustment). Diagnosis of a mental disorder was associated with a 7.87 (95% CI 5.16 to 12.01; p<0.001) odds ratio of suicide and attempted suicide compared to no diagnosis (after adjustment). Involuntary job loss was associated with increased odds of suicide and attempts when these were modelled separately, but results did not reach statistical significance.

Conclusions: Involuntary job loss was associated with increased odds of suicide and attempted suicide. The strength of this relationship was attenuated after adjustment for socio-economic status and mental disorders, which indicates that these may have a stronger influence on suicide than job loss.

Is transition to disability pension in young people associated with changes in risk of attempted suicide?

Mittendorfer-Rutz E, Alexanderson K, Westerlund H, Lange T (Sweden, Denmark)
Psychological Medicine. Published online: 17 January 2014. doi: 10.1017/S0033291713003097, 2014

Background: The aim of the present study was to investigate trajectories of suicide attempt risks before and after granting of disability pension in young people.

Method: The analytic sample consisted of all persons 16-30 years old and living in Sweden who were granted a disability pension in the years 1995-1997; 2000-2002 as well as 2005-2006 (n = 26 624). Crude risks and adjusted odds ratios for suicide attempt were computed for the 9-year window around the year of disability pension receipt by repeated-measures logistic regressions.

Results: The risk of suicide attempt was found to increase continuously up to the year preceding the granting of disability pension in young people, after which the risk declined. These trajectories were similar for women and men and for disability pension due to mental and somatic diagnoses. Still, the multivariate odds ratios for suicide attempts for women and for disability pension due to mental disorders were 2.5- and 3.8-fold increased compared with the odds ratios for men and disability pension due to somatic disorders, respectively. Trajectories of suicide attempts differed for young individuals granted a disability pension during 2005-2006 compared with those granted during 1995-1997 and 2000-2002.

Conclusions: We found an increasing risk of suicide attempt up until the granting of a disability pension in young individuals, after which the risk decreased. It is of clinical importance to monitor suicide attempt risk among young people waiting for the granting of a disability pension.

Past suicide attempts in depressed inpatients: Clinical versus research assessment

Molero P, Grunebaum MF, Galfalvy HC, Bongiovi MA, Lowenthal D, Almeida MG, Burke AK, Stevenson E, Mann JJ, Oquendo MA (USA)
Archives of Suicide Research 18, 50-57, 2013

Objective: To compare structured clinical assessment versus research measurement of suicidal risk among inpatients with major depression.

Methods: 50 depressed inpatients underwent a structured clinical and an independent research assessment of suicidal risk. Agreement between both assessments and its impact upon time to first readmission was tested.

Results: A false negative rate of 25% in the clinical screening of past suicide attempts was associated with older age, concealment and reported lower frequency of suicidal thoughts. Mean times to first readmission (2.5-years follow-up) were 74 weeks (discordant responders) and 118 weeks (concordant responders).

Conclusion: A failure to detect 25% of patients with past suicide attempt history in the clinical assessment was associated with older age and concealment of suicidal thoughts.

Association of training on attitudes towards self-injuring clients across health professionals

Muehlenkamp JJ, Claes L, Quigley K, Prosser E, Claes S, Jans D (USA, Belgium)

Archives of Suicide Research 17, 462-468, 2013

The objective of this study was to evaluate associations between self-injury training and attitudes across different health care professions. In the study, 342 psychologists, social workers, psychiatric, and medical nurses were recruited from 12 hospitals in Belgium. Participants completed a confidential questionnaire assessing attitudes, perceived knowledge/competence in self-injury, and prior self-injury training. Professionals with training reported more positive empathy, less negative attitudes, and greater perceived knowledge/competence, which was related to positive attitudes. Mental health providers had more positive attitudes than medical professionals. Conclusions: Attitudes towards self-injuring patients are multifaceted and vary across health professions. Training on self-injury should be incorporated into the educational curriculum of all health care professions.

A review of ketamine in affective disorders: Current evidence of clinical efficacy, limitations of use and pre-clinical evidence on proposed mechanisms of action

Naughton M, Clarke G, Oleary OF, Cryan JF, Dinan TG (Ireland)

Journal of Affective Disorders 156, 24-35, 2013

Introduction: Recent research has seen low-dose ketamine emerge as a novel, rapid-acting antidepressant. Ketamine, an N-methy-d-aspartate (NMDA) receptor antagonist, leads to effects on the glutamatergic system and abnormalities in this neurotransmittor system are present in depression. This article aims to (1) review the clinical literature on low-dose ketamine as a rapid-acting antidepressant in affective disorders, (2) provide a critical overview of the limitations of ketamine and research attempts to overcome these (3) discuss the proposed mechanisms of action of ketamine and (4) point towards future research directions.

Method: The electronic database Pubmed, Web of Science and sciencedirect were searched using the keywords: ketamine, N-methyl-d-aspartate receptor antagonist, rapid-acting antidepressant, depression, treatment-resistant depression, bipolar depression, suicidal ideation, electroconvulsive therapy, mechanism of action.

Result: The literature demonstrates evidence supporting a rapid-acting antidepressant effect of low-dose intravenous ketamine in major depressive disorder, in bipolar depression and in depression with suicidal ideation. There are mixed results as to whether ketamine leads to a reduction in time to remission in patients undergoing electroconvulsive therapy (ECT). Efforts to unravel ketamine s therapeutic mechanism of action have implicated the mammalian target of rapamycin (mTOR)-dependent synapse formation in the rat prefrontal cortex, eukaryotic elongation factor 2 phosphorylation (p-eEF2) and glycogen synthase kinase (GSK-3). Ketamine s limiting factors are the transient nature of its antidepressant effect and concerns regarding abuse, and research efforts to overcome these are reviewed.

Conclusion: Current and future research studies are using ketamine as a promising tool to evaluate the glutamatergic neurotransmittor system to learn more about the pathophysiology of depression and develop more specific rapid-acting antidepressant treatments.

Characteristics of U.S. Suicide decedents in 2005-2010 who had received mental health treatment

Niederkrotenthaler T, Logan JE, Karch DL, Crosby A (USA)
Psychiatric Services 65, 387-390, 2014

Objective: To inform suicide prevention efforts in mental health treatment, the study assessed associations between recent mental health treatment, personal characteristics, and circumstances of suicide among suicide decedents.

Methods: Data from 18 states reporting to the National Violent Death Reporting System between 2005 and 2010 (N=57,877 suicides) were used to compare circumstances among adult decedents receiving any or no type of mental health treatment within two months before death.

Results: Of suicide decedents, 28.5% received treatment before suicide. Several variables were associated with higher odds of receiving treatment, including death by poisoning with commonly prescribed substances (adjusted odds ratio [AOR]=3.04, 95% confidence interval [CI]=2.84-3.26), a history of suicide attempts (AOR=2.77, CI=2.64-2.90), depressed mood (AOR=1.69, CI=1.62-1.76), and nonalcoholic substance abuse or dependence (AOR=1.13, CI=1.07-1.19).

Conclusions: For nearly a third of all suicide decedents, better mental health care might have prevented death. Efforts to reduce access to lethal doses of prescription medications seem warranted to prevent overdosing with commonly prescribed substances.

Prevalence and correlates of suicidal behavior among soldiers: Results from the army study to assess risk and resilience in servicemembers (army STARRS)

Nock MK, Stein MB, Heeringa SG, Ursano RJ, Colpe LJ, Fullerton CS, Hwang I, Naifeh JA, Sampson NA, Schoenbaum M, Zaslavsky AM, Kessler RC (USA)

JAMA Psychiatry. Published online: 3 March 2014. doi:10.1001/jamapsychiatry.2014.30, 2014

Importance: The suicide rate among US Army soldiers has increased substantially in recent years.

Objectives: To estimate the lifetime prevalence and sociodemographic, Army career, and psychiatric predictors of suicidal behaviors among nondeployed US Army soldiers.

Design, Setting, and Participants: A representative cross-sectional survey of 5428 nondeployed soldiers participating in a group self-administered survey.

Main Outcomes and Measures: Lifetime suicidal ideation, suicide plans, and suicide attempts.

Results: The lifetime prevalence estimates of suicidal ideation, suicide plans, and suicide attempts are 13.9%, 5.3%, and 2.4%. Most reported cases (47.0%-58.2%) had pre-enlistment onsets. Pre-enlistment onset rates were lower than in a prior national civilian survey (with imputed/simulated age at enlistment), whereas post-enlistment onsets of ideation and plans were higher, and post-enlistment first attempts were equivalent to civilian rates. Most reported onsets of plans and attempts among ideators (58.3%-63.3%) occur within the year of onset of ideation. Post-enlistment attempts are positively related to being a woman (with an odds ratio [OR] of 3.3 [95% CI, 1.5-7.5]), lower rank (OR = 5.8 [95% CI, 1.8-18.1]), and previously deployed (OR = 2.4-3.7) and are negatively related to being unmarried (OR = 0.1-0.8) and assigned to Special Operations Command (OR = 0.0 [95% CI, 0.0-0.0]). Five mental disorders predict post-enlistment first suicide attempts in multivariate analysis: pre-enlistment panic disorder (OR = 0.1 [95% CI, 0.0-0.8]), pre-enlistment posttraumatic stress disorder (OR = 0.1 [95% CI, 0.0-0.7]), post-enlistment depression (OR = 3.8 [95% CI, 1.2-11.6]), and both pre- and post-enlistment intermittent explosive disorder (OR = 3.7-3.8). Four of these 5 ORs (posttraumatic stress disorder is the exception) predict ideation, whereas only post-enlistment intermittent explosive disorder predicts attempts among ideators. The population-attributable risk proportions of lifetime mental disorders predicting post-enlistment suicide attempts are 31.3% for pre-enlistment onset disorders, 41.2% for post-enlistment onset disorders, and 59.9% for all disorders.

Conclusions and Relevance: The fact that approximately one-third of post-enlistment suicide attempts are associated with pre-enlistment mental disorders suggests that pre-enlistment mental disorders might be targets for early screening and intervention. The possibility of higher fatality rates among Army suicide attempts than among civilian suicide attempts highlights the potential importance of means control (ie, restricting access to lethal means [such as firearms]) as a suicide prevention strategy.

Correlates of suicidal ideation in physically injured trauma survivors

O'Connor SS, Dinsio K, Wang J, Russo J, Rivara FP, Love J, McFadden C, Lapping-Carr L, Peterson R, Zatzick DF (USA)

Suicide and Life-Threatening Behavior. Published online: 24 February 2014. doi: 10.1111/sltb.12085, 2014

Epidemiologic studies have documented that injury survivors are at increased risk for suicide. We evaluated 206 trauma survivors to examine demographic, clinical, and injury characteristics associated with suicidal ideation during hospitalization and across 1 year. Results indicate that mental health functioning, depression symptoms, and history of mental health services were associated with suicidal ideation in the hospital; being a parent was a protective factor. Pre-injury post-traumatic stress disorder symptoms, assaultive injury mechanism, injury-related legal proceedings, and physical pain were significantly associated with suicidal ideation across 1 year. Readily identifiable risk factors early after traumatic injury may inform hospital-based screening and intervention procedures.

Feeling that life is not worth living (death thoughts) among middle-aged, Australian women providing unpaid care

O'Dwyer ST, Moyle W, Pachana NA, Sung B, Barrett S (Australia)

Maturitas 77, 375-379, 2014

Objective: To identify the proportion of female carers who experience death thoughts and the factors associated with these thoughts, using data from the Australian Longitudinal Study on Women's Health (ALSWH).

Methods: A cross-sectional analysis of the fifth ALSWH survey was conducted. 10,528 middle-aged women provided data on caring and death thoughts, 3077 were carers and 2005 of those were included in the multivariate analysis.

Results: 7.1% of female carers had felt life was not worth living in the previous week and were classified as having experienced death thoughts, compared with 5.7% of non-carers (p = .01). Carers with death thoughts had poorer physical and mental health, higher levels of anxiety, lower levels of optimism, and reported less social support (p < .01). In a multivariate model social support, mental health, carer satisfaction, and depressive symptoms significantly predicted death thoughts. Carers with clinically significant depressive symptoms were four times more likely to experience death thoughts than those without. Carers who were satisfied with their role were 50% less likely to have experienced death thoughts than those who were dissatisfied.

Conclusions: A small but significant proportion of female carers experience death thoughts and may be at risk for suicide. These findings add to the growing body of evidence on suicide-related thoughts and behaviours in carers and have implications for health professionals and service providers.

A diffusion tensor imaging study of suicide attempters

Olvet DM, Peruzzo D, Thapa-Chhetry B, Sublette ME, Sullivan GM, Oquendo MA, Mann JJ, Parsey RV (USA, Italy)

Journal of Psychiatric Research 51, 60-67, 2014

Background: Few studies have examined white matter abnormalities in suicide attempters using diffusion tensor imaging (DTI). This study sought to identify white matter regions altered in individuals with a prior suicide attempt.

Methods: DTI scans were acquired in 13 suicide attempters with major depressive disorder (MDD), 39 non-attempters with MDD, and 46 healthy participants (HP). Fractional anisotropy (FA) and apparent diffusion coefficient (ADC) were determined in the brain using two methods: region of interest (ROI) and tract-based spatial statistics (TBSS). ROIs were limited a priori to white matter adjacent to the caudal anterior cingulate cortex, rostral anterior cingulate cortex, dorsomedial prefrontal cortex, and medial orbitofrontal cortex.

Results: Using the ROI approach, suicide attempters had lower FA than MDD non-attempters and HP in the dorsomedial prefrontal cortex. Uncorrected TBSS results confirmed a significant cluster within the right dorsomedial prefrontal cortex indicating lower FA in suicide attempters compared to non-attempters. There were no differences in ADC when comparing suicide attempters, non-attempters and HP groups using ROI or TBSS methods.

Conclusions: Low FA in the dorsomedial prefrontal cortex was associated with a suicide attempt history. Converging findings from other imaging modalities support this finding, making this region of potential interest in determining the diathesis for suicidal behavior.

Effectiveness of a multimodal community intervention program to prevent suicide and suicide attempts: A quasi-experimental study

Ono Y, Sakai A, Otsuka K, Uda H, Oyama H, Ishizuka N, Awata S, Ishida Y, Iwasa H, Kamei Y, Motohashi Y, Nakamura J, Nishi N, Watanabe N, Yotsumoto T, Nakagawa A, Suzuki Y, Tajima M, Tanaka E, Sakai H, Yonemoto N (Japan)

PLoS ONE. Published online: 9 October 2013. doi: 10.1371/journal.pone.0074902, 2013

Background: Multilevel and multimodal interventions have been suggested for suicide prevention. However, few studies have reported the outcomes of such interventions for suicidal behaviours.

Methods: We examined the effectiveness of a community-based multimodal intervention for suicide prevention in rural areas with high suicide rates, compared with a parallel prevention-as-usual control group, covering a total of 631,133 persons. The effectiveness was also examined in highly populated areas near metropolitan cities (1,319,972 persons). The intervention started in July 2006, and continued for 3.5 years. The primary outcome was the incidence of composite outcome, consisting of completed suicides and suicide attempts requiring admission to an emergency ward for critical care. We compared the rate ratios (RRs) of the outcomes adjusted by sex, age group, region, period and interaction terms. Analyses were performed on an intention-to-treat basis and stratified by sex and age groups.

Findings: In the rural areas, the overall median adherence of the intervention was significantly higher. The RR of the composite outcome in the intervention group decreased 7% compared with that of the control group. Subgroup analyses demonstrated heterogeneous effects among subpopulations: the RR of the composite outcome in the intervention group was significantly lower in males (RR = 0.77, 95% CI 0.59-0.998, p = 0.0485) and the RR of suicide attempts was significantly lower in males (RR = 0.39, 95% CI 0.22-0.68, p = 0.001) and the elderly (RR = 0.35, 95% CI 0.17-0.71, p = 0.004). The intervention had no effect on the RR of the composite outcome in the highly populated areas.

Interpretation: Our findings suggest that this community-based multimodal intervention for suicide prevention could be implemented in rural areas, but not in highly populated areas. The effectiveness of the intervention was shown for males and for the elderly in rural areas.

Life events: A complex role in the timing of suicidal behavior among depressed patients

Oquendo M, Perez-Rodriguez M, Poh E, Sullivan G, Burke Ak, Sublette Me, Mann Jj, Galfalvy H (USA)

Molecular Psychiatry. Published online: 15 October 2013. doi: 10.1038/mp.2013.128, 2013

Suicidal behavior is often conceptualized as a response to overwhelming stress. Our model posits that given a propensity for acting on suicidal urges, stressors such as life events or major depressive episodes (MDEs) determine the timing of suicidal acts. Depressed patients (n=415) were assessed prospectively for suicide attempts and suicide, life events and MDE over 2 years. Longitudinal data were divided into 1-month intervals characterized by MDE (yes/no), suicidal behavior (yes/no) and life event scores. Marginal logistic regression models were fit, with suicidal behavior as the response variable and MDE and life event score in either the same or previous month, respectively, as time-varying covariates. Among 7843 person-months, 33% had MDE and 73% had life events. MDE increased the risk for suicidal behavior (odds ratio (OR)=4.83, P 0.0001). Life event scores were unrelated to the timing of suicidal behavior (OR=1.06 per 100 point increase, P=0.32), even during a MDE (OR=1.12, P=0.15). However, among those without borderline personality disorder (BPD), both health- and work-related life events were key precipitants, as was recurrent MDE, with a 13-fold effect. The relationship of life events to suicidal behavior among those with BPD was more complex. Recurrent MDE was a robust precipitant for suicidal behavior, regardless of BPD comorbidity. The specific nature of life events is key to understanding the timing of suicidal behavior. Given unanticipated results regarding the role of BPD and study limitations, these findings require replication. Of note, that MDE, a treatable risk factor, strongly predicts suicidal behaviors is cause for hope.

Suicide bereavement and risk for suicide attempt: A national cross-sectional survey of young adults

Pitman A, Osborn D, King M (UK)

The Lancet 383, S82, 2014

Background: Provision of support to people bereaved by suicide has become a key priority for suicide prevention strategies in the UK and many other developed countries. Stigma, social modelling, depression, heritability, and other factors are thought to increase this group's risk of suicidality. Few studies have described the nature or magnitude of the effects of suicide bereavement on family, friends, and other contacts, or assessed the effectiveness of post-bereavement support. We tested the hypothesis that young adults bereaved by the suicide of a close contact have an increased risk of suicidal thoughts and suicide attempts and poorer social functioning than those bereaved by other causes of sudden death.

Methods: We used a sample of 635?000 staff and students on the email distribution lists of 37 UK higher education institutions in 2010. Via mass email, we invited adults who had experienced a sudden bereavement to complete an online survey measuring outcomes relating to suicidal thoughts, suicide attempts, and social functioning. Inclusion criteria were current age 18-40 years, and sudden bereavement of a close contact since the age of 10 years. Multiple regression was used to compare those bereaved by suicide, those bereaved by accidental death, and those bereaved by sudden natural death (the baseline group), adjusting for covariates chosen a priori: age, sex, social class, family history of suicide (excluding an index suicide), past psychological problems, and kinship to the deceased (non-relativevsblood relative).

Findings: Of 3685 bereaved adults (from 4631 consenting to participate), 658 had been bereaved by suicide, 761 by sudden accidental death, and 2266 by sudden death due to natural causes. 20% were male. Because the denominator for the population of people exposed to sudden bereavement could not be estimated reliably, calculation of a response rate was not possible. Multiple logistic regression showed a non-significant excess risk of suicidal ideation (odds ratio 1·10, 95% CI 0·87-1·40) and a significant excess risk of suicide attempt (1·63, 1·06-2·50) in the group bereaved by suicide. No statistically significant interactions were found between type of bereavement and kinship to the deceased.

Interpretation: Our findings suggest that young adults who have been exposed to suicide bereavement might be at increased risk of suicide attempts and poor social functioning compared with young adults bereaved by other causes of sudden death, whether or not they were related to the deceased. Clinically, this finding suggests that inquiring about a history of suicide in unrelated close contacts should be added to family history of suicide within routine psychosocial assessments. From a public health policy perspective the findings confirm that this population of young adults is vulnerable to suicidal behaviour. Further work is needed to identify the nature and effectiveness of the support needed for this group.

Insomnia as a predictor of high-lethality suicide attempts

Pompili M, Innamorati M, Forte A, Longo L, Mazzetta C, Erbuto D, Ricci F, Palermo M, Stefani H, Seretti ME, Lamis DA, Perna G, Serafini G, Amore M, Girardi P (Italy, USA, The Netherlands)
International Journal of Clinical Practice 67, 1311-1316, 2013

Summary: Introduction Research has demonstrated that patients with insomnia are at an increased risk of experiencing suicidal ideation and/or making a suicide attempt.

Objectives: To evaluate the relation between insomnia and suicidal behaviour.

Aims: To examine factors associated with a diagnosis of insomnia in patients admitted to an Emergency Department (ED) and assessed by the psychiatrist in charge.

Methods: Participants were 843 patients consecutively admitted to the ED of Sant'Andrea Hospital in Rome, between January 2010 and December 2011. All patients admitted were referred to a psychiatrist. A clinical interview based on the Mini International Neuropsychiatric Interview (MINI) and a semi-structured interview was conducted. Patients were asked about 'ongoing' suicidal ideation or plans for suicide.

Results: Forty-eight percent of patients received a diagnosis of bipolar disorder (BD), major depressive disorder (MDD) or an anxiety disorder; whereas, 17.1% were diagnosed with Schizophrenia or other non-affective psychosis. Patients with insomnia (compared to patients without insomnia) more frequently had a diagnosis of BD (23.9% vs. 12.4%) or MDD (13.3% vs. 9.5%; p < 0.001). Moreover, patients with insomnia less frequently had attempted suicide in the past 24 h (5.3% vs. 9.5%; p < 0.05) as compared with other patients, but those patients with insomnia who attempted suicide more frequently used a violent method (64.3% vs. 23.6%; p < 0.01) compared to other suicide attempters.

Conclusions: Our results do not support an association between insomnia and suicidal behaviour. However, suicide attempters with insomnia more frequently used violent methods, and this phenomenon should be taken into serious consideration by clinicians.

Predicting the risk of suicide by analyzing the text of clinical notes

Poulin C, Shiner B, Thompson P, Vepstas L, Young-Xu Y, Goertzel B, Watts B, Flashman L, McAllister T (USA)

PLoS ONE. Published online: 28 January 2014. doi: 10.1371/journal.pone.0085733, 2014

We developed linguistics-driven prediction models to estimate the risk of suicide. These models were generated from unstructured clinical notes taken from a national sample of U.S. Veterans Administration (VA) medical records. We created three matched cohorts: veterans who committed suicide, veterans who used mental health services and did not commit suicide, and veterans who did not use mental health services and did not commit suicide during the observation period (n = 70 in each group). From the clinical notes, we generated datasets of single keywords and multi-word phrases, and constructed prediction models using a machine-learning algorithm based on a genetic programming framework. The resulting inference accuracy was consistently 65% or more. Our data therefore suggests that computerized text analytics can be applied to unstructured medical records to estimate the risk of suicide. The resulting system could allow clinicians to potentially screen seemingly healthy patients at the primary care level, and to continuously evaluate the suicide risk among psychiatric patients.

Combined effects of physical illness and comorbid psychiatric disorder on risk of suicide in a national population study

Qin P, Hawton K, Mortensen PB, Webb R (Denmark, UK)

British Journal of Psychiatry. Published online: 27 February 2014. doi: 10.1192/bjp.bp.113.128785, 2014

Background: People with physical illness often have psychiatric disorder and this comorbidity may have a specific influence on their risk of suicide.

Aims: To examine how physical illness and psychiatric comorbidity interact to influence risk of suicide, with particular focus on relative timing of onset of the two types of illness.

Method: Based on the national population of Denmark, individual-level data were retrieved from five national registers on 27 262 suicide cases and 468 007 gender- and birth-date matched living controls. Data were analysed using conditional logistic regression.

Results: Both suicides and controls with physical illness more often had comorbid psychiatric disorder than their physically healthy counterparts. Although both physical and psychiatric illnesses constituted significant risk factors for suicide, their relative timing of onset in individuals with comorbidity significantly differentiated the associated risk of suicide. While suicide risk was highly elevated when onsets of both physical and psychiatric illness occurred close in time to each other, regardless which came first, psychiatric comorbidity developed some time after onset of physical illness exacerbated the risk of suicide substantially.

Conclusions: Suicide risk in physically ill people varies substantially by presence of psychiatric comorbidity, particularly the relative timing of onset of the two types of illness. Closer collaboration between general and mental health services should be an essential component of suicide prevention strategies.

Canada-wide effect of regulatory warnings on antidepressant prescribing and suicide rates in boys and girls

Rhodes AE, Skinner R, McFaull S, Katz LY (Canada)

Canadian Journal of Psychiatry 58, 640-645, 2013

Objective: To examine the impact of the Health Canada regulatory warnings regarding antidepressant (AD) prescribing on suicide rates in boys and girls under the age of 18 and aged 18 to 19 years in Canada between 2004 and 2009. We hypothesized that an increase in suicide rates would be specific to girls, refecting higher AD prescribing rates in girls than boys.

Method: We graphed and tested the difference between Canada-wide suicide rates before and after the regulatory warning periods (either from 1995 to 2006 or from 1995 to 2009) in boys and girls under the age of 18 or aged 18 to 19 years. For comparison with prior studies, we estimated rate ratios and 95% confidence intervals using either Poisson regression or negative binomial regression.

Results: There was no statistically significant increase in suicide rates in girls under the age of 18, or aged 18 to 19 years in response to the AD regulatory warnings. In boys under the age of 18 or aged 18 to 19 years, suicide rates declined after 2003.

Conclusions: We did not find increased rates of suicide after the AD regulatory warnings in boys or girls under the age of 18 or aged 18 to 19 years in Canada-wide rates. However, this does not rule out the possibility that such an effect occurred in some jurisdictions in girls and (or) the regulatory warnings prevented the trend toward declining suicide rates. Factors infuencing the downward trend in boys merit further attention.

"Talk" about male suicide? Learning from community programmes

Robinson M, Braybrook D, Robertson S (UK)

Mental Health Review Journal 18, 115-127, 2013

Purpose: The purpose of this paper is to examine the contribution of public awareness campaigning in developing community capacity toward preventing male suicide and explores emerging considerations for suicide prevention programme development.

Design/Methodology/Approach: The paper draws on campaign evaluation data, specifically qualitative discussion groups with the general public, to report results concerning campaign processes, and "interim" effectiveness in changing public awareness and attitudes, and then discusses how progress is to be lasting and transformational.

Findings: The campaign raised the awareness of a substantial proportion of those targeted, and affected attitudes and behaviour of those who were highly aware. The community settings approach was effective in reaching younger men, but there were challenges targeting the public more selectively, and engaging communities in a sustained way.

Practical Implications: The paper discusses emerging considerations for suicide prevention, focusing on gender and approaches and materials for engaging with the public as "influencers". There are challenges to target audiences more specifically, provide a clear call to action, and engage the public in a sustained way.

Social Implications: The paper discusses emerging considerations for suicide prevention, focusing on gender and approaches and materials for engaging with the public as "influencers". There are challenges to target audiences more specifically, provide a clear call to action, and engage the public in a sustained way.

Originality/Value: The paper adds fresh evidence of gendered communication processes, including their effects on public awareness, attitudes and engagement. Application of a theory of change model leads to systems level findings for sustaining programme gains.

Heavy episodic drinking and deliberate self-harm in young people: A longitudinal cohort study

Rossow I, Norström T (Norway)
Addiction. Published online: 24 February 2014. doi: 10.1111/add.12527, 2014

Aim: To assess the association between heavy episodic drinking (HED) and deliberate self-harm (DSH) in young people in Norway.

Design, Setting, Participants, and Measurements: We analysed data on past year HED and DSH from the second (1994) and third (1999) waves of the Young in Norway Longitudinal Study (cumulative response rate: 68.1%, n = 2681). Associations between HED and DSH were obtained as odds ratios and population attributable fractions (PAF) applying fixed-effects modelling, which eliminates the effects of time-invariant confounders.

Findings: An increase in HED was associated with a 64 % increase in risk of DSH (OR = 1.64, P = 0.013), after controlling for time-varying confounders. The estimated PAF was 28% from fixed-effects modelling and 51 % from conventional modelling.

Conclusion: Data on Norwegian youths show a statistically significant association between heavy episodic drinking and deliberate self-harm.

Facing a patient who seeks help after a suicide attempt

Rothes IA, Henriques MR, Leal JB, Lemos MS (Portugal)
Crisis 35, 110-122, 2013

Background: Although intervention with suicidal patients is one of the hardest tasks in clinical practice, little is known about health professionals' perceptions about the difficulties of working with suicidal patients.

Aims: The aims of this study were to: (1) describe the difficulties of professionals facing a suicidal patient; (2) analyze the differences in difficulties according to the sociodemographic and professional characteristics of the health professionals; and (3) identify the health professionals' perceived skills and thoughts on the need for training in suicide.

Method: A self-report questionnaire developed for this purpose was filled out by 196 health professionals. Exploratory principal components analyses were used.

Results: Four factors were found: technical difficulties; emotional difficulties; relational and communicational difficulties; and family-approaching and logistic difficulties. Differences were found between professionals who had or did not have training in suicide, between professional groups, and between the number of patient suicide attempts. Sixty percent of the participants reported a personal need for training and 85% thought it was fundamental to implement training plans targeted at health professionals.

Conclusion: Specific training is fundamental. Experiential and active methodologies should be used and technical, relational, and emotional questions must be included in the training syllabus.

Smoking and suicidality in patients with a psychotic disorder

Sankaranarayanan A, Mancuso S, Castle D (Australia)

Psychiatry Research 215, 634-640, 2013

Background: Cigarette smoking has been associated with an increased risk of suicide. Patients with psychosis are more likely to smoke cigarettes and are also at an increased risk of suicide. The aim of this study was to compare risk for suicidal behavior among patients with psychosis who were current smokers, previous smokers and nonsmokers.

Methods: We studied 1812 of the 1825 participants who took part in the Australian Survey of High Impact Psychosis (SHIP) for whom smoking data was available. We identified predictors for lifetime suicide attempts using univariate logistic regression analysis. These variables were retained for the multiple logistic regression models if they were a significant predictor of lifetime suicide attempts. A series of multiple logistic regressions were then conducted to predict lifetime suicide attempts using current smoking status and lifetime smoking status as independent variables, respectively, while controlling for the retained predictor variables.

Results: Current smoking and lifetime smoking were statistically significant predictors of lifetime suicide attempts. However adding the covariates to a logistic regression model reduced this association to non-significance. The strongest predictors were self-harm in the past 12 months, the presence of lifetime depressive symptoms and a diagnosis of psychotic depression.

Conclusions: Identification of suicide risk factors is essential for successful suicide prevention. While previous research highlights the importance of cigarette smoking as an important risk factor for suicidal behaviors including in patients with psychosis, these results must be interpreted within the context of methodological issues.

Suicidal ideation and physical illness: Does the link lie with depression?

Sanna L, Stuart AL, Pasco JA, Kotowicz MA, Berk M, Girardi P, Williams LJ (Australia)

Journal of Affective Disorders 152-154, 422-426, 2014

Objective: Medical illness is a risk factor for suicidality; however, disorder-specific risks are not well-known and these relationships are often explained by major depressive disorder (MDD). We aimed to investigate the relationship between suicidal ideation, MDD and medical illnesses in an age-stratified, population-based sample of men participating in the Geelong Osteoporosis Study.

Methods: Suicidal ideation and medical conditions were self-reported. Medical conditions were confirmed by medical records, medication use or clinical data where possible. MDD was determined using the Structured Clinical Interview for DSM-IV-TR Research Version, Non-patient edition.

Results: Of the 907 men, 8.5% reported suicidal ideation. Thyroid disorders (OR

3.85, 95%CI 1.2-12.1), syncope and seizures (OR 1.96, 95%CI 1.1-3.5), liver disorders (OR 3.53, 95%CI 1.1-11.8; younger men only) and alcoholism (OR 2.15, 95%CI 1.1-4.4) were associated with increased odds of suicidal ideation, independent of age and MDD. Major vascular events doubled the odds of suicidal ideation but this was explained by MDD. No association was evident with high medical burden, musculoskeletal disease, metabolic factors, gastrointestinal disorders, headaches, cardiovascular disease, COPD, cancer and psoriasis.

Conclusion: Health care professionals should focus on identification, assessment and management of suicidal ideation in the medically ill in patients both with and without MDD.

Service use in adolescents at risk of depression and self-harm: Prospective longitudinal study

Sayal K, Yates N, Spears M, Stallard P (UK)
Social Psychiatry and Psychiatric Epidemiology. Published online: 26 February 2014. doi: 10.1007/s00127-014-0843-y, 2014

Purpose: Although depression and self-harm are common mental health problems in adolescents, there are barriers to accessing help. Using a community-based sample, this study investigates predictors of service contacts for adolescents at high risk of depression and self-harm.

Methods: Three thousand seven hundred and forty-nine (3,749) 12- to 16-year-olds in UK secondary (high) schools provided baseline and 6 months' follow-up data on mood, self-harm and service contacts with a range of primary and secondary healthcare services.

Results: Although most adolescents at high risk of depression or self-harm had seen their general practitioner (GP) in the previous 6 months, less than one-third had used primary or secondary healthcare services for emotional problems. 5 % of adolescents who reported self-harm had seen specialist child and adolescent mental health services in the previous 6 months. In longitudinal analyses, after adjustment for confounders, both depression and self-harm predicted the use of any healthcare services [adjusted odds ratio (AOR) = 1.34 (95 % CI 1.09, 1.64); AOR = 1.38 (95 % CI 1.02, 1.86), respectively] and of specialist mental health services [AOR = 5.48 (95 % CI 2.27, 13.25); AOR = 2.58 (95 % CI 1.11, 6.00), respectively]. Amongst those with probable depression, 79 % had seen their GP and 5 % specialist mental health services in the preceding year.

Conclusions: Most adolescents at high risk of depression or self-harm see their GP over a 6-month period although only a minority of them access specialist mental health services. Their consultations within primary care settings provide a potential opportunity for their identification and for signposting to appropriate specialist services.

Collective levels of stigma and national suicide rates in 25 European countries

Schomerus G, Evans-Lacko S, Rusch N, Mojtabai R, Angermeyer MC, Thornicroft G (Germany, UK, USA, Italy, Austria)

Epidemiology and Psychiatric Sciences. Published online: 27 February 2014. doi: 10.1017/S2045796014000109, 2014

Aims: There is substantial diversity in national suicide rates, which has mainly been related to socio-economic factors, as well as cultural factors. Stigma is a cultural phenomenon, determining the level of social acceptance or rejection of persons with mental illness in a society. In this study, we explore whether national suicide rates are related to the degree of mental illness stigma in that country.

Methods: We combine the data on country-level social acceptance (Eurobarometer) with the data on suicide rates and socio-economic indicators (Eurostat) for 25 European countries.

Results: In a linear regression model controlling for socio-economic indicators, the social acceptance of someone with a significant mental health problem in 2010 was negatively correlated with age standardised national suicide rates in the same year (beta -0.46, p = 0.014). This association also held true when combining national suicide rates with death rates due to events of undetermined intent.

Conclusions: Stigma towards persons with mental health problems may contribute to differences in suicide rates in a country. We hypothesise possible mechanisms explaining this link, including stigma as a stressor and social isolation as a consequence of stigma.

Which symptoms of post-traumatic stress disorder are associated with suicide attempts?

Selaman ZMH, Chartrand HK, Bolton JM, Sareen J (Canada)

Journal of Anxiety Disorders 28, 246-251, 2014

Individuals with post-traumatic stress disorder are at increased risk for suicide attempts. The present study aimed to determine which of the specific DSM-IV symptoms of post-traumatic stress disorder (PTSD) are independently associated with suicide attempts. Data came from Wave 2 of the National Epidemiologic Survey on Alcohol and Related Conditions (NESARC). The NESARC has a sample size of N = 34 653. The full sample size included in analyses was 2322 individuals with PTSD. Among individuals with lifetime PTSD, after adjusting for sociodemographic factors, as well as any mood, substance, personality, or anxiety disorder (excluding PTSD), increasing numbers of re-experiencing and avoidance symptoms were significantly correlated with suicide attempts. Of the specific symptoms, having physical reactions by reminders of the trauma, being unable to recall some part of it, and having the sense of a foreshortened future, were all associated with suicide attempts. These findings will help extend our understanding of the elevated risk for suicide attempts in individuals with PTSD.

Persistence and resolution of suicidal ideation during treatment of depression in patients with significant suicidality at the beginning of treatment: The crescend study

Seo HJ, Jung YE, Jeong S, Kim JB, Lee MS, Kim JM, Yim HW, Jun TY (Korea)

Journal of Affective Disorders 155, 208-215, 2013

Background: The appropriate length of time for patients who visit clinics with significant suicidal ideation to be closely monitored is a critical issue for clinicians. We evaluated the course of suicidal ideation and associated factors for persistent suicidality in patients who entered treatment for depression with significant suicidal ideation.

Methods: A total of 565 patients who had both moderate to severe depression (Hamilton Depression Rating Scale (HAMD) score ≥14) and significant suicidal ideation (Beck Scale for Suicide Ideation (SSI-B) score ≥6) were recruited from 18 hospitals in South Korea. Participants were assessed using the SSI-B, HAMD, Hamilton Anxiety Rating Scale, and Clinical Global Impression Scale-severity during a 12-week naturalistic treatment with antidepressant intervention. Participants were classified into resolved suicidality or persistent suicidality groups according to whether their suicidal ideation improved to SSI-B scores <6 and were sustained for 12 weeks.

Results: During the 12-week treatment, 206 (36.4%) patients were classified in the resolved suicidality group. Persistent suicidality was associated with intervention with SSRIs, higher SSI-B baseline score, and no HAMD or HAMA remission. The proportions of participants who had persistent suicidal ideation even with HAMD remission or response were 0.25 and 0.34, respectively.

Limitations: This study was observational, and the treatment modality was naturalistic.

Conclusions: A considerable number of patients had persistent suicidal ideation despite 12 weeks of antidepressant treatment. Close monitoring for suicidal ideation may be needed beyond the initial weeks of treatment and even after a response to antidepressants is observed.

Suicidal ideations and attempts among adolescents subjected to childhood sexual abuse and family conflict/violence: The mediating role of anger and depressed mood

Sigfusdottir ID, Asgeirsdottir BB, Gudjonsson GH, Sigurdsson JF (Iceland, USA, UK)

Journal of Adolescence 36, 1227-1236, 2013

Based on a sample of 9085 16- to 19-year-old students attending all high schools in Iceland in 2004, the current study examines depressed mood and anger as potential mediators between family conflict/violence and sexual abuse, on the one hand, and suicidal ideations and suicide attempts on the other. Agnew's general strain theory provides the theoretical framework for the study. Structural equation modelling (SEM) was conducted allowing explicit modelling of both direct and mediating effects using observed and latent variables. The findings showed that both depressed mood and anger mediated the relationship between family conflict/violence and sexual abuse and suicidal attempts. However, when testing the mediating pathways between sexual abuse and family conflict/violence and suicidal ideations, only depressed mood but not anger turned out to be a significant mediator. The authors discuss how these finding may inform and facilitate the design and development of interventions to reduce the likelihood of suicide attempts among young people.

Characterizing suicide in Toronto: An observational study and cluster analysis

Sinyor M, Schaffer A, Streiner DL (Canada)

Canadian Journal of Psychiatry 59, 26-33, 2014

Objective: To determine whether people who have died from suicide in a large epidemiologic sample form clusters based on demographic, clinical, and psychosocial factors.

Method: We conducted a coroner's chart review for 2886 people who died in Toronto, Ontario, from 1998 to 2010, and whose death was ruled as suicide by the Office of the Chief Coroner of Ontario. A cluster analysis using known suicide risk factors was performed to determine whether suicide deaths separate into distinct groups. Clusters were compared according to person- and suicide-specific factors.

Results: Five clusters emerged. Cluster 1 had the highest proportion of females and nonviolent methods, and all had depression and a past suicide attempt. Cluster 2 had the highest proportion of people with a recent stressor and violent suicide methods, and all were married. Cluster 3 had mostly males between the ages of 20 and 64, and all had either experienced recent stressors, suffered from mental illness, or had a history of substance abuse. Cluster 4 had the youngest people and the highest proportion of deaths by jumping from height, few were married, and nearly one-half had bipolar disorder or schizophrenia. Cluster 5 had all unmarried people with no prior suicide attempts, and were the least likely to have an identified mental illness and most likely to leave a suicide note.

Conclusions: People who die from suicide assort into different patterns of demographic, clinical, and death-specific characteristics. Identifying and studying subgroups of suicides may advance our understanding of the heterogeneous nature of suicide and help to inform development of more targeted suicide prevention strategies.

Suicide bereavement and the media: A qualitative study

Skehan J, Maple M, Fisher J, Sharrock G (Australia)
Advances in Mental Health 11, 223-237, 2013

While there has been international interest in the reporting of suicide and the potential impact on community behaviour, research has yet to consider the specific impact of media reporting on those bereaved by suicide. Nor has the research considered the potential impact that reports focussed on suicide bereavement may have on community behaviour. The suicide bereavement literature has generally focussed on describing the unique experiences and needs of people bereaved by suicide, but specific considerations, such as interaction with the media, are generally absent from the discussion. In the present study a series of focus groups with people bereaved by suicide and key informant interviews with media professionals, postvention workers, police, coroners and people bereaved by suicide were conducted. Results show that there can be considerable variation in how people bereaved by suicide view media coverage and the reported impacts that exposure to, or involvement in, stories about suicide can have. It highlights a need to consider resources and service models to brief and support those bereaved by suicide when interacting with the media and expansion of current resources and training for journalists that considers the challenges of interacting with people who are bereaved.

Mental health follow-up among adolescents with suicidal behaviors after emergency department discharge

Sobolewski B, Richey L, Kowatch RA, Grupp-Phelan J (USA)
Archives of Suicide Research 17, 323-334, 2013

The objective of this study was to examine mental health follow-up patterns and need for additional urgent ED evaluation in adolescents discharged home from a pediatric ED after an evaluation for suicidal ideation or attempt. In the study, the parent or guardian of suicidal youth ages 11 to 18 years who were discharged from the pediatric ED were interviewed by telephone between 1 and 2 months following the initial visit and asked about their child's suicide risk, mental health follow-up, return ED visits, and previous mental health experiences. ED records were also examined for return visits. A parent or guardian of 100 suicidal adolescents was interviewed by telephone. Most (66%) successfully followed up with a mental health provider. Mental health follow-up was more likely in those with an existing psychiatric diagnosis (OR: 3.03 [95% CI: 1.02-9.05]). The majority of those that returned to the ED within 2 months of their initial evaluation for mental health reasons were admitted [92% (19/21)]. The odds of an ED return visit were increased by a prior inpatient psychiatric admission (OR: 5.23 [95% CI: 1.80-15.16]), and a suicide attempt immediately prior to the initial ED visit (OR: 4.87 [95% CI: 1.04-22.69]). Many suicidal youth who are discharged from the ED successfully follow up with an outpatient mental health provider. However, a significant number do return to the ED within 2 months and require inpatient psychiatric admission. Future ED based interventions should focus on adolescents who attempt suicide and those with a history of prior inpatient admission.

Suicide attempts in chronic pain patients. A register-based study

Stenager E, Christiansen E, Handberg G, Jensen B (Denmark)
Scandinavian Journal of Pain 5, 4-7, 2013

Background: There are several studies about the relationship between depression and chronic non-malignant pain. These studies have shown that up to 50% of chronic pain patients are suffering from depression. It is, therefore, reasonable to expect that pain patients would also have an increased risk of suicidal behaviour. This problem is not well studied. Since 1990 the Centre for Suicide Research, Odense, Denmark has registered all suicide attempts in patients residing in the Region of Funen, Denmark. The Pain Clinic, Odense University Hospital receives patients with chronic pain from the entire Region of Southern Denmark.

Purpose: The purpose of the study has been:. To investigate, whether patients treated in the Pain Clinic during the period from 1 January 2004 to 31 December 2009 had an increased risk of suicide attempts compared with the background population.

Materials and Methods: The Register for Suicide Attempts (RSA) is a product of the WHO research programme WHO/EURO Multicentre Study on Para suicide. The RSA is a longitudinal person-based register. It contains information about people who have been in contact with the health care system in the County of Funen as a result of a suicide attempt. The Pain Clinic, Odense University Hospital receives patients with non-malignant chronic pain from the Region of Southern Denmark with 1,194,659 inhabitants. Data about age, sex, and time of treatment for patients treated in the Pain Clinic during the period were registered. Time and method of the suicide attempts were registered in the RSA. By registry linkages between the patient registers it was possible to calculate any excess risk of suicide attempts in chronic pain patients in the study period. We used a cohort design and calculated incidence rates (IR) and incidence rate ratios (IRRs) for suicide attempts, based on data from RSA. Poisson Regression analyses were used for calculation of IR and IRR for suicide attempts.

Results: In the study period from 1 January 2004 to 31 December 2009 1871 patients residing in the Region of Funen in Denmark were referred to The Pain Clinic. In the patient group 258 suicide attempts in 110 persons were registered. In all 6% of the patient group had attempted suicide. An increased risk of suicide attempts was found in the pain population as the incidence rate ratio (IRR) was 3.76 95% CI (3.22; 4.40). No statistical significant differences between men and women were found.

Conclusion: In a chronic non-malignant pain population, referred to a pain clinic, the risk of suicide attempts was increased.

Implications: It is important to be aware of risk factors for suicidal behaviour, i.e. pain history, depression, anxiety, abuse problems, and social problems when caring for patients with chronic pain. More knowledge and training of the staff caring for chronic pain patients are needed to decrease the risk of suicidal behaviour.

Sexual orientation and suicide ideation, plans, attempts, and medically serious attempts: Evidence from local youth risk behavior surveys, 2001-2009

Stone DM, Luo F, Ouyang L, Lippy C, Hertz MF, Crosby AE (USA)
American Journal of Public Health 104, 262-271, 2013

Objectives: We examined the associations between 2 measures of sexual orientation and 4 suicide risk outcomes (SROs) from pooled local Youth Risk Behavior Surveys.

Methods: We aggregated data from 5 local Youth Risk Behavior Surveys from 2001 to 2009. We defined sexual minority youths (SMYs) by sexual identity (lesbian, gay, bisexual) and sex of sexual contacts (same- or both-sex contacts). Survey logistic regression analyses controlled for a wide range of suicide risk factors and sample design effects.

Results: Compared with non-SMYs, all SMYs had increased odds of suicide ideation; bisexual youths, gay males, and both-sex contact females had greater odds of suicide planning; all SMYs, except same-sex contact males, had increased odds of suicide attempts; and lesbians, bisexuals, and both-sex contact youths had increased odds of medically serious attempts. Unsure males had increased odds of suicide ideation compared with heterosexual males. Not having sexual contact was protective of most SROs among females and of medically serious attempts among males.

Conclusions: Regardless of sexual orientation measure used, most SMY subgroups had increased odds of all SROs. However, many factors are associated with SROs.

Suicide attempts and mortality in eating disorders: A follow-up study of eating disorder patients

Suokas JT, Suvisaari JM, Grainger M, Raevuori A, Gissler M, Haukka J (Finland)

General Hospital Psychiatry 36, 355-357, 2014

Objective: The aim of this study is to explore the prevalence of hospital-treated suicide attempts in a large clinical population of eating disorder patients.

Method: Follow-up study of adults (N= 2462, 95% women, age 18-62 years) admitted to the Eating Disorder Clinic of Helsinki University Central Hospital in the period 1995-2010. For each patient, four controls were selected and matched for age, sex and place of residence. The end point events were modeled using Cox's proportional hazard model, taking matching into account.

Results: We identified 156 patients with eating disorder (6.3%) and 139 controls (1.4%) who had required hospital treatment for attempted suicide. Of them, 66 (42.3%) and 37 (26.6%) had more than one attempt. The rate ratio (RR) for suicide attempt in patients with eating disorder was 4.70 [95% confidence interval (CI) 1.41-15.74]. In anorexia nervosa, RR was 8.01 (95% CI 5.40-11.87), and in bulimia nervosa, it was 5.08 (95% CI 3.46-7.42). In eating disorder patients with a history of suicide attempt, the risk of death from any cause was 12.8%, suicide being the main cause in 45% of the deaths.

Conclusion: Suicide attempts and repeated attempts are common among patients with eating disorders. Suicidal ideation should be routinely assessed from patients with eating disorders.

How to decrease suicide rates in both genders? An effectiveness study of a community-based intervention (EAAD)

Székely A, Thege BK, Mergl R, Birkás E, Rózsa S, Purebl G, Hegerl U (Hungary, Canada, Germany)

PLoS ONE. Published online: 23 September 2013. doi: 10.1371/journal.pone.0075081, 2013

Background: The suicide rate in Hungary is high in international comparison. The two-year community-based four-level intervention programme of the European Alliance Against Depression (EAAD) is designed to improve the care of depression and to prevent suicidal behaviour. Our aim was to evaluate the effectiveness of a regional community-based four-level suicide prevention programme on suicide rates.

Method: The EAAD programme was implemented in Szolnok (population 76,311), a town in a region of Hungary with an exceptionally high suicide rate. Effectiveness was assessed by comparing changes in suicide rates in the intervention region after the intervention started with changes in national suicide rates and those in a control region (Szeged) in the corresponding period.

Results: For the duration of the programme and the follow-up year, suicide rates in Szolnok were significantly lower than the average of the previous three years (p = .0076). The suicide rate thus went down from 30.1 per 100,000 in 2004 to 13.2

in 2005 (-56.1 %), 14.6 in 2006 (-51.4 %) and 12.0 in 2007 (-60.1 %). This decrease of annual suicide rates in Szolnok after the onset of the intervention was significantly stronger than that observed in the whole country (p = .017) and in the control region (p = .0015). Men had the same decrease in suicide rates as women. As secondary outcome, an increase of emergency calls to the hotline service (200%) and outpatient visits at the local psychiatry clinic (76%) was found.

Conclusions: These results seem to provide further support for the effectiveness of the EAAD concept. Whilst the majority of suicide prevention programs mainly affect female suicidal behaviour, this programme seems to be beneficial for both sexes. The sustainability and the role of the mediating factors (social service and health care utilization, community attitudes about suicide) should be key points in future research.

Smoking cessation treatment and risk of depression, suicide, and self harm in the clinical practice research datalink: Prospective cohort study

Thomas KH, Martin RM, Davies NM, Metcalfe C, Windmeijer F, Gunnell D (UK)
British Medical Journal 347, f5704, 2013

Objective: To compare the risk of suicide, self harm, and depression in patients prescribed varenicline or bupropion with those prescribed nicotine replacement therapy.

Design: Prospective cohort study within the Clinical Practice Research Datalink.

Setting: 349 general practices in England.

Participants: 119546 men and women aged 18 years and over who used a smoking cessation product between 1 September 2006 and 31 October 2011. There were 81545 users of nicotine replacement products (68.2% of all users of smoking cessation medicines), 6741 bupropion (5.6%), and 31260 varenicline (26.2%) users.

Main Outcome Measures: Outcomes were treated depression and fatal and non-fatal self harm within three months of the first smoking cessation prescription, determined from linkage with mortality data from the Office for National Statistics (for suicide) and Hospital Episode Statistics data (for hospital admissions relating to non-fatal self harm). Hazard ratios or risk differences were estimated using Cox multivariable regression models, propensity score matching, and instrumental variable analysis using physicians' prescribing preferences as an instrument. Sensitivity analyses were performed for outcomes at six and nine months.

Results: We detected 92 cases of fatal and non-fatal self harm (326.5 events per 100000 person years) and 1094 primary care records of treated depression (6963.3 per 100000 person years). Cox regression analyses showed no evidence that patients prescribed varenicline had higher risks of fatal or non-fatal self harm (hazard ratio 0.88, 95% confidence interval 0.52 to 1.49) or treated depression (0.75, 0.65 to 0.87) compared with those prescribed nicotine replacement therapy.

There was no evidence that patients prescribed bupropion had a higher risk of fatal or non-fatal self harm (0.83, 0.30 to 2.31) or of treated depression (0.63, 0.46 to 0.87) compared with patients prescribed nicotine replacement therapy. Similar findings were obtained using propensity score methods and instrumental variable analyses.

Conclusions: There is no evidence of an increased risk of suicidal behaviour in patients prescribed varenicline or bupropion compared with those prescribed nicotine replacement therapy. These findings should be reassuring for users and prescribers of smoking cessation medicines.

The effects of media reports of suicides by well-known figures between 1989 and 2010 in Japan

Ueda M, Mori K, Matsubayashi T (Japan)

International Journal of Epidemiology. Published online: 16 March 2014. doi: 10.1093/ije/dyu056, 2014

Background: Many studies have shown that media reporting of suicide incidents can trigger suicidal behaviours in viewers and readers. Yet little is known about the exact timing and duration of the imitative effects.

Methods: We estimated the Poisson regression model using original data on 109 celebrity suicides and daily suicide counts (n = 8035) in Japan from 1989 through 2010. Various fixed effects were included in the model to control for the effects of seasonal variations and time-specific shocks.

Results: The media reports on celebrity suicides were associated with an immediate increase in total suicides. The total number of suicides increased by 4.6% (95% confidence interval (CI): 2.4-6.7) on the day that media reports on celebrity suicides were published. The increase during the post-report period lasted for about 10 days after the publication of news reports. The average effect of celebrity suicides on total suicides over the 10-day post-reporting period was estimated to be highest when the suicide by nationally recognized politicians was reported (14.8%; CI: 10.9-18.7), whereas reports on the deaths of entertainment celebrities were followed by a 4.7% increase (CI: 2.9-6.5) in suicide counts.

Conclusions: This study presents evidence that media reports on celebrity suicides have an immediate impact on the number of suicides in the general population. Our findings also highlight the importance of responsible and cautious media reporting on suicide.

What factors determine disclosure of suicide ideation in adults 60 and older to a treatment provider?

Unützer J, Lin EH, Vannoy SD, Duberstein PR, Cukrowicz KC (USA)
Suicide and Life-Threatening Behavior. Published online: 3 February 2014. doi: 10.1111/sltb.12075, 2014

Correlates of patient disclosure of suicide ideation to a primary care or mental health provider were identified. Secondary analyses of IMPACT trial data were conducted. Of the 107 patients 60 years of age or older who endorsed thoughts of ending their life at least "a little bit" during the past month, 53 indicated they had disclosed these thoughts to a mental health or primary care provider during this period. Multiple logistic regression was used to identify predictors of disclosure to a provider. Significant predictors included poorer quality of life and prior mental health specialty treatment. Among participants endorsing thoughts of suicide, the likelihood of disclosing these thoughts to a provider was 2.96 times higher if they had a prior history of mental health specialty treatment and 1.56 times higher for every one-unit decrease in quality of life. Variation in disclosure of thoughts of suicide to a mental health or primary care provider depends, in part, on patient characteristics. Although the provision of evidence-based suicide risk assessment and guidelines could minimize unwanted variation and enhance disclosure, efforts to routinize the process of suicide risk assessment should also consider effective ways to lessen potential unintended consequences.

The effect of shame-proneness, guilt-proneness, and internalizing tendencies on nonsuicidal self-injury

Vanderhei S, Rojahn J, Stuewig J, McKnight PE (USA)
Suicide and Life-Threatening Behavior. Published online: 7 December 2013. doi: 10.1111/sltb.12069, 2013

Nonsuicidal self-injury is especially common in adolescents and young adults. Self-injury may be related to shame or guilt-two moral emotions-as these differentially predict other maladaptive behaviors. Using a college sample, we examined not only how shame-proneness, guilt-proneness, and internalizing emotional tendencies related to self-injury, but also whether these moral emotions moderate the relation between internalizing tendencies and self-injury. High shame-proneness was associated with higher frequencies of self-injury. High guilt-proneness was associated with less self-injury, although this effect was mitigated at higher levels of internalizing tendencies. These results suggest shame-proneness is a risk factor for self-injury, while guilt-proneness is protective.

"Rebuilding our community": Hearing silenced voices on Aboriginal youth suicide

Walls ML, Hautala D, Hurley J (USA)

Transcultural Psychiatry 51, 47-72, 2013

This paper brings forth the voices of adult Aboriginal First Nations community members who gathered in focus groups to discuss the problem of youth suicide on their reserves. Our approach emphasizes multilevel (e.g., individual, family, and broader ecological systems) factors viewed by participants as relevant to youth suicide. Wheaton's conceptualization of stressors and Evans-Campbell's multilevel classification of the impacts of historical trauma are used as theoretical and analytic guides. Thematic analysis of qualitative data transcripts revealed a highly complex intersection of stressors, traumas, and social problems seen by community members as underlying mechanisms influencing heightened levels of Aboriginal youth suicidality. Our multilevel coding approach revealed that suicidal behaviors were described by community members largely as a problem with deep historical and contemporary structural roots, as opposed to being viewed as individualized pathology.

Suicidality in primary care patients with somatoform disorders

Wiborg JF, Gieseler D, Fabisch AB, Voigt K, Lautenbach A, Lowe B (Germany)

Psychosomatic Medicine 75, 800-806, 2013

Objective: To examine rates of suicidality in primary care patients with somatoform disorders and to identify factors that might help to understand and manage active suicidal ideation in these patients.

Methods: We conducted a cross-sectional study screening 1645 primary care patients. In total, 142 patients fulfilled the criteria for a somatoform disorder. Suicidality and illness perceptions were assessed in these patients.

Results: Of the 142 patients, 23.9% had active suicidal ideation during the previous 6 months; 17.6% had attempted to commit suicide in the past, the majority after onset of the somatoform symptoms. We tested two models with suicidal ideation as a dependent variable. In the first model, comorbid symptoms of depression (odds ratio [OR] = 1.17, 95% confidence interval [CI] = 1.03-1.33) and previous suicide attempts (OR= 3.02, 95% CI = 1.06-8.62) were significantly associated with suicidal ideation. Comorbid symptoms of anxiety did not yield significance. Illness perceptions and age of onset of the symptoms were then added to this model to test the role of somatoform-specific factors in addition to previous factors. In the complete model, comorbid symptoms of depression (OR = 1.15, 95% CI = 1.00-1.32) and dysfunctional illness perceptions (OR = 1.06, 95% CI = 1.01-1.11) were independently associated with active suicidal ideation, whereas the other factors did not yield significance.

Conclusions: According to our data, suicidality seems to be a substantial problem in primary care patients with somatoform disorders. Dysfunctional illness perceptions may play a vital role in the understanding and management of active suicidal ideation in these patients, in addition to more established factors.

The relationship between suicide and violence in schizophrenia: Analysis of the clinical antipsychotic trials of intervention effectiveness (CATIE) dataset

Witt K, Hawton K, Fazel S (UK)
Schizophrenia Research 154, 61-67, 2014

Background: Suicide and violence often co-occur in the general population as well as in mentally ill individuals. Few studies, however, have assessed whether these suicidal behaviors are predictive of violence risk in mental illness.

Aims: The aim of this study is to investigate whether suicidal behaviors, including suicidal ideation, threats, and attempts, are significantly associated with increased violence risk in individuals with schizophrenia.

Method: Data for these analyses were obtained from the Clinical Antipsychotic Trials of Intervention Effectiveness (CATIE) trial, a randomized controlled trial of antipsychotic medication in 1460 adults with schizophrenia. Univariate Cox regression analyses were used to calculate hazard ratios (HRs) for suicidal ideation, threats, and attempts. Multivariate analyses were conducted to adjust for common confounding factors, including: age, alcohol or drug misuse, major depression, antisocial personality disorder, depression, hostility, positive symptom, and poor impulse control scores. Tests of discrimination, calibration, and reclassification assessed the incremental predictive validity of suicidal behaviors for the prediction of violence risk.

Results: Suicidal threats and attempts were significantly associated with violence in both males and females with schizophrenia with little change following adjustment for common confounders. Only suicidal threats, however, were associated with a significant increase in incremental validity beyond age, diagnosis with a comorbid substance use disorder, and recent violent behavior.

Conclusions: Suicidal threats are independently associated with violence risk in both males and females with schizophrenia, and may improve violence risk prediction.

Detection of suicide among the elderly in a long term care facility

Wongpakaran T, Wongpakaran N (Thailand)
Clinical Interventions in Aging 8, 1553-1559, 2013

Purpose: The aim of this study was to establish the level of correlation between the suicide item contained within the Core Symptom Index (CSI), and the presence of suicidal thoughts as assessed by the Mini-International Neuropsychiatric Interview (MINI) and the Cornell Scale of Depression in Dementia (CSDD).

Patients and Methods: Seventy elderly residents in a long term care facility were included in this study. All of these patients completed a CSI and a geriatric depression scale (GDS), plus were interviewed using CSDD, MINI (suicide module), and MMSE. Test characteristics of item two of the CSI (suicidal thoughts) and MINI were compared. Gwet's AC1 and Cohen's Kappa were also used to test the level of agreement between raters, and univariate analysis was used to determine predictors for the severity of any suicidal thoughts present.

Results: There was found to be a significant correlation between suicidal ideation, as assessed by item two of the CSI, and the suicidal ideation score as assessed by MINI and CSDD (r=0.773 and r=0.626, P<0.001, respectively). The level of agreement across all three instruments was good (Gwet's AC1 =0.907). The CSI yielded a high level of sensitivity (100%) and specificity (90.32%) for suicidal thoughts as measured by MINI, with an area under the curve of 97%. When assessing predictors of the severity of suicidal thoughts, only item two of the CSI predicted severity, while the depression, GDS, and total scores obtained from the CSI did not.

Conclusion: CSI item two has the ability to detect suicidal ideation, regardless of whether the patient has cognitive impairment and/or depression or not, and is currently the best predictor of its presence. Therefore, it shows promise as a measure for screening the presence of suicidal thoughts among the elderly in long term care facilities.

Suicide among older people in relation to their subjective and objective well-being in different European regions

Wu J, Värnik A, Tooding LM, Värnik P, Kasearu K (Estonia)
European Journal of Ageing. Published online: 23 October 2013. doi: 10.1007/s10433-013-0297-1, 2013

The aim of this study was to establish how different types of welfare states shape the context of the everyday life of older people by influencing their subjective well-being, which in turn might manifest itself in suicide rates. Twenty-two European countries studied were divided into Continental, Nordic, Island, Southern, and post-socialist countries, which were subdivided into Baltic, Slavic, and Central-Eastern groups based on their socio-political and welfare organization. Suicide rates, subjective well-being data, and objective well-being data were used as parameters of different welfare states and obtained from the World Health Organization European Mortality Database, European Social Survey, and Eurostat Database. This study revealed that the suicide rates of older people were the highest in the Baltic countries, while in the Island group, the suicide rate was the lowest. The suicide rate ratios between the age groups 65+ and 0-64 were above 1 (from 1.2 to 2.5), except for the group of the Island countries with a suicide rate ratio of 0.8. Among subjective well-being indicators, relatively high levels of life satisfaction and happiness were revealed in Continental, Nordic, and Island countries. Objective well-being indicators like old age pension, expenditure on old age, and social protection benefits in GDP were the highest in the Continental countries. The expected inverse relationship between subjective well-being indicators and suicide rates among older people was found across the 22 countries. We conclude that welfare states shape the context and exert influence on subjective well-being, and thus may lead to variations in risk of suicide at the individual level.

Citation List

FATAL SUICIDAL BEHAVIOR

Epidemiology

Abd-Elwahab Hassan D, Ghaleb SS, Kotb H, Agamy M, Kharoshah M (2013). Suicidal hanging in Kuwait: Retrospective analysis of cases from 2010 to 2012. *Journal of Forensic and Legal Medicine* 20, 1118-1121.

Agampodi S, Wickramage K, Agampodi T, Thennakoon U, Jayathilaka N, Karunarathna D, Alagiyawanna S (2014). Maternal mortality revisited: The application of the new ICD-MM classification system in reference to maternal deaths in Sri Lanka. *Reproductive Health* 11, 17.

Ahmedani B, Simon G, Stewart C, Beck A, Waitzfelder B, Lynch F, Owen-Smith A, Rossom R, Whiteside U, Coffey MJ, Solberg L (2013). Examining health service utilization in the year prior to suicide death. *Clinical Medicine and Research* 11, 168.

Amore M, Innamorati M, Vittorio CD, Weinberg I, Turecki G, Sher L, Paris J, Girardi P, Pompili M (2013). Suicide attempts in major depressed patients with personality disorder. *Suicide and Life-Threatening Behavior*. Published online: 19 October 2013. doi: 10.1111/sltb.12059.

Antonowicz D, Winterdyk J (2013). A review of deaths in custody in three Canadian provinces. *Canadian Journal of Criminology and Criminal Justice* 56, 85-103.

Arnautovska U, McPhedran S, De Leo D (2013). A regional approach to understanding farmer suicide rates in Queensland. *Social Psychiatry and Psychiatric Epidemiology* 49, 593-599.

Assareh M, Moghaddam MF, Rakhshani T, Nikoo MA, Effatpanah M, Rai A, Rezaie L (2013). The motives behind the decision for choosing self-immolation as a method for suicide. *Life Science Journal* 10, 1610-1614.

Austin AE, van den Heuvel C, Byard RW (2014). Prison suicides in South Australia: 1996-2010. *Journal of Forensic Sciences*. Published online: 18 March 2014. doi: 10.1111/1556-4029.12454.

Bacopoulou F, Petridou E, Korpa TN, Deligeoroglou E, Chrousos GP (2013). External-cause mortality among adolescents and young adults in Greece over the millennium's first decade 2000-09. *Journal of Public Health*. Published online: doi: 10.1093/pubmed/fdt115.

Balint L, Döme P, Daroczi G, Gonda X, Rihmer Z (2013). Investigation of the marked and long-standing spatial inhomogeneity of the Hungarian suicide rate: A spatial regression approach. *Journal of Affective Disorders* 155, 180-185.

Bansal A, Patel A, Mittal P, Bhoot R, Merchant S, Patel P (2013). Pattern of spot death cases brought to V.S. General hospital, Ahmedabad: A retrospective study. *Journal of Indian Academy of Forensic Medicine* 35, 131-133.

Bori evi Maršani V, Margeti BA, Ze evi I, Herceg M (2013). The prevalence and psychosocial correlates of suicide attempts among inpatient adolescent offspring of Croatian PTSD male war veterans. *Child Psychiatry and Human Development*. Published online: 14 December 2013. doi: 10.1007/s10578-013-0426-2.

Burrows S, Auger N, Gamache P, Hamel D (2013). Leading causes of unintentional injury and suicide mortality in Canadian adults across the urban-rural continuum. *Public Health Reports* 128, 443-453.

Callaghan RCP, Sanches MM, Gatley JMB, Cunningham JKP (2013). Effects of the minimum legal drinking age on alcohol-related health service use in hospital settings in Ontario: A regression-discontinuity approach. *American Journal of Public Health* 103, 2284-2291.

Carson HJ, Dudley MH, Knight LD, Lingamfelter D (2013). Psychosocial complications of crohn's disease and cause of death. *Journal of Forensic Sciences* 59, 568-570.

Chan YC, Tse ML, Lau FL (2013). Hong Kong poison information centre: Annual report 2012. *Hong Kong Journal of Emergency Medicine* 20, 371-381.

Chang EC, Yu EA, Kahle ER, Jeglic EL, Hirsch JK (2013). Is doubling up on positive future cognitions associated with lower suicidal risk in Latinos?: A look at hope and positive problem orientation. *Cognitive Therapy and Research* 37, 1285-1293.

Chaudhary B, Pradeep Y, Mukesh K, Rahul B (2013). Mortality profile of burn injuries: A postmortem study in Lady Hardinge Medical College, New Delhi. *Journal of Indian Academy of Forensic Medicine* 35, 123-126.

Chaudhury S, Murthy PS, Srivastava K, Bakhla AK, Rathee SP (2013). Socio-demographic and clinical correlates of attempted suicide. *Pravara Medical Review* 4, 20-25.

Chen J, Yu B, Wang Y, Tang M, Hu Y, Cai T, Zhang F, Von Zinkernagel D, Harwell JI, Huang ZJ (2014). Expansion of HIV care and treatment in Yunnan province, China: Treatment outcomes with scale up of combination antiretroviral therapy. *AIDS Care* 26, 633-641.

Cornutiu O (2013). Statistical profile of suicide attempts. *Romanian Journal of Legal Medicine* 21, 193-196.

Craig J, Hull-Jilly DC (2013). Suicide in Alaska: Exploring inter- and intra-regional differences. *International Journal of Circumpolar Health* 72, 262.

Crosby AE, Ortega L, Stevens MR (2013). Suicides - United States, 2005-2009. *MMWR Surveillance Summaries* 62, 179-183.

Darke S, Torok M, Duflou J (2014). Circumstances and toxicology of sudden or unnatural deaths involving alprazolam. *Drug and Alcohol Dependence.* Published online: 12 February 2014. doi: 10.1016/j.drugalcdep.2014.01.023.

De Koning E, Piette MH (2014). A retrospective study of murder-suicide at the forensic institute of Ghent university, Belgium: 1935-2010. *Medicine, Science and the Law* 54, 88-98.

Degenhardt L, Whiteford HA, Ferrari AJ, Baxter AJ, Charlson FJ, Hall WD, Freedman G, Burstein R, Johns N, Engell RE, Flaxman A, Murray CJL, Vos T (2013). Global burden of disease attributable to illicit drug use and dependence: Findings from the global burden of disease study 2010. *The Lancet* 382, 1564-1574.

Desel H, Müller D (2013). Common causes of poisoning: Etiology, diagnosis and treatment. *Deutsches Ärzteblatt International* 110, 690-700.

Doyon S, Klein-Schwartz W, Lee S, Beuhler MC (2013). Fatalities involving acetaminophen combination products reported to United States poison centers. *Clinical Toxicology* 51, 941-948.

Eckes L, Tsokos M, Herre S, Gapert R, Hartwig S (2014). Post-mortem evidence of doxylamine in toxicological analyses. *Science & Justice* 54, 61-65.

Ehren K, Hertenstein C, Kümmerle T, Vehreschild JJ, Fischer J, Gillor D, Wyen C, Lehmann C, Cornely OA, Jung N, Gravemann S, Platten M, Wasmuth JC, Rockstroh JK, Boesecke C, Schwarze-zander C, Fätkenheuer G (2014). Causes of death in HIV-infected patients from the cologne-bonn cohort. *Infection* 42, 135-140.

Elo IT, Beltrán-Sánchez H, Macinko J (2013). The contribution of health care and other interventions to black-white disparities in life expectancy, 1980-2007. *Population Research and Policy Review* 33, 97-126.

Ferrari AJ, Charlson FJ, Norman RE, Patten SB, Freedman G, Murray CJL, Vos T, Whiteford HA (2013). Burden of depressive disorders by country, sex, age, and year: Findings from the Global Burden of Disease study 2010. *PLoS Medicine* 10, e1001547.

Fleming TM, Clark T, Denny S, Bullen P, Crengle S, Peiris-John R, Robinson E, Rossen FV, Sheridan J, Lucassen M (2013). Stability and change in the mental health of New Zealand secondary school students 2007-2012: Results from the national adolescent health surveys. *Australian and New Zealand Journal of Psychiatry*. Published online: 6 December 2013. doi: 10.1177/0004867413514489.

Garnett BR, Masyn KE, Austin SB, Miller M, Williams DR, Viswanath K (2013). The intersectionality of discrimination attributes and bullying among youth: An applied latent class analysis. *Journal of Youth and Adolescence*. Published online: 8 December 2013. doi: 10.1007/s10964-013-0073-8.

Gijzen S, Boere-Boonekamp MM, L'Hoir M P, Need A (2013). Child mortality in the Netherlands in the past decades: An overview of external causes and the role of public health policy. *Journal of Public Health Policy* 35, 43-59.

Gjertsen F, Leenaars A, Vollrath ME (2014). Mixed impact of firearms restrictions on fatal firearm injuries in males: A national observational study. *International Journal of Environmental Research and Public Health* 11, 487-506.

Holopainen J, Helama S, Bjorkenstam C, Partonen T (2013). Variation and seasonal patterns of suicide mortality in Finland and Sweden since the 1750s. *Environmental Health and Preventive Medicine* 18, 494-501.

Hong J, Knapp M (2013). Geographical inequalities in suicide rates and area deprivation in South Korea. *Journal of Mental Health Policy and Economics* 16, 109-119.

Houle J, Guillou-Ouellette C (2014). Coroners' records on suicide mortality in Montréal: Limitations and implications in suicide prevention strategies. *Chronic Diseases and Injuries in Canada* 34, 23-29.

Hoye A, Jacobsen BK, Hansen V (2013). Sex differences in mortality of admitted patients with personality disorders in north Norway - a prospective register study. *BMC Psychiatry* 13, 317.

Huguet N, Kaplan MS, McFarland BH (2013). The effects of misclassification biases on veteran suicide rate estimates. *American Journal of Public Health* 104, 151-155.

Ichikawa M, Inada H, Kumeji M (2013). Reconsidering the effects of blue-light installation for prevention of railway suicides. *Journal of Affective Disorders* 152, 183-185.

Inoue K, Fukunaga T, Nata M, Abe S, Okazaki Y (2013). Discussion of extensive suicide prevention based on suicide statistics from 2006 to 2009 in Mie prefecture, Japan. *International Medical Journal* 20, 646-648.

Ionides EL, Wang Z, Granados JAT (2013). Macroeconomic effects on mortality revealed by panel analysis with nonlinear trends. *Annals of Applied Statistics* 7, 1362-1385.

Iqbal Khokhar J, Iqbal M, Nadar S (2013). Predominance of homicidal fire-arms deaths in medico-legal autopsies in Lahore. *Medical Forum Monthly* 24, 86-90.

Irgens A, Grønning M, Thorsen E, Troland K (2013). Mortality among professional divers in Norway. *Occupational Medicine* 63, 537-543.

Ismael MA, Sherif MM, El-Dabah FH, Mohamed YS, Mohammed IN, Gaber MA (2013). Cases with toxicity of anticholinesterase enzyme and factors affecting outcome. *Journal of Pharmacology and Toxicology* 8, 90-97.

Jiménez-Ornelas RA, Cardiel-Téllez L (2013). Suicide and social trends in Mexico: 1990-2011. *Papeles de Poblacion* 19, 205-229.

Jollant F, Malafosse A, Docto R, Macdonald C (2014). A pocket of very high suicide rates in a non-violent, egalitarian and cooperative population of south-east Asia. *Psychological Medicine*. Published online: 17 January 2014. doi: 10.1017/S0033291713003176.

Jors E, Christoffersen M, Veirum NH, Aquilar GC, Morant RC, Konradsen F (2013). Suicide attempts and suicides in Bolivia from 2007 to 2012: Pesticides are the preferred method - females try but males commit suicide! *International Journal of Adolescent Medicine and Health*. Published online: 11 October 2013. doi: 10.1515/ijamh-2013-0309.

Joshi SC, Prakash C, Joshi A, Joshi G (2013). Profile of organophosphorus poisoning at tertiary care hospital in Uttarakhand. *Journal of Indian Academy of Forensic Medicine* 35, 346-348.

Ju Ji N, Young Lee W, Seok Noh M, Yip PSF (2013). The impact of indiscriminate media coverage of a celebrity suicide on a society with a high suicide rate: Epidemiological findings on copycat suicides from South Korea. *Journal of Affective Disorders* 156, 56-61.

Kalesan B, French C, Fagan JA, Fowler DL, Galea S (2013). Firearm-related hospitalizations and in-hospital mortality in the United States, 2000-2010. *American Journal of Epidemiology* 179, 303-312.

Kamat MA, Edgar L, Niblock P, McDowell C, Kelly CB (2013). Association between antidepressant prescribing and suicide rates in OECD countries: An ecological study. *Pharmacopsychiatry* 47, 18-21.

Karbeyaz K, Akkaya H, Balci Y (2013). Analysis of suicide deaths in a 15-year period in Eskisehir, Western Anatolia, Turkey and the determination of risk factors. *Annals of Saudi Medicine* 33, 377-381.

Karthik SK, Balaji PA, Mohan VJ, Varne SR, Poornima S, Ali SS, Jayaprakash G (2013). A preventable death: Suicidal patterns among women in Metro-city Bangalore, India. *Journal of South India Medicolegal Association* 5, 50-57.

Kato K, Mikami K, Kimoto K, Kimoto K, Takahashi Y, Sato R, Matsumoto H (2014). Changes in the frequency and clinical features of suicide attempts in the midwestern area of Kanagawa after the great east Japan earthquake. *Journal of Forensic Science* 59, 417-419.

Kim DR, Ali M, Thiem VD, Wierzba TF (2014). Socio-ecological risk factors for prime-age adult death in two coastal areas of Vietnam. *PloS ONE* 9, e89780.

Kimberley Molina D, DiMaio VJM, Cave R (2013). Handgun wounds: A review of range and location as pertaining to manner of death. *American Journal of Forensic Medicine and Pathology* 34, 342-347.

Kõlves K, De Leo D (2013). Suicide in medical doctors and nurses: An analysis of the Queensland Suicide Register. *Journal of Nervous and Mental Disease* 201, 987-990.

Kristiansen T, Lossius HM, Rehn M, Kristensen P, Gravseth HM, Roislien J, Soreide K (2014). Epidemiology of trauma: A population-based study of geographical risk factors for injury deaths in the working-age population of Norway. *Injury* 45, 23-30.

Kumar S, Verma AK, Ali W, Singh US (2014). Homeless and unclaimed persons' deaths in north India (Jan 2008-Nov 2012): A retrospective study. *Medicine, Science and the Law*. Published online: 17 February 2014. doi: 10.1177/0025802414523585.

Kumar S, Verma AK, Bhattacharya S, Singh US (2013). Epidemiology & preventive aspects of railway suicides and fatalities related to trespassing accidents. *Journal of Forensic and Legal Medicine* 20, 1052-1056.

Kunst AE, van Hooijdonk C, Droomers M, Mackenbach JP (2013). Community social capital and suicide mortality in the Netherlands: A cross-sectional registry-based study. *BMC Public Health* 13, 969.

Leventhal JM, Gaither JR, Sege R (2014). Hospitalizations due to firearm injuries in children and adolescents. *Pediatrics*. Published online: 27 January 2014. doi: 10.1542/peds.2013-1809.

Levin B, Bhardwaj A (2013). Chronic traumatic encephalopathy: A critical appraisal. *Neurocritical Care* 20, 334-344.

Lockley A, Cheung YTD, Cox G, Robinson J, Williamson M, Harris M, Machlin A, Moffat C, Pirkis J (2014). Preventing suicide at suicide hotspots: A case study from Australia. *Suicide and Life-Threatening Behavior*. Published online: 15 February 2014. doi: 10.1111/sltb.12080.

Lu TH, Hsiao A, Chang PC, Chao YC, Hsu CC, Peng HC, Chen LH, Kawachi I (2013). Counting injury deaths: A comparison of two definitions and two countries. *Injury Prevention*. Published online: 17 December 2013. doi: 10.1136/injuryprev-2013-040974.

Lukaschek K, Baumert J, Erazo N, Ladwig KH (2014). Stable time patterns of railway suicides in Germany: Comparative analysis of 7,187 cases across two observation periods (1995-1998; 2005-2008). *BMC Public Health* 14, 124.

Mashreky SR, Rahman F, Rahman A (2013). Suicide kills more than 10,000 people every year in Bangladesh. *Archives of Suicide Research* 17, 387-396.

McCarthy JF, Szymanski BR, Karlin BE, Katz IR (2013). Suicide mortality following nursing home discharge in the department of veterans affairs health system. *American Journal of Public Health* 103, 2261-2266.

Mene T (2013). Underestimation of suicide: A study of the Idu Mishmi tribe of Arunachal Pradesh. *Economic and Political Weekly* 48, 129-133.

Mishra N, Shrestha D, Poudyal RB, Mishra P (2013). Retrospective study of suicide among children and young adults. *Journal of Nepal Paediatric Society* 33, 110-116.

Molina DK, DiMaio V, Cave R (2013). Gunshot wounds a review of firearm type, range, and location as pertaining to manner of death. *American Journal of Forensic Medicine and Pathology* 34, 366-371.

Molina DK, DiMaio VJM, Cave R (2013). Handgun wounds a review of range and location as pertaining to manner of death. *American Journal of Forensic Medicine and Pathology* 34, 342-347.

Moore EC, Pilcher DV, Bailey MJ, Stephens H, Cleland H (2013). The burns evaluation and mortality study (BEAMS): Predicting deaths in Australian and New Zealand burn patients admitted to intensive care with burns. *Journal of Trauma and Acute Care Surgery* 75, 298-303.

Morovatdar N, Moradi-Lakeh M, Malakouti SK, Nojomi M (2013). Most common methods of suicide in eastern Mediterranean region of WHO: A systematic review and meta-analysis. *Archives of Suicide Research* 17, 335-344.

Music E, Jacobsson L, Renberg ES (2014). Suicide in Bosnia and Herzegovina and the city of Sarajevo: With special reference to ethnicity. *Crisis* 35, 42-50.

Najafi F, Hasanzadeh J, Moradinazar M, Faramarzi H, Nematollahi A (2013). An epidemiological survey of the suicide incidence trends in the southwest Iran: 2004-2009. *International Journal of Health Policy and Management* 1, 219-222.

Najim H, Shaik R (2013). A critical review of patients under section 5(2) of the mental health act of 1983. *Psychiatria Danubina* 25 Suppl 2, 241-243.

Nevalainen O, Raitanen J, Ansakorpi H, Artama M, Isojärvi J, Auvinen A (2013). Long-term mortality risk by cause of death in newly diagnosed patients with epilepsy in Finland: A nationwide register-based study. *European Journal of Epidemiology* 28, 981-990.

Ngwena J (2013). Black and minority ethnic groups (BME) suicide, admission with suicide or self-harm: An inner city study. *Journal of Public Health* 22, 155-163.

Nielsen M, Hansen J, Ritz B, Nordahl H, Schernhammer E, Wermuth L, Hulvej Rod N (2013). Cause-specific mortality among spouses of parkinson disease patients. *Epidemiology* 25, 225-232.

O'Connor N, Hunt GE, O'Hara-Aarons M, Hall A, Snars J, Storm V, Lambert T (2014). The Sydney mental health client mortality audit: What does it tell us and what are we to do? *Australasian Psychiatry*. Published online: 23 January 2014. doi: 10.1177/1039856213519690.

Obiorah CC, Amakiri CN (2013). Review of population based coroners autopsy findings in Rivers state of Nigeria. *Forensic Science International* 233, 1-6.

Okamura T, Ito K, Morikawa S, Awata S (2013). Suicidal behavior among homeless people in Japan. *Social Psychiatry and Psychiatric Epidemiology* 49, 573-582.

Opoliner A, Azrael D, Barber C, Fitzmaurice G, Miller M (2014). Explaining geographic patterns of suicide in the U.S.: The role of firearms and antidepressants. *Injury Epidemiology* 1, 6.

Orellana JDY, Basta PC, de Souza MLP (2013). Mortality by suicide: A focus on municipalities with a high proportion of self-reported Indigenous people in the state of Amazonas, Brazil. *Revista Brasileira de Epidemiologia* 16, 658-669.

Papadimitriou G, Giotakos O, Tsouvelas G, Kontaxakis V, Havaki-Kontaxaki B, Papaslanis T (2013). Suicide in Greece: 2001-2011. *Psychiatrike* 24, 170-174.

Paraschakis A, Michopoulos I, Douzenis A, Christodoulou C, Lykouras L, Koutsaftis F (2014). Switching suicide methods in order to achieve lethality: A study of Greek suicide victims. *Death Studies*. Published online: 13 November 2013. doi: 10.1080/07481187.2013.780111.

Parks SE, Johnson LL, McDaniel DD, Gladden M (2014). Surveillance for violent deaths - national violent death reporting system, 16 states, 2010. *MMWR Surveillance Summaries* 63, 1-33.

Peshin SS, Srivastava A, Halder N, Gupta YK (2014). Pesticide poisoning trend analysis of 13 years: A retrospective study based on telephone calls at the national poisons information centre, all India Institute of Medical Sciences, New Delhi. *Journal of Forensic and Legal Medicine* 22, 57-61.

Pompili M, Vichi M, Innamorati M, Lester D, Yang B, De Leo D, Girardi P (2013). Suicide in Italy during a time of economic recession: Some recent data related to age and gender based on a nationwide register study. *Health and Social Care in the Community*. Published online: 6 December 2013. doi: 10.1111/hsc.12086.

Procter NG, De Leo D, Newman L (2013). Suicide and self-harm prevention for people in immigration detention. *Medical Journal of Australia* 199, 730-732.

Rodrigues Alves MM, Alves SV, de Cerqueira Antunes MB, Pereira dos Santos DL (2013). External causes of maternal mortality: Proposal for classification. *Revista De Saude Publica* 47, 283-291.

Rosta J, Aasland OG (2013). Changes in the lifetime prevalence of suicidal feelings and thoughts among Norwegian doctors from 2000 to 2010: A longitudinal study based on national samples. *BMC Psychiatry* 13, 322.

Sabre L, Rekand T, Asser T, Korv J (2013). Mortality and causes of death after traumatic spinal cord injury in Estonia. *Journal of Spinal Cord Medicine* 36, 687-694.

Sakelliadis EI, Vlachodimitropoulos DG, Goutas ND, Panousi PI, Logiopoulou API, Delicha EM, Spiliopoulou CA (2013). Forensic investigation of suicide cases in major Greek correctional facilities. *Journal of Forensic and Legal Medicine* 20, 953-958.

Santhosh CS, Nawaz B (2013). Pattern of suicidal deaths at district hospital Davangere a cross-sectional study. *Journal of Indian Academy of Forensic Medicine* 35, 233-235.

Santos SA, Legay LF, Lovisi GM, de Santos JFC, Lima LA (2013). Suicide and attempts suicide by exogenous intoxication in Rio De Janeiro: Analysis of data from official health information systems, 2006-2008. *Revista Brasileira de Epidemiologia* 16, 376-387.

Scalfari A, Knappertz V, Cutter G, Goodin DS, Ashton R, Ebers GC (2013). Mortality in patients with multiple sclerosis. *Neurology* 81, 184-192.

Searles VB, Valley MA, Hedegaard H, Betz ME (2013). Suicides in urban and rural counties in the United States, 2006-2008. *Crisis* 35, 18-26.

Shakirov BM, Ahmedov YM, Hakimov EA, Tagaev KR, Karabaev BH (2013). Suicidal burns in Samarkand burn centers and their consequences. *Annals of Burns and Fire Disasters* 26, 217-220.

Shelef A, Hiss J, Cherkashin G, Berger U, Aizenberg D, Baruch Y, Barak Y (2014). Psychosocial and medical aspects of older suicide completers in Israel: A 10-year survey. *International Journal of Geriatric Psychiatry*. Published online: 14 January 2014. doi: 10.1002/gps.4070.

Shumilov OI, Kasatkina EA, Novikova TB, Sutinen ML, Chramov AV, Enykeev AV (2014). Natural and man-made influences on suicides in northwestern Russia. *Natural Hazards*. Published online: 14 February 2014. doi: 10.1007/s11069-014-1078-7.

Simpson K, Chen SY, Wu A, Boulanger L, Chambers R, Nedrow K, Tawadrous M, Pashos C, Haider S (2014). Costs of adverse events among patients with HIV infection treated with non-nucleoside reverse transcriptase inhibitors. *HIV Medicine*. Published online: 18 March 2014. doi: 10.1111/hiv.12145.

Singh GK, Siahpush M (2013). Widening rural-urban disparities in all-cause mortality and mortality from major causes of death in the USA, 1969-2009. *Journal of Urban Health*. Published online: 24 December 2013. doi: 10.1007/s11524-013-9847-2.

Singh GK, Siahpush M (2014). Widening rural-urban disparities in life expectancy, U.S., 1969-2009. *American Journal of Preventive Medicine* 46, e19-e29.

Sinyor M, Schaffer A, Streiner DL (2014). Characterizing suicide in Toronto: An observational study and cluster analysis. *Canadian Journal of Psychiatry* 59, 26-33.

Srivastava A (2013). Psychological attributes and socio-demographic profile of hundred completed suicide victims in the state of Goa, India. *Indian Journal of Psychiatry* 55, 268-272.

Tahir MN, Akbar AH, Naseer R, Khan QO, Khan F, Yaqub I (2013). Suicide and attempted suicide trends in Mianwali, Pakistan: Social perspective. *Eastern Mediterranean Health Journal* 19, s111-s114.

Termorshuizen F, Wierdsma AI, Smeets HM, Visser E, Drukker M, Nijman H, Sytema S (2013). Cause-specific mortality among patients with psychosis: Disentangling the effects of age and illness duration. *Psychosomatics* 54, 536-545.

Tóth, Adam S, Birkás E, Szekely A, Stauder A, Purebl G (2014). Gender differences in deliberate self-poisoning in Hungary. *Crisis*. Published online: 3 February 2014. doi: 10.1027/0227-5910/a000245.

Toygar M, Türker T, Erolu M, Kaldirim U, Poyrazolu Y, Eyi YE, Durusu M, Eryilmaz M (2013). An analysis of firearms-related deaths between 1993-2010: A retrospective study. *Ulusal Travma ve Acil Cerrahi Dergisi* 19, 536-542.

Tsai CP, Chang BH, Lee CT (2013). Underlying cause and place of death among patients with amyotrophic lateral sclerosis in Taiwan: A population-based study, 2003-2008. *Journal of Epidemiology* 23, 424-428.

Urban D, Rao A, Bressel M, Neiger D, Solomon B, Mileshkin L (2013). Suicide in lung cancer: Who is at risk? *Chest* 144, 1245-1252.

Verzeletti A, Russo MC, Bin P, Leide A, De Ferrari F (2014). Homicide in Brescia county (northern Italy): A thirty-year review. *Journal of Forensic and Legal Medicine* 22, 84-89.

Viklund Å, Björnstig J, Larsson M, Björnstig U (2013). Car crash fatalities associated with fire in Sweden. *Traffic Injury Prevention* 14, 823-827.

Wagenaar BH, Kohrt BA, Hagaman AK, McLean KE, Kaiser BN (2013). Determinants of care seeking for mental health problems in rural Haiti: Culture, cost, or competency. *Psychiatric Services* 64, 366-372.

Wang C-W, Chan CLW, Yip PSF (2013). Suicide rates in China from 2002 to 2011: An update. *Social Psychiatry and Psychiatric Epidemiology*. Published online: 16 November 2013. doi: 10.1007/s00127-013-0789-5 .

Wang Z, Qin Y, Zhang Y, Zhang B, Li L, Li T, Ding L (2013). Prevalence and correlated factors of lifetime suicidal ideation in adults in Ningxia, China. *Shanghai Archives of Psychiatry* 25, 287-295.

Whiteford HA, Degenhardt L, Rehm J, Baxter AJ, Ferrari AJ, Erskine HE, Charlson FJ, Norman RE, Flaxman AD, Johns N, Burstein R, Murray CJL, Vos T (2013). Global burden of disease attributable to mental and substance use disorders: Findings from the global burden of disease study 2010. *The Lancet* 382, 1575-1586.

Wiborg JF, Gieseler D, Fabisch AB, Voigt K, Lautenbach A, Lowe B (2013). Suicidality in primary care patients with somatoform disorders. *Psychosomatic Medicine* 75, 800-806.

Wilson N, Summers JA, Baker MG, Thomson G, Harper G (2013). Fatal injury epidemiology among the New Zealand military forces in the first world war. *The New Zealand Medical Journal* 126, 13-25.

Wu J, Värnik A, Tooding LM, Värnik P, Kasearu K (2013). Suicide among older people in relation to their subjective and objective well-being in different European regions. *European Journal of Ageing.* Published online: 23 October 2013. doi: 10.1007/s10433-013-0297-1.

Yano Y, Yamamoto A, Sakane T, Fujimoto A, Motohashi H (2013). Social factors of mental disorder and suicide in Japan—for understanding circumstance of suicides in each prefecture. *Yakugaku Zasshi* 133, 1235-1241.

Yoshioka E, Hanley SJ, Kawanishi Y, Saijo Y (2014). Epidemic of charcoal burning suicide in Japan. *British Journal of Psychiatry.* Published online: 16 January 2014. doi: 10.1192/bjp.bp.113.135392

Zaridze D, Lewington S, Boroda A, Scélo G, Karpov R, Lazarev A, Konobeevskaya I, Igitov V, Terechova T, Boffetta P, Sherliker P, Kong X, Whitlock G, Boreham J, Brennan P, Peto R (2014). Alcohol and mortality in Russia: Prospective observational study of 151000 adults. *Lancet.* Published online: 31 January 2014. doi: 10.1016/S0140-6736(13)62247-3.

Zhang J (2014). The gender ratio of Chinese suicide rates: An explanation in confucianism. *Sex Roles* 70, 146-154.

Zhang L, Li Z, Li X, Zhang J, Zheng L, Jiang C, Li J (2014). Study on the trend and disease burden of injury deaths in Chinese population, 2004-2010. *PLoS ONE* 9, e85319.

Zhang M, Fang X, Zhou L, Su L, Zheng J, Jin M, Zou H, Chen G (2013). Pesticide poisoning in Zhejiang, China: A retrospective analysis of adult cases registration by occupational disease surveillance and reporting systems from 2006 to 2010. *British Medical Journal Open* 3, e003510.

Risk and protective factors

Anonymous (2013). Call for papers: Suicide prevention, nontraditional career paths, and lessons of leadership. *Academic Psychiatry* 37, 407

Akpotuzor Josephine O, Akpan Patience A, Akwiwu Euphoria C (2013). Perception level of voluntary counselling/testing and knowledge/ awareness of HIV/aids among adult population in Ugep town of cross-river state of Nigeria. *Journal of AIDS and Clinical Research* 4, 234.

Altangerel U, Liou J-C, Yeh P-M (2013). Prevalence and predictors of suicidal behavior among Mongolian high school students. *Community Mental Health Journal* 50, 362-372.

Alvarado-Esquivel C, Sanchez-Anguiano LF, Arnaud-Gil CA, Lopez-Longoria JC, Molina-Espinoza LF, Estrada-Martinez S, Liesenfeld O, Hernandez-Tinoco J, Sifuentes-Alvarez A, Salas-Martinez C (2013). Toxoplasma gondii infection and suicide attempts: A case-control study in psychiatric outpatients. *Journal of Nervous and Mental Disease* 201, 948-952.

Anderson DM, Rees DI, Sabia JJ (2014). Medical marijuana laws and suicides by gender and age. *American Journal of Public Health.* Published online: 16 January 2014. doi: 10.2105/AJPH.2013.301612.

Antypa N, Serretti A (2014). Family history of a mood disorder indicates a more severe bipolar disorder. *Journal of Affective Disorders* 156, 178-186.

Arias F, Szerman N, Vega P, Mesias B, Basurte I, Morant C, Ochoa E, Poyo F, Babin F (2013). Alcohol abuse or dependence and other psychiatric disorders. Madrid study on the prevalence of dual pathology. *Mental Health and Substance Use: Dual Diagnosis* 6, 339-350.

Arnautovska U, Sveticic J, De Leo D (2013). What differentiates homeless persons who died by suicide from other suicides in Australia? A comparative analysis using a unique mortality register. *Social Psychiatry and Psychiatric Epidemiology* 49, 583-589.

Asoglu M, Bulbul F, Altindag A (2013). Evaluation of suicide attempts that referred to a university hospital emergency department. *Dusunen Adam* 26, 376-380.

Aziz R, Steffens DC (2013). What are the causes of late-life depression? *Psychiatric Clinics of North America* 36, 497-516.

Baek JH, Kang E-S, Fava M, Mischoulon D, Nierenberg AA, Yu B-H, Lee D, Jeon HJ (2014). Serum lipids, recent suicide attempt and recent suicide status in patients with major depressive disorder. *Progress in Neuro-Psychopharmacology and Biological Psychiatry* 51, 113-118.

Bagaric D, Brecic P, Ostojic D, Jukic V, Goles A (2013). The relationship between depressive syndrome and suicidal risk in patients with acute schizophrenia. *Croatian Medical Journal* 54, 436-443.

Balazs J, Miklosi M, Kereszteny A, Dallos G, Gadoros J (2014). Attention-deficit hyperactivity disorder and suicidality in a treatment naive sample of children and adolescents. *Journal of Affective Disorders* 152, 282-287.

Ballard ED, Horowitz LM, Jobes DA, Wagner BM, Pao M, Teach SJ (2013). Association of positive responses to suicide screening questions with hospital admission and repeated emergency department visits in children and adolescents. *Pediatric Emergency Care* 29, 1070-1074.

Bamonti PM, Price EC, Fiske A (2013). Depressive symptoms and suicide risk in older adults: Value placed on autonomy as a moderator for men but not women. *Suicide and Life-Threatening Behavior.* Published online: 13 November 2013. doi: 10.1111/sltb.12062.

Bansal YS, Medhi B, Prakash A, Attrey SD, Singh D (2013). Study to evaluate correlation of serum cholesterol and serotonin levels in suicidal deaths. *Journal of Indian Academy of Forensic Medicine* 35, 339-342.

Barker E, O'Gorman J, De Leo D (2014). Suicide around public holidays. *Australasian Psychiatry.* Published online: 4 February 2014. doi: 10.1177/1039856213519293.

Barzilay S, Apter A (2014). Predictors of suicide in adolescents and adults with mood and common comorbid disorders. *Neuropsychiatry* 4, 81-93.

Beck A, Heinz A (2013). Alcohol-related aggression-social and neurobiological factors. *Deutsches Arzteblatt International* 110, 711-U724.

Behera C, Rautji R, Sikary AK, Kumar R, Vidua RK, Millo T, Gupta SK (2014). Triple hanging in filicide-suicide: An unusual case report. *Medicine, Science, and the Law.* Published online: 18 March 2014. doi: 10.1177/0025802414524951.

Berman M (2013). Suicide among young Alaska native men: Community risk factors and alcohol control. *International Journal of Circumpolar Health* 72, 263.

Blasco-Fontecilla H, Lopez-Castroman J, Giner L, Baca-Garcia E, Oquendo MA (2013). Predicting suicidal behavior: Are we really that far along? Comment on "discovery and validation of blood biomarkers for suicidality". *Current Psychiatry Reports* 15, 1-3.

Blosnich JR, Brown GR, Shipherd JC, Kauth M, Piegari RI, Bossarte RM (2013). Prevalence of gender identity disorder and suicide risk among transgender veterans utilizing veterans health administration care. *American Journal of Public Health* 103, e27-e32.

Bohnert KM, Ilgen MA, McCarthy JF, Ignacio RV, Blow FC, Katz IR (2013). Tobacco use disorder and the risk of suicide mortality. *Addiction* 109, 155-162.

Brière FN, Rohde P, Seeley JR, Klein D, Lewinsohn PM (2013). Comorbidity between major depression and alcohol use disorder from adolescence to adulthood. *Comprehensive Psychiatry* 55, 526-533.

Briggs JT, Tabarrok A (2014). Firearms and suicides in U.S. states. *International Review of Law and Economics* 37, 180-188.

Britton PC, Van Orden KA, Hirsch JK, Williams GC (2014). Basic psychological needs, suicidal ideation, and risk for suicidal behavior in young adults. *Suicide and Life-Threatening Behavior.* Published online: 3 Feburary 2014. doi: 10.1111/sltb.12074.

Brown VM, Strauss JL, Labar KS, Gold AL, McCarthy G, Morey RA (2014). Acute effects of trauma-focused research procedures on participant safety and distress. *Psychiatry Research* 215, 154-158.

Bryan CJ, Bryan AO, Ray-Sannerud BN, Etienne N, Morrow CE (2013). Suicide attempts before joining the military increase risk for suicide attempts and severity of suicidal ideation among military personnel and veterans. *Comprehensive Psychiatry* 55, 534-541.

Carli V, Hoven CW, Wasserman C, Chiesa F, Guffanti G, Sarchiapone M, Apter A, Balazs J, Brunner R, Corcoran P, Cosman D, Haring C, Iosue M, Kaess M, Kahn JP, Keeley H, Postuvan V, Saiz P, Varnik A, Wasserman D (2014). A newly identified group of adolescents at "invisible" risk for psychopathology and suicidal behavior: Findings from the SEYLE study. *World Psychiatry* 13, 78-86.

Chang EC, Yu EA, Kahle ER, Jeglic EL, Hirsch JK (2013). Is doubling up on positive future cognitions associated with lower suicidal risk in Latinos?: A look at hope and positive problem orientation. *Cognitive Therapy and Research* 37, 1285-1293.

Chang JC, Yen AMF, Lee CS, Chen SLS, Chiu SYH, Fann JCY, Chen HH (2013). Metabolic syndrome and the risk of suicide: A community-based integrated screening samples cohort study. *Psychosomatic Medicine* 75, 807-814.

Chapman A, Gratz K, Turner B (2013). Risk-related and protective correlates of nonsuicidal self-injury and co-occurring suicide attempts among incarcerated women. *Suicide and Life-Threatening Behavior.* Published online: 19 October 2013. doi: 10.1111/sltb.12058.

Chen C-Y, Yeh H-H, Huang N, Lin Y-C (2013). Socioeconomic and clinical characteristics associated with repeat suicide attempts among young people. *Journal of Adolescent Health.* Published online: 9 December 2013. doi: 10.1016/j.jadohealth.2013.10.008.

Chen L, Liu YH, Zheng QW, Xiang YT, Duan Yp, Yang Fd, Wang G, Fang YR, Lu Z, Yang HC, Hu J, Chen ZY, Huang Y, Sun J, Wang XP, Li HC, Zhang JB, Chen DF, Si TM (2013). Suicide risk in major affective disorder: Results from a national survey in China. *Journal of Affective Disorders* 155, 174-179.

Chen YJ, Tsai YF, Ku YC, Lee SH, Lee HL (2013). Perceived reasons for, opinions about, and suggestions for elders considering suicide: Elderly outpatients' perspectives. *Aging and Mental Health*. Published online: 12 December 2013. doi: 10.1080/13607863.2013.860424

Cheng CC, Yen WJ, Chang WT, Wu KC, Ko MC, Li CY (2013). Risk of adolescent offspring's completed suicide increases with prior history of their same-sex parents' death by suicide. *Psychological Medicine*. Published online: 24 September 2013. doi: 10.1017/S0033291713002298

Chiang YC, Lee TS, Yen LL, Wu CC, Lin DC, Hurng BS, Chang HY (2013). Influence of stressors and possible pathways of onset of seventh graders' suicidal ideation in urban and rural areas in Taiwan. *BMC Public Health* 13, 1233.

Chistopolskaya KA, Enikolopov SN (2013). Terror management after a recent suicide attempt. *Psychology in Russia: State of the Art* 6, 142-156.

Choo C, Diederich J, Song I, Ho R (2013). Cluster analysis reveals risk factors for repeated suicide attempts in a multi-ethnic Asian population. *Asian Journal of Psychiatry* 8, 38-42.

Christodoulou NG, Christodoulou GN (2013). The financial crisis and its impact on mental health. *Psychiatrike* 24, 95-98.

Clark CB, Waesche MC, Hendricks PS, McCullumsmith CB, Redmond N, Katiyar N, Lawler RM, Cropsey KL (2013). The relationship between prior suicidal behavior and mortality among individuals in community corrections. *Crisis* 34, 428-433.

Clark TC, Lucassen MFG, Bullen P, Denny SJ, Fleming TM, Robinson EM, Rossen FV (2014). The health and well-being of Transgender high school students: Results from the New Zealand adolescent health survey (youth'12). *Journal of Adolescent Health*. Published online 14 January 2014. doi: 10.1016/j.jadohealth.2013.11.008.

Class QA, Abel KM, Khashan AS, Rickert ME, Dalman C, Larsson H, Hultman CM, Långström N, Lichtenstein P, D'Onofrio BM (2014). Offspring psychopathology following preconception, prenatal and postnatal maternal bereavement stress. *Psychological Medicine* 44, 71-84.

Cook LC, Borrill J (2013). Identifying suicide risk in a metropolitan probation trust: Risk factors and staff decision making. *Legal and Criminological Psychology*. Published online: 4 December 2013. doi: 10.1111/lcrp.12034.

Cooper WO, Callahan ST, Shintani A, Fuchs DC, Shelton RC, Dudley JA, Graves AJ, Ray WA (2014). Antidepressants and suicide attempts in children. *Pediatrics*. Published online: 6 January 2014. doi: 10.1542/peds.2013-0923.

Copeland L, Sun F, Haller I, Roberts M, Bailey-Davis L, Vanwormer J, Gessert C, Behl A, Shapiro G, Morales L, Elliott T (2013). Ps3-47: Rural health research initiative in the Hmorn: A new scientific interest group. *Clinical Medicine & Research* 11, 142.

Cukrowicz KC, Jahn DR, Graham RD, Poindexter EK, Williams RB (2013). Suicide risk in older adults: Evaluating models of risk and predicting excess zeros in a primary care sample. *Journal of Abnormal Psychology* 122, 1021-1030.

Currier JM, Holland JM, Jones HW, Sheu S (2014). Involvement in abusive violence among Vietnam veterans: Direct and indirect associations with substance use problems and suicidality. *Psychological Trauma: Theory, Research, Practice, and Policy* 6, 73-82.

Czyz EK, King CA (2013). Longitudinal trajectories of suicidal ideation and subsequent suicide attempts among adolescent inpatients. *Journal of Clinical and Child Adolescent Psychology*. Published online: 30 September 2013. doi: 10.1080/15374416.2013.836454.

Dalca IM, McGirr A, Renaud J, Turecki G (2013). Gender-specific suicide risk factors: A case-control study of individuals with major depressive disorder. *Journal of Clinical Psychiatry* 74, 1209-1216.

Daly MC, Wilson DJ, Johnson NJ (2013). Relative status and well-being: Evidence from U.S. Suicide deaths. *Review of Economics and Statistics* 95, 1480-1500.

Davies NM, Gunnell D, Thomas KH, Metcalfe C, Windmeijer F, Martin RM (2013). Physicians' prescribing preferences were a potential instrument for patients' actual prescriptions of anti-depressants. *Journal of Clinical Epidemiology* 66, 1386-1396.

de la Grandmaison GL, Watier L, Cavard S, Charlier P (2013). Are suicide rates higher in the cancer population? An investigation using forensic autopsy data. *Medical Hypotheses* 82, 16-19.

Dell'Osso L, Mandelli L, Carlini M, Bouanani S, Rotondo A, Conversano C, Serretti A, Marazziti D (2013). Temperamental and genetic predictors of suicide attempt and self-muti-lation. *Neuropsychobiology* 68, 250-257.

Demirci S, Dogan KH, Deniz I, Erkol Z (2014). Evaluation of shotgun suicides in Konya, Turkey between 2000 and 2007. *American Journal of Forensic Medicine and Pathology* 35, 45-49.

Denney JT (2014). Families, resources, and suicide: Combined effects on mortality. *Journal of Marriage and Family* 76, 218-231.

Dewey L, Allwood M, Fava J, Arias E, Pinizzotto A, Schlesinger L (2013). Suicide by cop: Clini-cal risks and subtypes. *Archives of Suicide Research* 17, 448-461.

Dias D, Mendonça MC, Real FC, Vieira DN, Teixeira HM (2013). Suicides in the centre of Por-tugal: Seven years analysis. *Forensic Science International* 234, 22-28.

Dong X-Y, Wang W-Q, Zhao Y, Li X-D, Fang Z-G, Lin D-J, Xiao R-Z, Huang R-W, Pan G-J, Liu J-J (2013). Antibody-directed double suicide gene therapy targeting of MUC1-positive leukemia cells in vitro and in vivo. *Current Gene Therapy* 13, 346-357.

Dougall N, Lambert P, Maxwell M, Dawson A, Sinnott R, McCafferty S, Morris C, Clark D, Springbett A (2014). Deaths by suicide and their relationship with general and psychiatric hospital discharge: 30-year record linkage study. *British Journal of Psychiatry*. Published online: 30 January 2014. doi: 10.1192/bjp.bp.112.122.

Duthé G, Hazard A, Kensey A, Pan Ké Shon JL (2013). Suicide among male prisoners in France: A prospective population-based study. *Forensic Science International* 233, 273-277.

Encrenaz G, Miras A, Contrand B, Galera C, Pujos S, Michel G, Lagarde E (2014). Inmate-to-inmate violence as a marker of suicide attempt risk during imprisonment. *Journal of Forensic and Legal Medicine* 22, 20-25.

Eskandarieh S, Hajebi A, Saberi-Zafarghandi MB, Vares-Vazirian M, Asadi A (2013). Demo-graphic risk factors of suicide in Savojbolagh city of Tehran province: 2007-2009. *Studies on Ethno-Medicine* 7, 143-148.

Evren C, Yigiter S, Bozkurt M, Cagil D, Ozcetinkaya S, Can Y, Mutlu E (2013). Personality dimensions and defense styles that are related with relapse during 12 month follow-up in male alcohol dependents. *Dusunen Adam* 26, 248-257.

Eynan R, Bergmans Y, Antony J, Cutcliffe JR, Harder HG, Ambreen M, Balderson K, Links PS (2013). The effects of suicide ideation assessments on urges to self-harm and suicide. *Crisis* 35, 123-131.

Fábregas BC, Abreu MNS, dos Santos AKD, Moura AS, Carmo RA, Teixeira AL (2014). Impul-siveness in chronic hepatitis C patients. *General Hospital Psychiatry*. Published online: 23 December 2013. doi: 10.1016/j.genhosppsych.2013.12.006.

Faresjo A, Theodorsson E, Chatziarzenis M, Sapouna V, Claesson H-P, Koppner J, Faresjo T (2013). Higher perceived stress but lower cortisol levels found among young Greek adults living in a stressful social environment in comparison with Swedish young adults. *PLoS ONE*. Published online: 16 September 2013.

Farias DR, Pinto TdJP, Teofilo MMA, Vilela AAF, Vaz JdS, Nardi AE, Kac G (2013). Prevalence of psychiatric disorders in the first trimester of pregnancy and factors associated with current suicide risk. *Psychiatry Research* 210, 962-968.

Fazel S, Wolf A, Pillas D, Lichtenstein P, Långström N (2014). Suicide, fatal injuries, and other causes of premature mortality in patients with traumatic brain injury: A 41-year Swedish population study. *JAMA Psychiatry* 71, 326-333.

Ferrer P, Ballarín E, Sabaté M, Vidal X, Rottenkolber M, Amelio J, Hasford J, Schmiedl S, Ibáñez L (2014). Antiepileptic drugs and suicide: A systematic review of adverse effects. *Neuroepidemiology* 42, 107-120.

Finseth PI, Sønderby IE, Djurovic S, Agartz I, Malt UF, Melle I, Morken G, Andreassen OA, Vaaler AE, Tesli M (2014). Association analysis between suicidal behaviour and candidate genes of bipolar disorder and schizophrenia. *Journal of Affective Disorders*. Published online: 27 December 2013. doi: 10.1016/j.jad.2013.12.018.

Ford-Paz RE, Reinhard C, Kuebbeler A, Contreras R, Sanchez B (2013). Culturally tailored depression/suicide prevention in Latino youth: Community perspectives. *Journal of Behavioral Health Services and Research*. Published online: 17 October 2013. doi: 10.1007/s11414-013-9368-5.

Fusar-Poli P, Nelson B, Valmaggia L, Yung AR, McGuire PK (2014). Comorbid depressive and anxiety disorders in 509 individuals with an at-risk mental state: Impact on psychopathology and transition to psychosis. *Schizophrenia Bulletin* 40, 120-131.

Germain ML (2014). Work-related suicide: An analysis of U.S. government reports and recommendations for human resources. *Employee Relations* 36, 148-164.

Giotakos O, Nisianakis P, Tsouvelas G, Giakalou VV (2013). Lithium in the public water supply and suicide mortality in Greece. *Biological Trace Element Research* 156, 376-379.

Gjorup Pedersen C, Wallenstein Jensen SO, Gradus J, Paaske Johnsen S, Mainz J (2013). Systematic suicide risk assessment for patients with schizophrenia: A national population-based study. *Psychiatric Servies*. Published online: 1 February 2014. doi: 10.1176/appi.ps.201200021.

Goldman-Mellor S, Caspi A, Harrington H, Hogan S, Nada-Raja S, Poulton R, Moffitt T (2013). Young people's suicide attempts during an economic recession: A signal for long-term healthcare and social needs. *Comprehensive Psychiatry* 54, e15.

Güleç MY, Ýnanç L, Yanartath O, Üzer A, Güleç H (2013). Predictors of suicide in patients with conversion disorder. *Comprehensive Psychiatry* 55, 457-462.

Gvion Y, Horresh N, Levi-Belz Y, Fischel T, Treves I, Weiser M, David HS, Stein-Reizer O, Apter A (2014). Aggression-impulsivity, mental pain, and communication difficulties in medically serious and medically non-serious suicide attempters. *Comprehensive Psychiatry* 55, 40-50.

Haddock G, Eisner E, Davies G, Coupe N, Barrowclough C (2013). Psychotic symptoms, self-harm and violence in individuals with schizophrenia and substance misuse problems. *Schizophrenia Research* 151, 215-220.

Harris KM, McLean JP, Sheffield J (2014). Suicidal and online: How do online behaviors inform us of this high-risk population? *Death Studies*. Published online: 18 October 2013. doi: 10.1080/07481187.2013.768313.

Hawkins KA, Cougle JR (2013). A test of the unique and interactive roles of anger experience and expression in suicidality: Findings from a population-based study. *Journal of Nervous and Mental Disease* 201, 959-963.

Hawkins KA, Hames JL, Ribeiro JD, Silva C, Joiner TE, Cougle JR (2014). An examination of the relationship between anger and suicide risk through the lens of the interpersonal theory of suicide. *Journal of Psychiatric Research* 50, 59-65.

Hawton K, Turecki G (2013). Psychosocial influences on suicide. *British Journal of Psychiatry* 203, 333.

Herrell RK, Bliese PD, Hoge CW (2013). PTSD, depression, anxiety, and suicidality in a sample of U.S. soldiers. *Comprehensive Psychiatry* 54, e15.

Hettige NC, Kennedy JL, De Luca V (2014). Does a history of suicide attempt predict higher antipsychotic dosage in schizophrenia? *Psychopharmacology.* Published online: 9 January 2014. doi: 10.1007/s00213-013-3419-8.

Hikiji W, Fukunaga T (2014). Suicide of physicians in the special wards of Tokyo metropolitan area. *Journal of Forensic and Legal Medicine* 22, 37-40.

Hiratori Y, Tachikawa H, Nemoto K, Endo G, Aiba M, Matsui Y, Asada T (2014). Network analysis for motives in suicide cases: A cross-sectional study. *Psychiatry and Clinical Neurosciences* 68, 299-307.

Hirsch JK, Webb JR, Kaslow NJ (2013). Daily hassles and suicide ideation in African-American female suicide attempters: Moderating effect of spiritual well-being. *Mental Health, Religion and Culture* 17, 529-541.

Ho Choi K, Wang SM, Yeon B, Suh SY, Oh Y, Lee HK, Kweon YS, Tai Lee C, Lee KU (2013). Risk and protective factors predicting multiple suicide attempts. *Psychiatry Research* 210, 957-961.

Holland JM, Malott J, Currier JM (2013). Meaning made of stress among veterans transitioning to college: Examining unique associations with suicide risk and life-threatening behavior. *Suicide and Life-Threatening Behavior.* Published online: 5 December 2013. doi: 10.1111/sltb.12061.

Hsiao FH, Lai YM, Chen YT, Yang TT, Liao SC, Ho RTH, Ng SM, Chan CLW, Jow GM (2013). Efficacy of psychotherapy on diurnal cortisol patterns and suicidal ideation in adjustment disorder with depressed mood. *General Hospital Psychiatry* 36, 214-219.

Hu J, Chan LF, Souza RP, Tampakeras M, Kennedy JL, Zai C, De Luca V (2014). The role of tyrosine hydroxylase gene variants in suicide attempt in schizophrenia. *Neuroscience Letters* 559, 39-43.

Huber RS, Coon H, Kim N, Renshaw PF, Kondo DG (2014). Altitude is a risk factor for completed suicide in bipolar disorder. *Medical Hypotheses* 82, 377-381.

Jang SI, Lee KS, Park EC (2013). Relationship between current sleep duration and past suicidal ideation or attempt among Korean adolescents. *Journal of Preventive Medicine and Public Health* 46, 329-335.

Jia Z, Wang Y, Huang X, Kuang W, Wu Q, Lui S, Sweeney JA, Gong Q (2013). Impaired frontothalamic circuitry in suicidal patients with depression revealed by diffusion tensor imaging at 3.0 T. *Journal of Psychiatry & Neuroscience* 38, 130023.

Jones T, Hillier L (2013). Comparing trans-spectrum and same-sex-attracted youth in Australia: Increased risks, increased activisms. *Journal of LGBT Youth* 10, 287-307.

Kanchan T, Krishan K (2013). Inverse association between body mass index and suicide? *International Journal of Legal Medicine* 21, e334-e442.

Kang SG, Lee YJ, Kim SJ, Lim W, Lee HJ, Park YM, Cho IH, Cho SJ, Hong JP (2013). Weekend catch-up sleep is independently associated with suicide attempts and self-injury in Korean adolescents. *Comprehensive Psychiatry* 55, 319-325.

Karhumaa T, Hakko H, Nauha R, Rasanen P (2013). Season of birth in suicides: Excess of births during the summer among schizophrenic suicide victims. *Neuropsychobiology* 68, 238-242.

Kato T (2013). Insomnia symptoms, depressive symptoms, and suicide ideation in Japanese white-collar employees. *International Journal of Behavioral Medicine.* Published online: 18 October 2013. doi: 10.1007/s12529-013-9364-4.

Kessler RC, Adler LA, Berglund P, Green JG, McLaughlin KA, Fayyad J, Russo LJ, Sampson NA, Shahly V, Zaslavsky AM (2013). The effects of temporally secondary co-morbid mental disorders on the associations of DSM-IV adhd with adverse outcomes in the U.S. National Comorbidity Survey Replication Adolescent Supplement (NCS-A). *Psychological Medicine.* Published online: 8 October 2013. doi: 10.1017/S0033291713002419.

Kim B, Kang ES, Fava M, Mischoulon D, Soskin D, Yu BH, Lee D, Lee DY, Park HD, Jeon HJ (2013). Follicle-stimulating hormone (FSH), current suicidal ideation and attempt in female patients with major depressive disorder. *Psychiatry Research* 210, 951-956.

Kim J-H, Park E-C, Nam J-M, Park S, Cho J, Kim S-J, Choi J-W, Cho E (2013). The werther effect of two celebrity suicides: An entertainer and a politician. *PLoS ONE.* Published online: 26 December 2013. doi: 10.1371/journal.pone.0084876.

Kim S, Ha JH, Yu J, Park DH, Ryu SH (2013). Path analysis of suicide ideation in older people. *International Psychogeriatrics* 26, 509-515.

Kindrick C, Gathright M, Cisler JM, Messias E (2013). Sadness, suicide, and sexual behavior in Arkansas: Results from the youth risk behavior survey 2011. *Journal of the Arkansas Medical Society* 110, 134-136.

Kiviniemi M, Suvisaari J, Isohanni M, Saarento O, Hakkinen U, Pirkola S, Hakko H (2013). The characteristics and outcomes of hospitalised and outpatient-treated first-onset schizophrenia patients: A 5-year register linkage study. *International Journal of Clinical Practice* 67, 1105-1112.

Kleiman EM, Liu RT (2013). Prospective prediction of suicide in a nationally representative sample: Religious service attendance as a protective factor. *British Journal of Psychiatry.* Published online: 10 October 2013. doi: 10.1192/bjp.bp.113.128900.

Kleiman EM, Liu RT, Riskind JH (2013). Integrating the interpersonal psychological theory of suicide into the depression/suicidal ideation relationship: A short-term prospective study. *Behavior Therapy* 45, 212-221.

Kleiman EM, Riskind JH, Schaefer KE (2014). Social support and positive events as suicide resiliency factors: Examination of synergistic buffering effects. *Archives of Suicide Research.* Published online: 12 March 2014. doi: 10.1080/13811118.2013.826155.

Kochanski-Ruscio KM, Carreno-Ponce JT, DeYoung K, Grammer G, Ghahramanlou-Holloway M (2014). Diagnostic and psychosocial differences in psychiatrically hospitalized military service members with single versus multiple suicide attempts. *Comprehensive Psychiatry* 55, 450-456.

Kupferschmid S, Gysin-Maillart A, Buhler SK, Steffen T, Michel K, Schimmelmann BG, Reisch T (2013). Gender differences in methods of suicide attempts and prevalence of previous suicide attempts. *Zeitschrift fur Kinder- und Jugendpsychiatrie und Psychotherapie* 41, 401-405.

Kwon M, Yang S, Park KR, Kim DJ (2013). Factors that affect substance users' suicidal behavior: A view from the addiction severity index in Korea. *Annals of General Psychiatry* 12, 35.

Lai YC, Huang MC, Chen HC, Lu MK, Chiu YH, Shen WW, Lu RB, Kuo PH (2013). Familiality and clinical outcomes of sleep disturbances in major depressive and bipolar disorders. *Journal of Psychosomatic Research* 76, 61-67.

Lakey CE, Hirsch JK, Nelson LA, Nsamenang SA (2013). Effects of contingent self-esteem on depressive symptoms and suicidal behavior. *Death Studies*. Published online: 5 February 2014. doi: 10.1080/07481187.2013.809035.

Lamis DA, Wilson CK, Shahane AA, Kaslow NJ (2013). Mediators of the childhood emotional abuse-hopelessness association in African American women. *Child Abuse and Neglect*. Published online: 19 December 2013. doi: 10.1016/j.chiabu.2013.11.006.

Large M, Ryan C, Walsh G, Stein-Parbury J, Patfield M (2013). Nosocomial suicide. *Australasian Psychiatry*. Published online: 27 November 2013. doi: 10.1177/1039856213511277.

Latas M, Milovanovic S (2014). Personality disorders and anxiety disorders: What is the relationship? *Current Opinion in Psychiatry* 27, 57.

Leadholm AKK, Rothschild AJ, Nielsen J, Bech P, Østergaard SD (2014). Risk factors for suicide among 34,671 patients with psychotic and non-psychotic severe depression. *Journal of Affective Disorders* 156, 119-125.

Lee A, Pridmore S (2013). Emerging correlations between measures of population well-being, suicide and homicide: A look at global and Australian data. *Australasian Psychiatry*. Published online: 4 November 2013. doi: 10.1177/1039856213510577.

Lee ES (2013). The ambiguous practices of the inauthentic Asian American woman. *Hypatia* 29, 146-163.

Leszczynska-Rodziewicz A, Szczepankiewicz A, Pawlak J, Dmitrzak-Weglarz M, Hauser J (2013). Association, haplotype, and gene-gene interactions of the HPA axis genes with suicidal behaviour in affective disorders. *Scientific World Journal*. Published online: 22 October 2013. doi: 10.1155/2013/207361.

Levi-Belz Y, Gvion Y, Horesh N, Fischel T, Treves I, Or E, Stein-Reisner O, Weiser M, David HS, Apter A (2013). Mental pain, communication difficultiesand medically serious suicide attempts: A case-control study. *Archives of Suicide Research* 18, 74-87.

Liem M, Reichelmann A (2014). Patterns of multiple family homicide. *Homicide Studies* 18, 44-58.

Lindner R, Foerster R, von Renteln-Kruse W (2013). Physical distress and relationship problems - exploring the psychosocial and intrapsychic world of suicidal geriatric patients. *Zeitschrift fur Gerontologie und Geriatrie*. Published online: 9 November 2013. doi: 10.1007/s00391-013-0563-z.

Lorenzo-Luaces L, Phillips JA (2013). Racial and ethnic differences in risk factors associated with suicidal behavior among young adults in the USA. *Ethnicity & Health*. Published online: 18 October 2013. doi: 10.1080/13557858.2013.846299.

Lucas M, O'Reilly EJ, Mirzaei F, Okereke OI, Unger L, Miller M, Ascherio A (2013). Cigarette smoking and completed suicide: Results from 3 prospective cohorts of American adults. *Journal of Affective Disorders* 151, 1053-1058.

Luckhoff M, Koen L, Jordaan E, Niehaus D (2013). Attempted suicide in a xhosa schizophrenia and schizoaffective disorder population. *Suicide and Life-Threatening Behavior*. Published online: 29 November 2013. doi: 10.1111/sltb.12066.

Lundholm L, Thiblin I, Runeson B, Leifman A, Fugelstad A (2013). Acute influence of alcohol, THC or central stimulants on violent suicide: A Swedish population study. *Journal of Forensic Sciences*. Published online: 25 November 2013. doi: 10.1111/1556-4029.12353.

Manetta AA, Cox LE (2014). Suicidal behavior and HIV/aids: A partial test of Joiner's theory of why people die by suicide. *Social Work in Mental Health* 12, 20-35.

Massaro JF, Cao Y, Devivo MJ, Chen Y, Krause JS (2013). Suicide mortality after spinal cord injury in the United States: Injury cohorts analysis. *Archives of Physical Medicine and Rehabilitation* 95, 230-235.

Mattei G, Ferrari S, Pingani L, Rigatelli M (2014). Short-term effects of the 2008 great recession on the health of the Italian population: An ecological study. *Social Psychiatry and Psychiatric Epidemiology*. Published online: 21 January 2014. doi: 10.1007/s00127-014-0818-z.

McPhedran S, De Leo D (2013). Risk factors for suicide among rural men: Are farmers more socially isolated? *The International Journal of Sociology and Social Policy* 33, 762-772 .

Miller M, Warren M, Hemenway D, Azrael D (2013). Firearms and suicide in U.S. cities. *Injury Prevention*. Published online: 3 December 2013. doi: 10.1136/injuryprev-2013-040969.

Mills PD, Vince Watts B, Hemphill RR (2014). Suicide attempts and completions on medical-surgical and intensive care units. *Journal of Hospital Medicine* 9, 182-185.

Milner A, Spittal MJ, Pirkis J, Lamontagne AD (2013). Suicide by occupation: Systematic review and meta-analysis. *British Journal of Psychiatry* 203, 409-416.

Minden SL, Feinstein A, Kalb RC, Miller D, Mohr DC, Patten SB, Bever C, Jr., Schiffer RB, Gronseth GS, Narayanaswami P (2014). Evidence-based guideline: Assessment and management of psychiatric disorders in individuals with MS: Report of the guideline development subcommittee of the American academy of neurology. *Neurology* 82, 174-181.

Mitter N, Subramaniam M, Abdin E, Poon LY, Verma S (2013). Predictors of suicide in Asian patients with first episode psychosis. *Schizophrenia Research* 151, 274-278.

Mork E, Walby FA, Harkavy-Friedman JM, Barrett EA, Steen NE, Lorentzen S, Andreassen OA, Melle I, Mehlum L (2013). Clinical characteristics in schizophrenia patients with or without suicide attempts and non-suicidal self-harm - a cross-sectional study. *BMC Psychiatry* 13, 255.

Morley KC, Haber PS, Tucker P, Sitharthan T (2013). The efficacy of an opportunistic cognitive behavioral intervention package (OCB) on substance use and comorbid suicide risk: A multisite randomized controlled trial. *Journal of Consulting and Clinical Psychology* 82, 130-140.

Motohashi H, Fujimoto A, Sakane T, Yamamoto A, Yano Y (2013). Social factors of mental disorder and suicide in Japan -for understanding circumstance of suicides in each prefecture. *Yakugaku Zasshi* 133, 1235-1241.

Murphy MM, Verjee MA, Bener A, Gerber LM (2013). The hopeless age? A qualitative exploration of the experience of menopause in Arab women in Qatar. *Climacteric* 16, 550.

Mustanski B, Andrews R, Herrick A, Stall R, Schnarrs PW (2013). A syndemic of psychosocial health disparities and associations with risk for attempting suicide among young sexual minority men. *American Journal of Public Health* 104, 287-294.

Nadorff MR, Anestis MD, Nazem S, Claire Harris H, Samuel Winer E (2013). Sleep disorders and the interpersonal-psychological theory of suicide: Independent pathways to suicidality? *Journal of Affective Disorders* 152-154, 505-512.

Nanri A, Mizoue T, Poudel-Tandukar K, Noda M, Kato M, Kurotani K, Goto A, Oba S, Inoue M, Tsugane S (2013). Dietary patterns and suicide in Japanese adults: Health centre-based prospective study. *British Journal of Psychiatry* 203, 422-427.

Nanri A, Mizoue T, Poudel-Tandukar K, Noda M, Kato M, Kurotani K, Goto A, Oba S, Inoue M, Tsugane S, Japan Publ Hlth Ctr B (2013). Dietary patterns and suicide in Japanese adults: The Japan public health center-based prospective study. *British Journal of Psychiatry* 203, 422-427.

Nicolayeva VV, Onaybayeva ZK (2013). Search for the causes of suicidal behavior among teenagers. *Education and Science Without Borders* 4, 89-91.

Norstrom T (2014). Commentary on pridemore (2014): Drinking and suicide in Russia-strong evidence of a strong link. *Addiction* 109, 189-190.

O'Hare T, Shen C, Sherrer M (2013). Lifetime trauma and suicide attempts in people with severe mental illness. *Community Mental Health Journal.* Published online: 27 November 2013. doi: 10.1007/s10597-013-9658-7.

Okello J, Nakimuli-Mpungu E, Musisi S, Broekaert E, Derluyn I (2013). War-related trauma exposure and multiple risk behaviors among school-going adolescents in northern Uganda: The mediating role of depression symptoms. *Journal of Affective Disorders* 151, 715-721.

Oquendo Ma, Perez-Rodriguez Mm, Poh E, Sullivan G, Burke Ak, Sublette Me, Mann Jj, Galfalvy H (2013). Life events: A complex role in the timing of suicidal behavior among depressed patients. *Molecular Psychiatry.* Published online: 15 August 2013. doi: 10.1038/mp.2013.128

Osborne B (2014). Suicide risk among farmers. *Veterinary Record* 174, 22.

Owen DC, Armstrong ML, Koch J, Roberts A (2013). College students with body art: Well-being or high-risk behavior? *Journal of Psychosocial Nursing & Mental Health Services* 51, 20-28.

Park BC, Soo Im J, Strother Ratcliff K (2013). Rising youth suicide and the changing cultural context in South Korea. *Crisis* 35, 102-109.

Park J-Y, Chung I-J (2014). Adolescent suicide triggered by problems at school in Korea: Analyses focusing on depression, suicidal ideation, plan, and attempts as four dimensions of suicide. *Child Indicators Research* 7, 75-88.

Park S, Cho S-C, Kim B-N, Kim J-W, Yoo HJ, Hong JP (2013). Increased use of lethal methods and annual increase of suicide rates in Korean adolescents: Comparison with adolescents in the United States. *Journal of Child Psychology and Psychiatry* 55, 258-263.

Park S, Yi KK, Na R, Lim A, Hong JP (2013). No association between serum cholesterol and death by suicide in patients with schizophrenia, bipolar affective disorder, or major depressive disorder. *Behavioral and Brain Functions* 9, 45.

Pellegrini LC, Rodriguez-Monguio R (2013). Unemployment, medicaid provisions, the mental health industry, and suicide. *Social Science Journal* 50, 482-490.

Petersen L, Sorensen TIA, Andersen PK, Mortensen PB, Hawton K (2014). Y genetic and familial environmental effects on suicide attempts: A study of Danish adoptees and their biological and adoptive siblings. *Journal of Affective Disorders* 155, 273-277.

Petersen L, Sørensen TIA, Andersen PK, Mortensen PB, Hawton K (2013). Genetic and familial environmental effects on suicide - an adoption study of siblings. *PLoS ONE* 8, e77973.

Phillips JA, Nugent CN (2013). Antidepressant use and method of suicide in the United States: Variation by age and sex, 1998-2007. *Archives of Suicide Research* 17, 360-372.

Polling C, Dutta R (2014). Adolescents with emotional, conduct and hyperkinetic disorders who are experiencing psychotic symptoms may be at increased risk of suicide attempt. *Evidence-Based Mental Health* 17, 19.

Pompili M, Innamorati M, Forte A, Longo L, Mazzetta C, Erbuto D, Ricci F, Palermo M, Stefani H, Seretti ME, Lamis DA, Perna G, Serafini G, Amore M, Girardi P (2013). Insomnia as a predictor of high-lethality suicide attempts. *International Journal of Clinical Practice* 67, 1311-1316.

Pompili M, Venturini P, Montebovi F, Forte A, Palermo M, Lamis DA, Serafini G, Amore M, Girardi P (2013). Suicide risk in dialysis: Review of current literature. *International Journal of Psychiatry in Medicine* 46, 85-108.

Pompili M, Serafini G, Innamorati M, Biondi M, Girardi N, Murri MB, Amore M, Lester D, Girardi P (2013). Impulsivity, aggression, and suicide risk in patients with schizophrenia. *Psychiatric Annals* 43, 458-462.

Poulin C, Shiner B, Thompson P, Vepstas L, Young-Xu Y, Goertzel B, Watts B, Flashman L, McAllister T (2014). Predicting the risk of suicide by analyzing the text of clinical notes. *PLoS ONE.* Published online: 28 January 2014. doi: 10.1371/journal.pone.0085733

Pregelj P, Agius M, Rokavec T, Korosec Jagodic H (2013). Availability of mental health service providers and suicide rates in Slovenia: A nationwide ecological study. *Croatian Medical Journal* 54, 444-452.

Pridmore S, Walter G (2013). Culture and suicide set points. *German Journal of Psychiatry* 16, 143-151.

Pritchard C, Roberts S, Pritchard CE (2013). 'Giving a voice to the unheard'? Is female youth (15-24 years) suicide linked to restricted access to family planning? Comparing two catholic continents. *International Social Work* 56, 798.

Pugh MJ, Hesdorffer D, Wang CP, Amuan ME, Tabares JV, Finley EP, Cramer JA, Kanner AM, Bryan CJ (2013). Temporal trends in new exposure to antiepileptic drug monotherapy and suicide-related behavior. *Neurology* 81, 1900-1906.

Rahimipour Anaraki N, Boostani D (2013). Living in and living out: A qualitative study of incarcerated mothers' narratives of their children's living condition. *Quality and Quantity.* Published online: 25 October 2013. doi: 10.1007/s11135-013-9943-0.

Ralphs A (2014). Suicide risk among farming patients and the effects of HS2. *British Journal of General Practice* 64, 69-70.

Randall JR, Doku D, Wilson ML, Peltzer K (2014). Suicidal behaviour and related risk factors among school-aged youth in the republic of Benin. *PLoS ONE.* Published online: 5 February 2014. doi: 10.1371/journal.pone.0088233.

Rappaport LM, Moskowitz DS, Galynker I, Yaseen ZS (2014). Panic symptom clusters differentially predict suicide ideation and attempt. *Comprehensive Psychiatry.* Published online: 17 December 2013. doi: 10.1016/j.comppsych.2013.10.017.

Rasmussen ML, Haavind H, Dieserud G, Dyregrov K (2013). Exploring vulnerability to suicide in the developmental history of young men: A psychological autopsy study. *Death Studies.* Published online: 19 December 2013. doi: 10.1080/07481187.2013.780113.

Reutfors J, Bahmanyar S, Jönsson EG, Brandt L, Bodén R, Ekbom A, Ösby U (2013). Medication and suicide risk in schizophrenia: A nested case-control study. *Schizophrenia Research* 150, 416-420.

Riihimäki K, Vuorilehto M, Isometsä E (2013). Borderline personality disorder among primary care depressive patients: A five-year study. *Journal of Affective Disorders* 155, 303-306.

Rojas Y, Stickley A (2014). Informal social capital in childhood and suicide among adolescent and young adult women: A cross-sectional analysis with 30 countries. *Women's Studies International Forum* 42, 1-8.

Runfola CD, Thornton LM, Pisetsky EM, Bulik CM, Birgegård A (2013). Self-image and suicide in a Swedish national eating disorders clinical register. *Comprehensive Psychiatry* 55, 439-449.

Sabella RA, Patchin JW, Hinduja S (2013). Cyberbullying myths and realities. *Computers in Human Behavior* 29, 2703-2711.

Sadkowski M, Dennis B, Clayden RC, ElSheikh W, Rangarajan S, DeJesus J, Samaan Z (2013). The role of the serotonergic system in suicidal behavior. *Neuropsychiatric Disease and Treatment* 9, 1699-1716.

Sadr S, Seghatoleslam T, Habil H, Zahiroddin A, Bejanzadeh S, Seghatoleslam N, Ardakani A, Rashid R (2013). Risk factors for multiple suicide attempts: A critical appraisal of Iranian psychology. *International Medical Journal* 20, 418-422.

Saewyc EM, Chen W (2013). To what extent can adolescent suicide attempts be attributed to violence exposure? A population-based study from western Canada. *Canadian Journal of Community Mental Health* 32, 79-94.

Sankaranarayanan A, Mancuso S, Castle D (2013). Smoking and suicidality in patients with a psychotic disorder. *Psychiatry Research* 30, 634-640.

Sareen J, Isaak C, Bolton S-L, Enns MW, Elias B, Deane F, Munro G, Stein MB, Chateau D, Gould M, Katz LY (2013). Gatekeeper training for suicide prevention in first nations community members: A randomized controlled trial. *Depression and Anxiety* 30, 1021-1029.

Scanavino MdT, Ventuneac A, Najjar Abdo CH, Tavares H, Sant'Ana do Amaral ML, Messina B, dos Reis SC, Lian Branco Mattins JP, Parsons JT (2013). Compulsive sexual behavior and psychopathology among treatment-seeking men in Sao Paulo, Brazil. *Psychiatry Research* 209, 518-524.

Schneider B, Lukaschek K, Baumert J, Meisinger C, Erazo N, Ladwig KH (2013). Living alone, obesity, and smoking increase risk for suicide independently of depressive mood findings from the population-based Monica/Kora Augsburg cohort study. *Journal of Affective Disorders* 152-154, 416-421.

Serafini G, Pompili M, Hansen KF, Obrietan K, Dwivedi Y, Shomron N, Girardi P (2013). The involvement of microRNAs in major depression, suicidal behavior, and related disorders: A focus on miR-185 and miR-491-3p. *Cellular and Molecular Neurobiology* 34, 17-30.

Shoval G, Shmulewitz D, Wall MM, Aharonovich E, Spivak B, Weizman A, Hasin D (2013). Alcohol dependence and suicide-related ideation/behaviors in an Israeli household sample, with and without major depression. *Alcoholism: Clinical and Experimental Research* 38, 820-825.

Sigfusdottir ID, Asgeirsdottir BB, Gudjonsson GH, Sigurdsson JF (2013). Suicidal ideations and attempts among adolescents subjected to childhood sexual abuse and family conflict/violence: The mediating role of anger and depressed mood. *Journal of Adolescence* 36, 1227-1236.

Singh AB, Bousman CA, Ng CH, Berk M (2013). High impact child abuse may predict risk of elevated suicidality during antidepressant initiation. *Australian and New Zealand Journal of Psychiatry* 47, 1191-1195.

Snider AM, McPhedran S (2013). Religiosity, spirituality, mental health, and mental health treatment outcomes in Australia: A systematic literature review. *Mental Health, Religion and Culture* 17, 568-581.

Solmi F, Hatch SL, Hotopf M, Treasure J, Micali N (2014). Prevalence and correlates of disordered eating in a general population sample: The south east London community health (SELCOH) study. *Social Psychiatry and Psychiatric Epidemiology*. Published online: 5 January 2014. doi: 10.1007/s00127-014-0822-3.

Stein D, Zinman D, Halevy L, Yaroslavsky A, Bachar E, Kreitler S, Orbach I (2013). Attitudes toward life and death and suicidality among inpatient female adolescents with eating disorders. *Journal of Nervous and Mental Disease* 201, 1066-1071.

Stenager E, Christiansen E, Handberg G, Jensen B (2013). Suicide attempts in chronic pain patients. A register-based study. *Scandinavian Journal of Pain*. Published online: 28 October 2013. doi: 10.1016/j.sjpain.2013.09.001.

Sugawara N, Yasui-Furukori N, Ishii N, Iwata N, Terao T (2013). Lithium in tap water and suicide mortality in Japan. *International Journal of Environmental Research and Public Health* 10, 6044-6048.

Suh S, Chang Y, Kim N (2014). Quantitative exponential modelling of copycat suicides: Association with mass media effect in South Korea. *Epidemiology and Psychiatric Sciences.* Published online: 4 February 2014. doi: 10.1017/S204579601400002X

Suliman S, Troeman Z, Stein DJ, Seedat S (2013). Are neuropsychological deficits after trauma associated with ASD severity? *Comprehensive Psychiatry* 55, 145-154.

Sunbury T, Luvsandagva N (2013). An exploration of suicide risk factors in Alaska 2003-2006: Combining the Alaska trauma registry and Alaska injury prevention center data. *International Journal of Circumpolar Health* 72, 263-264.

Suresh Kumar PN, Rajmohan V, Sushil K (2013). An exploratory analysis of personality factors contributed to suicide attempts. *Indian Journal of Psychological Medicine* 35, 378-384.

Suttajit S, Paholpak S, Choovanicvong S, Kittiwattanagul K, Pratoomsri W, Srisurapanont M (2013). Correlates of current suicide risk among Thai patients with bipolar I disorder: Findings from the thai bipolar disorder registry. *Neuropsychiatric Disease and Treatment* 9, 1751-1757.

Takeuchi A, Sakano N, Miyatake N (2014). Combined effects of working hours, income, and leisure time on suicide in all 47 prefectures of Japan. *Industrial Health.* Published online: 27 January 2014. doi: 10.2486/indhealth.2013-0182.

Teicher MH, Samson JA (2013). Childhood maltreatment and psychopathology: A case for ecophenotypic variants as clinically and neurobiologically distinct subtypes. *The American Journal of Psychiatry* 170, 1114-1133.

Teismann T, Förtsch EMAD, Baumgart P, Het S, Michalak J (2013). Influence of violent video gaming on determinants of the acquired capability for suicide. *Psychiatry Research* 215, 217-222.

Thibodeau MA, Welch PG, Sareen J, Asmundson GJG (2013). Anxiety disorders are independently associated with suicide ideation and attempts: Propensity score matching in two epidemiological samples. *Depression and Anxiety* 30, 947-954.

Tibi L, van Oppen P, Aderka IM, van Balkom AJLM, Batelaan NM, Spinhoven P, Penninx BW, Anholt GE (2013). Examining determinants of early and late age at onset in panic disorder: An admixture analysis. *Journal of Psychiatric Research* 47, 1870-1875.

Torchalla I, Li K, Strehlau V, Linden IA, Krausz M (2014). Religious participation and substance use behaviors in a Canadian sample of homeless people. *Community Mental Health Journal.* Published online: 7 February 2014. doi: 10.1007/s10597-014-9705-z.

Tovilla-Zarate CA, Gonzalez-Castro TB, Juarez-Rojop I, Pool Garcia S, Velazquez-Sanchez MP, Villar-Soto M, Genis A, Nicolini H, Lopez-Narvaez ML, Jimenez-Santos MA (2014). Study on genes of the serotonergic system and suicidal behavior: Protocol for a case-control study in Mexican population. *BMC Psychiatry* 14, 29.

Travasso SM, Rajaraman D, Heymann SJ (2014). A qualitative study of factors affecting mental health amongst low-income working mothers in Bangalore, India. *BMC Womens Health* 14, 22.

Tsafrir S, Chubarov E, Shoval G, Levi M, Nahshoni E, Ratmansky M, Weizman A, Zalsman G (2013). Cognitive traits in inpatient adolescents with and without prior suicide attempts and non-suicidal self-injury. *Comprehensive Psychiatry* 55, 370-373.

Turner BJ, Layden BK, Butler SM, Chapman AL (2013). How often, or how many ways: Clarifying the relationship between non-suicidal self-injury and suicidality. *Archives of Suicide Research* 17, 397-415.

Umut G, Altun ZO, Danismant BS, Kucukparlak I, Karamustafalioglu N, Ilnem MC (2013). The correlation of suicide attempt and suicidal ideation with insight, depression and severity of illness in schizophrenic patients. *Dusunen Adam* 26, 341-350.

Vanderhei S, Rojahn J, Stuewig J, McKnight PE (2013). The effect of shame-proneness, guilt-proneness, and internalizing tendencies on nonsuicidal self-injury. *Suicide and Life-Threatening Behavior*. Published online: 7 December 2013. doi: 10.1111/sltb.12069.

von Renteln-Kruse W, Foerster R, Lindner R (2013). Physical distress and relationship problems: Exploring the psychosocial and intrapsychic world of suicidal geriatric patients. *Zeitschrift fur Gerontologie*. Published online: 9 November 2013. doi: 10.1007/s00391-013-0563-z.

Voracek M (2013). Regional analysis of big five personality factors and suicide rates in Russia. *Psychological Reports* 113, 1043-1047.

Voracek M (2013). Regional intelligence and suicide rate in Germany, revisited. *Psychological Reports* 113, 1114-1118.

Walls ML, Hautala D, Hurley J (2013). "Rebuilding our community": Hearing silenced voices on Aboriginal youth suicide. *Transcultural Psychiatry* 51, 47-72.

Wang M, Alexanderson K, Runeson B, Head J, Melchior M, Perski A, Mittendorfer-Rutz E (2013). Are all-cause and diagnosis-specific sickness absence, and sick-leave duration risk indicators for suicidal behaviour? A nationwide register-based cohort study of 4.9 million inhabitants of Sweden. *Occupational and Environmental Medicine* 71, 12-20.

Wang Z, Qin Y, Zhang Y, Zhang B, Li L, Li T, Ding L (2013). Prevalence and correlated factors of lifetime suicidal ideation in adults in Ningxia, China. *Shanghai Archives of Psychiatry* 25, 287-295.

Wei HS, Chen JK (2014). Filicide-suicide ideation among Taiwanese parents with school-aged children: Prevalence and associated factors. *Child Abuse and Neglect*. Published online: 15 January 2014. doi: 10.1016/j.chiabu.2013.12.004.

Wnuk S, McMain S, Links PS, Habinski L, Murray J, Guimond T (2013). Factors related to dropout from treatment in two outpatient treatments for borderline personality disorder. *Journal of Personality Disorders* 27, 716-726.

Yalch MM, Hopwood CJ, Fehon DC, Grilo CM (2013). The influence of borderline personality features on inpatient adolescent suicide risk. *Personality Disorders* 5, 26-31.

Zahreddine N, Hady RT, Chammai R, Kazour F, Hachem D, Richa S (2013). Psychiatric morbidity, phenomenology and management in hospitalized female foreign domestic workers in Lebanon. *Community Mental Health Journal*. Published online: 27 December 2013. doi: 10.1007/s10597-013-9682-7.

Zerach G, Levi-Belz Y, Solomon Z (2013). Trajectories of suicidal ideation and posttraumatic stress symptoms among former prisoners of war: A 17-year longitudinal study. *Journal of Psychiatric Research* 49, 83-89.

Zhou R, Zhang J (2013). Effects of community stress and problems on residents' psychopathology. *Psychiatry Research* 215, 394-400.

Zhu Y, Zhang H, Shi S, Gao J, Li Y, Tao M, Zhang K, Wang X, Gao C, Yang L, Li K, Shi J, Wang G, Liu L, Zhang J, Du B, Jiang G, Shen J, Zhang Z, Liang W, Sun J, Hu J, Liu T, Wang X, Miao G, Meng H, Li Y, Hu C, Huang G, Li G, Ha B, Deng H, Mei Q, Zhong H, Gao S, Sang H, Zhang Y, Fang X, Yu F, Yang D, Liu T, Chen Y, Hong X, Wu W, Chen G, Cai M, Song Y, Pan J, Dong J, Pan R, Zhang W, Shen Z, Liu Z, Gu D, Wang X, Liu X, Zhang Q, Li Y, Chen Y, Kendler KS, Flint J, Liu Y (2013). Suicidal risk factors of recurrent major depression in Han Chinese women. *PLoS ONE*. Published online: 27 November 2013. doi: 10.1371/journal.pone.0080030

Zupanc T, Agius M, Paska AV, Pregelj P (2013). Blood alcohol concentration of suicide victims by partial hanging. *Journal of Forensic and Legal Medicine* 20, 976-979.

Prevention

Ahmedani BK, Coffey MJ, Coffey CE (2013). Collecting mortality data to drive real-time improvement in suicide prevention. *American Journal of Managed Care* 19, e386-e390.

Akotia CS, Knizek BL, Kinyanda E, Hjelmeland H (2013). "I have sinned": Understanding the role of religion in the experiences of suicide attempters in Ghana. *Mental Health, Religion and Culture* 17, 437-448.

Allen J, Charles W, Rasmus S (2013). Cultural intervention for suicide prevention: The Qunagsvik projects with Indigenous youth in Alaska. *International Journal of Circumpolar Health* 72, 264.

Barekatain M, Aminoroaia M, Samimi SMA, Rajabi F, Attari A (2013). Educational needs assessment for psychiatry residents to prevent suicide: A qualitative approach. *International Journal of Preventive Medicine* 4, 1200-1205.

Barker E, Kõlves K, De Leo D (2014). Management of suicidal and self-harming behaviors in prisons: Systematic literature review of evidence-based activities. *Archives of Suicide Research.* Published online: 10 March 2014. doi: 10.1080/13811118.2013.824830.

Best P, Foye U, Taylor B, Hazlett D, Manktelow R (2013). Online interactive suicide support services: Quality and accessibility. *Mental Health Review Journal* 18, 226-239.

Biddle VS, Kern J, Brent DA, Thurkettle MA, Puskar KR, Sekula LK (2014). Student assistance program outcomes for students at risk for suicide. *Journal of School Nursing.* Published online: 18 March 2014. doi: 10.1177/1059840514525968.

Bocquier A, Pambrun E, Dumesnil H, Villani P, Verdoux H, Verger P (2013). Physicians' characteristics associated with exploring suicide risk among patients with depression: A French panel survey of general practitioners. *PloS ONE* 8, e80797.

Bryant L, Gamham B (2013). Beyond discourses of drought: The micro-politics of the wine industry and farmer distress. *Journal of Rural Studies* 32, 1-9.

Cerel J, Bolin MC, Moore MM (2013). Suicide exposure, awareness and attitudes in college students. *Advances in Mental Health* 12, 46-53.

Chan WI, Batterham P, Christensen H, Galletly C (2014). Suicide literacy, suicide stigma and help-seeking intentions in Australian medical students. *Australasian Psychiatry.* Published online: 13 February 2014. doi: 10.1177/1039856214522528.

Cheng Q, Fu KW, Caine E, Yip PS (2013). Why do we report suicides and how can we facilitate suicide prevention efforts? *Crisis* 35, 74-81.

Cimini MD, Rivero EM, Bernier JE, Stanley JA, Murray AD, Anderson DA, Wright HR, Bapat M (2014). Implementing an audience-specific small-group gatekeeper training program to respond to suicide risk among college students: A case study. *Journal of American College Health* 62, 92-100.

Davidson L, Stern E (2013). Psychiatric/psychosocial rehabilitation (PSR) in relation to social and leisure environments: Friends and recreation. *Current Psychiatry Reviews* 9, 207-213.

Davis M-C, Ibrahim JE, Ranson D, Ozanne-Smith J, Routley V (2013). Work-related musculoskeletal injury and suicide: Opportunities for intervention and therapeutic jurisprudence. *Journal of Law and Medicine* 21, 110-121.

de Schweinitz P, Nation C, DeCou C, Stewart T, Allen J (2013). The village wellness project: Building community resilience and preventing suicide in rural Alaska. *International Journal of Circumpolar Health* 72, 264.

de Schweinitz P, Nation C, Sam C (2013). The Huslia wellness team documentary: Suicide prevention through community empowerment. *International Journal of Circumpolar Health* 72, 265.

Edlavitch SA, Byrns PJ (2014). Primary prevention research in suicide. *Crisis* 35, 69-73.

Erickson A, Abel NR (2013). A high school counselor's leadership in providing school-wide screenings for depression and enhancing suicide awareness. *Professional School Counseling* 16, 283-289.

Ghoncheh R, Kerkhof AJ, Koot HM (2014). Effectiveness of adolescent suicide prevention e-learning modules that aim to improve knowledge and self-confidence of gatekeepers: Study protocol for a randomized controlled trial. *Trials* 15, 52.

Huertas IB, Fernández Rodríguez MDC (2013). Suicide prevention in college students: A collaborative approach. *Interamerican Journal of Psychology* 47, 53-60.

Jashinsky J, Burton SH, Hanson CL, West J, Giraud-Carrier C, Barnes MD, Argyle T (2014). Tracking suicide risk factors through twitter in the U.S. *Crisis* 35, 51-59

Jun WH, Lee EJ, Park JS (2013). Effects of a suicide prevention programme for hospitalised patients with mental illness in South Korea. *Journal of Clinical Nursing*. Published online: 20 November 2014. doi: 10.1111/jocn.12417.

Kessler RC, Colpe LJ, Fullerton CS, Gebler N, Naifeh JA, Nock MK, Sampson NA, Schoenbaum M, Zaslavsky AM, Stein MB, Ursano RJ, Heeringa SG (2013). Design of the army study to assess risk and resilience in servicemembers (Army STARRS). *International Journal of Methods in Psychiatric Research* 22, 267-275.

Kõlves K, Arnautovska U, Gioannis AD, Leo DD (2013). Community care of individuals at risk of suicide: The life promotion clinic model. *Mental Illness* 5, 41-45.

Kowal J, Wilson KG, Henderson PR, McWilliams LA (2013). Change in suicidal ideation following interdisciplinary treatment of chronic pain. *Clinical Journal of Pain*. Published online: 25 November 2013. doi: 10.1097/AJP.0000000000000003.

Lai MH, Maniam T, Chan LF, Ravindran AV (2014). Caught in the web: A review of web-based suicide prevention. *Journal of Medical Internet Research* 16, e30.

Lancaster PG, Moore JT, Putter SE, Chen PY, Cigularov KP, Baker A, Quinnett P (2014). Feasibility of a web-based gatekeeper training: Implications for suicide prevention. *Suicide and Life-Threatening Behavior*. Published online: 27 February 2014. doi: 10.1111/sltb.12086.

Li HC, Hsiao YL, Tang CH, Miao NF (2014). Nursing inequalities in elderly suicides: An empirical study of Taiwan. *International Journal of Gerontology*. Published online: 14 March 2014. doi: 10.1016/j.ijge.2013.10.005

Luxton DD, Thomas EK, Chipps J, Relova RM, Brown D, McLay R, Lee T, Smolenski DJ (2014). Caring letters for suicide prevention: Implementation of a multi-site randomized clinical trial in the U.S. Military and veteran affairs healthcare systems. *Contemporary Clinical Trials* 37, 252-260.

Matsubayashi T, Ueda M, Sawada Y (2013). The effect of public awareness campaigns on suicides: Evidence from Nagoya, Japan. *Journal of Affective Disorders* 152-154, 526-529.

Matthieu MM, Swensen AB (2014). Suicide prevention training program for gatekeepers working in community hospice settings. *Journal of Social Work in End-of-life and Palliative Care* 10, 95-105.

McLaughlin AM, Scotece T, Rodríguez-Campos L (2013). Metaevaluation of a suicide prevention program focused on youth. *International Journal of Interdisciplinary Social and Community Studies* 7, 1-14.

Ono Y, Sakai A, Otsuka K, Uda H, Oyama H, Ishizuka N, Awata S, Ishida Y, Iwasa H, Kamei Y, Motohashi Y, Nakamura J, Nishi N, Watanabe N, Yotsumoto T, Nakagawa A, Suzuki Y, Tajima M, Tanaka E, Sakai H, Yonemoto N (2013). Effectiveness of a multimodal community intervention program to prevent suicide and suicide attempts: A quasi-experimental study. *PLoS ONE* 8, e74902.

Ornstein A, Bowes M, Shouldice M, Yanchar NL (2013). The importance of child and youth death review. *Paediatrics and Child Health* 18, 425-428.

Oyama H, Sakashita T (2014). Effects of universal screening for depression among middle-aged adults in a community with a high suicide rate. *Journal of Nervous and Mental Disease* 202, 280-286.

Pil L, Pauwels K, Muijzers E, Portzky G, Annemans L (2013). Cost-effectiveness of a helpline for suicide prevention. *Journal of Telemedicine and Telecare* 19, 273-281.

Pollock N, Jong M, Mulay S, Chaulk K, Wight J, Al-Krenawi A (2013). The role of community consultations in suicide prevention research in Labrador. *International Journal of Circumpolar Health* 72, 265.

Ranahan P (2013). Pathways for preparation: Locating suicide education in preparing professionals for encounters with suicidal adolescents. *Child and Youth Services* 34, 387-401.

Reilly S, Planner C, Gask L, Hann M, Knowles S, Druss B, Lester H (2013). Collaborative care approaches for people with severe mental illness. *Cochrane Database of Systematic Reviews* 11, CD009531.

Robinson J, Pirkis J (2013). Research priorities in suicide prevention: An examination of Australian-based research 2007-11. *Australian Health Review* 38, 18-24.

Robinson M, Braybrook D, Robertson S (2013). "Talk" about male suicide? Learning from community programmes. *Mental Health Review Journal* 18, 115-127.

Rothes IA, Henriques MR, Leal JB, Lemos MS (2013). Facing a patient who seeks help after a suicide attempt. *Crisis* 35, 110-122.

Ryan B (2013). Reducing the risk of suicide or trespass on railways: Developing better interventions through understanding behaviours of people. *Proceedings of the Institution of Mechanical Engineers Part F-Journal of Rail and Rapid Transit* 227, 715-723.

Sáiz PA, Bobes J (2014). Suicide prevention in Spain: An uncovered clinical need. *Revista de Psiquiatría y Salud Mental* 7, 1-4.

Sakamoto S, Tanaka E, Kameyama A, Takizawa T, Takizawa S, Fujishima S, Nara M, Sakashita T, Oyama H, Ono Y (2014). The effects of suicide prevention measures reported through a psychoeducational video: A practice in Japan. *International Journal of Social Psychiatry*. Published online: 29 January 2014. doi: 10.1177/0020764013518689.

Shahtahmasebi S (2013). De-politicizing youth suicide prevention. *Frontiers in Pediatrics* 1, 8.

Sirey JA, Greenfield A, Depasquale A, Weiss N, Marino P, Alexopoulos GS, Bruce ML (2013). Improving engagement in mental health treatment for home meal recipients with depression. *Clinical Interventions in Aging* 8, 1305-1312.

Sobolewski B, Richey L, Kowatch RA, Grupp-Phelan J (2013). Mental health follow-up among adolescents with suicidal behaviors after emergency department discharge. *Archives of Suicide Research* 17, 323-334.

Székely A, Thege BK, Mergl R, Birkás E, Rózsa S, Purebl G, Hegerl U (2013). How to decrease suicide rates in both genders? An effectiveness study of a community-based intervention (EAAD). *PLoS ONE*. Published online: 23 September 2013. doi: 10.1371/journal.pone.0075081.

Whiteside U, Lungu A, Richards J, Simon GE, Clingan S, Siler J, Snyder L, Ludman E (2014). Designing messaging to engage patients in an online suicide prevention intervention: Survey results from patients with current suicidal ideation. *Journal of Medical Internet Research* 16, e42.

Winter D, Bradshaw S, Bunn F, Wellsted D (2014). A systematic review of the literature on counselling and psychotherapy for the prevention of suicide: 2. Qualitative studies. *Counselling and Psychotherapy Research* 14, 64.

Postvention and Bereavement

Anonymous (2013). Medically assisted aid in dying? Vermont is now the fourth state to permit mercy. *The West Virginia Medical Journal* 109, 7.

Abbott CH, Prigerson HG, Maciejewski PK (2013). The influence of patients' quality of life at the end of life on bereaved caregivers' suicidal ideation. *Journal of Pain and Symptom Management.* Published online: 6 December 2013. doi: 10.1016/j.jpainsymman.2013.09.011.

Abel KM, Heuvelman HP, Jorgensen L, Magnusson C, Wicks S, Susser E, Hallkvist J, Dalman C (2014). Severe bereavement stress during the prenatal and childhood periods and risk of psychosis in later life: Population based cohort study. *British Medical Journal* 348, f7679.

Abidin Z, Davoren M, Naughton L, Gibbons O, Nulty A, Kennedy HG (2013). Susceptibility (risk and protective) factors for in-patient violence and self-harm: Prospective study of structured professional judgement instruments start and saprof, dundrum-3 and dundrum-4 in forensic mental health services. *BMC Psychiatry* 13, 197.

Burke LA, Neimeyer RA (2014). Complicated spiritual grief I: Relation to complicated grief symptomatology following violent death bereavement. *Death Studies* 38, 259-267.

Castelli Dransart DA, Gutjahr E, Gulfi A, Kaufmann Didisheim N, Séguin M (2013). Patient suicide in institutions: Emotional responses and traumatic impact on Swiss mental health professionals. *Death Studies* 38, 315-321.

Crenshaw MR (2013). Attitudes of African American clergy regarding the postvention needs of African American suicide survivors. *Pastoral Psychology.* Published online: 29 November 2013. doi: 10.1007/s11089-013-0581-1.

de Groot M (2013). Course of bereavement over 8-10 years in first degree relatives and spouses of people who committed suicide: Longitudinal community based cohort study. *British Medical Journal* 347, F6649.

Dickens N (2014). Prevalence of complicated grief and posttraumatic stress disorder in children and adolescents following sibling death. *Family Journal* 22, 119-126.

Gall TL, Henneberry J, Eyre M (2014). Two perspectives on the needs of individuals bereaved by suicide. *Death Studies.* Published online: 13 November 2013. doi: 10.1080/07481187.2013.772928.

Goodwin-Smith I, Hicks N, Hawke M, Alver G, Raftery P (2013). Living beyond Aboriginal suicide: Developing a culturally appropriate and accessible suicide postvention service for aboriginal communities in South Australia. *Advances in Mental Health* 11, 238-245.

Jackson D, Peters K, Murphy G (2014). Suicide of a close family member through the eyes of a child: A narrative case study report. *Journal of Child Health Care.* Published online: 31 January 2014. doi: 10.1177/1367493513519297.

Jacobs AS (2013). A crisis in counseling: Questioning the role of crisis counselors within police departments. *Health Communication.* Published online: 30 October 2013. doi: 10.1080/10410236.2013.796437.

Kaplow JB, Howell KH, Layne CM (2014). Do circumstances of the death matter? Identifying socioenvironmental risks for grief-related psychopathology in bereaved youth. *Journal of Traumatic Stress* 27, 42-49.

Kola V, Kola E, Petrela E, Zaimi E (2013). Trends of attempted suicide in Albanian children and adolescents. *Archives of Psychiatry and Psychotherapy* 15, 39-44.

Lachter B (2013). The stress of work, with bonus vaudeville section. *Australasian Psychiatry* 21, 486-489.

Ljung T, Sandin S, Langstrom N, Runeson B, Lichtenstein P, Larsson H (2013). Offspring death and subsequent psychiatric morbidity in bereaved parents: Addressing mechanisms in a total population cohort. *Psychological Medicine*. Published online: 1 November 2013. doi: 10.1017/S0033291713002572.

McKay K, Tighe J (2013). Talking through the dead: The impact and interplay of lived grief after suicide. *OMEGA* 68, 111-121.

Pitman A, Osborn D, King M (2014). Suicide bereavement and risk for suicide attempt: A national cross-sectional survey of young adults. *The Lancet* 383, s82.

Pompili M, Shrivastava A, Serafini G, Innamorati M, Milelli M, Erbuto D, Ricci F, Lamis DA, Scocco P, Amore M, Lester D, Girardi P (2013). Bereavement after the suicide of a significant other. *Indian Journal of Psychiatry* 55, 256-263.

Powell KA, Matthys A (2013). Effects of suicide on siblings: Uncertainty and the grief process. *Journal of Family Communication* 13, 321-339.

Rostila M, Saarela J, Kawachi I (2013). "The psychological skeleton in the closet": Mortality after a sibling's suicide. *Social Psychiatry and Psychiatric Epidemiology*. Published online: 15 October 2013. doi: 10.1007/s00127-013-0780-1.

Ryan M, Giljohann A (2013). 'I needed to know': Imparting graphic and distressing details about a suicide to the bereaved. *Bereavement Care* 32, 111-116.

Ryan M, Lister R, Flynn L (2013). Giving voice to those bereaved by suicide: The 'nothing prepared me for this' project1. *Advances in Mental Health* 11, 213-222.

Saindon C, Rheingold AA, Baddeley J, Wallace MM, Brown C, Rynearson EK (2014). Restorative retelling for violent loss: An open clinical trial. *Death Studies* 38, 251-258 .

Salska A, Plesiewicz I, Zieli ska M, Chizy ski K (2013). A family member suicide causes "broken heart syndrome" - two cases of the tako-tsubo cardiomyopathy. *Archives of Psychiatry and Psychotherapy* 15, 27-29.

Schotanus-Dijkstra M, Havinga P, van Ballegooijen W, Delfosse L, Mokkenstorm J, Boon B (2013). What do the bereaved by suicide communicate in online support groups? *Crisis* 35, 27-35.

Skehan J, Maple M, Fisher J, Sharrock G (2013). Suicide bereavement and the media: A qualitative study. *Advances in Mental Health* 11, 223-237.

Visser VS, Comans TA, Scuffham PA (2014). Evaluation of the effectiveness of a community-based crisis intervention program for people bereaved by suicide. *Journal of Community Psychology* 42, 19-28 .

Xu G, Li N (2014). A comparison study on mental health status between suicide survivors and survivors of accidental deaths in rural China. *Journal of Psychiatric and Mental Health Nursing*. Published online: 20 March 2014. doi: 10.1111/jpm.12147.

NON FATAL SUICIDAL BEHAVIOR

Epidemiology

Allroggen M, Kleinrahm R, Rau TAD, Weninger L, Ludolph AG, Plener PL (2014). Nonsuicidal self-injury and its relation to personality traits in medical students. *Journal of Nervous and Mental Disease* 202, 300-304.

Althaus F, Stucki S, Guyot S, Trueb L, Moschetti K, Daeppen J-B, Bodenmann P (2013). Characteristics of highly frequent users of a swiss academic emergency department: A retrospective consecutive case series. *European Journal of Emergency Medicine* 20, 413-419.

Alves VdM, Silva AMSd, Magalhaes APNd, Andrade TGd, Faro ACMe, Nardi AE (2014). Suicide attempts in a emergency hospital. *Arquivos de Neuro-Psiquiatria* 72, 123-128.

Ansari-Moghaddam A, Baghbanian A, Dogoonchi M, Chooban B, Mostaghim-Roudi M, Torkfar G (2013). Epidemiology of burn injuries in south-eastern Iran: A retrospective study. *Journal of the Pakistan Medical Association* 63, 1476-1481.

Bammigatti C, Surynarayana Bs, Harichandra Kumar Kt, Ganesh Kumar S (2013). Pattern and outcome of cleistanthus collinus (Oduvanthalai) poisoning in a tertiary care teaching hospital in south India. *Journal of Forensic and Legal Medicine* 20, 959-961.

Banerjee S, Chowdhury AN, Schelling E, Weiss MG (2013). Household survey of pesticide practice, deliberate self-harm, and suicide in the sundarban region of West Bengal, India. *BioMed Research International.* Published online: 30 July 2013. doi: 10.1155/2013/949076.

Bhola P, Rekha DP, Sathyanarayanan V, Daniel S, Thomas T (2013). Self-reported suicidality and its predictors among adolescents from a pre-university college in Bangalore, India. *Asian Journal of Psychiatry* 7, 38-45.

Bolton S-L, Elias B, Enns MW, Sareen J, Beals J, Novins DK, Prevention Team TSCS, Team TA-S (2013). A comparison of the prevalence and risk factors of suicidal ideation and suicide attempts in two American Indian and a general population sample. *Transcultural Psychiatry* 51, 3-22.

Bryan C, Bryan A (2014). Nonsuicidal self-injury among a sample of United States military personnel and veterans enrolled in college classes. *Journal of Clinical Psychology.* Published online: 11 March 2014. doi: 10.1002/jclp.22075.

Calcaterra SL, Beaty B, Mueller SR, Min S-J, Binswanger IA (2014). The association between social stressors and drug use/hazardous drinking among former prison inmates. *Journal of Substance Abuse Treatment.* Published online: 1 March 2014. doi: 10.1016/j.jsat.2014.02.002.

Carroll R, Benger J, Bramley K, Williams S, Griffin L, Potokar J, Gunnell D (2013). Epidemiology, management and outcome of paracetamol poisoning in an inner city emergency department. *Emergency Medicine Journal.* Published online: 7 October 2013. doi: 10.1136/emermed-2013-202518.

Carter MW, Reymann MR (2014). ED use by older adults attempting suicide. *American Journal of Emergency Medicine.* Published online: 10 February 2014. doi: 10.1016/j.ajem.2014.02.003.

Chakravarthy B, Toohey S, Rezaimehr Y, Anderson CL, Hoonpongsimanont W, Menchine M, Lotfipour S (2014). National differences between ED and ambulatory visits for suicidal ideation and attempts and depression. *American Journal of Emergency Medicine.* Published online: 26 December 2012. doi: 10.1016/j.ajem.2013.12.044.

Choi JH, Kim SH, Kim SP, Jung KY, Ryu JY, Choi SC, Park IC (2014). Characteristics of intentional fall injuries in the ED. *American Journal of Emergency Medicine.* Published online: 4 February 2014. doi: 10.1016/j.ajem.2014.01.053.

Cuypers PJV, Danckaerts M, Sabbe M, Demyttenaere K, Bruffaerts R (2013). The paediatric psychiatric emergency population in a university teaching hospital in Belgium (2003-2008). *European Journal of Emergency Medicine*. Published online: 27 November 2013. doi: 10.1097/MEJ.0000000000000096.

Deans AK, Boerma CJ, Fordyce J, De Souza M, Palmer DJ, Davis JS (2013). Use of Royal Darwin Hospital emergency department by immigration detainees in 2011. *Medical Journal of Australia* 199, 776-778.

Dickens G, Picchioni M, Long C (2013). Aggression in specialist secure and forensic inpatient mental health care: Incidence across care pathways. *Journal of Forensic Practice* 15, 206-217.

Eskin M, Palova E, Krokavcova M (2013). Suicidal behavior and attitudes in Slovak and Turkish high school students: A cross-cultural investigation. *Archives of Suicide Research* 18, 58-73.

Evren C, Evren B, Bozkurt M, Can Y (2014). Non-suicidal self-harm behavior within the previous year among 10th-grade adolescents in Istanbul and related variables. *Nordic Journal of Psychiatry*. Published online: 24 January 2014. doi: 10.3109/08039488.2013.872699.

Fanning JR, Pietrzak RH (2013). Suicidality among older male veterans in the United States: Results from the national health and resilience in veterans study. *Journal of Psychiatric Research* 47, 1766-1775.

Gilyoma JM, Hauli KA, Chalya PL (2014). Cut throat injuries at a university teaching hospital in northwestern Tanzania: A review of 98 cases. *BMC Emergency Medicine* 14, 1.

Gmitrowicz A, Zalewska-Janowska A, Kropiwnicki P, Kostulski A (2013). Cutaneous deliberate self-harm in Polish school teenagers: An inter-disciplinary challenge. *Acta Dermato-venereologica*. Published online: 6 November 2013. doi: 10.2340/00015555-1690.

Gojd K, Bak-Sosnowska M, Kołodziej S, Skrzypulec-Plinta V (2013). Quality of life of female physicians aged 45-55 years. *Przeglad Menopauzalny* 17, 213-215.

Guo Y, Wang J, Yu Y, Ahmed NI, Ma Y, Tang J (2013). Association of aggression and non-suicidal self injury: A school-based sample of adolescents. *PLoS ONE* 8, e78149.

Hawton K, Linsell L, Adeniji T, Sariaslan A, Fazel S (2013). Self-harm in prisons in England and Wales: An epidemiological study of prevalence, risk factors, clustering, and subsequent suicide. *The Lancet* 383, 1147-1154.

Hawton K, Saunders K, Topiwala A, Haw C (2013). Psychiatric disorders in patients presenting to hospital following self-harm: A systematic review. *Journal of Affective Disorders* 151, 821-830.

Holden KB, Bradford LD, Hall SP, Belton AS (2013). Prevalence and correlates of depressive symptoms and resiliency among African American women in a community-based primary health care center. *Journal of Health Care for the Poor and Underserved* 24, 79-93.

Hoodin F, Zhao L, Carey J, Levine JE, Kitko C (2013). Impact of psychological screening on routine outpatient care of hematopoietic cell transplantation survivors. *Biology of Blood and Marrow Transplantation* 19, 1493-1497.

Jang H-S, Kim J-Y, Choi S-H, Yoon Y-H, Moon S-W, Hong Y-S, Lee S-W (2013). Comparative analysis of acute toxic poisoning in 2003 and 2011: Analysis of 3 academic hospitals. *Journal of Korean Medical Science* 28, 1424-1430.

Jeon HJ, Walker RS, Inamori A, Hong JP, Cho MJ, Baer L, Clain A, Fava M, Mischoulon D (2013). Differences in depressive symptoms between Korean and American outpatients with major depressive disorder. *International Clinical Psychopharmacology*. Published online: 29 May 2014. doi: 10.1097/YIC.0000000000000019.

Joe S, Ford BC, Taylor RJ, Chatters LM (2013). Prevalence of suicide ideation and attempts among black Americans in later life. *Transcultural Psychiatry*. Published online: 9 October 2013. doi:10.1177/1363461513503381.

Jureidini J, Tonkin A, Jureidini E (2013). Combination pharmacotherapy for psychiatric disorders in children and adolescents: Prevalence, efficacy, risks and research needs. *Pediatric Drugs* 15, 377-391.

Kang HJ, Stewart R, Jeong BO, Kim SY, Bae KY, Kim SW, Kim JM, Shin IS, Yoon JS (2013). Suicidal ideation in elderly Korean population: A two-year longitudinal study. *International Psychogeriatrics* 26, 59-67.

Kati C, Karakus A, Altunta M, Duran L, Ilkaya F, Kaya C, Alaçam H, Yavuz Y (2013). Evaluation of acute poisonings in geriatric patients attended to a university emergency clinic. *Turk Geriatri Dergisi* 16, 286-291.

Kennedy JL, Altar CA, Taylor DL, Degtiar I, Hornberger JC (2014). The social and economic burden of treatment-resistant schizophrenia: A systematic literature review. *International Clinical Psychopharmacology* 29, 63-76.

Klaas SJ, Kelly EH, Anderson CJ, Vogel LC (2014). Depression and anxiety in adolescents with pediatric-onset spinal cord injury. *Topics in Spinal Cord Injury Rehabilitation* 20, 13-22.

Kola V, Kola E, Petrela E, Zaimi E (2013). Trends of attempted suicide in Albanian children and adolescents. *Archives of Psychiatry and Psychotherapy* 15, 39-44.

Koylu R, Dundar ZD, Koylu O, Akinci E, Akilli NB, Gonen MO, Cander B (2014). The experiences in a toxicology unit: A review of 623 cases. *Journal of Clinical Medicine Research* 6, 59-65.

Liu Y, Lee RB (2013). Prevalence and associated factors of suicide ideaton among university students: Evidence from large-scale surveys. *Asia-Pacific Social Science Review* 13, 79-86.

Loh C, Teo YW, Lim L (2013). Deliberate self-harm in adolescent psychiatric outpatients in Singapore: Prevalence and associated risk factors. *Singapore Medical Journal* 54, 491-495.

Masoumi G, Ganjei Z, Teymoori E, Sabzghabaee AM, Yaraghi A, Akabri M, Eizadi-Mood N (2013). Evaluating the prevalence of intentional and unintentional poisoning in vulnerable patients admitted to a referral hospital. *Journal of Isfahan Medical School* 31, 1452-1460.

McKibben JB, Fullerton CS, Herberman Mash HB, Nock MK, Naifeh JA, Kessler RC, Stein MB, Ursano RJ (2013). Suicidal behaviors and the use of mental health services among active duty army soldiers. *Psychiatric Services* 65, 374-380.

McMahon A, Brohan J, Donnelly M, Fitzpatrick GJ (2013). Characteristics of patients admitted to the intensive care unit following self-poisoning and their impact on resource utilisation. *Irish Journal of Medical Science.* Published online: 8 October 2013. doi: 10.1007/s11845-013-1026-7.

Mohseni Saravi B, Kabirzadeh A, Asghari Z, Reza Zadeh I, Bagherian Farahabbadi E, Siamian H (2013). Prevalence of non-drug poisoning in patients admitted to hospitals of Mazandaran University of Medical Sciences, 2010-2011. *Acta Informatica Medica* 21, 192-195.

Muula AS, Siziya S, Rudatsikira E (2013). Self-inflicted serious injuries among adolescents in Zambia. *Tanzania Journal of Health Research* 15, 1-8.

Najavits L, Lung J, Froias A, Paull N, Bailey G (2013). A study of multiple behavioral addictions in a substance abuse sample. *Substance Use and Misuse* 49, 479-484.

Netto LR, Cavalcanti-Ribeiro P, Pereira JL, Nogueira JF, Santos LL, Lira SB, Guedes GM, Teles CA, UFBA TADSG, Koenen KC, Quarantini LC (2013). Clinical and socio-demographic characteristics of college students exposed to traumatic experiences: A census of seven college institutions in northeastern Brazil. *PLoS ONE* 8, e78677.

Nguyen DT, Dedding C, Pham TT, Bunders J (2013). Perspectives of pupils, parents, and teachers on mental health problems among vietnamese secondary school pupils. *BMC Public Health* 13, 1046.

Nguyen DT, Dedding C, Pham TT, Wright P, Bunders J (2013). Depression, anxiety, and suicidal ideation among Vietnamese secondary school students and proposed solutions: A cross-sectional study. *BMC Public Health* 13, 1195.

O'Neill S, Ferry F, Murphy S, Corry C, Bolton D, Devine B, Ennis E, Bunting B (2014). Patterns of suicidal ideation and behavior in northern Ireland and associations with conflict related trauma. *PLoS ONE* 9, e91532.

Özenir M, Selçuk Duru N, Elevli M, Karaku A, Çivilibal M (2013). The familial factors and demographic characteristics of children with drug poisoning. *Haseki Tip Bulteni* 51, 157-161.

Padmakumar K, Maheshkrishna BG, Jaghadheeswararaj J, Natarajan A (2013). Incidence of poisoning reported at a tertiary care hospital. *Journal of South India Medicolegal Association* 5, 58-62.

Page RM, Saumweber J, Hall PC, Crookston BT, West JH (2013). Multi-country, cross-national comparison of youth suicide ideation: Findings from global school-based health surveys. *School Psychology International* 34, 540-555.

Pérez Fominaya M, de Leon-Martinez V, Garcia-Nieto R, Díaz de Neira M, Carballo JJ, Baca-Garcia E (2013). Prevalence and functions of self-injurious thoughts and behaviors in a sample of Spanish adolescents assessed in mental health outpatient departments. *Revista de Psiquiatría y Salud Mental.* Published online: 6 November 2013. doi: 10.1016/j.rpsm.2013.09.003.

Pisetsky EM, Thornton LM, Lichtenstein P, Pedersen NL, Bulik CM (2013). Suicide attempts in women with eating disorders. *Journal of Abnormal Psychology* 122, 1042-1056.

Pratt LA, Brody DJ (2013). Implications of two-stage depression screening for identifying persons with thoughts of self-harm. *General Hospital Psychiatry* 36, 119-1123.

Rakofsky JJ, Schettler PJ, Kinkead BL, Frank E, Judd LL, Kupfer DJ, Rush AJ, Thase ME, Yonkers KA, Rapaport MH (2013). The prevalence and severity of depressive symptoms along the spectrum of unipolar depressive disorders: A post hoc analysis. *Journal of Clinical Psychiatry* 74, 1084-1091.

Rosta J, Aasland OG (2014). Correction: Changes in the lifetime prevalence of suicidal feelings and thoughts among Norwegian doctors from 2000 to 2010: A longitudinal study based on national samples. *BMC Psychiatry* 14, 1.

Sansone RA, Sansone LA (2013). Preventing wounds from healing: Clinical prevalence and relationship to borderline personality. *Innovations in Clinical Neuroscience* 10, 23-27.

Schwartz S, Correll CU (2014). Efficacy and safety of atomoxetine in children and adolescents with attention-deficit/hyperactivity disorder: Results from a comprehensive meta-analysis and metaregression. *Journal of the American Academy of Child and Adolescent Psychiatry* 53, 174-187.

Sepehrmanesh Z, Ahmadvand A, Akkasheh G, Saei R (2014). Prevalence of psychiatric disorders and related factors in male prisoners. *Iranian Red Crescent Medical Journal* 16, e15205.

Shadnia S, Rahimi M, Hassanian-Moghaddam H, Soltaninejad K, Noroozi A (2013). Methadone toxicity: Comparing tablet and syrup formulations during a decade in an academic poison center of Iran. *Clinical Toxicology* 51, 777-782.

Shellman L, Beckstrand RL, Callister LC, Luthy KE, Freeborn D (2013). Postpartum depression in immigrant Hispanic women: A comparative community sample. *Journal of the American Association of Nurse Practitioners.* Published online: 25 November 2013. doi: 10.1002/2327-6924.12088.

Shilubane HN, Ruiter RA, van den Borne B, Sewpaul R, James S, Reddy PS (2013). Suicide and related health risk behaviours among school learners in South Africa: Results from the 2002 and 2008 national youth risk behaviour surveys. *BMC Public Health* 13, 926.

Singh B (2013). Profile of acute poisoning by agricultural and horticultural chemicals in ICU, at Pravara rural medical college, Loni. *Pravara Medical Review* 5, 4-7.

Stallard P, Spears M, Montgomery AA, Phillips R, Sayal K (2013). Self-harm in young adolescents (12—16 years): Onset and short-term continuation in a community sample. *BMC Psychiatry* 13, 328.

Suokas JT, Suvisaari JM, Grainger M, Raevuori A, Gissler M, Haukka J (2014). Suicide attempts and mortality in eating disorders: A follow-up study of eating disorder patients. *General Hospital Psychiatry.* Published online: 13 January 2014. doi: 10.1016/j.genhosppsych.2014.01.002.

Swannell SV, Martin GE, Page A, Hasking P, St John NJ (2014). Prevalence of nonsuicidal self-injury in nonclinical samples: Systematic review, meta-analysis and meta-regression. *Suicide and Life-Threatening Behavior.* Published online: 15 January 2014. doi: 10.1111/sltb.12070.

Takeuchi T, Nakao M (2013). The relationship between suicidal ideation and symptoms of depression in Japanese workers: A cross-sectional study. *British Medical Journal Open* 3, e003643.

Taussig HN, Harpin SB, Maguire SA (2014). Suicidality among preadolescent maltreated children in foster care. *Child Maltreatment.* Published online: 24 February 2014. doi:10.1177/1077559514525503.

Urban M, Navrátil T, Pelclová D (2013). Trends in cns affecting drugs in the calls to the toxicological information center from 1997 to 2012. *Neuroendocrinology Letters* 34, 25-30.

Viner R, Patten SB, Berzins S, Bulloch AGM, Fiest KM (2014). Prevalence and risk factors for suicidal ideation in a multiple sclerosis population. *Journal of Psychosomatic Research* 76, 312-316.

Yu SS, Sung HE, Mellow J, Shlosberg A (2013). Prevalence and correlates of suicidal ideation among parolees. *Psychiatric Services* 65, 381-386.

Zanone Poma S, Vicentini S, Siviero F, Grossi A, Toniolo E, Cocchio S, Baldo V, De Leo D (2014). Life span history of non-fatal suicidal behaviours in a large sample of general practitioners' patients: Data from Rovigo, northern Italy. *Community Mental Health Journal.* Published online: 22 February 2014. doi: 10.1007/s10597-014-9715-x.

Zhang J, Sun L (2014). Suicide ideation and acceptability among females aged 15 to 34 years in rural China. *Journal of Nervous and Mental Disease* 202, 161-166.

Risk and protective factors

Acun P, Yilmaz I, Denizliolu B, Demirta Y, Aksay E (2013). Demographic characteristics of patients, who attempted suicide with paracetamol in a research hospital. *Duzce Medical Journal* 15, 33-36.

Adeosun II, Jeje O (2013). Symptom profile and severity in a sample of Nigerians with psychotic versus nonpsychotic major depression. *Depression Research and Treatment* 2013, Article ID 815456.

Akdemir D, Zeki A, Ünal DY, Kara M, Çuhadarolu Çetin F (2013). Identity status and self-esteem in adolescents with non-suicidal self-injurious behavior. *Anadolu Psikiyatri Dergisi* 14, 69-76.

Allan NP, Capron DW, Raines AM, Schmidt NB (2014). Unique relations among anxiety sensitivity factors and anxiety, depression, and suicidal ideation. *Journal of Anxiety Disorders* 28, 266-275.

Angkaw AC, Ross BS, Pittman JOE, Kelada AMY, Valencerina MAM, Baker DG (2013). Post-traumatic stress disorder, depression, and aggression in OEF/OIF veterans. *Military Medicine* 178, 1044-1050.

Anikeeva O, Bi P, Hiller JE, Ryan P, Roder D, Han GS (2014). Trends in migrant mortality rates in Australia 1981-2007: A focus on the national health priority areas other than cancer. *Ethnicity and Health*. Published online: 6 February 2014. doi: 10.1080/13557858.2014.883368.

Annerback EM, Sahlqvist L, Wingren G (2013). A cross-sectional study of victimisation of bullying among schoolchildren in Sweden: Background factors and self-reported health complaints. *Scandinavian Journal of Public Health*. Published online: 5 December 2013. doi: 10.1177/1403494813514142.

Anthenelli RM, Morris C, Ramey TS, Dubrava SJ, Tsilkos K, Russ C, Yunis C (2013). Effects of varenicline on smoking cessation in adults with stably treated current or past major depression: A randomized trial. *Annals of Internal Medicine* 159, 390-400.

Apfelbaum S, Regalado P, Herman L, Teitelbaum J, Gagliesi P (2013). Comorbidity between bipolar disorder and cluster b personality disorders as indicator of affective dysregulation and clinical severity. *Actas Espanolas De Psiquiatria* 41, 269-278.

Arias ACA, Bruce A, Herrán D, Arango AM, Muñoz K, Abella P (2013). Variables associated with the risk of suicide in patients with chronic pain seen in a hospital outpatient clinic in Bogotá. *Revista Colombiana de Anestesiologia* 41, 267-273.

Armstrong LL, Manion IG (2013). Meaningful youth engagement as a protective factor for youth suicidal ideation. *Journal of Research on Adolescence*, Published online: 23 November 2013. doi: 10.1111/jora.12098.

Asbridge M, Azagba S, Langille DB, Rasic D (2014). Elevated depressive symptoms and adolescent injury: Examining associations by injury frequency, injury type, and gender. *BMC Public Health* 14, 190.

Assari S, Moghani Lankarani M, Moghani Lankarani R (2013). Ethnicity modifies the additive effects of anxiety and drug use disorders on suicidal ideation among black adults in the United States. *International Journal of Preventive Medicine* 4, 1151-1157.

Austad G, Joa I, Johannessen JO, Larsen TK (2013). Gender differences in suicidal behaviour in patients with first-episode psychosis. *Early Intervention in Psychiatry*. Published online: 5 December 2013. doi: 10.1111/eip.12113.

Ayub M, Mushtaq I, Mushtaq S, Hafeez MA, Helal N, Irfan M, Hassan B, Tiffin P, Naeem F (2013). Domestic violence, mental illness and suicidal ideation - a study from Lahore, Pakistan. *Journal of Mental Health* 22, 474-481.

Bani-Fatemi A, Polsinelli G, Kennedy J, De Luca V (2013). Ethnicity and suicide attempt: Analysis in bipolar disorder and schizophrenia. *BMC Psychiatry* 13, 252.

Barbosa LP, Quevedo L, da Silva GDG, Jansen K, Pinheiro RT, Branco J, Lara D, Oses J, da Silva RA (2014). Childhood trauma and suicide risk in a sample of young individuals aged 14-35 years in southern Brazil. *Child Abuse and Neglect.* Published online: 12 March 2014. doi: 10.1016/j.chiabu.2014.02.008.

Barton JJ, Meade T, Cumming S, Samuels A (2013). Suicide attempts and deliberate self harm in a substance abusing inmate population. *Drug and Alcohol Review* 32, 24-25.

Bauer RL, Chesin MS, Jeglic EL (2013). Depression, delinquency, and suicidal behaviors among college students. *Crisis* 35, 36-41.

Bedi R, Muller RT, Classen CC (2013). Cumulative risk for deliberate self-harm among treatment-seeking women with histories of childhood abuse. *Psychological Trauma: Theory, Research, Practice, and Policy* ,

Bersani FS, Corazza O, Simonato P, Mylokosta A, Levari E, Lovaste R, Schifano F (2013). Drops of madness? Recreational misuse of tropicamide collyrium; early warning alerts from Russia and Italy. *General Hospital Psychiatry* 35, 571-573.

Błazek M, Kazmierczak M, Besta T (2014). Sense of purpose in life and escape from self as the predictors of quality of life in clinical samples. *Journal of Religion and Health.* Published online: 14 February 2014. doi: 10.1007/s10943-014-9833-3.

Blüml V, Kapusta ND, Doering S, Brähler E, Wagner B, Kersting A (2013). Personality factors and suicide risk in a representative sample of the German general population. *PLoS ONE.* Published online: 4 October 2013. doi: 10.1371/journal.pone.0076646.

Bossarte RM, Blosnich JR, Piegari RI, Hill LL, Kane V (2013). Housing instability and mental distress among U.S. Veterans. *American Journal of Public Health* 103, S213-S216.

Brabant M-E, Hébert M, Chagnon F (2014). Predicting suicidal ideations in sexually abused female adolescents: A 12-month prospective study. *Journal of Child Sexual Abuse.* Published online: 18 March 2014. doi: 10.1080/10538712.2014.896842.

Bracken-Minor KL, McDevitt-Murphy ME (2013). Differences in features of non-suicidal self-injury according to borderline personality disorder screening status. *Archives of Suicide Research* 18, 88-103.

Bresin K (2013). Five indices of emotion regulation in participants with a history of nonsuicidal self-injury: A daily diary study. *Behavior Therapy* 45, 56-66.

Brinkman TM, Zhang N, Recklitis CJ, Kimberg C, Zeltzer LK, Muriel AC, Stovall M, Srivastava DK, Sklar CA, Robison LL, Krull KR (2013). Suicide ideation and associated mortality in adult survivors of childhood cancer. *Cancer* 20, 271-277.

Brunner R, Kaess M, Parzer P, Fischer G, Carli V, Hoven CW, Wasserman C, Sarchiapone M, Resch F, Apter A, Balazs J, Barzilay S, Bobes J, Corcoran P, Cosmanm D, Haring C, Iosuec M, Kahn JP, Keeley H, Meszaros G, Nemes B, Podlogar T, Postuvan V, Saiz PA, Sisask M, Tubiana A, Varnik A, Wasserman D (2013). Life-time prevalence and psychosocial correlates of adolescent direct self-injurious behavior: A comparative study of findings in 11 European countries. *Journal of Child Psychology and Psychiatry* 55, 337-348.

Bucchianeri MM, Eisenberg ME, Wall MM, Piran N, Neumark-Sztainer D (2014). Multiple types of harassment: Associations with emotional well-being and unhealthy behaviors in adolescents. *Journal of Adolescent Health.* Published online: 24 December 2013. doi: 10.1016/j.jadohealth.2013.10.205.

Bunevicius R, Liaugaudaite V, Peceliuniene J, Raskauskiene N, Bunevicius A, Mickuviene N (2014). Factors affecting the presence of depression, anxiety disorders, and suicidal ideation in patients attending primary health care service in Lithuania. *Scandinavian Journal of Primary Health Care* 32, 24-29.

Caci HM, Morin AJS, Tran A (2014). Prevalence and correlates of attention deficit hyperactivity disorder in adults from a French community sample. *Journal of Nervous and Mental Disease* 202, 324-332.

Calandre EP, Navajas-Rojas MA, Ballesteros J, Garcia-Carrillo J, Garcia-Leiva JM, Rico-Villademoros F (2014). Suicidal ideation in patients with fibromyalgia: A cross-sectional study. *Pain Practice.* Published online: 17 January 2014. doi: 10.1111/papr.12164.

Capron DW, Allan NP, Norr AM, Zvolensky MJ, Schmidt NB (2014). The effect of successful and unsuccessful smoking cessation on short-term anxiety, depression, and suicidality. *Addictive Behaviors* 39, 782-788.

Cardwell JM, Lewis EG, Smith KC, Holt ER, Baillie S, Allister R, Adams VJ (2013). A cross-sectional study of mental health in UK veterinary undergraduates. *The Veterinary Record* 173, 266.

Carroll D, Hallett V, McDougle CJ, Aman MG, McCracken JT, Tierney E, Arnold LE, Sukhodolsky DG, Lecavalier L, Handen BL, Swiezy N, Johnson C, Bearss K, Vitiello B, Scahill L (2014). Examination of aggression and self-injury in children with autism spectrum disorders and serious behavioral problems. *Child and Adolescent Psychiatric Clinics of North America* 23, 57.

Cederbaum JA, Gilreath TD, Benbenishty R, Astor RA, Pineda D, DePedro KT, Esqueda MC, Atuel H (2013). Well-being and suicidal ideation of secondary school students from military families. *Journal of Adolescent Health.* Published online: 7 November 2013. doi: 10.1016/j.jadohealth.2013.09.006.

Chakravorty S, Grandner MA, Mavandadi S, Perlis ML, Sturgis EB, Oslin DW (2013). Suicidal ideation in veterans misusing alcohol: Relationships with insomnia symptoms and sleep duration. *Addictive Behaviors* 39, 399-405.

Chang SS, Chen YY, Heron J, Kidger J, Lewis G, Gunnell D (2013). IQ and adolescent self-harm behaviours in the ALSPAC birth cohort. *Journal of Affective Disorders* 152-154, 175-182.

Chen J, Cai Y, Cong E, Liu Y, Gao J, Li Y, Tao M, Zhang K, Wang X, Gao C, Yang L, Li K, Shi J, Wang G, Liu L, Zhang J, Du B, Jiang G, Shen J, Zhang Z, Liang W, Sun J, Hu J, Liu T, Wang X, Miao G, Meng H, Li Y, Hu C, Huang G, Li G, Ha B, Deng H, Mei Q, Zhong H, Gao S, Sang H, Zhang Y, Fang X, Yu F, Yang D, Liu T, Chen Y, Hong X, Wu W, Chen G, Cai M, Song Y, Pan J, Dong J, Pan R, Zhang W, Shen Z, Liu Z, Gu D, Wang X, Liu X, Zhang Q, Li Y, Chen Y, Kendler KS, Shi S, Flint J (2014). Childhood sexual abuse and the development of recurrent major depression in Chinese women. *PLoS ONE* 9, e87569.

Chen XR, Kuang L, Cao J, Ai M, Chen JM, Wang W, Niu YJ, Phillips MR (2014). Correlation of suicidal ideation with social support and quality of life among college students. *Academic Journal of Second Military Medical University* 35, 74-78.

Chesin MS, Moster AN, Jeglic EL (2013). Non-suicidal self-injury among ethnically and racially diverse emerging adults: Do factors unique to the minority experience matter? *Current Psychology* 32, 318-328.

Choi Y-N, Kim Y-A, Yun YH, Kim S, Bae J-M, Kim Y-W, Ryu KW, Lee JH, Noh J-H, Sohn T-S (2013). Suicide ideation in stomach cancer survivors and possible risk factors. *Supportive Care in Cancer* 22, 331-337.

Chun S, Reid EA, Yun M (2013). The association of alcohol drinking pattern and self-inflicted intentional injury in Korea: A cross-sectional who collaborative emergency room study. *British Medical Journal Open* 3, e002469.

Chung MS, Chiu HJ, Sun WJ, Lin CN, Kuo CC, Huang WC, Chen YS, Cheng HP, Chou P (2013). Association among depressive disorder, adjustment disorder, sleep disturbance, and suicidal ideation in Taiwanese adolescent. *Asia-Pacific Psychiatry.* Published online: 3 December 2013. doi: 10.1111/appy.12112.

Ciuhodaru T, Romedea SN, Iorga M (2013). Study on characteristics of patients with suicide attempt, near-lethal harm and deliberate suicide. *Procedia - Social and Behavioral Sciences* 84, 321-326.

Claes L, Luyckx K, Bijttebier P (2014). Non-suicidal self-injury in adolescents: Prevalence and associations with identity formation above and beyond depression. *Personality and Individual Differences* 61-62, 101-104.

Claes L, Muehlenkamp J (2013). The relationship between the UPPS-P impulsivity dimensions and nonsuicidal self-injury characteristics in male and female high-school students. *Psychiatry Journal* 2013, 654847.

Claes L, Norré J, Van Assche L, Bijttebier P (2013). Non-suicidal self-injury (functions) in eating disorders: Associations with reactive and regulative temperament. *Personality and Individual Differences* 57, 65-69.

Coughlan H, Tiedt L, Clarke M, Kelleher I, Tabish J, Molloy C, Harley M, Cannon M (2014). Prevalence of DSM-IV mental disorders, deliberate self-harm and suicidal ideation in early adolescence: An Irish population-based study. *Journal of Adolescence* 37, 1-9.

Courtney-Seidler EA, Klein D, Miller AL (2013). Borderline personality disorder in adolescents. *Clinical Psychology-Science and Practice* 20, 425-444.

Crane C, Barnhofer T, Duggan DS, Eames C, Hepburn S, Shah D, Williams JMG (2013). Comfort from suicidal cognition in recurrently depressed patients. *Journal of Affective Disorders* 155, 241-246.

D'Onofrio BM, Class QA, Rickert ME, Larsson H, Langstrom N, Lichtenstein P (2013). Preterm birth and mortality and morbidity: A population-based quasi-experimental study. *JAMA Psychiatry* 70, 1231-1240.

Dallos G, Keresztény A, Miklósi M, Bals J, Gádoros J (2013). Attention-deficit hyperactivity disorder and suicidality in a treatment naïve sample of children and adolescents. *Journal of Affective Disorders* 152-154, 282-287.

Davis MT, Witte TK, Weathers FW (2013). Posttraumatic stress disorder and suicidal ideation: The role of specific symptoms within the framework of the interpersonal-psychological theory of suicide. *Psychological Trauma: Theory, Research, Practice, and Policy*. Published online: 14 October 2013. doi: 10.1037/a0033941.

De Genna NM, Feske U (2013). Phenomenology of borderline personality disorder: The role of race and socioeconomic status. *The Journal of Nervous and Mental Disease* 201, 1027-1034.

Debeer BB, Kimbrel NA, Meyer EC, Gulliver SB, Morissette SB (2014). Combined PTSD and depressive symptoms interact with post-deployment social support to predict suicidal ideation in operation enduring freedom and operation Iraqi freedom veterans. *Psychiatry Research* 216, 357-362.

Deeley ST, Love AW (2013). Longitudinal analysis of the emotion self-confidence model of suicidal ideation in adolescents. *Advances in Mental Health* 12, 34-45.

Deshpande SS, Kalmegh B, Patil PN, Ghate MR, Sarmukaddam S, Paralikar VP (2014). Stresses and disability in depression across gender. *Depression Research and Treatment* 2014, 735307.

Duncan DT, Hatzenbuehler ML (2014). Lesbian, gay, bisexual, and transgender hate crimes and suicidality among a population-based sample of sexual-minority adolescents in Boston. *American Journal of Public Health* 104, 272-278.

Dyrbye LN, West CP, Satele D, Boone S, Tan L, Sloan J, Shanafelt TD (2014). Burnout among U.S. Medical students, residents, and early career physicians relative to the general U.S. Population. *Academic Medicine* 89, 443-451.

Eisenberg D, Golberstein E, Whitlock JL (2014). Peer effects on risky behaviors: New evidence from college roommate assignments. *Journal of Health Economics* 33, 126-138.

Erchull MJ, Liss M, Lichiello S (2013). Extending the negative consequences of media internalization and self-objectification to dissociation and self-harm. *Sex Roles* 69, 583-593.

Erdem Ö, Kara IH, Ayyildiz O (2013). The analysis of relationship between suicide attempt and the level of serum lipid. *Duzce Medical Journal* 15, 41-45.

Eskin M (2013). The effects of individualistic-collectivistic value orientations on non-fatal suicidal behavior and attitudes in Turkish adolescents and young adults. *Scandinavian Journal of Psychology* 54, 493-501.

Falhammar H, Butwicka A, Landen M, Lichtenstein P, Nordenskjold A, Nordenstrom A, Frisen L (2013). Increased psychiatric morbidity in men with congenital adrenal hyperplasia due to 21-hydroxylase deficiency. *Journal of Clinical Endocrinology and Metabolism.* Published online: 4 December 2013. doi: 10.1210/jc.2013-3707.

Farias DR, Pereira Pinto TdJ, Alves Teofilo MM, Freitas Vilela AA, Vaz JdS, Nardi AE, Kac G (2013). Prevalence of psychiatric disorders in the first trimester of pregnancy and factors associated with current suicide risk. *Psychiatry Research* 210, 962-968.

Ford JD, Grasso DJ, Hawke J, Chapman JF (2013). Poly-victimization among juvenile justice-involved youths. *Child Abuse and Neglect* 37, 788-800.

Forkmann T, Scherer A, Bocker M, Pawelzik M, Gauggel S, Glaesmer H (2014). The relation of cognitive reappraisal and expressive suppression to suicidal ideation and suicidal desire. *Suicide and Life-Threatening Behavior.* Published online: 3 February 2014. doi: 10.1111/sltb.12076.

Francis KA (2014). General strain theory, gender, and the conditioning influence of negative internalizing emotions on youth risk behaviors. *Youth Violence and Juvenile Justice* 12, 58-76.

Fuller-Thomson E, Schrumm M, Brennenstuhl S (2013). Migraine and despair: Factors associated with depression and suicidal ideation among Canadian migraineurs in a population-based study. *Depression Research and Treatment* 2013, 401487.

Galán F, Ríos-Santos Jv, Polo J, Rios-Carrasco B, Bullón P (2013). Burnout, depression and suicidal ideation in dental students. *Medicina Oral, Patologia Oral y Cirugia Bucal.* Published online: 13 October 2013. doi: 10.4317/medoral.19281.

Gallagher M, Prinstein MJ, Simon V, Spirito A (2014). Social anxiety symptoms and suicidal ideation in a clinical sample of early adolescents: Examining loneliness and social support as longitudinal mediators. *Journal of Abnormal Child Psychology.* Published online: 5 January 2014. doi: 10.1007/s10802-013-9844-7.

Gallant J, Snyder GS, von der Embse NP (2014). Characteristics and psychosocial predictors of adolescent nonsuicidal self-injury in residential care. *Preventing School Failure* 58, 26.

Goldman-Mellor SJ, Caspi A, Harrington H, Hogan S, Nada-Raja S, Poulton R, Moffitt TE (2013). Suicide attempt in young people: A signal for long-term health care and social needs. *JAMA Psychiatry* 71, 119-127.

Gonzalez-Rodriguez A, Molina-Andreu O, Navarro V, Gasto C, Penades R, Catalan R (2014). Delusional disorder: No gender differences in age at onset, suicidal ideation, or suicidal behavior. *Revista Brasileira de Psiquiatria.* Published online: 28 January 2014. doi: 10.1590/1516-4446-2013.1205.

Grunebaum MF, Keilp JG, Ellis SP, Sudol K, Bauer N, Burke AK, Oquendo MA, Mann JJ (2013). SSRI versus bupropion effects on symptom clusters in suicidal depression: Post hoc analysis of a randomized clinical trial. *Journal of Clinical Psychiatry* 74, 872-879.

Gulliver P, Fanslow J (2013). Exploring risk factors for suicidal ideation in a population-based sample of New Zealand women who have experienced intimate partner violence. *Australian and New Zealand Journal of Public Health* 37, 527-533.

Hahm HC, Gonyea JG, Chiao C, Koritsanszky LA (2014). Fractured identity: A framework for understanding young Asian American women's self-harm and suicidal behaviors. *Race and Social Problems* 6, 56-68.

Halvorsen JA, Lien L, Dalgard F, Bjertness E, Stern RS (2014). Suicidal ideation, mental health problems and social function in adolescents with eczema: A population-based study. *Journal of Investigative Dermatology*. Published online: 4 February 2014. doi: 10.1038/jid.2014.70.

Hardoff D (2013). Health issues in adolescents' internet use - benefits and risks. *Georgian Medical News* 99-103.

Harford TC, Yi H-Y, Grant BF (2013). Other- and self-directed forms of violence and their relationships to DSM-IV substance use and other psychiatric disorders in a national survey of adults. *Comprehensive Psychiatry* 54, 731-739.

Harris IM, Roberts LM (2013). Exploring the use and effects of deliberate self-harm websites: An internet-based study. *Journal of Medical Internet Research* 15, E285.

Hatzenbuehler ML, Birkett M, Van Wagenen A, Meyer IH (2014). Protective school climates and reduced risk for suicide ideation in sexual minority youths. *American Journal of Public Health* 104, 279-286.

Heylens G, Verroken C, De Cock S, T'Sjoen G, De Cuypere G (2013). Effects of different steps in gender reassignment therapy on psychopathology: A prospective study of persons with a gender identity disorder. *Journal of Sexual Medicine* 11, 119-126.

Hjorthoj CR, Madsen T, Agerbo E, Nordentoft M (2014). Risk of suicide according to level of psychiatric treatment: A nationwide nested case-control study. *Social Psychiatry and Psychiatric Epidemiology*. Published online: 18 March 2014. doi: 10.1007/s00127-014-0860-x.

Hoch J, Symons F, Sng S (2013). Sequential analysis of autonomic arousal and self-injurious behavior. *American Journal on Intellectual and Developmental Disabilities* 118, 435-446.

Hollander P, Gupta AK, Plodkowski R, Greenway F, Bays H, Burns C, Klassen P, Fujioka K (2013). Effects of naltrexone sustained-release/bupropion sustained-release combination therapy on body weight and glycemic parameters in overweight and obese patients with type2 diabetes. *Diabetes Care* 36, 4022-4029.

Holma KM, Haukka J, Suominen K, Valtonen HM, Mantere O, Melartin TK, Sokero TP, Oquendo MA, Isometsä ET (2014). Differences in incidence of suicide attempts between bipolar I and II disorders and major depressive disorder. *Bipolar Disorders*. Published online: 17 March 2014. doi: 10.1111/bdi.12195.

Hua J, Emrick CB, Golin CE, Liu K, Pan J, Wang M, Wan X, Chen W, Jiang N (2013). HIV and stigma in Liuzhou, China. *AIDS Behavior* 18 Suppl 2, S203-S211.

Husky MM, Guignard R, Beck F, Michel G (2013). Risk behaviors, suicidal ideation and suicide attempts in a nationally representative French sample. *Journal of Affective Disorders* 151, 1059-1065.

Iacobelli S, Robillard PY, Gouyon JB, Nichols M, Boukerrou M, Barau G, Bonsante F (2014). Longitudinal health outcome and wellbeing of mother-infant pairs after adolescent pregnancy in Reunion Island, Indian Ocean. *International Journal of Gynecology and Obstetrics* 125, 44-48.

Iliceto P, Fino E, Sabatello U, Candilera G (2014). Personality and suicidal ideation in the elderly: Factorial invariance and latent means structures across age. *Aging and Mental Health*. Published online: 30 January 2014. doi: 10.1080/13607863.2014.880404.

Irwin JA, Coleman JD, Fisher CM, Marasco VM (2013). Correlates of suicide ideation among LGBT Nebraskans. *Journal of Homosexuality*. Published online: 17 December 2013. doi: 10.1080/00918369.2014.872521.

Ismail Z, Fischer C, McCall WV (2013). What characterizes late-life depression? *Psychiatric Clinics of North America* 36, 483-496.

Jablonska B, Ostberg V, Hjern A, Lindberg L, Rasmussen F, Modin B (2013). School effects on risk of non-fatal suicidal behaviour: A national multilevel cohort study. *Social Psychiatry and Psychiatric Epidemiology* 49, 609-618.

Jang JH, Lee YJ, Cho S-J, Cho IH, Shin NY, Kim SJ (2014). Psychotic-like experiences and their relationship to suicidal ideation in adolescents. *Psychiatry Research* 215, 641-645.

Jang JM, Park JI, Oh KY, Lee KH, Kim MS, Yoon MS, Ko SH, Cho HC, Chung YC (2014). Predictors of suicidal ideation in a community sample: Roles of anger, self-esteem, and depression. *Psychiatry Research* 216, 74-81.

Jang SY, Choi B, Ju EY, Kim YM, Kang SB, Park S, Yang SH, Joo MH, Kim IH (2014). Association between restriction of activity related to chronic diseases and suicidal ideation in older adults in Korea. *Geriatrics and Gerontology International*. Published online: 24 January 2014. doi: 10.1111/ggi.12202.

Jankovic J, Bremner S, Bogic M, Lecic-Tosevski D, Ajdukovic D, Franciskovic T, Galeazzi GM, Kucukalic A, Morina N, Popovski M, Schützwohl M, Priebe S (2013). Trauma and suicidality in war affected communities. *European Psychiatry* 28, 514-520.

Jovet-Toledo GG, Clatts MC, Rodriguez-Diaz CE, Goldsamt L, Vargas-Molina RL (2014). Risk factors for suicide attempts in a clinic-based sample of people living with HIV in Puerto Rico. *AIDS Care*. Published online: 13 March 2014. doi: 10.1080/09540121.2014.894618.

Junker A, Bjørngaard JH, Gunnell D, Bjerkeset O (2014). Sleep problems and hospitalization for self-harm: A 15-year follow-up of 9,000 Norwegian adolescents. The young-hunt study. *Sleep* 37, 579-585.

Kadotani H, Nagai Y, Sozu T (2013). Railway suicide attempts are associated with amount of sunlight in recent days. *Journal of Affective Disorders* 152-154, 162-168.

Kaplan SG, Ali SK, Simpson B, Britt V, McCall WV (2013). Associations between sleep disturbance and suicidal ideation in adolescents admitted to an inpatient psychiatric unit. *International Journal of Adolescent Medicine and Health*. Published online: 19 December 2013. doi: 10.1515/ijamh-2013-0318.

Kaspar V (2013). Long-term depression and suicidal ideation outcomes subsequent to emancipation from foster care: Pathways to psychiatric risk in the Métis population. *Psychiatry Research* 215, 347-354.

Kim BJ, Ahn J (2013). Factors that influence suicidal ideation among elderly Korean immigrants: Focus on diatheses and stressors. *Aging and Mental Health*. Published online: 12 December 2013. doi: 10.1080/13607863.2013.866631.

Kim J, Shin DH, Lee WJ (2013). Suicidal ideation and occupational pesticide exposure among male farmers. *Environmental Research* 128, 52-56.

Kim JH, Park EC, Cho WH, Park JY, Choi WJ, Chang HS (2013). Association between total sleep duration and suicidal ideation among the Korean general adult population. *Sleep* 36, 1563-1572.

Kim M-H, Noh H-J (2013). Characteristics of elderly suicide attempters in Korea; distinction between "young-old" vs "old-old". *International Journal of Psychiatry in Clinical Practice* 17, 27.

Kim SM, Han DH, Trksak GH, Lee YS (2013). Gender differences in adolescent coping behaviors and suicidal ideation: Findings from a sample of 73,238 adolescents. *Anxiety Stress Coping*. Published online: 21 January 2014. doi: 10.1080/10615806.2013.876010.

Kindrick K, Castro J, Messias E (2013). Sadness, suicide, and bullying in Arkansas: Results from the youth risk behavior survey — 2011. *Journal of the Arkansas Medical Society* 110, 90-91.

King KA, Vidourek RA (2013). Getting inked: Tattoo and risky behavioral involvement among university students. *Social Science Journal* 50, 540-546.

Kwok CL, Yip PS, Gunnell D, Kuo CJ, Chen YY (2014). Non-fatal repetition of self-harm in Taipei City, Taiwan: Cohort study. *British Journal of Psychiatry*. Published online: 30 January 2014. doi: 10.1192/bjp.bp.113.130179.

Kwon JA, Lee M, Yoo K-B, Park E-C (2013). Does the duration and time of sleep increase the risk of allergic rhinitis? Results of the 6-year nationwide Korea youth risk behavior web-based survey. *PLoS ONE* 8, e72507.

Lämmle L, Oedl C, Ziegler M (2014). Don't threaten me and my dark side or even self-harm won't stop me from hurting you. *Personality and Individual Differences*. Published online: 8 February 2014. doi: 10.1016/j.paid.2013.12.024.

Lance EI, York JM, Lee LC, Zimmerman AW (2014). Association between regression and self injury among children with autism. *Research in Developmental Disabilities* 35, 408-413.

Landgraf S, Blumenauer K, Osterheider M, Eisenbarth H (2013). A clinical and demographic comparison between a forensic and a general sample of female patients with schizophrenia. *Psychiatry Research* 210, 1176-1183.

Landsberger SA, Diaz DR, Spring NZ, Sheward J, Sculley C (2014). Psychiatric diagnoses and psychosocial needs of outpatient deaf children and adolescents. *Child Psychiatry and Human Development* 45, 42-51.

Larkin C, Blasi ZD, Arensman E (2014). Risk factors for repetition of self-harm: A systematic review of prospective hospital-based studies. *PLoS ONE* 9, e84282.

Larkin C, Corcoran P, Perry I, Arensman E (2013). Severity of hospital-treated self-cutting and risk of future self-harm: A national registry study. *Journal of Mental Health* 23, 115-119.

Larkin C, Di Blasi Z, Arensman E (2014). Correction: Risk factors for repetition of self-harm: A systematic review of prospective hospital-based studies. *PloS ONE* 9, e84282.

Latalova K, Prasko J, Grambal A, Havlikova P, Jelenova D, Mainerova B, Kamaradova D, Ociskova M, Sedlackova Z, Sandoval A (2013). Bipolar disorder and anxiety disorders. *Neuroendocrinology Letters* 34, 738-744.

Lee H, Iglewicz A, Golshan S, Zisook S (2013). A tale of two veterans: Homeless vs domiciled veterans presenting to a psychiatric urgent care clinic. *Annals of Clinical Psychiatry* 25, 275-282.

Lehuluante A, Fransson P (2014). Are there specific health-related factors that can accentuate the risk of suicide among men with prostate cancer? *Support Care Cancer*. Published online: 11 February 2014. doi: 10.1007/s00520-014-2150-2.

Leszczynska-Rodziewicz A, Szczepankiewicz A, Narozna B, Skibinska M, Pawlak J, Dmitrzak-Weglarz M, Hauser J (2014). Possible association between haplotypes of the FKBP5 gene and suicidal bipolar disorder, but not with melancholic depression and psychotic features, in the course of bipolar disorder. *Neuropsychiatric Disease and Treatment* 10, 243-248.

Liang S, Yan J, Zhang T, Zhu C, Situ M, Du N, Fu X, Huang Y (2013). Differences between non-suicidal self injury and suicide attempt in chinese adolescents. *Asian Journal of Psychiatry* 8, 76-83.

Macaron G, Fahed M, Matar D, Bou-Khalil R, Kazour F, Nehme-Chlela D, Richa S (2013). Anxiety, depression and suicidal ideation in Lebanese patients undergoing hemodialysis. *Community Mental Health Journal* 50, 235-238.

MacLean SJ, Kutin J, Best D, Bruun A, Green R (2014). Risk profiles for early adolescents who regularly use alcohol and other drugs compared with older youth. *Vulnerable Children and Youth Studies* 9, 17-27.

Maniam T, Marhani M, Firdaus M, Kadir AB, Mazni MJ, Azizul A, Salina AA, Fadzillah AR, Nurashikin I, Ang KT, Jasvindar K, Noor Ani A (2013). Risk factors for suicidal ideation, plans and attempts in Malaysia - results of an epidemiological survey. *Comprehensive Psychiatry* 55 Suppl 1, S121-S125.

March J, Sareen J, Gawaziuk JP, Doupe M, Chateau D, Hoppensack M, Nour S, Husarewycz W, Palitsky D, Khan S, Leslie WD, Enns MW, Stein MB, Asmundson GJ, Medved M, Logsetty S (2014). Increased suicidal activity following major trauma: A population-based study. *Journal of Trauma and Acute Care Surgery* 76, 180-184.

Marshall SK, Faaborg-Andersen P, Tilton-Weaver LC, Stattin H (2013). Peer sexual harassment and deliberate self-injury: Longitudinal cross-lag investigations in Canada and Sweden. *Journal of Adolescent Health* 53, 717-722.

Matamura M, Tochigi M, Usami S, Yonehara H, Fukushima M, Nishida A, Togo F, Sasaki T (2014). Associations between sleep habits and mental health status and suicidality in a longitudinal survey of monozygotic twin adolescents. *Journal of Sleep Research*. Published online: 24 January 2014. doi: 10.1111/jsr.12127.

McGarrity LA, Huebner DM, McKinnon RK (2013). Putting stigma in context: Do perceptions of group stigma interact with personally experienced discrimination to predict mental health? *Group Processes and Intergroup Relations* 16, 684-698.

McGlinchey EL, Harvey AG (2014). Risk behaviors and negative health outcomes for adolescents with late bedtimes. *Journal of Youth and Adolescence*. Published online: 6 March 2014. doi: 10.1007/s10964-014-0110-2.

McGuire AW, Eastwood JA, Hays RD, Macabasco-O'Connell A, Doering LV (2014). Depressed or not depressed: Untangling symptoms of depression in patients hospitalized with coronary heart disease. *American Journal of Critical Care* 23, 106-116.

McKenzie KC, Gross JJ (2014). Nonsuicidal self-injury: An emotion regulation perspective. *Psychopathology*. Published online: 12 February 2014. doi: 10.1159/000358097.

McKercher C, Patton GC, Schmidt MD, Venn AJ, Dwyer T, Sanderson K (2013). Physical activity and depression symptom profiles in young men and women with major depression. *Psychosomatic Medicine* 75, 366-374.

Medeiros K, Rojahn J, Moore LL, van Ingen DJ (2014). Functional properties of behaviour problems depending on level of intellectual disability. *Journal of Intellectual Disability Research* 58, 151-161.

Mellqvist Fassberg M, Ostling S, Braam AW, Backman K, Copeland JR, Fichter M, Kivela SL, Lawlor BA, Lobo A, Magnusson H, Prince MJ, Reischies FM, Turrina C, Wilson K, Skoog I, Waern M (2014). Functional disability and death wishes in older europeans: Results from the EURODEP concerted action. *Social Psychiatry and Psychiatric Epidemiology*. Published online: 20 February 2014. doi: 10.1007/s00127-014-0840-1.

Melville JD, Kellogg ND, Perez N, Lukefahr JL (2014). Assessment for self-blame and trauma symptoms during the medical evaluation of suspected sexual abuse. *Child Abuse and Neglect*. Published online: 10 March 2014. doi: 10.1016/j.chiabu.2014.01.020.

Miller AB, Esposito-Smythers C (2013). How do cognitive distortions and substance-related problems affect the relationship between child maltreatment and adolescent suicidal ideation? *Psychology of Violence* 3, 340-353.

Miller M, Pate V, Swanson Sa, Azrael D, White A, Stürmer T (2013). Antidepressant class, age, and the risk of deliberate self-harm: A propensity score matched cohort study of SSRI and SNRI users in the USA. *CNS Drugs* 28, 79-88.

Miranda R, Shaffer D (2013). Understanding the suicidal moment in adolescence. *Annals of the New York Academy of Sciences* 1304, 14-21.

Misdrahi D, Denard S, Swendsen J, Jaussent I, Courtet P (2014). Depression in schizophrenia: The influence of the different dimensions of insight. *Psychiatry Research* 216, 12-16.

Mittendorfer-Rutz E, Alexanderson K, Westerlund H, Lange T (2014). Is transition to disability pension in young people associated with changes in risk of attempted suicide? *Psychological Medicine.* Published online: 17 January 2014. doi: 10.1017/S0033291713003097.

Mok CC, Chan KL, Cheung EFC, Yip PSF (2013). Suicidal ideation in patients with systemic lupus erythematosus: Incidence and risk factors. *Rheumatology (Oxford)* 53, 714-721.

Morris C, Simpson J, Sampson M, Beesley F (2013). Emotion and self-cutting: Narratives of service users referred to a personality disorder service. *Clinical Psychology and Psychotherapy.* Published online: 1 October 2013. doi: 10.1002/cpp.1870.

Mossige S, Huang L, Straiton M, Roen K (2014). Suicidal ideation and self-harm among youths in Norway: Associations with verbal, physical and sexual abuse. *Child and Family Social Work.* Published online: 22 January 2014. doi: 10.1111/cfs.12126.

Mota NP, Medved M, Whitney D, Hiebert-Murphy D, Sareen J (2013). Protective factors for mental disorders and psychological distress in female, compared with male, service members in a representative sample. *Canadian Journal of Psychiatry* 58, 570-578.

Mundt JC, Greist JH, Jefferson JW, Federico M, Mann JJ, Posner K (2013). Prediction of suicidal behavior in clinical research by lifetime suicidal ideation and behavior ascertained by the electronic Columbia-Suicide Severity Rating Scale. *Journal of Clinical Psychiatry* 74, 887-893.

Nahaliel S, Sommerfeld E, Orbach I, Weller A, Apter A, Zalsman G (2014). Mental pain as a mediator of suicidal tendency: A path analysis. *Comprehensive Psychiatry* 55, 944-951.

Najavits LM, Johnson KM (2014). Pilot study of creating change, a new past-focused model for PTSD and substance abuse. *American Journal on Addictions.* Published online: 15 March 2014. doi: 10.1111/j.1521-0391.2014.12127.

Noori R, Rafiey H, Azizabadi-Farahani M, Khoddami-Vishteh HR, Mirabi P, Farhadi MH, Narenjiha H (2013). Corrigendum to "risk factors of suicidal ideation and attempt in women with drug user spouse". *Journal of the Chinese Medical Association* 76, 727.

O'Neil Rodriguez KA, Kendall PC (2014). Suicidal ideation in anxiety-disordered youth: Identifying predictors of risk. *Journal of Clinical Child and Adolescent Psychology* 43, 51-62.

Odebrecht Vargas Nunes S, Pizzo de Castro MR, Ehara Watanabe MA, Losi Guembarovski R, Odebrecht Vargas H, Vissoci Reiche EM, Kaminami Morimoto H, Dodd S, Berk M (2014). Genetic polymorphisms in glutathione-s-transferases are associated with anxiety and mood disorders in nicotine dependence. *Psychiatric Genetics.* Published online: 14 March 2014. doi: 10.1097/YPG.0000000000000023.

Olema DK, Catani C, Ertl V, Saile R, Neuner F (2014). The hidden effects of child maltreatment in a war region: Correlates of psychopathology in two generations living in northern Uganda. *Journal of Traumatic Stress* 27, 35-41.

Olvet DM, Peruzzo D, Thapa-Chhetry B, Sublette ME, Sullivan GM, Oquendo MA, Mann JJ, Parsey RV (2014). A diffusion tensor imaging study of suicide attempters. *Journal of Psychiatric Research* 51, 60-67.

Park S (2013). Gender-specific factors of suicide ideation among adolescents in the republic of Korea: A nationally representative population-based study. *Archives of Psychiatric Nursing* 27, 253-259.

Patil V, Pattanayak RD, Mishra AK (2013). Predictors of suicide attempt in early-onset psychosis: Methodological issues and concerns. *Journal of Clinical Psychiatry* 74, 1264.

Pedrelli P, Nyer M, Holt D, Bakow BR, Fava M, Baer L, Cassiello C, Mulligan M, Cusin C, Farabaugh A (2013). Correlates of irritability in college students with depressive symptoms. *The Journal of Nervous and Mental Disease* 201, 953-958.

Petersen L, Sørensen TIA, Kragh Andersen P, Bo Mortensen P, Hawton K (2013). Genetic and familial environmental effects on suicide attempts: A study of danish adoptees and their biological and adoptive siblings. *Journal of Affective Disorders* 155, 273-277.

Peterson CM, Davis-Becker K, Fischer S (2014). Interactive role of depression, distress tolerance and negative urgency on non-suicidal self-injury. *Personality and Mental Health* 8, 151-160.

Petty JL, Bacarese-Hamilton M, Davies LE, Oliver C (2014). Correlates of self-injurious, aggressive and destructive behaviour in children under five who are at risk of developmental delay. *Research in Developmental Disabilities* 35, 36-45.

Pfeiffer PN, Brandfon S, Garcia E, Duffy S, Ganoczy D, Myra Kim H, Valenstein M (2013). Predictors of suicidal ideation among depressed veterans and the interpersonal theory of suicide. *Journal of Affective Disorders* 152-154, 277-281.

Pigeon WR, Woosley JA, Lichstein KL (2014). Insomnia and hypnotic medications are associated with suicidal ideation in a community population. *Archives of Suicide Research*. Published online: 12 March 2014. doi: 10.1080/13811118.2013.824837.

Power J, Brown SL, Usher AM (2013). Non-suicidal self-injury in women offenders: Motivations, emotions, and precipitating events. *International Journal of Forensic Mental Health* 12, 192-204.

Ragot A, Guiho-Bailly M-P, Tanguy M, Gohier B, Garre J-B, Roquelaure Y (2013). Psychiatric disorders observed in the angers hospital occupational psychopathology clinic. *Sante Publique* 25, 729-736.

Rahim T, Saeed B (2013). Suicidal ideation among a group of Kurdish schizophrenic patients. *Middle East Current Psychiatry* 20, 229-234.

Rasing SPA, Creemers DHM, Janssens JMAM, Scholte RHJ (2013). Effectiveness of depression and anxiety prevention in adolescents with high familial risk: Study protocol for a randomized controlled trial. *BMC Psychiatry* 13, 316.

Ringback Weitoft G, Berglund M, Lindstrom EA, Nilsson M, Salmi P, Rosen M (2014). Mortality, attempted suicide, re-hospitalisation and prescription refill for clozapine and other antipsychotics in Sweden-a register-based study. *Pharmacoepidemiology and Drug Safety* 23, 290-298.

Roberts DL, Shanafelt TD, Dyrbye LN, West CP (2014). A national comparison of burnout and work-life balance among internal medicine hospitalists and outpatient general internists. *Journal of Hospital Medicine* 9, 176-181.

Rocha-Leite CI, Borges-Oliveira R, Araújo-de-Freitas L, Machado PRL, Quarantini LC (2014). Mental disorders in leprosy: An underdiagnosed and untreated population. *Journal of Psychosomatic Research* 76, 422-425.

Romeo LAP, Balducci CP, Quintarelli EMD, Riolfi AMD, Pelizza LM, Serpelloni AM, Tisato SMD, Perbellini LFP (2013). MMPI-2 personality profiles and suicidal ideation and behavior in victims of bullying at work: A follow-up study. *Violence and Victims* 28, 1000-1014.

Rossow I, Norström T (2014). Heavy episodic drinking and deliberate self-harm in young people: A longitudinal cohort study. *Addiction*. Published online: 24 February 2014. doi: 10.1111/add.12527.

Rowe C, Spelman L, Oziemski M, Ryan A, Manoharan S, Wilson P, Daubney M, Scott J (2013). Isotretinoin and mental health in adolescents: Australian consensus. *Australasian Journal of Dermatology* 55, 162-167.

Russell PSS, Nair Mkc, Chandra A, Subramaniam VS, Bincymol K, George B, Samuel B (2013). Suicidal behavior in anxiety disorders among adolescents in a rural community population in India. *Indian Journal of Pediatrics* 80 Suppl 2, S175-S180.

Salvatore P, Baldessarini RJ, Khalsa H-MK, Indic P, Maggini C, Tohen M (2013). Negative affective features in 516 cases of first psychotic disorder episodes: Relationship to suicidal risk. *Journal of Depression and Anxiety* 2, 1-11.

Sanna L, Stuart AL, Pasco JA, Kotowicz MA, Berk M, Girardi P, Williams LJ (2014). Suicidal ideation and physical illness: Does the link lie with depression? *Journal of Affective Disorders* 152-154, 422-426.

Sarajlija M, Jugovi A, Živaljevi D, Merdovi B, Sarajlija A (2014). Assessment of health status and quality of life of homeless persons in Belgrade, Serbia. *Vojnosanitetski Pregled* 71, 167-174.

Sarchiapone M, Mandelli L, Carli V, Iosue M, Wasserman C, Hadlaczky G, Hoven CW, Apter A, Balazs J, Bobes J, Brunner R, Corcoran P, Cosman D, Haring C, Kaess M, Keeley H, Keresztény A, Kahn JP, Postuvan V, Mars U, Saiz PA, Varnik P, Sisask M, Wasserman D (2014). Hours of sleep in adolescents and its association with anxiety, emotional concerns, and suicidal ideation. *Sleep Medicine* 15, 248-254.

Schenk AM, Fremouw WJ, Keelan CM (2013). Characteristics of college cyberbullies. *Computers in Human Behavior* 29, 2320-2327.

Schoenleber M, Berenbaum H, Motl R (2013). Shame-related functions of and motivations for self-injurious behavior. *Personality Disorders* 5, 204-211.

Sedlackova Z, Sedlacek M, Ociskova M, Kamaradova D, Latalova K, Prasko J (2013). The relationship of personality disorders to treatment outcome in depressed patient - two years follow up in retrospective study. *Activitas Nervosa Superior Rediviva* 55, 27-32.

Selby EA, Nock MK, Kranzler A (2014). How does self-injury feel? Examining automatic positive reinforcement in adolescent self-injurers with experience sampling. *Psychiatry Research* 215, 417-423.

Selby EA, Yen S (2013). Six-month trajectory of suicidal ideation in adolescents with borderline personality disorder. *Suicide and Life-Threatening Behavior* 44, 89-100.

Selemogwe MP, White DP (2013). An overview of gay, lesbian and bisexual issues in Botswana. *Journal of Gay & Lesbian Mental Health* 17, 406.

engül MCB, Kaya V, en CA, Kaya K (2014). Association between suicidal ideation and behavior, and depression, anxiety, and perceived social support in cancer patients. *Medical Science Monitor* 20, 329-336.

Slade K, Edelmann R, Worrall M, Bray D (2014). Applying the cry of pain model as a predictor of deliberate self-harm in an early-stage adult male prison population. *Legal and Criminological Psychology* 19, 131-146.

Smith PN, Selwyn CN, Wolford-Clevenger C, Mandracchia JT (2014). Psychopathic personality traits, suicide ideation, and suicide attempts in male prison inmates. *Criminal Justice and Behavior* 41, 364-379.

Soler L, Segura A, Kirchner T, Forns M (2013). Polyvictimization and risk for suicidal phenomena in a community sample of Spanish adolescents. *Violence and Victims* 28, 899-912.

Spears M, Montgomery AA, Gunnell D, Araya R (2013). Factors associated with the development of self-harm amongst a socio-economically deprived cohort of adolescents in Santiago, Chile. *Social Psychiatry and Psychiatric Epidemiology* 49, 629-637.

Spivak HR, Jenkins L, Vanaudenhove K, Lee D, Kelly M, Iskander J (2014). CDC grand rounds: A public health approach to prevention of intimate partner violence. *Morbidity and Mortality Weekly Report* 63, 38-41.

Sprengelmeyer R, Orth M, Muller HP, Wolf RC, Gron G, Depping MS, Kassubek J, Justo D, Rees EM, Haider S, Cole JH, Hobbs NZ, Roos RA, Durr A, Tabrizi SJ, Sussmuth SD, Landwehrmeyer GB (2013). The neuroanatomy of subthreshold depressive symptoms in huntington's disease: A combined diffusion tensor imaging (DTI) and voxel-based morphometry (VBM) study. *Psychological Medicine.* Published online: 7 October 2013. doi: 10.1017/S003329171300247X.

Steinberg JR, McCulloch CE, Adler NE (2014). Abortion and mental health: Findings from the national comorbidity survey-replication. *Obstetrics and Gynecology* 123, 263-270.

Stephens T, Holliday RC (2014). Predictors of suicide ideation and risk for HIV among juvenile offenders in Georgia. *International Journal of Adolescent Medicine and Health* 26, 137-143.

Stone DM, Luo F, Ouyang L, Lippy C, Hertz MF, Crosby AE (2013). Sexual orientation and suicide ideation, plans, attempts, and medically serious attempts: Evidence from local youth risk behavior surveys, 2001-2009. *American Journal of Public Health* 104, 262-271.

Su S, Li X, Zhang L, Lin D, Zhang C, Zhou Y (2014). Age group differences in HIV risk and mental health problems among female sex workers in southwest China. *AIDS Care.* Published online: 13 January 2014. doi: 10.1080/09540121.2013.878780.

Svensson T, Inoue M, Charvat H, Sawada N, Iwasaki M, Sasazuki S, Shimazu T, Yamaji T, Ikeda A, Kawamura N, Mimura M, Tsugane S (2014). Coping behaviors and suicide in the middle-aged and older Japanese general population: The Japan public health center-based prospective study. *Annals of Epidemiology* 24, 199-205.

Swanson EN, Owens EB, Hinshaw SP (2013). Pathways to self-harmful behaviors in young women with and without adhd: A longitudinal examination of mediating factors. *Journal of Child Psychology and Psychiatry and Allied Disciplines* 55, 505-515.

Swogger MT, Walsh Z, Maisto SA, Conner KR (2014). Reactive and proactive aggression and suicide attempts among criminal offenders. *Criminal Justice and Behavior* 41, 337-344.

Tait RJ, Anstey KJ (2013). Risk factors for self-harm and substance use in the general adult population. *Drug and Alcohol Review* 32, 67.

Tamam L, Bican M, Keskin N (2014). Impulse control disorders in elderly patients. *Comprehensive Psychiatry* 55, 1022-1028.

Tatnell R, Kelada L, Hasking P, Martin G (2013). Longitudinal analysis of adolescent NSSI: The role of intrapersonal and interpersonal factors. *Journal of Abnormal Child Psychology.* Published online: 17 December 2013. doi: 10.1007/s10802-013-9837-6.

Taymur I, Özdel K, Duyan V, Emre Sargin A, Dem G, Türkçapar MH (2014). The relationship between temperament and character features, and social problem solving in psychiatric patients who attempted suicide with drugs: Preliminary results. *Anadolu Psikiyatri Dergisi* 15, 31-38.

Testa RJ, Jimenez CL, Rankin S (2014). Risk and resilience during transgender identity development: The effects of awareness and engagement with other transgender people on affect. *Journal of Gay and Lesbian Mental Health* 18, 31-46.

Thon N, Preuss UW, Pölzleitner A, Quantschnig B, Scholz H, Kühberger A, Bischof A, Rumpf HJ, Wurst FM (2014). Prevalence of suicide attempts in pathological gamblers in a nationwide Austrian treatment sample. *General Hospital Psychiatry* 36, 342-346.

To WT, Neirynck S, Vanderplasschen W, Vanheule S, Vandevelde S (2014). Substance use and misuse in persons with intellectual disabilities (ID): Results of a survey in ID and addiction services in Flanders. *Research in Developmental Disabilities* 35, 1-9.

Tsirigotis K, Gruszczynski W, Tsirigotis-Maniecka M (2013). Gender differentiation in indirect self-destructiveness and suicide attempt methods (gender, indirect self-destructiveness, and suicide attempts). *Psychiatric Quarterly* 85, 197-209.

Tuisku V, Kiviruusu O, Pelkonen M, Karlsson L, Strandholm T, Marttunen M (2013). Depressed adolescents as young adults - predictors of suicide attempt and non-suicidal self-injury during an 8-year follow-up. *Journal of Affective Disorders* 152-154, 313-319.

Tuna E, Bozo O (2014). Exploring the link between emotional and behavioral dysregulation: A test of the emotional cascade model. *Journal of General Psychology* 141, 1-17.

Udell JA, Lu H, Redelmeier DA (2013). Long-term cardiovascular risk in women prescribed fertility therapy. *Journal of the American College of Cardiology* 62, 1704-1712.

Ulke C, Klein AM, von Klitzing K (2014). Relational stressors as predictors for repeat aggressive and self-harming incidents in child and adolescent psychiatric inpatient settings. *International Journal of Adolescent Medicine and Health.* Published online: 3 February 2014. doi: 10.1515/ijamh-2013-0339.

Umamaheswari V, Avasthi A, Grover S (2014). Risk factors for suicidal ideations in patients with bipolar disorder. *Bipolar Disorders.* Published online: 28 January 2014. doi: 10.1111/bdi.12179.

Van Eck K, Ballard E, Hart S, Newcomer A, Musci R, Flory K (2014). ADHD and suicidal ideation: The roles of emotion regulation and depressive symptoms among college students. *Journal of Attention Disorders.* Published online: 27 January 2014. doi: 10.1177/1087054713518238.

van Nierop M, van Os J, Gunther N, van Zelst C, de Graaf R, ten Have M, van Dorsselaer S, Bak M, Myin-Germeys I, Van Winkel R (2013). Does social defeat mediate the association between childhood trauma and psychosis? Evidence from the NEMESIS-2 study. *Acta Psychiatrica Scandinavica.* Published online: 25 November 2013. doi: 10.1111/acps.12212.

Vanderoost F, Van Der Wielen S, Van Nunen K, Van Hal G (2013). Employment loss during economic crisis and suicidal thoughts in Belgium: A survey in general practice. *British Journal of General Practice* 63, e691-e697.

Venta A, Sharp C (2014). Attachment organization in suicide prevention research: Preliminary findings and future directions in a sample of inpatient adolescents. *Crisis* 35, 60-66.

Verma A, Kumar A, Mishra A, Pandey AK (2014). Long-term treatment and poor management of psychiatric manifestations in mesial temporal sclerosis leading to suicidality in a young male. *Epilepsy and Behavior Case Reports* 2, 17-18.

Verschueren S, Berends T, Kool-Goudzwaard N, van Huigenbosch E, Gamel C, Dingemans A, van Elburg A, van Meijel B (2014). Patients with anorexia nervosa who self-injure: A phenomenological study. *Perspectives in Psychiatric Care.* Published online: 17 January 2014. doi: 10.1111/ppc.12061.

Viner R, Fiest KM, Bulloch AGM, Williams JVA, Lavorato DH, Berzins S, Jetté N, Metz LM, Patten SB (2014). Point prevalence and correlates of depression in a national community sample with multiple sclerosis. *General Hospital Psychiatry* 36, 352-354.

Voon D, Hasking P, Martin G (2013). The roles of emotion regulation and ruminative thoughts in non-suicidal self-injury. *British Journal of Clinical Psychology* 53, 95-113.

Voon V, Howell NA, Krack P (2013). Psychiatric considerations in deep brain stimulation for parkinson's disease. *Handbook of Clinical Neurology* 116, 147-154.

Vrbová K, Praško J, Kamarádová D, erná M, Ocisková M, Látalová K, Sedlá ková Z (2013). Comorbid anxiety disorders in patients with schizophrenia. *Activitas Nervosa Superior Rediviva* 55, 40-46.

Vuorilehto M, Valtonen HM, Melartin T, Sokero P, Suominen K, Isometsa ET (2013). Method of assessment determines prevalence of suicidal ideation among patients with depression. *European Psychiatry.* Published online: 28 October 2013. doi: 10.1016/j.eurpsy.2013.08.005.

Wardenaar KJ, Conradi HJ, de Jonge P (2014). Data-driven course trajectories in primary care patients with major depressive disorder. *Depression and Anxiety*. Published online: 3 January 2014. doi: 10.1002/da.22228.

Warf CW, Clark LF, Desai M, Rabinovitz SJ, Agahi G, Calvo R, Hoffmann J (2013). Coming of age on the streets: Survival sex among homeless young women in Hollywood. *Journal of Adolescence* 36, 1205-1213.

Weinstock LM, Gaudiano BA, Epstein-Lubow G, Tezanos K, Celis-deHoyos CE, Miller IW (2014). Medication burden in bipolar disorder: A chart review of patients at psychiatric hospital admission. *Psychiatry Research* 216, 24-30.

Westers NJ, Rehfuss M, Olson L, Wiemann CM (2013). An exploration of adolescent nonsuicidal self-injury and religious coping. *International Journal of Adolescent Medicine and Health*. Published online: 11 October 2013. doi: 10.1515/ijamh-2013-0314.

Wilhelm K, Robins L, Gillis I, Glennon S (2013). Substance use related lifestyle behaviours in people attending a clinic following self-harm/suicidal presentations. *Drug and Alcohol Review* 32, 73.

Wisco BE, Marx BP, Holowka DW, Vasterling JJ, Han SC, Chen MS, Gradus JL, Nock MK, Rosen RC, Keane TM (2014). Traumatic brain injury, PTSD, and current suicidal ideation among Iraq and Afghanistan U.S. Veterans. *Journal of Traumatic Stress* 27, 244-248.

Wong YJ, Kim BS, Nguyen CP, Cheng JK, Saw A (2013). The interpersonal shame inventory for Asian Americans: Scale development and psychometric properties. *Journal of Counseling Psychology* 61, 119-132.

Wright N, Horton M, Tennant A, Meade T (2013). Assessing the risk of self-harm in an adult prison population. *Drug and Alcohol Review* 32, 74.

Xie W, Li H, Luo X, Fu R, Ying X, Wang N, Yin Q, Zou Y, Cui Y, Wang X, Shi C (2013). Anhedonia and pain avoidance in the suicidal mind: Behavioral evidence for motivational manifestations of suicidal ideation in patients with major depressive disorder. *Journal of Clinical Psychology*. Published online: 4 December 2013. doi: 10.1002/jclp.22055.

Yang M, Wong SCP, Coid JW (2013). Violence, mental health and violence risk factors among community women: An epidemiological study based on two national household surveys in the UK. *BMC Public Health* 13, 1020.

Yang Y-C, Tu H-P, Hong C-H, Chang W-C, Fu H-C, Ho J-C, Chang W-P, Chuang H-Y, Lee C-H (2014). Female gender and acne disease are jointly and independently associated with the risk of major depression and suicide: A national population-based study. *Biomed Research International* 2014, 504279.

Yen CF, Lai CY, Ko CH, Liu TL, Tang TC, Wu YY, Yang P (2013). The associations between suicidal ideation and attempt and anxiety symptoms and the demographic, psychological and social moderators in Taiwanese adolescents. *Archives of Suicide Research* 18, 104-116.

Yeol LS, Hong J (2013). The effect of self esteem and social support on suicidal ideation among elderly in a city of Korea: Focused on the mediating effect of depressive symptoms. *International Journal of Psychiatry in Clinical Practice* 17, 33.

Youngblut JM, Brooten D, Cantwell GP, Del Moral T, Totapally B (2013). Parent health and functioning 13 months after infant or child NICU/PICU death. *Pediatrics* 132, e1295-e1301.

Yuan H, Zhang N, Wang C, Luo BY, Shi Y, Li J, Zhou Y, Wang Y, Zhang T, Zhou J, Zhao X (2014). Factors of hamilton depression rating scale (17 items) at 2 weeks correlated with poor outcome at 1 year in patients with ischemic stroke. *Neurological Sciences* 35, 171-177.

Zaroff CM, Wong HL, Ku L, Van Schalkwyk G (2014). Interpersonal stress, not depression or hopelessness, predicts suicidality in university students in Macao. *Australas Psychiatry* 22, 127-131.

Zeichner JA (2013). Evaluating and treating the adult female patient with acne. *Journal of Drugs in Dermatology* 12, 1418-1427.

Zhang C, Li X, Hong Y, Su S, Zhou Y (2013). Relationship between female sex workers and gatekeeper: The impact on female sex worker's mental health in China. *Psychology, Health and Medicine.* Published online: 17 December 2013. doi: 10.1080/13548506.2013.869612.

Zimmerman M, Martinez JH, Morgan TA, Young D, Chelminski I, Dalrymple K (2013). Distinguishing bipolar ii depression from major depressive disorder with comorbid borderline personality disorder: Demographic, clinical, and family history differences. *Journal of Clinical Psychiatry* 74, 880-886.

Prevention

Bragazzi NL (2013). A google trends-based approach for monitoring NSSI. *Psychology Research and Behavior Management* 7, 1-8.

Gandy M, Sharpe L, Nicholson Perry K, Thayer Z, Miller L, Boserio J, Mohamed A (2014). Cognitive behaviour therapy to improve mood in people with epilepsy: A randomised controlled trial. *Cognitive Behaviour Therapy,* 43, 153-166.

Gelinas BL, Wright KD (2013). The cessation of deliberate self-harm in a university sample: The reasons, barriers, and strategies involved. *Archives of Suicide Research* 17, 373-386

Gibson S, Boden ZVR, Benson O, Brand SL (2014). The impact of participating in suicide research online. *Suicide and Life-Threatening Behavior.* Published online: 15 February 2014. doi: 10.1111/sltb.12082.

Jones JE, Siddarth P, Gurbani S, Shields WD, Caplan R (2013). Screening for suicidal ideation in children with epilepsy. *Epilepsy and Behavior* 29, 521-526.

Shand FL, Ridani R, Tighe J, Christensen H (2013). The effectiveness of a suicide prevention app for Indigenous Australian youths: Study protocol for a randomized controlled trial. *Trials* 14, 396.

Simpson A, Flood C, Rowe J, Quigley J, Henry S, Hall C, Evans R, Sherman P, Bowers L (2014). Results of a pilot randomised controlled trial to measure the clinical and cost effectiveness of peer support in increasing hope and quality of life in mental health patients discharged from hospital in the UK. *BMC Psychiatry* 14, 30.

Care and support

Aktepe E, Kocaman O, I ik A, Erolu FÖ (2013). An evaluation of the child and adolescent psychiatry consultation services requested in a university hospital. *TAF Preventive Medicine Bulletin* 12, 539-544.

Arias F, Szerman N, Vega P, Mesias B, Basurte I, Morant C, Ochoa E, Poyo F, Babin F (2013). Alcohol abuse or dependence and other psychiatric disorders. Madrid study on the prevalence of dual pathology. *Mental Health and Substance Use* 6, 339.

Ballard ED, Tingey L, Lee A, Suttle R, Barlow A, Cwik M (2014). Emergency department utilization among American Indian adolescents who made a suicide attempt: A screening opportunity. *Journal of Adolescent Health* 54, 357-359.

Beeley C, Sarkar J (2013). Experiences of staff managing self-harm algorithmically. *Journal of Forensic Practice* 15, 249-258.

Bendit N (2013). Reputation and science: Examining the effectiveness of DBT in the treatment of borderline personality disorder. *Australasian Psychiatry*. Published online: 4 November 2013. doi: 10.1177/1039856213510959.

Bilén K, Pettersson H, Owe-Larsson B, Ekdahl K, Ottosson C, Castrén M, Ponzer S (2013). Can early follow-up after deliberate self-harm reduce repetition? A prospective study of 325 patients. *Journal of Affective Disorders* 152-154, 320-325.

Brent DA, McMakin DL, Kennard BD, Goldstein TR, Mayes TL, Douaihy AB (2013). Protecting adolescents from self-harm: A critical review of intervention studies. *Journal of the American Academy of Child and Adolescent Psychiatry* 52, 1260-1271.

Brüne M, Dimaggio G, Edel MA (2013). Mentalization-based group therapy for inpatients with borderline personality disorder: Preliminary findings. *Clinical Neuropsychiatry* 10, 196-201.

Brunoni AR, Junior RF, Kemp AH, Lotufo PA, Bensenor IM, Fregni F (2013). Differential improvement in depressive symptoms for TDCS alone and combined with pharmacotherapy: An exploratory analysis from the sertraline vs. Electrical current therapy for treating depression clinical study. *International Journal of Neuropsychopharmacology* 17, 53-61.

Chakravarthy B, Frumin E, Lotfipour S (2014). Increasing suicide rates among middle-age persons and interventions to manage patients with psychiatric complaints. *Western Journal of Emergency Medicine* 15, 11-13.

Chi MT, Long A, Jeang SR, Ku YC, Lu T, Sun FK (2013). Healing and recovering after a suicide attempt: A grounded theory study. *Journal of Clinical Nursing*. Published online: 20 November 2013. doi: 10.1111/jocn.12328.

Cooper J, Steeg S, Bennewith O, Lowe M, Gunnell D, House A, Hawton K, Kapur N (2013). Are hospital services for self-harm getting better? An observational study examining management, service provision and temporal trends in England. *British Medical Journal Open* 3, e003444.

Davies NM, Gunnell D, Thomas KH, Metcalfe C, Windmeijer F, Martin RM (2013). Physicians' prescribing preferences were a potential instrument for patients' actual prescriptions of antidepressants. *Journal of Clinical Epidemiology* 66, 1386-1396.

de Beurs DP, de Groot MH, Bosmans JE, de Keijser J, Mokkenstorm J, Verwey B, van Duijn E, de Winter RF, Kerkhof AJ (2013). Reducing patients' suicide ideation through training mental health teams in the application of the dutch multidisciplinary practice guideline on assessment and treatment of suicidal behavior: Study protocol of a randomized controlled trial. *Trials* 14, 372.

Diamond GM (2013). Attachment-based family therapy interventions. *Psychotherapy* 51, 15-19.

Dickstein BD, Walter KH, Schumm JA, Chard KM (2013). Comparing response to cognitive processing therapy in military veterans with subthreshold and threshold posttraumatic stress disorder. *Journal of Traumatic Stress* 26, 703-709.

Dobscha SK, Denneson LM, Kovas AE, Corson K, Helmer DA, Bair MJ (2014). Primary care clinician responses to positive suicidal ideation risk assessments in veterans of Iraq and Afghanistan. *General Hospital Psychiatry.* Published online: 4 December 2013. doi: 10.1016/j.genhosppsych.2013.11.007.

Donker T, Petrie K, Proudfoot J, Clarke J, Birch M-R, Christensen H (2013). Smartphones for smarter delivery of mental health programs: A systematic review. *Journal of Medical Internet Research* 15, e247.

Findling RL, Groark J, Chiles D, Ramaker S, Yang L, Tourian KA (2014). Safety and tolerability of desvenlafaxine in children and adolescents with major depressive disorder. *Journal of Child and Adolescent Psychopharmacology.* Published online: 10 March 2014. doi: 10.1089/cap.2012.0126.

Findling RL, Robb A, Bose A (2013). Escitalopram in the treatment of adolescent depression: A randomized, double-blind, placebo-controlled extension trial. *Journal of Child and Adolescent Psychopharmacology* 23, 468-480.

Gangadhar BN, Naveen GH, Rao MG, Thirthalli J, Varambally S (2013). Positive antidepressant effects of generic yoga in depressive out-patients: A comparative study. *Indian Journal of Psychiatry* 55, s369-s373.

Geddes K, Dziurawiec S, Lee CW (2013). Dialectical behaviour therapy for the treatment of emotion dysregulation and trauma symptoms in self-injurious and suicidal adolescent females: A pilot programme within a community-based child and adolescent mental health service. *Psychiatry Journal* 2013, 145219.

Goldman-Mellor SJ, Caspi A, Harrington HL, Hogan S, Nada-Raja S, Poulton R, Moffitt TE (2014). Suicide attempt in young people a signal for long-term health care and social needs. *JAMA Psychiatry* 71, 119-127.

Gordon M, Melvin G (2013). Selective serotonin re-uptake inhibitors: A review of the side effects in adolescents. *Australian Family Physician* 42, 620-623.

Gratz KL, Dixon-Gordon KL, Tull MT (2014). Predictors of treatment response to an adjunctive emotion regulation group therapy for deliberate self-harm among women with borderline personality disorder. *Personality Disorders* 5, 97-107.

Gray J, Haji Ali Afzali H, Beilby J, Holton C, Banham D, Karnon J (2014). Practice nurse involvement in primary care depression management: An observational cost-effectiveness analysis. *BMC Family Practice* 15, 10.

Groos AD, Shakespeare-Finch J (2013). Positive experiences for participants in suicide bereavement groups: A grounded theory model. *Death Studies* 37, 1-24.

Guaiana G, Gupta S, Chiodo D, Davies SJ, Haederle K, Koesters M (2013). Agomelatine versus other antidepressive agents for major depression. *Cochrane Database of Systematic Reviews* 12, CD008851.

Hagan CC, Graham JME, Widmer B, Holt RJ, Ooi C, van Nieuwenhuizen AO, Fonagy P, Reynolds S, Target M, Kelvin R, Wilkinson PO, Bullmore ET, Lennox BR, Sahakian BJ, Goodyer I, Suckling J (2013). Magnetic resonance imaging of a randomized controlled trial investigating predictors of recovery following psychological treatment in adolescents with moderate to severe unipolar depression: Study protocol for magnetic resonance-improving mood with psychoanalytic and cognitive therapies (MR-IMPACT). *BMC Psychiatry* 13, 247.

Harned MS, Korslund KE, Linehan MM (2014). A pilot randomized controlled trial of dialectical behavior therapy with and without the dialectical behavior therapy prolonged exposure protocol for suicidal and self-injuring women with borderline personality disorder and PTSD. *Behaviour Research and Therapy* 55C, 7-17.

Hay A, Majumder P, Fosker H, Karim K, O'Reilly M (2013). The views and opinions of camhs professionals on their role and the role of others in attending to children who self-harm. *Clinical and Child Psychology and Psychiatry*. Published online: 23 December 2013. doi: 10.1177/1359104513514068.

Hedman E, Ljótsson B, Kaldo V, Hesser H, El Alaoui S, Kraepelien M, Andersson E, Rück C, Svanborg C, Andersson G, Lindefors N (2013). Effectiveness of internet-based cognitive behaviour therapy for depression in routine psychiatric care. *Journal of Affective Disorders* 155, 49-58.

Huffman JC, DuBois CM, Healy BC, Boehm JK, Kashdan TB, Celano CM, Denninger JW, Lyubomirsky S (2013). Feasibility and utility of positive psychology exercises for suicidal inpatients. *General Hospital Psychiatry* 36, 88-94.

Jagodic HK, Agius M, Pregelj P (2013). Psychopharmacotherapy prescription and suicidal behaviour. *Psychiatria Danubina* 25, 324-328.

Kelly DL, Wehring HJ, Earl AK, Sullivan KM, Dickerson FB, Feldman S, McMahon RP, Buchanan RW, Warfel D, Keller WR, Fischer BA, Shim J-C (2013). Treating symptomatic hyperprolactinemia in women with schizophrenia: Presentation of the ongoing daamsel clinical trial (dopamine partial agonist, aripiprazole, for the management of symptomatic elevated prolactin). *BMC Psychiatry* 13, 214.

Khalatbari J, Tarkhan M, Rahnama S (2013). Effectiveness of imagery rescripting and reprocessing therapy on suicidal ideation in individuals with suicide attempt history. *Procedia - Social and Behavioral Sciences* 84, 1095-1099.

Korczak DJ (2013). Use of selective serotonin reuptake inhibitor medications for the treatment of child and adolescent mental illness. *Paediatrics and Child Health* 18, 1-6.

Lana F, Isabel Fernandez-San Martin M (2013). To what extent are specific psychotherapies for borderline personality disorders efficacious? A systematic review of published randomised controlled trials. *Actas Espanolas De Psiquiatria* 41, 242-252.

Lees D, Procter N, Fassett D (2014). Therapeutic engagement between consumers in suicidal crisis and mental health nurses. *International Journal of Mental Health Nursing*. Published online: 27 February 2014. doi: 10.1111/inm.12061

Leon SC, Stoner AM, Usher AML, Carey D (2013). Measuring children's response to inpatient treatment: Use of practice-based evidence. *Psychiatric Services* 64, 252-256.

Mackenzie DW (2013). Applying the anderson-darling test to suicide clusters. *Crisis* 34, 434-437.

Madsen T, Nordentoft M (2013). Changes in inpatient and postdischarge suicide rates in a nationwide cohort of Danish psychiatric inpatients, 1998-2005. *Journal of Clinical Psychiatry* 74, e1190-e1194.

Mahdi I, Jevertson J, Schrader R, Nelson A, Ramos MM (2014). Survey of New Mexico school health professionals regarding preparedness to support sexual minority students. *The Journal of School Health* 84, 18-24.

Marshall E, York J, Magruder K, Yeager D, Knapp R, De Santis ML, Burriss L, Mauldin M, Sulkowski S, Pope C, Jobes DA (2014). Implementation of online suicide-specific training for VA providers. *Academic Psychiatry*. Published online: 22 February 2014. doi: 10.1007/s40596-014-0039-5

Martin C, Chapman R (2013). A mixed method study to determine the attitude of Australian emergency health professionals towards patients who present with deliberate self-poisoning. *International Emergency Nursing* 22, 98-104.

McAuliffe C, McLeavey BC, Fitzgerald T, Corcoran P, Carroll B, Ryan L, O'Keeffe B, Fitzgerald E, Hickey P, O'Regan M, Mulqueen J, Arensman E (2014). Group problem-solving skills training for self-harm: Randomised controlled trial. *British Journal of Psychiatry*. Published online: 16 January 2014. doi: 10.1192/bjp.bp.111.101816.

Milner A, Kõlves K, Kõlves K, Gladman B, De Leo D (2013). Treatment priority for suicide ideation and behaviours at an Australian emergency department. *World Journal of Psychiatry* 3, 34-40.

Mooney T (2014). Preventing psychological distress in patients with acne. *Nursing Standard* 28, 42-48.

Naughton M, Clarke G, Oleary OF, Cryan JF, Dinan TG (2014). A review of ketamine in affective disorders: Current evidence of clinical efficacy, limitations of use and pre-clinical evidence on proposed mechanisms of action. *Journal of Affective Disorders* 156, 24-35.

Neacsiu AD, Lungu A, Harned MS, Rizvi SL, Linehan MM (2014). Impact of dialectical behavior therapy versus community treatment by experts on emotional experience, expression, and acceptance in borderline personality disorder. *Behaviour Research and Therapy* 53, 47-54.

Nelson KJ (2013). Managing borderline personality disorder on general psychiatric units. *Psychodynamic Psychiatry* 41, 563-574.

Nordentoft M, Melau M, Iversen T, Petersen L, Jeppesen P, Thorup A, Bertelsen M, Hjorthoj CR, Hastrup LH, Jorgensen P (2013). From research to practice: How opus treatment was accepted and implemented throughout Denmark. *Early Intervention in Psychiatry*. Published online: 5 December 2013. doi: 10.1111/eip.12108.

O'Connell B, Dowling M (2013). Dialectical behaviour therapy (DBT) in the treatment of borderline personality disorder. *Journal of Psychiatric and Mental Health Nursing*. Published online: 5 November 2013. doi: 10.1111/jpm.12116.

Perugi G, Medda P, Reis J, Rizzato S, Giorgi Mariani M, Mauri M (2013). Clinical subtypes of severe bipolar mixed states. *Journal of Affective Disorders* 151, 1076-1082.

Piette JD, Aikens JE, Trivedi R, Parrish D, Standiford C, Marinec NS, Striplin D, Bernstein SJ (2013). Depression self-management assistance using automated telephonic assessments and social support. *American Journal of Managed Care* 19, 892-900.

Prološi J, Zeli SB, Peitl MV, Bistrovi IL (2013). Intensive psychiatric care - psychiatric emergencies. *Medicina Fluminensis* 49, 463-467.

Reijas T, Ferrer E, Gonzalez A, Iglesias F (2013). Evaluation of an intensive intervention program in suicidal behaviour. *Actas Espanolas De Psiquiatria* 41, 279-286.

Riva-Posse P, Hermida AP, McDonald WM (2013). The role of electroconvulsive and neuromodulation therapies in the treatment of geriatric depression. *Psychiatric Clinics of North America* 36, 607.

Robillard R, Naismith SL, Hickie IB (2013). Recent advances in sleep-wake cycle and biological rhythms in bipolar disorder. *Current Psychiatry Reports* 15, 402.

Sayal K, Yates N, Spears M, Stallard P (2014). Service use in adolescents at risk of depression and self-harm: Prospective longitudinal study. *Social Psychiatry and Psychiatric Epidemiology*. Published online: 26 February 2014. doi: 10.1007/s00127-014-0843-y.

Schlaepfer TE, Bewernick BH (2013). Deep brain stimulation for major depression. *Handbook of Clinical Neurology* 116, 235-243.

Schweitzer I, Menon R (2013). Recognising the suicidal patient. *Medicine Today* 14, 73-75.

Seo HJ, Jung YE, Jeong S, Kim JB, Lee MS, Kim JM, Yim HW, Jun TY (2013). Persistence and resolution of suicidal ideation during treatment of depression in patients with significant suicidality at the beginning of treatment: The crescend study. *Journal of Affective Disorders* 155, 208-215.

Smith EG, Deligiannidis KM, Ulbricht CM, Landolin CS, Patel JK, Rothschild AJ (2013). Antidepressant augmentation using the n-methyl-d-aspartate antagonist memantine: A randomized, double-blind, placebo-controlled trial. *Journal of Clinical Psychiatry* 74, 966-973.

Spijker AJ, Straten Av, Kerkhof JF (2014). Effectiveness of online self-help for suicidal thoughts: Results of a randomised controlled trial. *PLoS ONE*. Published online: 27 February 2014. doi: 10.1371/journal.pone.0090118.

Stikkelbroek Y, Bodden DH, Dekovi M, van Baar AL (2013). Effectiveness and cost effectiveness of cognitive behavioral therapy (CBT) in clinically depressed adolescents: Individual CBT versus treatment as usual (TAU). *BMC Psychiatry* 13, 314.

Sun FK, Long A, Tsao LI, Huang HM (2013). The healing process following a suicide attempt: Context and intervening conditions. *Archives of Psychiatric Nursing* 28, 55-61.

Tauch D, Winkel S, Quante A (2013). Psychiatric consultations and therapy recommendations following a suicide attempt in a general hospital and their associations with selected parameters in a one year period. *International Journal of Psychiatry in Clinical Practice*. Published online: 13 December 2013. doi: 10.3109/13651501.2013.865756.

Taylor D, Lenox-Smith A, Bradley A (2013). A review of the suitability of duloxetine and venlafaxine for use in patients with depression in primary care with a focus on cardiovascular safety, suicide and mortality due to antidepressant overdose. *Therapeutic Advances in Psychopharmacology* 3, 151-161.

Unützer J, Lin EH, Vannoy SD, Duberstein PR, Cukrowicz KC (2014). What factors determine disclosure of suicide ideation in adults 60 and older to a treatment provider? *Suicide and Life-Threatening Behavior*. Published online: 3 February 2014. doi: 10.1111/sltb.12075.

van Ballegooijen W, Riper H, Klein B, Ebert DD, Kramer J, Meulenbeek P, Cuijpers P (2013). An internet-based guided self-help intervention for panic symptoms: Randomized controlled trial. *Journal of Medical Internet Research* 15, 33-44.

Vatne M, Nåden D (2013). Patients' experiences in the aftermath of suicidal crises. *Nursing Ethics* 21, 163-175.

Walker X, Lee J, Koval L, Kirkwood A, Taylor J, Gibbs J, Ng S, Steele L, Thompson P, Celi LA (2013). Predicting ICU admissions from attempted suicide presentations at an emergency department in central Queensland. *Australasian Medical Journal* 6, 536-541.

Waszynski C, Veronneau P, Therrien K, Brousseau M, Massa A, Levick S (2013). Decreasing patient agitation using individualized therapeutic activities. *American Journal of Nursing* 113, 32-39.

Wijlaars LPMM, Nazareth I, Whitaker HJ, Evans SJW, Petersen I (2013). Suicide-related events in young people following prescription of SSRIs and other antidepressants: A self-controlled case series analysis. *British Medical Journal Open* 3, e003247.

Wills KA (2013). What does recovery mean to adults who self-injure? An interpretative phenomenological analysis. *International Journal of Psychosocial Rehabilitation* 17, 93-116.

Wong J, Brownson C, Rutkowski L, Nguyen C, Becker M (2014). A mediation model of professional psychological help seeking for suicide ideation among Asian American and white American college students. *Archives of Suicide Research*. Published online: 12 March 2014. doi: 10.1080/13811118.2013.824831.

Wong YJ, Maffini CS, Shin M (2014). The racial-cultural framework: A framework for addressing suicide-related outcomes in communities of color. *Counseling Psychologist* 42, 13-54.

Wortzel HS, Homaifar B, Matarazzo B, Brenner LA (2014). Therapeutic risk management of the suicidal patient: Stratifying risk in terms of severity and temporality. *Journal of Psychiatric Practice* 20, 63-67.

Wright B, Hooke N, Neupert S, Nyein C, Ker S (2013). Young people who cut themselves: Can understanding the reasons guide the treatment? *Advances in Psychiatric Treatment* 19, 446-456.

Yaseen ZS, Briggs J, Kopeykina I, Orchard KM, Silberlicht J, Bhingradia H, Galynker II (2013). Distinctive emotional responses of clinicians to suicide-attempting patients - a comparative study. *BMC Psychiatry* 13, 230.

Zunszain PA, Horowitz MA, Cattaneo A, Lupi MM, Pariante CM (2013). Ketamine: Synaptogenesis, immunomodulation and glycogen synthase kinase-3 as underlying mechanisms of its antidepressant properties. *Molecular Psychiatry* 18, 1236-1241.

Case Reports

Abhilash K, Arul J, Bala D (2013). Fatal overdose of iron tablets in adults. *Indian Journal of Critical Care Medicine* 17, 311-313.

Acera Pozzi R, Yee LM, Brown K, Driscoll KE, Rajan PV (2014). Pregnancy in the severely mentally ill patient as an opportunity for global coordination of care. *American Journal of Obstetrics and Gynecology* 210, 32-37.

Aggrawal A, Pradhan M, Sreenivas M (2014). Nail injury to the brain obfuscated by a fall from height - homicide or suicide? A case report. *Medicine, Science, and the Law*. Published online: 21 February 2014. doi: 10.1177/0025802414524191.

Ahuja AK, Biesaga K, Sudak DM, Draper J, Womble A (2014). Suicide on facebook. *Journal of Psychiatric Practice* 20, 141-146.

Algahtani HA, Aldarmahi AA, Al-Rabia MW, Almalki WH, Bryan Young G (2014). Generalized myoclonus and spasticity induced by lamotrigine toxicity: A case report and literature review. *Clinical Neuropharmacology* 37, 52-54.

Arnestad M, Eldor KBB, Stray-Pedersen A, Bachs L, Karinen R (2013). Suicide due to cyclizine overdose. *Journal of Analytical Toxicology* 38, 110-112.

Arslan MN, Melez DO, Gulbeyaz H, Hosukler B, Sam B, Koc S (2013). Possible death mechanisms other than respiratory asphyxia in a suicidal hanging case. *Romanian Journal of Legal Medicine* 21, 169-172.

Arun P, Sahni S (2014). Methylphenidate and suicidal ideation: Report of two cases. *Indian Journal of Psychiatry* 56, 79-81.

Atigari OV, Hogan C, Healy D (2013). Doxycycline and suicidality. *British Medical Journal Case Reports*. Published online: 17 December 2013. doi: 10.1136/bcr-2013-200723.

Balla I, Karafotias I, Christopoulos C (2013). Intentional overdose with tinzaparin: Management dilemmas. *Journal of Emergency Medicine* 46, 197-201.

Behera C, Krishna K, Singh Hr (2014). Antitubercular drug-induced violent suicide of a hospitalised patient. *British Medical Journal Case Reports*. Published online: 6 January 2014. doi: 10.1136/bcr-2013-201469.

Behera C, Rautji R, Sikary AK, Kumar R, Vidua RK, Millo T, Gupta SK (2014). Triple hanging in filicide-suicide: An unusual case report. *Medicine, Science, and the Law*. Published online: 18 March 2014. doi: 10.1177/0025802414524951.

Bennett A, Pourmand A, Shokoohi H, Shesser R, Sanchez J, Joyce J (2014). Impacts of social networking sites on patient care in the emergency department. *Telemedicine Journal and E-Health* 20, 94-96.

Blässer K, Tatschner T, Bohnert M (2013). Suicidal carbon monoxide poisoning using a gas-powered generator. *Forensic Science International* 236, e19-e21.

Byard RW (2013). Suicide attempts involving power drills. *Journal of Forensic and Legal Medicine* 20, 1032-1034.

Byers DS (2013). "Do they see nothing wrong with this?": Bullying, bystander complicity, and the role of homophobic bias in the Tyler Clementi case. *Families in Society* 94, 251-258.

Campana C, Griffin PL, Simon EL (2014). Caffeine overdose resulting in severe rhabdomyolysis and acute renal failure. *American Journal of Emergency Medicine* 32, 111.e113-111.e114.

Chan SK, Pang KY, Wong CK (2014). Transnasal penetrating intracranial injury with a chopstick. *Hong Kong Medical Journal* 20, 67-69.

Chowdhury FR, Bari MS, Alam MJ, Rahman MM, Bhattacharjee B, Qayyum JA, Mridha MS (2014). Organophosphate poisoning presenting with muscular weakness and abdominal pain- a case report. *BMC Research Notes* 7, 140.

de Santana NO, de Góis AFT (2013). Rhabdomyolysis as a manifestation of clomipramine poisoning. *Sao Paulo Medical Journal* 131, 432-435.

Dissanayake VL, Nasr I (2014). Betrayed mood in public view: Taking a myspace history. *Western Journal of Emergency Medicine* 15, 31-34.

Dogan KH, Demirci S, Fusun Baba Z, Buken B (2013). Suicide in two patients with epilepsy and cystic degeneration areas of their brains. *Romanian Journal of Legal Medicine* 21, 271-274.

Dorfman D, George MC, Tamler R, Lushing J, Nmashie A, Simpson DM (2014). Pruritus induced self injury behavior: An overlooked risk factor for amputation in diabetic neuropathy? *Diabetes Research and Clinical Practice.* Published online: 26 December 2013. doi: 10.1016/j.diabres.2013.12.013.

Edwards RT, McCormick-Deaton C, Hosanagar A (2014). Acute urinary retention secondary to buprenorphine administration. *The American Journal of Emergency Medicine* 32, 109.

Erden A, Karagoz H, Gümüscü HH, Karahan S, Basak M, Aykas F, Bulut K, Cetinkaya A, Avci D, Poyrazoglu OK (2013). Colchicine intoxication: A report of two suicide cases. *Therapeutics and Clinical Risk Management* 9, 505-509.

Franchitto N, Pelissier F, Lauque D, Simon N, Lancon C (2014). Self-intoxication with baclofen in alcohol-dependent patients with co-existing psychiatric illness: An emergency department case series. *Alcohol and Alcoholism* 49, 79-83.

Fuke C, Nagai T, Ninomiya K, Fukasawa M, Ihama Y, Miyazaki T (2014). Detection of imidacloprid in biological fluids in a case of fatal insecticide intoxication. *Legal Medicine* 16, 40-43.

Garlich FM, Goldman M, Pepe J, Nelson LS, Allan MJ, Goldstein DA, Goldfarb DS, Hoffman RS (2014). Hemodialysis clearance of glyphosate following a life-threatening ingestion of glyphosate-surfactant herbicide. *Clinical Toxicology* 52, 66-71.

Gaur S, Bist Hk, Sinha V, Gupta M (2013). An unusual case of self-inflicted multiple needles injuries to eye. *Indian Journal of Ophthalmology* 61, 516-517.

Griwan MS, Singh BJ, Rajan KY, Pal N, Lohchab SS (2013). Isolated vertebral artery injury secondary to suicidal neck stab. *Indian Journal of Thoracic and Cardiovascular Surgery* 29, 203-206.

Harada K, Itoi Y, Kanawaku Y, Nakatsumi T, Kanetake J (2014). An unusual case of suicide by handcrafted shotgun and slug. *Legal Medicine* 16, 95-97.

Herbst J, Stanley W, Byard RW (2014). Autopsy reenactment - a useful technique in the evaluation of adhesive tape asphyxia. *Journal of Forensic Science.* Published online: 6 February 2014. doi: 10.1111/1556-4029.12378.

Hoppner AC, Fauser S, Kerling F (2013). Clinical course of intoxication with the new anticonvulsant drug perampanel. *Epileptic Disorders* 15, 362-364.

Innamorato L, Pentone A, Introna F (2013). Dying transfixing his own heart: A rare case of suicide by stabbing. *American Journal of Forensic Medicine and Pathology* 34, 318-320.

Isabelle LB-L, Clarot F, Vaz E, Jean Pierre G, Proust B (2014). Disopyramide and mianserin intoxication: A unique fatal case - review of the literature. *Journal of Forensic Sciences.* Published online: 6 February 2014. doi: 10.1111/1556-4029.12392.

Karaci M, Özçetin M, Dilsiz G, Güçlü-Songür YG (2013). Severe childhood amitriptyline intoxication and plasmapheresis: A case report. *Turkish Journal of Pediatrics* 55, 645-647.

Karthik K, Behera C, Gupta S, Bhardwaj D (2013). Cut wrists, electrocution and subsequent drowning in a water drum: An unusual combination of methods in complex suicide. *Medico-Legal Journal* 81, 124-127.

Kobidze T, Urushadze O, Afandiyev I, Nemsadze G, Loladze D (2014). Clinical manifestation and management of intravenous mercury injection: A case report. *Georgian Medical News* 226, 11-16.

Kocourkova J, Dudova I, Koutek J (2013). Asperger syndrome related suicidal behavior: Two case studies. *Neuropsychiatric Disease and Treatment* 9, 1815-1819.

Kowlgi NG, Gowani SA, Mota P, Haider J (2013). Self-inflicted vertebral artery dissection: A case report and review of literature. *Connecticut Medicine* 77, 551-552.

Kumar S, Ali W, Verma AK, Pandey A, Rathore S (2013). Epidemiology and mortality of burns in the Lucknow region, India - a 5 year study. *Burns* 39, 1599-1605.

Kundavaram PPA, Majumdar S, Das S (2013). Intra-aural route of insecticide poisoning. *Toxicology International* 20, 192-193.

Lardi C, Vogt S, Pollak S, Thierauf A (2013). Complex suicide with homemade nicotine patches. *Forensic Science International* 236, e14-e18.

Madentzoglou MS, Kastanaki AE, Nathena D, Kranioti EF, Michalodimitrakis M (2013). Nitrogen-plastic bag suicide: A case report. *American Journal of Forensic Medicine and Pathology* 34, 311-314.

Mahmood K, Khan AM, Ramanan AV, Martin K (2013). Intentional overdose of azathioprine in a patient with systemic lupus erythematosus. *Scottish Medical Journal* 58, e3-e4.

Maiese A, Gitto L, Dell'aquila M, Bolino G (2014). A peculiar case of suicide enacted through the ancient Japanese ritual of Jigai. *American Journal of Forensic Medicine and Pathology* 35, 8-10.

Malkarnekar S, Anjanappa R, Naveen L, Kiran B (2014). Acute methemoglobinemia with hemolytic anemia following bio-organic plant nutrient compound exposure: Two case reports. *Indian Journal of Critical Care Medicine* 18, 115-117.

Matsuda T, Fujita H, Kunimoto Y, Kimura T, Maeda T, Yamakawa J, Maeda N, Takano K, Maruyama S, Uenaka Y, Ogino K (2013). Thoracoscopic esophagectomy in the prone position for corrosive stricture after esophageal perforation due to balloon dilatation. *Esophagus* 11, 146-151.

McDonald H (2013). Et ego in atlantis: A possible source for quentin cornpson's suicide. *Southern Literary Journal* 46, 36-47.

Miltner RS, Selleck CS, Moore RL, Patrician PA, Froelich KD, Eagerton GS, Harper DC (2013). Equipping the nursing workforce to care for the unique needs of veterans and their families. *Nurse Leader* 11, 45-48.

Mishra A, Pandya HV, Dave N, Mehta M (2013). Multi-organ dysfunction syndrome with dual organophosphate pesticides poisoning. *Toxicology International* 20, 275-277.

Mortaz Hejri S, Faizi M, Babaeian M (2013). Zolpidem-induced suicide attempt: A case report. *Daru* 21, 77.

Murat D, Arman A (2013). Suicidal attempt with high dose long-acting methylphenidate: A case report. *Marmara Medical Journal* 26, 165-167.

Namera A, Konuma K, Kawamura M, Saito T, Nakamoto A, Yahata M, Ohta S, Miyazaki S, Shiraishi H, Nagao M (2014). Time-course profile of urinary excretion of intravenously administered alpha-pyrrolidinovalerophenone and alpha-pyrrolidinobutiophenone in a human. *Forensic Toxicology* 32, 68-74.

Neely LL, Irwin K, Ponce JTC, Perera K, Grammer G, Ghahramanlou-Holloway M (2013). Post-admission cognitive therapy (PACT) for the prevention of suicide in military personnel with histories of trauma: Treatment development and case example. *Clinical Case Studies* 12, 457-473.

Nicholson L (2013). Risk of suicide in patients with dementia: A case study. *Nursing Standard* 28, 43-49.

Norgaard ML, Melchior T, Wagner T, Haugan K (2013). Suicide attempt by complete self-removal of a 12-year-old permanent pacemaker system: Case report. *Journal of Cardiovascular Electrophysiology* 25, 99-100.

Otasowie J, Hambleton BA (2013). Aggression and homicidal thoughts in a patient with primary hyperparathyroidism: A case report. *British Journal of Medical Practitioners* 6, a630.

Park YM, Kim YS (2014). Secondary mania in a patient with delayed anoxic encephalopathy after carbon monoxide intoxication caused by a suicide attempt. *General Hospital Psychiatry* 36, 125 e123-e124.

Patra BN, Sharma A, Mehra A, Singh S (2014). Complicated alcohol withdrawal presenting as self mutilation. *Journal of Forensic and Legal Medicine* 21, 46-47.

Pawlas N, Mi kiewicz Ł, Motyka S, Nowakowski R, Pajak J, Celi ski R, Kłopotowski T (2013). Fatal suicidal poisoning with antituberculosis agents with ST elevation and acute coronary syndrome symptoms—a case report. *Przeglad Lekarski* 70, 657-660.

Pentone A, Innamorato L, Introna F (2013). Dying transfixing his own heart a rare case of suicide by stabbing. *American Journal of Forensic Medicine and Pathology* 34, 318-320.

Philip R, Patidar PP, Agarwal P, Gupta KK (2013). A young diabetic with suicidal risk: Rare disease with a rarer presentation. *Indian Journal of Endocrinology and Metabolism* 17, 920-921.

Priya S, Siva N (2013). Dissociative identity disorder: An uncommon psychiatric disorder reported. *Indian Journal of Psychiatry* 55, 403-404.

Rastogi P, Acharya J, Atreya A (2013). Fatal suicidal gun shot injury. *Journal of Punjab Academy of Forensic Medicine and Toxicology* 13, 30-32.

Rossi R, Lodise M, Lancia M, Bacci M, De-Giorgio F, Cascini F (2014). Trigemino-cardiac reflex as lethal mechanism in a suicidal fire death case. *Journal of Forensic Science*. Published online: 6 February 2014. doi: 10.1111/1556-4029.12408.

Sakai K, Fukuda T, Iwadate K, Maruyama-Maebashi K, Asakura K, Ozawa M, Matsumoto S (2013). A fatal fall associated with undiagnosed parenchymatous neurosyphilis. *American Journal of Forensic Medicine and Pathology* 35, 4-7.

Sautter J, Gapert R, Tsokos M, Oesterhelweg L (2013). Murder-suicide by carbon dioxide (co2) poisoning: A family case from Berlin, Germany. *Forensic Science, Medicine, and Pathology* 10, 97-102.

Sethi NK, Douyon P, Kaunzner U, Sethi PK, Torgovnick J, Cukierwar F, Marcus J (2013). Delayed status epilepticus due to bupropion and lamotrigine overdose. *Eastern Journal of Medicine* 18, 142-144.

Shimamoto S, Namiki M, Harada T, Takeda M, Moroi R, Yaguchi A (2013). Case of multiple organ failure due to benzine ingestion. *The Japanese Journal of Toxicology* 26, 234-239.

Sikary AK, Jhamad AR, Millo T (2013). A successful attempted suicidal hanging: A case report. *Journal of Punjab Academy of Forensic Medicine and Toxicology* 13, 38-40.

Sim SK, Theophilus SC, Noor Azman AR (2013). Multiple nail gun penetrating head injury: A case report. *International Medical Journal Malaysia* 12, 75-78.

Takeshita H, Nagai T, Sagi M, Chiba S, Kanno S, Takada M, Mukai T (2014). Forensic identification using multiple lot numbers of an implanted device. *Medicine, Science and the Law* 54, 51-53.

Tanaka N, Kinoshita H, Jamal M, Kumihashi M, Tobiume T, Tsutsui K, Ameno K (2013). Usefulness of intratracheal gas analysis in an autopsy case of helium inhalation. *Romanian Journal of Legal Medicine* 21, 237-238.

Tandon V, Mahajan V, Gillani Z, Mahajan A (2013). Pregabalin-induced self-harm behavior. *Indian Journal of Pharmacology* 45, 638-639.

Torimitsu S, Yajima D, Abe H, Kubo Y, Nagasawa S, Iwase H (2013). Homicide-suicide by oral administration of cyclobarbital. *Forensic Toxicology* 32, 180-185.

Toth AR, Kovacs K, Arok Z, Varga T, Kereszty E, Institoris L (2013). The role of stimulant designer drug consumption in three fatal cases in south-east Hungary in 2011. *Romanian Journal of Legal Medicine* 21, 275-280.

Tsuboi A, Satoh F, Seto Y, Osawa M (2013). Self-inflicted fatal shotgun wound from a home-made weapon. *Legal Medicine* 16, 81-83.

Tubbs RS, Mosier KM, Cohen-Gadol AA (2013). Geniculate neuralgia: Clinical, radiologic, and intraoperative correlates. *World Neurosurgery* 80, e353-e357.

Tzimas I, Bajanowski T, Pollak S, Trubner K, Thierauf A (2014). Suicidal ligature strangulation using gymnastics bands. *International Journal of Legal Medicine* 128, 313-316.

Wang F, Zheng S, Zhang Y (2013). Serious bromocriptine-induced psychosis: Suicide in the treatment of prolactinoma. *Neurosurgery Quarterly* 23, 249-251.

Webb DV, Stowman AM, Patterson JW (2013). Boric acid ingestion clinically mimicking toxic epidermal necrolysis. *Journal of Cutaneous Pathology* 40, 962-965.

Yadav A, Alam F, Kothari NS, Gahlot RK (2013). Suicidal endosulphan poisoning in a pregnant woman a case report. *Journal of Indian Academy of Forensic Medicine* 35, 187-188.

Yeh CF, Lee TL (2013). Critical airway induced by formalin injection: Case report. *Journal of Laryngology and Otology* 128, 107-109.

Zarzar T, McEvoy J (2013). Clozapine for self-injurious behavior in individuals with borderline personality disorder. *Therapeutic Advances in Psychopharmacology* 3, 272-274.

Zhuang S-T, Chan C-T (2013). A case report of application of existential approach in an elder cancer patient with suicide ideation. *Psycho-Oncology* 22, 180-181.

Zorro AR (2014). Asphyxial suicide by inhalation of chloroform inside a plastic bag. *Journal of Forensic and Legal Medicine* 21, 1-4.

Zupancic R, Kuhar M (2013). Oral rehabilitation with implant supported overdentures in patients with non-reconstructed segmental. Mandibulectomy: A report of two cases. *Zdravniski Vestnik-Slovenian Medical Journal* 82, 695-701.

Miscellaneous

Anonymous (2013). Blood test to predict suicide risk being studied. *Journal of Psychosocial Nursing and Mental Health Services* 51, 6.

Anonymous (2013). Call for papers: Suicide prevention, nontraditional career paths, and lessons of leadership. *Academic Psychiatry* 37, 407.

Anonymous (2013). Hospital treatment for patients who self-harm in England is 'as variable as ever'. *British Journal of Hospital Medicine* 74, 669.

Anonymous (2013). Minnesota's suicide trend ticks upward. *Minnesota Medicine* 96, 9.

Anonymous (2014). Correction: Predicting the risk of suicide by analyzing the text of clinical notes. *PLoS ONE* 9, e91602.

Aaron M (2014). Cinema and suicide: Necromanticism, dead-already-ness, and the logic of the vanishing point. *Cinema Journal* 53, 71-92.

Adamse P, van Egmond HP, Noordam MY, Mulder PPJ, De Nijs M (2014). Tropane alkaloids in food: Poisoning incidents. *Quality Assurance and Safety of Crops and Foods* 6, 15-24.

Aggarwal S, Gerrets R (2014). Exploring a Dutch paradox: An ethnographic investigation of gay men's mental health. *Culture Health & Sexuality* 16, 105-119.

Aghabiklooei A, Mostafazadeh B, Farzaneh E, Morteza A (2013). Does organophosphate poisoning cause cardiac injury? *Pakistan Journal of Pharmaceutical Sciences* 26, 1247-1250.

Agrawal A, Lynskey MT (2014). Cannabis controversies: How genetics can inform the study of comorbidity. *Addiction* 109, 360-370.

Ahuja AK, Biesaga K, Sudak DM, Draper J, Womble A (2014). Suicide on Facebook. *Journal of Psychiatric Practice* 20, 141-146.

Aishvarya S, Maniam T, Karuthan C, Sidi H, Ruzyanei N, T.P.S O (2013). Psychometric properties and validation of the reasons for living inventory in an outpatient clinical population in Malaysia. *Comprehensive Psychiatry* 55, S107-S113.

Aizenstein HJ, Khalaf A, Walker SE, Andreescu C (2013). Magnetic resonance imaging predictors of treatment response in late-life depression. *Journal of Geriatric Psychiatry and Neurology* 27, 24-32.

Akbari B, Rahmani Ma, Darvishi F, Rahbar M (2013). A comparison of relationship between early maladaptive schemas with depression severity in suicidal group and non-clinical sample. *Procedia - Social and Behavioral Sciences* 84, 1072-1077.

Akinci E, Akilli NB, Köylü R, Cander B (2013). A retrospective evaluation of the patients over 65 years old who treated in toxicology intensive care unit because of unintentional or suicidal poisoning. *Turk Geriatri Dergisi* 16, 330-334.

Al-Khafaji K, Loy J, Kelly A-M (2014). Characteristics and outcome of patients brought to an emergency department by police under the provisions (section 10) of the mental health act in Victoria, Australia. *International Journal of Law and Psychiatry*. Published online: 24 March 2014. doi: 10.1016/j.ijlp.2014.02.013.

Allen N (2013). The right to life in a suicidal state. *International Journal of Law and Psychiatry* 36, 350-357.

Allen RP, Chen C, Garcia-Borreguero D, Polo O, DuBrava S, Miceli J, Knapp L, Winkelman JW (2014). Comparison of pregabalin with pramipexole for restless legs syndrome. *New England Journal of Medicine* 370, 621-631.

Alves MM, Alves SV, Antunes MB, Santos DL (2013). External causes and maternal mortality: Proposal for classification. *Revista de Saude Publica* 47, 283-291.

Andover PH (2013). Dentist suicides. *British Dental Journal* 215, 592-593.

Anestis MD, Moberg FB, Arnau RC (2013). Hope and the interpersonal-psychological theory of suicidal behavior: Replication and extension of prior findings. *Suicide and Life-Threatening Behavior.* Published online: 16 November 2013. doi: 10.1111/sltb.12060.

Arai S, Matsui H, Ohki R, Miyazawa Y, Koike H, Hashita T, Katsuyama Y, Sekine Y, Nomura M, Shibata Y, Hatori M, Ito K, Yamamoto K, Ohmori S, Suzuki K (2014). Suicide attempt with an overdose of sunitinib. *British Journal of Clinical Pharmacology.* Published online: 19 March 2014. doi: 10.1111/bcp.12381.

Arias ACA, Bruce A, Herrán D, Arango AM, Muñoz K, Abella P (2013). Variables associated with the risk of suicide in patients with chronic pain seen in a hospital outpatient clinic in Bogotá. *Revista Colombiana de Anestesiologia* 41, 267-273.

Armiento JS, Hamza CA, Willoughby T (2014). An examination of disclosure of nonsuicidal self-injury among university students. *Journal of Community and Applied Social Psychology.* Published online: 20 February 2014. doi: 10.1002/casp.2190.

Arnautovska U, Kõlves K, Ide N, De Leo D (2013). Review of suicide-prevention programs in Queensland: State- and community-level activities. *Australian Health Review* 37, 660-665.

Ascher-Svanum H, Novick D, Maria Haro J, Bertsch J, McDonnell D, Detke H (2013). Predictors of psychiatric hospitalization during 6 months of maintenance treatment with olanzapine long-acting injection: Post hoc analysis of a randomized, double-blind study. *BMC Psychiatry* 13, 224.

Atal D, Naik S, Das S (2013). Hurt & grievous hurt in Indian context. *Journal of Indian Academy of Forensic Medicine* 35, 160-164.

Aubin HJ, Berlin I, Kornreich C (2013). The evolutionary puzzle of suicide. *International Journal of Environmental Research and Public Health* 10, 6873-6886.

Babacanoglu C, Basgut EC, Kasap Y, Durmus N, Artiran G, Kerman S, Aydinkarahaliloglu D (2013). Necessity of quantity limiting per package for oral olanzapine preparations to minimize the suicide risk. *Drug Safety* 36, 842-843.

Bagcchi S, Chaudhuri P (2013). Suicide and the law in India. *British Medical Journal (Clinical Research Ed.)* 347, f6975.

Baiocco R, Fontanesi L, Ioverno S, Santamaria F, Lonigro A, Baumgartner E, Laghi F (2014). Risk and protective factors for suicidal tendency among gay and lesbian young adults. *Journal of Sexual Medicine* 11, 106.

Balazs J, Keresztény A, Pelbát G, Sinka L, Szilvás F, Torzsa T (2013). Online media report on a Hungarian double suicide case: Comparison of consecutively published articles. *Psychiatria Danubina* 25, 248-254.

Baldwin DS, Pallanti S, Zwanzger P (2013). Developing a European research network to address unmet needs in anxiety disorders. *Neuroscience and Biobehavioral Reviews* 37, 2312-2317.

Banerjee R, Liu JJ, Minhas HM (2013). Lyme neuroborreliosis presenting with alexithymia and suicide attempts. *Journal of Clinical Psychiatry* 74, 981.

Bani-Fatemi A, Howe AS, De Luca V (2014). Epigenetic studies of suicidal behavior. *Neurocase.* Published online: 31 January 2014. doi: 10.1080/13554794.2013.826679.

Barekatain M, Maracy MR, Hassannejad R, Hosseini R (2013). Factors associated with readmission of patients at a university hospital psychiatric ward in Iran. *Psychiatry Journal* 2013, 685625.

Barzilay-Levkowitz S, Apter A (2014). Psychological models of suicide. *Archives of Suicide Research.* Published online: 25 February 2014. doi: 10.1080/13811118.2013.824825.

Batinic B, Duisin D, Barisi J (2013). Obsessive versus delusional jealousy. *Psychiatria Danubina* 25, 334-339.

Bayes A, Parker G, Fletcher K (2014). Clinical differentiation of bipolar II disorder from borderline personality disorder. *Current Opinion in Psychiatry* 27, 14.

Beghi M, Rosenbaum JF, Cerri C, Cornaggia CM (2013). Risk factors for fatal and nonfatal repetition of suicide attempts: A literature review. *Neuropsychiatric Disease and Treatment* 9, 1725-1735.

Bell R (2013). Erratum: Slave suicide, abolition and the problem of resistance (slavery and abolition. *Slavery and Abolition* 34, 782.

Berman AL, Silverman MM (2013). Suicide risk assessment and risk formulation part II: Suicide risk formulation and the determination of levels of risk. *Suicide and Life-Threatening Behavior*. Published online: 29 November 2013. doi: 10.1111/sltb.12067.

Bethel J (2013). Assessment of suicidal intent in emergency care. *Nursing Standard* 28, 52-58.

Biggs M (2013). How repertoires evolve: The diffusion of suicide protest in the twentieth century. *Mobilization* 18, 407-428.

Biswas S, Haldar M, Mondal KK, Dalai CK, Bhattacharyya S, Chatterjee S, Das AK (2013). Rationally used antidotes in organophosphorus poisoning prevents suicidal death. *Journal of Indian Academy of Forensic Medicine* 35, 51-54.

Bland P (2013). Lithium reduces suicide risk in mood disorders. *Practitioner* 257, 10-11.

Blier P (2013). Neurotransmitter targeting in the treatment of depression. *Journal of Clinical Psychiatry* 74, 19-24.

Boccio DE, Macari AM (2014). Workplace as safe haven: How managers can mitigate risk for employee suicide. *Journal of Workplace Behavioral Health* 29, 32-54.

Bonnewyn A, Shah A, Bruffaerts R, Schoevaerts K, Rober P, Van Parys H, Demyttenaere K (2014). Reflections of older adults on the process preceding their suicide attempt: A qualitative approach. *Death Studies*. Published online: 10 February 2014. doi: 10.1080/07481187.2013.835753.

Bossarte RM, Blosnich JR, Piegari RI, Hill LL, Kane V (2013). Housing instability and mental distress among U.S. veterans. *American Journal of Public Health* 103, S213-S216.

Boulougouris V, Malogiannis I, Lockwood G, Zervas I, Di Giovanni G (2013). Erratum to: Serotonergic modulation of suicidal behaviour: Integrating preclinical data with clinical practice and psychotherapy. *Experimental Brain Research* 231, 127.

Bowers L (2014). Safewards: A new model of conflict and containment on psychiatric wards. *Journal of Psychiatric and Mental Health Nursing*. Published online: 19 February 2014. doi: 10.1111/jpm.12129.

Bowman S, Alvarez-Jimenez M, Wade D, Howie L, McGorry P (2014). The impact of first episode psychosis on sibling quality of life. *Social Psychiatry and Psychiatric Epidemiology*. Published online: 22 January 2014. doi: 10.1007/s00127-013-0817-5.

Bradvik L (2013). Last suicide attempt before completed suicide in severe depression: An extended suicidal process may be found in men rather than women. *Archives of Suicide Research* 17, 426-433.

Bramoweth AD, Germain A (2013). Deployment-related insomnia in military personnel and veterans. *Current Psychiatry Reports* 15, 401.

Breivik H, Reme SE, Linton SJ (2013). High risk of depression and suicide attempt among chronic pain patients: Always explore catastrophizing and suicide thoughts when evaluating chronic pain patients. *Scandinavian Journal of Pain* 5, 1-3.

Brodbeck J, Goodyer IM, Abbott RA, Dunn VJ, St Clair MC, Owens M, Jones PB, Croudace TJ (2013). General distress, hopelessness-suicidal ideation and worrying in adolescence: Concurrent and predictive validity of a symptom-level bifactor model for clinical diagnoses. *Journal of Affective Disorders* 152-154, 299-305.

Bruckner TA, McClure C, Kim Y (2014). Google searches for suicide and risk of suicide. *Psychiatric Services* 65, 271-272.

Bryant L, Garnham B (2014). The fallen hero: Masculinity, shame and farmer suicide in Australia. *Gender, Place and Culture.* Published online: 7 February 2014. doi: 10.1080/0966369X.2013.855628.

Burke TA (2014). Nonsuicidal self-injury: Advances in psychotherapy, evidence-based practice. *Journal of the American Academy of Child and Adolescent Psychiatry* 53, 119-121.

Caine ED (2013). Changing the focus of suicide research in China from rural to urban communities. *Shanghai Archives of Psychiatry* 25, 174-175.

Calati R, Giegling I, Balestri M, Antypa N, Friedl M, Konte B, Hartmann AM, Serretti A, Rujescu D (2013). Influence of differentially expressed genes from suicide post-mortem study on personality traits as endophenotypes on healthy subjects and suicide attempters. *European Archives of Psychiatry and Clinical Neuroscience.* Published online: 16 November 2013. doi: 10.1007/s00406-013-0469-1.

Callaghan RC, Sanches M, Gatley JM, Cunningham JK (2013). Effects of the minimum legal drinking age on alcohol-related health service use in hospital settings in Ontario: A regression-discontinuity approach. *American Journal of Public Health* 103, 2284-2291.

Carr A (2014). The evidence base for family therapy and systemic interventions for child-focused problems. *Journal of Family Therapy* 36, 107-157.

Carroll LJ, Rothe JP (2014). Viewing vehicular violence through a wide angle lens: Contributing factors and a proposed framework. *Canadian Journal of Criminology and Criminal Justice* 56, 149.

Cavanna AE, Seri S (2013). Psychiatric adverse effects of zonisamide in patients with epilepsy and mental disorder comorbidities. *Epilepsy and Behavior* 29, 281-284.

Chan-Hyung K, Yoon-Young N (2013). Effect of polymorphisms in tryptophan hydroxylase 2 gene on suicide risk in Korean patients with major depressive disorder. *International Journal of Psychiatry in Clinical Practice* 17, 17.

Chan S, Lam L, Chiu H (2013). Enhancing the role of doctors in preventing suicide. *Hong Kong Medical Journal* 19, 372-373.

Chandra PS, Doraiswamy P, Padmanabh A, Philip M (2013). Do newspaper reports of suicides comply with standard suicide reporting guidelines? A study from Bangalore, India. *International Journal of Social Psychiatry.* Published online: 18 December 2013. doi: 10.1177/0020764013513438.

Chang E, Chen R, Ng J, Ruan J, Simon MA, Dong X (2013). A prevalence study of suicidal ideation and suicide attempts among U.S. Chinese older adults. *Gerontologist* 53, 157.

Chapman SCE, Horne R (2013). Medication nonadherence and psychiatry. *Current Opinion in Psychiatry* 26, 446-452.

Chapman SLC, Wu LT (2013). Suicide and substance use among female veterans: A need for research. *Drug and Alcohol Dependence* 136, 1-10.

Chartier KG, Vaeth PAC, Caetano R (2013). Focus on: Ethnicity and the social and health harms from drinking. *Alcohol Research-Current Reviews* 35, 229-237.

Chaudhary NS, Chakravorty S, Evenden JL, Sanuck N (2013). Insomnia severity is associated with decreased executive functioning in patients with suicidal ideation and drug abuse. *Primary Care Companion to the Journal of Clinical Psychiatry* 15, PCC.13l01548.

Chen J, Cai Y, Cong E, Liu Y, Gao J, Li Y, Tao M, Zhang K, Wang X, Gao C, Yang L, Li K, Shi J, Wang G, Liu L, Zhang J, Du B, Jiang G, Shen J, Zhang Z, Liang W, Sun J, Hu J, Liu T, Wang X, Miao G, Meng H, Li Y, Hu C, Huang G, Li G, Ha B, Deng H, Mei Q, Zhong H, Gao S, Sang H, Zhang Y, Fang X, Yu F, Yang D, Liu T, Chen Y, Hong X, Wu W, Chen G, Cai M, Song Y, Pan J, Dong J, Pan R, Zhang W, Shen Z, Liu Z, Gu D, Wang X, Liu X, Zhang Q, Li Y, Chen Y, Kendler KS, Shi S, Flint J (2014). Childhood sexual abuse and the development of recurrent major depression in Chinese women. *PLoS ONE* 9, e87569.

Christensen RC (2013). Commentary on suicide and homelessness: What differentiates homeless persons who died by suicide from other suicides in Australia? A comparative analysis using a unique mortality registry. *Social Psychiatry and Psychiatric Epidemiology* 49, 591-592.

Claes L, Smits D, Bijttebier P (2014). The Dutch version of the emotion reactivity scale validation and relation with various behaviors in a sample of high school students. *European Journal of Psychological Assessment* 30, 73-79.

Clark CB, P SH, Brown A, K LC (2014). Anxiety and suicidal ideation predict successful completion of substance abuse treatment in a criminal justice sample. *Substance Use and Misuse*. Published online: 5 February 2014. doi: 10.3109/10826084.2014.880722.

Clark JL (2014). Poetic renarration of disenfranchised grief in relation to client suicide. *Qualitative Inquiry* 20, 253.

Clements C, Morriss R, Jones S, Peters S, Roberts C, Kapur N (2013). Suicide in bipolar disorder in a national English sample, 1996-2009: Frequency, trends and characteristics. *Psychological Medicine* 43, 2593-2602.

Cloutier A-M, Greenfield B, Lavoie A, Lynd LD, Tournier M, Brabant M-J, Moride Y (2013). Effectiveness of risk communication interventions on the medical follow-up of youth treated with antidepressants. *Psychiatry Research* 209, 471-478.

Coffey CE, Coffey MJ, Ahmedani BK (2013). An update on perfect depression care. *Psychiatric Services* 64, 396.

Collins R (2013). Take leave of the world: Suicide in the west and in the east. *Contemporary Sociology* 42, 160-166.

Cooke BK (2013). Extended suicide with a pet. *Journal of the American Academy of Psychiatry and the Law* 41, 437-443.

Cooley DR (2013). "A kantian care ethics suicide duty". *International Journal of Law and Psychiatry* 36, 366-373.

Coon H, Darlington T, Pimentel R, Smith KR, Huff CD, Hu H, Jerominski L, Hansen J, Klein M, Callor WB, Byrd J, Bakian A, Crowell SE, McMahon WM, Rajamanickam V, Camp NJ, McGlade E, Yurgelun-Todd D, Grey T, Gray D (2013). Genetic risk factors in two Utah pedigrees at high risk for suicide. *Translational Psychiatry* 3, e325.

Corathers SD, Kichler J, Jones N-HY, Houchen A, Jolly M, Morwessel N, Crawford P, Dolan LM, Hood KK (2013). Improving depression screening for adolescents with type 1 diabetes. *Pediatrics* 132, e1395-1402.

Cossy LS, Miller LT (2013). A descriptive study of primary health care practices in Ontario's youth custody facilities. *Paediatrics and Child Health (Canada)* 18, 523-528.

Coughlin SS, Leo S (2013). Suicidal behavior and neurological illnesses. *Journal of Depression and Anxiety* Suppl 9, S9-001.

Cover R (2013). Conditions of living: Queer youth suicide, homonormative tolerance, and relative misery. *Journal of LGBT Youth* 10, 328-350.

Crona L, Mossberg A, Bradvik L (2013). Suicidal career in severe depression among long-term survivors: In a followup after 37-53 years suicide attempts appeared to end long before depression. *Depression Research and Treatment* 2013, 610245.

Crowell S, Yaptangco M (2013). Suicidal behaviours are common among U.S. adolescents and are associated with mental health disorders. *Evidence-Based Mental Health* 16, 106.

Cullen JG (2013). Towards an organisational suicidology. *Culture and Organization* 20, 40-52.

Curtis B, Curtis C, Fleet RW (2013). Socio-economic factors and suicide: The importance of inequality. *New Zealand Sociology* 28, 77-92.

Cyprien F, Guillaume S, Jaussent I, Lopez-Castroman J, Mercier G, Olie E, Courtet P (2014). Impact of axis-i comorbidity and suicidal behavior disorders on sensitivity and specificity of the mood disorder questionnaire in complex depressed inpatients. *Comprehensive Psychiatry*. Published online: 13 February 2014. doi: 10.1016/j.comppsych.2014.02.004.

Daine K, Hawton K, Singaravelu V, Stewart A, Simkin S, Montgomery P (2013). The power of the web: A systematic review of studies of the influence of the internet on self-harm and suicide in young people. *PLoS ONE*. Published online: 30 October 2013. doi: 10.1371/journal.pone.0077555.

Davies NM, Gunnell D, Thomas KH, Metcalfe C, Windmeijer F, Martin RM (2013). Physicians' prescribing preferences were a potential instrument for patients' actual prescriptions of anti-depressants. *Journal of Clinical Epidemiology* 66, 1386-1396.

Davis C, Shuss S, Lockhart L (2014). Assessing suicide risk. *Nursing Made Incredibly Easy* 12, 22-29.

De Gioannis A, De Leo D (2014). Oral ketamine augmentation for chronic suicidality in treatment-resistant depression. *Australian and New Zealand Journal of Psychiatry*. Published online: 22 January 2014. doi: 10.1177/0004867414520754.

Dedesma RK, Kallivayalil D, Albanese MJ, Eisen JC (2014). A slow suicide: The seemingly infinite cycle of alcohol and trauma in a middle-aged woman. *Harvard Review of Psychiatry* 22, 46-54.

Degenhardt L, Larney S, Randall D, Burns L, Hall W (2013). Causes of death in a cohort treated for opioid dependence between 1985 and 2005. *Addiction* 109, 90-99.

Dhiman GJ, Amber KT (2013). Pharmaceutical ethics and physician liability in side effects. *Journal of Medical Humanities* 34, 497-503.

Di Marco F (2013). Act or disease?: The making of modern suicide in early twentieth-century Japan. *The Journal of Japanese Studies* 39, 325-358.

Dodemaide P, Crisp BR (2013). Living with suicidal thoughts. *Health Sociology Review* 22, 308-317.

Dolton EC (2013). GPS may be the last port of call in suicide. *British Medical Journal* 347, f6472.

Döme P, Kapitány B, Faludi G, Gonda X, Rihmer Z (2013). Does economic environment influence the strength of the positive association between suicide and unemployment? *Journal of Epidemiology and Community Health* 67, 1074-1075.

Dray X, Cattan P (2013). Foreign bodies and caustic lesions. *Best Practice & Research in Clinical Gastroenterology* 27, 679-689.

Du L, Merali Z, Poulter MO, Palkovits M, Faludi G, Anisman H (2014). Catechol-o-methyltransferase val158met polymorphism and altered COMT gene expression in prefrontal cortex of suicide brains. *Progress in Neuro-Psychopharmacology and Biological Psychiatry* 3, 178-183.

Duff AJ, Chan CCA (2014). Investigating suicide as a career response. *Career Development International* 19, 4-26.

Duncan RE, Williams BJ, Knowles A (2013). Adolescents, risk behaviour and confidentiality: When would Australian psychologists breach confidentiality to disclose information to parents? *Australian Psychologist* 48, 408-419.

Dyer A, Hennrich L, Borgmann E, White AJ, Alpers GW (2013). Body image and noticeable self-inflicted scars. *Journal of Nervous and Mental Disease* 201, 1080-1084.

Eade DM, Henning D (2013). Chlamydia screening in young people as an outcome of a headss; home, education, activities, drug and alcohol use, sexuality and suicide youth psychosocial assessment tool. *Journal of Clinical Nursing* 22, 3280.

Eggertson L (2013). Inuit leaders announce national inuit suicide-prevention strategy. *Candian Medical Association Journal* 185, e703-e704.

Eggertson L (2013). Risk of suicide 40 times higher for Inuit boys. *Candian Medical Association Journal* 185, e701-e702.

Eggertson L (2013). Suicide prevention training saves lives in Nunavut. *Candian Medical Association Journal* 185, 1306-1307.

Eggertson L (2014). Nunavut calls inquest into record number of suicides. *Candian Medical Association Journal* 186, e109-e110.

Erchull MJ, Liss M, Lichiello S (2013). Extending the negative consequences of media internalization and self-objectification to dissociation and self-harm. *Sex Roles* 69, 583-593.

Evans J (2013). Research and practice priorities for suicide prevention in later life. *Gerontologist* 53, 593-594.

Fertleman C, Carroll W (2013). Protecting students and promoting resilience. *British Medical Journal* 347, F5266.

Filakovic P, Eric AP (2013). Pharmacotherapy of suicidal behaviour in major depression, schizophrenia and bipolar disorder. *Collegium Antropologicum* 37, 1039-1044.

Filgueiras A, Nunes ALS, Silveira LAS, de Assis da Silva R, da Silva RO, Landeira-Fernandez J, Cheniaux E (2014). Latent structure of the symptomatology of hospitalized patients with bipolar mania. *European Psychiatry*. Published online: 13 March 2014. doi: 10.1016/j.eurpsy.2014.02.003.

Fink M, Kellner CH, McCall WV (2013). The role of ECT in suicide prevention. *Journal of ECT* 30, 5-9.

Fish R (2013). Women who use secure services: Applying the literature to women with learning disabilities. *Journal of Forensic Practice* 15, 192-205.

Fish R, Judd A, Jungmann E, O'Leary C, Foster C (2013). Mortality in perinatally HIV-infected young people in England following transition to adult care: An HIV young persons network (HYPnet) audit. *HIV Medicine* 15, 239-244.

Fitzpatrick SJ, Hooker C, Kerridge I (2014). Suicidology as a social practice. *Social Epistemology*. Published online: 12 March 2014. doi: 10.1080/02691728.2014.895448.

Flaig B, Zedler B, Ackermann H, Bratzke H, Parzeller M (2013). Reply to commentary on "anthropometrical differences between suicide and other non-natural death circumstances: An autopsy study". *International Journal of Legal Medicine* 128, 397-399.

Fonseca L, Duarte J, Machado A, Sotiropoulos I, Lima C, Sousa N (2014). Suicidal behaviour in frontotemporal dementia patients-a retrospective study. *International Journal of Geriatric Psychiatry* 29, 217-218.

Forrester A, Slade K (2013). Preventing self-harm and suicide in prisoners: Job half done. *The Lancet* 383, 1109-1111.

Freuchen A, Grøholt B (2013). Characteristics of suicide notes of children and young adolescents: An examination of the notes from suicide victims 15 years and younger. *Clinical Child Psychology and Psychiatry*. Published online: 4 October 2013. doi: 10.1177/1359104513504312.

Friedman ES, Calabrese JR, Ketter TA, Leon AC, Thase ME, Bowden CL, Sylvia LG, Ostracher MJ, Severe J, Iosifescu DV, Nierenberg AA, Reilly-Harrington NA (2014). Using comparative effectiveness design to improve the generalizability of bipolar treatment trials data: Contrasting litmus baseline data with pre-existing placebo controlled trials. *Journal of Affective Disorders* 152-154, 97-104.

Geiger B (2013). Ethiopian males account for the double acts of murder and suicide committed by males in Ethiopian families postmigration to Israel. *International Criminal Justice Review* 23, 233.

Ghaziuddin N, King CA, Welch K, Ghaziuddin M (2013). Depressed suicidal adolescent males have an altered cortisol response to a pharmacological challenge. *Asian Journal of Psychiatry* 7, 28-33.

Gijzen S, Boere-Boonekamp MM, L'Hoir MP, Need A (2013). Child mortality in the netherlands in the past decades: An overview of external causes and the role of public health policy. *Journal of Public Health Policy* 35, 43-59.

Gilden A (2013). Cyberbullying and the innocence narrative. *Harvard Civil Rights* 48, 357-407.

Glendinning E (2013). Reinventing Lucretia: Rape, suicide and redemption from classical antiquity to the medieval era. *International Journal of the Classical Tradition* 20, 61-82.

Godlee F (2013). Editor's choice: Austerity, suicide, and screening. *British Medical Journal* 347, f5678.

Goldblatt MJ, Herbstman B, Maltsberger JT (2014). Superego distortions and self-attack. *Scandinavian Psychoanalytic Review*. Published online: 21 February 2014. doi: 10.1080/01062301.2014.891797.

Gonon A (2013). Vulnerability in times of disaster. *Iride* 26, 551-563.

Gordon MS, Melvin GA (2013). Suicide risk assessment: Where are we now? *Medical Journal of Australia* 199, 534.

Gould R (2014). Aaron Swartz's legacy. *Academe* 100, 19-23.

Graham M (2013). On deliberate self-harm and emergency departments. *Advances in Mental Health* 12, 2-7.

Green JG, Johnson RM, Dunn EC, Lindsey M, Xuan Z, Zaslavsky AM (2014). Mental health service use among high school students exposed to interpersonal violence. *Journal of School Health* 84, 141-149.

Gregoriano C, Ceschi A, Rauber-Lüthy C, Kupferschmidt H, Banner NR, Krähenbühl S, Taegtmeyer AB (2014). Acute thiopurine overdose: Analysis of reports to a national poison centre 1995-2013. *PLoS ONE*. Published online: 29 January 2014. doi: 10.1371/journal.pone.0086390.

Haddock G, Eisner E, Davies G, Coupe N, Barrowclough C (2013). Psychotic symptoms, self-harm and violence in individuals with schizophrenia and substance misuse problems. *Schizophrenia Research* 151, 215-220.

Hahn A, Jochai D, Caufield-Noll C, Hunt C, Allen L, Rios R, Cordts G (2013). Self-inflicted burns: A systematic review of the literature. *Journal of Burn Care and Research* 35, 102-119.

Hajebi A, Ahmadzad-Asl M, Ershadi M, Nikfarjam A, Davoudi F (2013). National registration system of suicide behaviors in Iran: Barriers and challenges. *Archives of Suicide Research* 17, 416-425.

Hales H, Freeman M, Edmondson A, Taylor P (2013). Witnessing suicide-related behavior in prison. *Crisis* 35, 10-17.

Hami H, Diallo T, Maiga A, Mokhtari A, Soulaymani-Bencheikh R, Soulaymani A (2013). Suicidal poisoning with drugs in Bamako, Mali. *Drug Safety* 36, 921.

Hammerton G, Zammit S, Potter R, Thapar A, Collishaw S (2014). Validation of a composite of suicide items from the mood and feelings questionnaire (MFQ) in offspring of recurrently depressed parents. *Psychiatry Research* 216, 82-88.

Han MA, Oh MG, Park J, Ryu SY, Choi SW (2013). Suicidal ideation and attempts in cancer survivors: Community health survey, 2008. *Gastroenterology* 144, S583.

Handley SA, Fisher DS, Flanagan RJ (2013). Fatal poisoning, antipsychotic drugs, England and Wales, 2000-2011. *Therapeutic Drug Monitoring* 35, 701.

Hardelid P, Gilbert R (2013). Accurate data on all injury deaths is vital for monitoring suicide prevention. *Archives of Disease in Childhood.* Published online: 18 October 2013. doi: 10.1136/archdischild-2013-304957.

Harden CL, Meador KJ (2013). Do antiepileptic drugs cause suicidal behavior? *Neurology* 81, 1889-1890.

Harrison DP, Stritzke WG, Fay N, Ellison TM, Hudaib AR (2014). Probing the implicit suicidal mind: Does the death/suicide implicit association test reveal a desire to die, or a diminished desire to live? *Psychological Assessment.* Published online: 10 March 2014. doi: 10.1037/pas0000001.

Hawcroft M (2013). Blood and teardrops: The suicide in the profane tragedies of Jean Racine. *French Studies* 67, 552-553.

Hawkes N (2014). Campaigners win fight to retain UK statistics on cancer deaths, lifestyle, and suicides *British Medical Journal* 348, G1504.

Healy D, Bechthold K, Tolias P (2014). Antidepressant-induced suicidality: How translational epidemiology incorporating pharmacogenetics into controlled trials can improve clinical care. *Personalized Medicine* 11, 79-88.

Hecht JM (2013). To live is an act of courage. *The American Scholar* 82, 41-49.

Heisel MJ, Flett GL (2013). Investigating the association between perceived autonomy and suicide ideation among older adults. *Gerontologist* 53, 386.

Hemenway D (2013). Preventing gun violence by changing social norms. *JAMA Internal Medicine* 173, 1167-1168.

Hemenway D (2014). Guns, suicide, and homicide: Individual-level versus population-level studies. *Annals of Internal Medicine* 160, 134-135.

Hendrikson H (2013). Preventable deaths on the rise: Growing numbers of overdoses, suicides, and brain injuries have lawmakers searching for solutions. *State Legislatures* 39, 30-31.

Heron M (2013). Deaths: Leading causes for 2010. *National Vital Statistics Reports* 62, 1-97.

Hilal MA, Mohamed KM, Aly NS (2013). Suicide and homicide by para-phenylenediamine poisoning in upper Egypt. *Therapeutic Drug Monitoring* 35, 710-711.

Hiriscau IE, Stingelin-Giles N, Stadler C, Schmeck K, Reiter-Theil S (2014). A right to confidentiality or a duty to disclose? Ethical guidance for conducting prevention research with children and adolescents. *European Child and Adolescent Psychiatry.* Published online: 12 March 2014. doi: 10.1007/s00787-014-0526-y.

Hjelmeland H, Osafo J, Akotia CS, Knizek BL (2013). The law criminalizing attempted suicide in Ghana. *Crisis* 35, 132-136.

Hollings J (2013). Reporting suicide in New Zealand: Time to end censorship. *Pacific Journalism Review* 19, 136-155.

Hoyo-Becerra C, Huebener A, Trippler M, Lutterbeck M, Liu ZJ, Truebner K, Bajanowski T, Gerken G, Hermann DM, Schlaak JF (2013). Concomitant interferon alpha stimulation and TRL3 activation induces neuronal expression of depression-related genes that are elevated in the brain of suicidal persons. *PLoS ONE* 8, e83149.

Hulse EJ, Clutton RE, Drummond G, Eddleston M (2013). Translational toxicological research: Investigating and preventing acute lung injury in organophosphorus insecticide poisoning. *Journal of the Royal Army Medical Corps.* Published online: 18 December 2013. doi: 10.1136/jramc-2013-000207.

Hunter E (2014). Mental health in Indigenous settings: Challenges for clinicians. *Australian Family Physician* 43, 26-28.

Içer M, Gülolu C, Orak M, Üstünda M (2013). Factors affecting mortality caused by falls from height. *Ulusal Travma ve Acil Cerrahi Dergisi* 19, 529-535.

Iessa N, Murray M, Wong I, Man K, Frank B, Santosh P, Sutcliffe A (2013). Leukotriene receptor antagonists and suicide: A self-controlled case series study. *Drug Safety* 36, 855.

In-Albon T, Ruf C, Schmid M (2013). Proposed diagnostic criteria for the DSM-5 of nonsuicidal self-injury in female adolescents: Diagnostic and clinical correlates. *Psychiatry Journal* 2013, 159208.

Inett A, Wright G, Roberts L, Sheeran A (2014). Predictive validity of the start with intellectually disabled offenders. *Journal of Forensic Practice* 16, 78-88.

Isacsson G, Rich CL (2014). Antidepressant drugs and the risk of suicide in children and adolescents. *Paediatric Drugs* 16, 115-122.

Iverson GL (2013). Chronic traumatic encephalopathy and risk of suicide in former athletes. *British Journal of Sports Medicine* 48, 162-165.

Jain S, Jain R (2014). Key steps to take when a patient commits suicide. *Current Psychiatry* 13, 79.

Janik M, Hejna P (2014). Comments on self-inflicted fatal shotgun wound from a homemade weapon. *Legal Medicine*. Published online: 12 February 2014. doi: 10.1016/j.legalmed.2014.02.001.

Jiménez Quenguan M, Hidalgo Bravo J, Camargo Santacruz C, Dulce Rosero PB (2014). Attempted suicide in a pediatric population, alarming reality. *Revista Ciencias de la Salud* 12, 59-92.

Joffe BI, Van Lieshout RJ, Duncan L, Boyle MH (2014). Suicidal ideation and behavior in adolescents aged 12-16 years: A 17-year follow-up. *Suicide and Life-Threatening Behavior*. Published online: 4 February 2014. doi: 10.1111/sltb.12077.

Juang KD, Yang CY (2014). Psychiatric comorbidity of chronic daily headache: Focus on traumatic experiences in childhood, post-traumatic stress disorder and suicidality. *Current Pain and Headache Reports* 18, 1-7.

Jung JH, Olson DVA (2014). Religion, stress, and suicide acceptability in South Korea. *Social Forces* 92, 1039-1059.

Kaess M, Brunner R, Parzer P, Carli V, Apter A, Balazs JA, Bobes J, Coman HG, Cosman D, Cotter P, Durkee T, Farkas L, Feldman D, Haring C, Iosue M, Kahn JP, Keeley H, Podlogar T, Postuvan V, Resch F, Saiz PA, Sisask M, Tubiana A, Varnik P, Sarchiapone M, Hoven CW, Wasserman D (2013). Risk-behaviour screening for identifying adolescents with mental health problems in Europe. *European Child and Adolescent Psychiatry*. Published online: 19 November 2013. doi: 10.1007/s00787-013-0490-y.

Kang C, Kim SC, Lee SH, Jeong JH, Kim DS, Kim DH (2013). Absolute lymphocyte count as a predictor of mortality in emergency department patients with paraquat poisoning. *PLoS ONE* 8, e78160.

Kanner AM (2013). Epilepsy psychiatric comorbidities and premature death in epilepsy. *Nature Reviews Neurology* 9, 606-608.

Kaplan MS, Giesbrecht N, Caetano R, Conner KR, Huguet N, McFarland BH, Nolte KB, Caine ED (2013). Acute alcohol consumption as a contributing factor to suicidal behavior/Caine responds. *American Journal of Public Health* 103, E2-E3.

Kawada T (2013). Screening strategy of depression in patients with systemic sclerosis with special reference to suicide. *Arthritis Care and Research* 66, 497.

Kempf A (2013). The suicide shop. *Library Journal* 138, 66.

Kerr DC, Gibson B, Leve LD, Degarmo DS (2014). Young adult follow-up of adolescent girls in juvenile justice using the Columbia suicide severity rating scale. *Suicide and Life-Threatening Behavior*. Published online: 22 January 2014. doi: 10.1111/sltb.12072.

Keyes KM, Cheslack-Postava K, Westhoff C, Heim CM, Haloossim M, Walsh K, Koenen K (2013). Association of hormonal contraceptive use with reduced levels of depressive symptoms: A national study of sexually active women in the United States. *American Journal of Epidemiology* 178, 1378-1388.

Khalil ZH, Naeem M, Adil M, Khan MZI, Abbas SH, Faqirullah (2013). Analysis of autopsy record of unnatural deaths in Peshawar district. *Journal of Postgraduate Medical Institute* 27, 392-396.

Kim JH, Park EC, Cho WH, Park CY, Choi WJ, Chang HS (2013). Association between total sleep duration and suicidal ideation among the Korean general adult population. *Sleep* 36, 1563.

Kim KR, Cho H-S, Kim SJ, Seok J-H, Lee E, Jon D-I (2013). Reevaluation of patients with bipolar disorder on manic episode improving the diagnosing of mixed episode. *Journal of Nervous and Mental Disease* 201, 686-690.

Kimberley Molina D, DiMaio V, Cave R (2013). Gunshot wounds: A review of firearm type, range, and location as pertaining to manner of death. *American Journal of Forensic Medicine and Pathology* 34, 366-371.

Kirsch B (2014). Preventing suicide in U.S. veterans remains challenging. *The Lancet* 383, 589-590.

Kleiman EM, Law KC, Anestis MD (2013). Do theories of suicide play well together? Integrating components of the hopelessness and interpersonal psychological theories of suicide. *Comprenensive Psychiatry* 55, 431-438.

Klonsky ED, May AM (2013). Differentiating suicide attempters from suicide ideators: A critical frontier for suicidology research. *Suicide and Life-Threatening Behavior* 44, 1-5.

Knizek BL, Kinyanda E, Akotia CS, Hjelmeland H (2013). Between hippocrates and God: Ugandan mental health professional's views on suicide. *Mental Health, Religion and Culture* 16, 767-780.

Knox KL, Bajorska A, Feng C, Tang W, Wu P, Tu XM (2013). Survival analysis for observational and clustered data: An application for assessing individual and environmental risk factors for suicide. *Shanghai Archives of Psychiatry* 25, 183-194.

Koirala DP, Rao KS, Malla KK, Malla T (2013). A study of clinical features, management and outcome of organophosphate and carbamate poisoning in children. *Journal of Nepal Paediatric Society* 33, 85-90.

Kounis NG, Soufras GD, Kounis GN, Hahalis G (2013). Suicidal anaphylactic death: Is kounis anaphylaxis associated syndrome the cause? *Forensic Science International* 232, E42-E43.

Kudo K, Otsuka K, Yagi J, Sanjo K, Koizumi N, Koeda A, Umetsu MY, Yoshioka Y, Mizugai A, Mita T, Shiga Y, Koizumi F, Nakamura H, Sakai A (2014). Predictors for delayed encephalopathy following acute carbon monoxide poisoning. *BMC Emergency Medicine*. Published online: 31 January 2014. doi: 10.1186/1471-227X-14-3.

Kumar PNS, Anish PK (2014). Methodological considerations in studying psycho-social aspects of suicide: Reply to the criticism. *Indian Journal of Psychiatry* 56, 98.

Kumar S, Verma A (2013). A study of elderly unnatural deaths in medico-legal autopsies at lucknow locality. *Medicine, Science and the Law*. Published online: 28 October 2013. doi: 10.1177/0025802413502783.

Kumar S, Verma AK, Ali W, Pandey A, Ahmad I, Singh US (2013). A study of unnatural female death profile in Lucknow, India. *American Journal of Forensic Medicine and Pathology* 34, 352-356.

Kumar V, Talwar R (2014). Determinants of psychological stress and suicidal behavior in Indian adolescents: A literature review. *Journal of Indian Association for Child and Adolescent Mental Health* 10, 47-68.

Kundagrami S, Mukherjee K, Datta M (2013). Self-harm: Are we doing enough? *Archives of Disease in Childhood* 99, 185.

Laas K, Reif A, Akkermann K, Kiive E, Domschke K, Lesch KP, Veidebaum T, Harro J (2013). Interaction of the neuropeptide s receptor gene asn107ile variant and environment: Contribution to affective and anxiety disorders, and suicidal behaviour. *International Journal of Neuropsychopharmacology* 17, 541-552.

Lambert E (2013). "Death will abide": A meditation on an adolescent suicide. *Raritan* 33, 122-147.

Lee K (2013). Depression and suicidal ideation in community dwelling elderly. *International Journal of Psychiatry in Clinical Practice* 17, 25.

Lemon TI (2013). Etiology of non-typical suicide patterns essential. *Indian Journal of Public Health* 57, 281-282.

Leong CH, Wu AM, Poon MM (2014). Measurement of perceived functions of non-suicidal self-injury for Chinese adolescents. *Archives of Suicide Research.* Published online: 25 February 2014. doi: 10.1080/13811118.2013.824828.

Leray E, Vukusic S, Confavreux C, Debouverie M, Clanet M, Brochet B, de Seze J, Zephir H, Lebrun-Frenay C, Defer G, Moreau T, Clavelou P, Pelletier J, Berger E, Camdessanche J, Yaouanq J, Le Page E, Edan G (2013). Suicide in multiple sclerosis: Insights from the survimus study, a large multicentre study on long-term mortality of French patients. *Multiple Sclerosis Journal* 19, 347-348.

Lester D (2013). Suicide prevention on campus - what direction? *Crisis* 34, 371-373.

Lester D, McSwain S, Gunn Iii JF (2013). Suicide and the internet: The case of Amanda Todd. *International Journal of Emergency Mental Health* 15, 179-180.

Levinger S, Holden RR (2014). Reliability and validation of the hebrew version of the reasons for attempting suicide questionnaire (RASQ-H) and its importance for mental pain. *Suicide and Life-Threatening Behavior.* Published online: 27 February 2014. doi. 10.1111/sltb.12087.

Li H, Chi I, Xu L (2013). Suicide ideation among older Chinese adults living in rural communities. *Gerontologist* 53, 218.

Lin PT, Dunn WA (2013). Suicidal carbon monoxide poisoning by combining formic acid and sulfuric acid within a confined space. *Journal of Forensic Sciences* 59, 271-273. doi: 10.1111/1556-4029.12297.

Lindor RA, Campbell RL, Pines JM, Melin GJ, Schipper AM, Goyal DG, Sadosty AT (2014). Emtala and patients with psychiatric emergencies: A review of relevant case law. *Annals of Emergency Medicine.* Published online: 31 January 2014. doi: 10.1016/j.annemergmed.2014.005.

Lopez Bernal J, Gasparrini A, Artundo C, McKee M (2014). Re: The effect of the late 2000s financial crisis on suicides in Spain: An interrupted time-series analysis. *European Journal of Public Health* 24, 183-184.

Loughlin AB, Gould MS, Kelleher C, Malone KM (2013). Completed suicide rates in later adolescence: Global trends. *Irish Journal of Medical Science* 182, S507.

Louis DM (2013). Bitch you must be crazy: Representations of mental illness in Ntozake Shange's for colored girls who consider suicide when the rainbow is enuf (1976). *Western Journal of Black Studies* 37, 197-211.

Lowen JT (2013). Warriors' hidden wounds: The VA tries to stem the rising suicide rate among veterans. *Minnesota Medicine* 96, 18-21.

Lowery AE, Starr T, Dhingra LK, Rogak L, Hamrick-Price JR, Farberov M, Kirsh KL, Saltz LB, Breitbart WS, Passik SD (2013). Frequency, characteristics, and correlates of pain in a pilot study of colorectal cancer survivors 1-10 years post-treatment. *Pain Medicine* 14, 1673-1680.

Lunetta P (2013). Atypical suicides or the first undiagnosed autoerotic deaths in Europe? *Journal of Forensic and Legal Medicine* 20, 1010-1013.

Luyten P, Blatt SJ, Fonagy P (2013). Impairments in self structures in depression and suicide in psychodynamic and cognitive behavioral approaches: Implications for clinical practice and research. *International Journal of Cognitive Therapy* 6, 265-279.

Lykouras L, Poulakou-Rebelakou E, Tsiamis C, Ploumpidis D (2013). Suicidal behaviour in the ancient Greek and Roman world. *Asian Journal of Psychiatry* 6, 548-551.

Lyoo YC, Ju S, Kim E, Kim JE, Lee JH (2013). The patient health questionnaire-15 and its abbreviated version as screening tools for depression in Korean college and graduate students. *Comprehensive Psychiatry* 55, 743-748.

Lysell H, Runeson B, Lichtenstein P, Långström N (2013). Risk factors for filicide and homicide: 36-year national matched cohort study. *Journal of Clinical Psychiatry* 75, 127-132.

Maignan M, Pommier P, Clot S, Saviuc P, Debaty G, Briot R, Carpentier F, Danel V (2013). Deliberate drug poisoning with slight symptoms on admission: Are there predictive factors for intensive care unit referral? A three-year retrospective study. *Basic and Clinical Pharmacology and Toxicology*. Published online: 3 September 2013. doi: 10.1111/bcpt.21232.

Malec K, Gasi ski M, Kuchta K, Kozok A (2013). Unsuccessful suicidal attempt with use of self-prepared bullet — case report. *Przeglad Lekarski* 70, 754-756.

Malphurs JE (2013). Suicide risk assessment for geriatric mental health populations in primary care settings. *Gerontologist* 53, 593.

Manca M, Presaghi F, Cerutti R (2013). Clinical specificity of acute versus chronic self-injury: Measurement and evaluation of repetitive non suicidal self-injury. *Psychiatry Research* 215, 111-119.

Manitt C, Eng C, Pokinko M, Ryan RT, Torres-Berrio A, Lopez JP, Yogendran SV, Daubaras MJ, Grant A, Schmidt ER, Tronche F, Krimpenfort P, Cooper HM, Pasterkamp RJ, Kolb B, Turecki G, Wong TP, Nestler EJ, Giros B, Flores C (2013). DCC orchestrates the development of the prefrontal cortex during adolescence and is altered in psychiatric patients. *Transl Psychiatry* 3, e338.

Marchand WR, Lee JN, Johnson S, Thatcher J, Gale P (2013). Striatal circuit function is associated with prior self-harm in remitted major depression. *Neuroscience Letters* 557, 154-158.

Marinelli LW, Thaker S, Borrup K, Shapiro DS, Bentley GC, Saleheen H, Lapidus G, Campbell BT (2013). Hartford's gun buy-back program: Are we on target? *Connecticut Medicine* 77, 453-459.

Martinaki S, Tsopelas C, Ploumpidis D, Douzenis A, Tzavara H, Skapinakis P, Mavreas V (2013). Evaluation of dangerousness of Greek mental patients. *Psychiatrike = Psychiatriki* 24, 185-196.

Marvasti JA, Wank AA (2013). Suicide in U.S. Veterans. *American Journal of Forensic Psychology* 31, 27-54.

Masuda N, Kurahashi I, Onari H (2014). Correction: Suicide ideation of individuals in online social networks. *PLoS ONE* 8, e62262.

Matarazzo BB, Barnes SM, Pease JL, Russell LM, Hanson JE, Soberay KA, Gutierrez PM (2014). Suicide risk among lesbian, gay, bisexual, and transgender military personnel and veterans: What does the literature tell us? *Suicide and Life-Threatening Behavior*. Published online: 3 February 2014. doi: 10.1111/sltb.12073.

Mawson AR, Xueyuan W (2013). Breastfeeding, retinoids, and postpartum depression: A new theory. *Journal of Affective Disorders* 150, 1129-1135.

Mbekou V, Gignac M, MacNeil S, Mackay P, Renaud J (2013). The CBCL dysregulated profile: An indicator of pediatric bipolar disorder or of psychopathology severity? *Journal of Affective Disorders* 155, 299-302.

McCall WV, Batson N, Webster M, Joshi I, Derreberry T, McDonough A, Farris S (2013). A psychometric cut-point to separate emergently suicidal depressed patients from stable depressed outpatients. *Indian Journal of Psychiatry* 55, 283-286.

McCarthy MJ, Wei H, Marnoy Z, Darvish RM, McPhie DL, Cohen BM, Welsh DK (2013). Genetic and clinical factors predict lithium's effects on PER2 gene expression rhythms in cells from bipolar disorder patients. *Translational Psychiatry* 3, e318.

McDonald H (2013). Et ego in Atlantis: A possible source for quentin cornpson's suicide. *Southern Literary Journal* 46, 36-47.

McGowan P (2013). Berryman, sexton and the possibilities of poetic language. *English* 62, 380-404.

McNamara RF, Ruys JF (2014). Unlocking the silences of the self-murdered: Textual approaches to suicidal emotions in the middle ages. *Exemplaria* 26, 58-80.

McRenolds DDO, Mehta PMD, Nasrallah HAMD (2013). Evaluation and treatment strategies in patients with schizophrenia and comorbid depression. *Psychiatric Annals* 43, 446-453.

Meixner C, O'Donoghue CR, Witt M (2013). Accessing crisis intervention services after brain injury: A mixed methods study. *Rehabilitation Psychology* 58, 377-385.

Mellanby RJ (2013). Improving wellbeing in the veterinary profession: Recent advances and future challenges. *Veterinary Record* 173, 264-265.

Mendelson D, Freckelton I (2013). The interface of the civil and criminal law of suicide at common law (1194-1845). *International Journal of Law and Psychiatry* 36, 343-349.

Mendez-Bustos P, de Leon-Martinez V, Miret M, Baca-Garcia E, Lopez-Castroman J (2013). Suicide reattempters: A systematic review. *Harvard Review of Psychiatry* 21, 281-295.

Mezuk B, Lohman M, Leslie M, Powell V (2013). Suicide risk in senior living communities: Evidence from the Virginia violent death reporting system. *Gerontologist* 53, 593.

Michas G (2013). Suicides in Greece: A light at the end of the tunnel. *British Medical Journal (Clinical Research Ed)* 347, f6249.

Miranda R, Shaffer D (2013). Understanding the suicidal moment in adolescence. *Annals of the New York Academy of Sciences* 1304, 14-21.

Młyniec K, Doboszewska U, Szewczyk B, Sowa-Ku ma M, Misztak P, Piekoszewski W, Trela F, Ostachowicz B, Nowak G (2014). The involvement of the GPR39-Zn(2+)-sensing receptor in the pathophysiology of depression. Studies in rodent models and suicide victims. *Neuropharmacology* 79, 290-297.

Moffitt LB, Garcia-Williams A, Berg JP, Calderon ME, Haas AP, Kaslow NJ (2014). Reaching graduate students at risk for suicidal behavior through the interactive screening program. *Journal of College Student Psychotherapy* 28, 23-34.

Molero P, Grunebaum MF, Galfalvy HC, Bongiovi MA, Lowenthal D, Almeida MG, Burke AK, Stevenson E, Mann JJ, Oquendo MA (2013). Past suicide attempts in depressed inpatients: Clinical versus research assessment. *Archives of Suicide Research* 18, 50-57.

Molloy L, Brady M, Beckett P, Pertile J (2014). Near-hanging and its management in the acute inpatient mental health setting. *Journal of Psychosocial Nursing and Mental Health Services.* Published online: 21 January 2014. doi: 10.3928/02793695-20140110-01.

Monsalve EM, García-Gutiérrez MS, Navarrete F, Giner S, Laborda J, Manzanares J (2013). Abnormal expression pattern of notch receptors, ligands, and downstream effectors in the dorsolateral prefrontal cortex and amygdala of suicidal victims. *Molecular Neurobiology* 49, 957-965.

Moon S (2013). Living memory of Roh Moo Hyun: Group cohesion, cultural politics, and the process of symbolic interaction. *Memory Studies* 6, 174-190.

Moore MD, Recker NL, Heirigs M (2014). Suicide and the creative class. *Social Indicators Research.* Published online: 11 January 2014. doi: 10.1007/s11205-013-0566-6.

Morey CM (2014). The influence of intergenerational family dynamics on suicidal behavior: Conceptualization, assessment, and intervention. *Smith College Studies in Social Work* 84, 5-22.

Muehlenkamp JJ, Claes L, Quigley K, Prosser E, Claes S, Jans D (2013). Association of training on attitudes towards self-injuring clients across health professionals. *Archives of Suicide Research* 17, 462-468.

Mumoli L, Ciriaco M, Gambardella A, Bombardiere G, Valentino P, Palleria C, Labate A, Russo E (2013). A possible case of natalizumab-dependent suicide attempt: A brief review about drugs and suicide. *Journal of Pharmacology and Pharmacotherapeutics* 4, S90-S93.

Nahvi S, Wu B, Richter KP, Bernstein SL, Arnsten JH (2013). Low incidence of adverse events following varenicline initiation among opioid dependent smokers with comorbid psychiatric illness. *Drug and Alcohol Dependence* 132, 47-52.

Neavyn MJ (2013). Suicide and the surrogate. *Journal of Medical Toxicology* 10, 3-6.

Nebhinani M, Nebhinani N, Tamphasana L, Gaikwad A (2013). Nursing students' attitude towards suicide attempters: A study from rural part of northern India. *Journal of Neurosciences in Rural Practice* 4, 400-407.

Nelson JC, Collins A, Foster T, Cooper SJ (2013). Religious beliefs and attitudes toward suicide in a cohort of medical students at Queen's university Belfast. *Ulster Medical Journal* 82, 194-195.

Nery-Fernandes F, Miranda-Scippa A (2013). Suicidal behavior in bipolar affective disorder and socio-demographic, clinical and neuroanatomical characteristics associated. *Revista de Psiquiatria Clinica* 40, 220-224.

Neufeld E (2013). Suicide prevention among older adults receiving home care: Evidence for risk and protective factors. *Gerontologist* 53, 487-487.

Nielsen T, Powell RA, Kuiken D (2013). Nightmare frequency is related to a propensity for mirror behaviors. *Consciousness and Cognition* 22, 1181-1188.

Nikolic S, Jukovic F, Zivkovic V (2013). An unusual complete laryngo-tracheal separation in a suicidal hanging with a drop effect. *Forensic Science, Medicine, and Pathology* 10, 133-135.

Nikolic S, Zivkovic V (2014). Cervical spine injuries in suicidal hanging without a long-drop-patterns and possible underlying mechanisms of injury: An autopsy study. *Forensic Science, Medicine, and Pathology* 10, 193-197.

Nikoli S, Živkovi V (2013). A train-related fatality-old dilemmas: Accident, suicide, or homicide? Premortem or postmortem decapitation? *Forensic Science, Medicine, and Pathology* 10, 278-283.

Novak H, Jacobs D (2013). Relational suicide assessment: Risks, resources, and possibilities for safety. *Psychiatric Services* 64, e02.

O'Brien KHM, Becker SJ, Spirito A, Simon V, Prinstein MJ (2014). Differentiating adolescent suicide attempters from ideators: Examining the interaction between depression severity and alcohol use. *Suicide and Life-Threatening Behavior* 44, 23-33.

O'Connor N, Large M, Oakley-Browne M, Paton M, Ryan C, Scott C, Keller A (2013). Clinical risk categorisation is valuable in the prevention of suicide and severe violence. *Australian and New Zealand Journal of Psychiatry* 47, 32-33.

O'Dowd A (2014). Share information about patients to tackle static suicide rate, doctors are told. *British Medical Journal (Clinical Research Ed)* 348, g400.

O'Leary FM, Lo MCI, Schreuder FB (2013). "Cuts are costly": A review of deliberate self-harm admissions to a district general hospital plastic surgery department over a 12-month period. *Journal of Plastic, Reconstructive and Aesthetic Surgery* 67, e109-e110.

O'Riley A, King D, Wood JR, Cross W (2013). Increase your suicide prevention skills with older veterans web-based training. *Gerontologist* 53, 359.

Obida M, Clark C, Govender I (2013). Reasons for parasuicide among patients admitted to Tshilidzini hospital, Limpopo province: A qualitative study. *South African Journal of Psychiatry* 19, 222-225.

Okazi A, Taghaddosinejad F, Mobaraki H, Kadkhodaei AR, Yousefinejad V (2014). "Bowel wall hemorrhage": A characteristic sign in hanging death. *Journal of Forensic and Legal Medicine* 21, 42-45.

Olfson M, Marcus SC, Bridge JA (2014). Focusing suicide prevention on periods of high risk. *JAMA* 311, 1107-1108.

Orkin AM, Rajaram N, Schwandt M (2013). Aboriginal populations and youth suicide. *Canadian Medical Association Journal* 185, 1347.

Pallett JR, Sutherland E, Glucksman E, Tunnicliff M, Keep JW (2014). A cross-sectional study of knife injuries at a London major trauma centre. *Annals of the Royal College of Surgeons of England* 96, 23-26.

Pandey GN, Rizavi HS, Ren X, Bhaumik R, Dwivedi Y (2014). Toll-like receptors in the depressed and suicide brain. *Journal of Psychiatric Research* 53, 62-68.

Park M, Jun H (2013). Elderly depression trajectory and suicide ideation in South Korea. *Gerontologist* 53, 288.

Park S, Ahn MH, Na R, Kim SO, Yoon JS, Park JH, Hong JP (2013). Factors associated with suicide method among psychiatric patients in a general hospital in Korea. *Psychiatry Research* 210, 945-950.

Paska AV, Zupanc T, Pregelj P (2013). The role of brain-derived neurotrophic factor in the pathophysiology of suicidal behavior. *Psychiatria Danubina* 25, 341-344.

Patnaik A, Mishra SS (2013). Self-inflicted penetrating injury to head with complete preservation of consciousness in a psychotic patient. *Journal of Neurosciences in Rural Practice* 4, 371-373.

Patton GC (2014). Youth suicide: New angles on an old problem. *Journal of Adolescent Health* 54, 245-246.

Paty JP (2013). Suicidal ideation and behavior: We can make a difference. *Applied Clinical Trials* 22, 42.

Pearson M, Zwi AB, Buckley NA, Manuweera G, Fernando R, Dawson AH, McDuie-Ra D (2013). Policymaking 'under the radar': A case study of pesticide regulation to prevent intentional poisoning in Sri Lanka. *Health Policy and Planning*. Published online: 20 December 2013. doi: 10.1093/heapol/czt096.

Pearson M, Zwi AB, Rouse AK, Fernando R, Buckley NA, McDuie-Ra D (2014). Taking stock - what is known about suicide in Sri Lanka. *Crisis* 35, 90-101.

Pelfrey Jr WV, Weber N (2013). Talking smack and the telephone game: Conceptualizing cyberbullying with middle and high school youth. *Journal of Youth Studies* 17, 397-414.

Pereira AR, Vieira DN, Magalhaes T (2013). Fatal intimate partner violence against women in Portugal: A forensic medical national study. *Journal of Forensic and Legal Medicine* 20, 1099-1107.

Petersen L, Sorensen TI, Andersen PK, Mortensen PB, Hawton K (2014). Correction: Genetic and familial environmental effects on suicide - an adoption study of siblings. *PLoS ONE*. Published online: 6 January 2014. doi: 10.1371/annotation/41113674-7ca2-42a5-a364-f646ff85c2e7.

Pitman AL, Osborn D, King M (2013). The effect of suicide bereavement on suicidal behaviour: A national cross-sectional survey of young adults in the UK. *The Lancet* 382, 81.

Podgorski C, Van Orden KA, Conwell Y (2013). Suicide risk among older adults: Identifying points of engagement. *Gerontologist* 53, 593.

Polling C, Dutta R (2014). Adolescents with emotional, conduct and hyperkinetic disorders who are experiencing psychotic symptoms may be at increased risk of suicide attempt. *Evidence-Based Mental Health* 17, 19.

Pompili M, Serafini G, Innamorati M, Biondi M, Girardi N, Murri MB, Amore M, Lester D, Girardi P (2013). Impulsivity, aggression, and suicide risk in patients with schizophrenia. *Psychiatric Annals* 43, 458-462.

Potard C, Kubiszewski V, Gimenes G, Courtois R (2013). Validation of the French version of the suicidal ideation questionnaire among adolescents. *Psychiatry Research* 215, 471-476.

Potticary J (2013). Biomarker series could help identify suicide risk. *Bioanalysis* 5, 2449.

Price EC (2013). Impulsivity and suicidal ideation or attempt in younger and older adults. *Gerontologist* 53, 359.

Pridemore WA (2014). Reply to norstrom (2014): The social epidemiology of alcohol and suicide-the struggle to formulate, debate and test social theory in the context of epidemiology and public health journals. *Addiction* 109, 191-192 .

Pridmore SA, Auchincloss S, Soh NL, Walter GJ (2013). Four centuries of suicide in opera. *Medical Journal of Australia* 199, 783-786.

Prokesch BC, Mangino JE (2013). Nail gun attempted suicide and traumatic ventricular perforations. *QJM*. Published online: 26 November 2013. doi: 10.1093/qjmed/hct237.

Püschel K, Gehl A, Tzikas A, Hasegawa I (2013). Suicidal cardiac tamponade by a skewer. *Forensic Science, Medicine, and Pathology* 9, 591-593.

Quaglio G, Karapiperis T, Van Woensel L, Arnold E, McDaid D (2013). Austerity and health in Europe. *Health Policy* 113, 13-19.

Rafnsson V, Kristbjornsdottir A (2014). Increased cardiovascular mortality and suicide after methyl chloride exposure. *American Journal of Industrial Medicine* 57, 108-113.

Raja M, Soleti F, Bentivoglio AR (2013). Lithium treatment in patients with huntington disease and suicidal behavior. *Journal of Clinical Psychopharmacology* 33, 819-821.

Ratta-Apha W, Hishimoto A, Mouri K, Shiroiwa K, Sasada T, Yoshida M, Okazaki S, Supriyanto I, Asano M, Ueno Y, Shirakawa O, Sora I (2013). Haplotype analysis of the DISC1 Ser704Cys variant in Japanese suicide completers. *Psychiatry Research* 215, 249-251.

Rau T, Plener P, Kliemann A, Fegert JM, Allroggen M (2013). Suicidality among medical students - a practical guide for staff members in medical schools. *GMS Zeitschrift für Medizinische Ausbildung* 30, Doc48.

Reavley NJ, Jorm AF (2014). Willingness to disclose a mental disorder and knowledge of disorders in others: Changes in Australia over 16 years. *Australian and New Zealand Journal of Psychiatry* 48, 162-168.

Redd CS, Lester D (2013). Lack of racial and sex stereotypes in the prediction of completed suicide. *Psychological Reports* 113, 987-993.

Renshaw J (2013). Dentist suicides. *British Dental Journal* 215, 593-594.

Rezaeian M (2013). Why it is so important to prevent self-immolation around the globe? *Burns* 39, 1322-1323.

Rhodes AE, Skinner R, McFaull S, Katz LY (2013). Canada-wide effect of regulatory warnings on antidepressant prescribing and suicide rates in boys and girls. *Canadian Journal of Psychiatry* 58, 640-645.

Ribbon G (2013). Campaigning against youth suicide. *Kai Tiaki Nursing New Zealand* 19, 34.

Ribeiro JD, Witte TK, Van Orden KA, Selby EA, Gordon KH, Bender TW, Joiner TE (2013). Fearlessness about death: The psychometric properties and construct validity of the revision to the acquired capability for suicide scale. *Psychological Assessment* 26, 115-126.

Rice T, Sher L (2013). Neuroendocrinology of emotion regulation and suicide risk in adolescents. *Neuropsychiatry* 3, 551-554.

Richard-Devantoy S, Annweiler C, Le Gall D, Beauchet O (2014). Cognitive deficits in a suicidal depressed alzheimer's patient: A specific vulnerability? *International Journal of Geriatric Psychiatry* 29, 326-328.

Richard-Devantoy S, Orsat M, Dumais A, Turecki G, Jollant F (2014). Neurocognitive vulnerability: Suicidal and homicidal behaviours in patients with schizophrenia. *Canadian Journal of Psychiatry* 59, 18-25.

Richards TN, Gillespie LK, Smith MD (2014). An examination of the media portrayal of femicide-suicides an exploratory frame analysis. *Feminist Criminology* 9, 24-44.

Richardson T, Elliott P, Roberts R (2013). The relationship between personal unsecured debt and mental and physical health: A systematic review and meta-analysis. *Clinical Psychology Review* 33, 1148-1162.

Roaldset JO, Linaker OM, Bjorkly S (2014). Triglycerides as a biological marker of repeated rehospitalization resulting from deliberate self-harm in acute psychiatry patients: A prospective observational study. *BMC Psychiatry* 14, 54.

Roca M, Gili M, Garcia-Campayo J, García-Toro M (2013). Economic crisis and mental health in Spain. *The Lancet* 382, 1977.

Rockett IRH, Kapusta ND, Coben JH (2014). Beyond suicide: Action needed to improve self-injury mortality accounting. *JAMA Psychiatry* 71, 231-232.

Rogers JR, Russell EJ (2014). A framework for bridging cultural barriers in suicide risk assessment: The role of compatibility heuristics. *Counseling Psychologist* 42, 55-72.

Romm J (2014). Dying every day: The suicides of Seneca and Nero. *Yale Review* 102, 1-32.

Roos L, Sareen J, Bolton JM (2013). Suicide risk assessment tools, predictive validity findings and utility today: Time for a revamp? *Neuropsychiatry* 3, 483-495.

Root R, Whiteside A (2013). A qualitative study of community home-based care and antiretroviral adherence in Swaziland. *Journal of the International AIDS Society* 16, 17978.

Rosellini AJ, Bagge CL (2014). Temperament, hopelessness, and attempted suicide: Direct and indirect effects. *Suicide and Life Threatening Behavior*. Published online: 4 February 2014. doi: 10.1111/sltb.12078.

Rottman J, Kelemen D, Young L (2014). Tainting the soul: Purity concerns predict moral judgments of suicide. *Cognition* 130, 217-226.

Roy-Byrne P (2013). Suicide: The long and winding road from research to practice. *Depression and Anxiety* 30, 893-895.

Roy A, Roy M, Deb S, Unwin G, Roy A (2014). Are opioid antagonists effective in reducing self-injury in adults with intellectual disability? A systematic review. *Journal of Intellectual Disability Research*. Published online: 7 January 2014. doi: 10.1111/jir.12111.

Russell PSS, Nair MKC (2013). Adad 1: Rationale and study design for anxiety disorders among adolescents in a rural community population in India. *Indian Journal of Pediatrics* 80 Suppl 2, 132-138.

Ryan CJ, Large M (2013). Suicide screening in general hospitals. *Psychosomatics* 54, 604-605.

Ryan CJ, Large MM, Callaghan S (2013). Re: Suicide risk assessment: Where are we now? *Medical Journal of Australia* 199, 534.

Salari S (2013). Loved to death? Media portrayals of murder suicide: Ageism, sexism and dangerous romantic themes. *Gerontologist* 53, 280-281.

Samples TC, Woods A, Davis TA, Rhodes M, Shahane A, Kaslow NJ (2014). Race of interviewer effect on disclosures of suicidal low-income African American women. *Journal of Black Psychology* 40, 27-46.

Sandberg-Thoma SE, Kamp Dush CM (2014). Indicators of adolescent depression and relationship progression in emerging adulthood. *Journal of Marriage and Family* 76, 191-206.

Sansone RA, Chang J, Sellbom M, Jewell B (2013). Bully victims and borderline personality symptomatology. *International Journal of Social Psychiatry* 59, 193-194.

Sansone RA, Sansone LA (2013). Sunshine, serotonin, and skin: A partial explanation for seasonal patterns in psychopathology? *Innovations in Clinical Neuroscience* 10, 20-24.

Sansone RA, Wiederman MW (2013). Exercising an injury on purpose: Relationships with borderline personality symptomatology. *Primary Care Companion to CNS Disorders* 15, 01424.

Savitsky TD, Dalal SR (2013). Bayesian non-parametric analysis of multirater ordinal data, with application to prioritizing research goals for prevention of suicide. *Journal of the Royal Statistical Society Series C: Applied Statistics.* Published online: 6 November 2013. doi: 10.1111/rssc.12049.

Seager M (2013). Male suicide and health inequality. *Psychologist* 26, 707.

Senarathna L, Hunter C, Dawson AH, Dibley MJ (2013). Social dynamics in rural Sri Lankan hospitals: Revelations from self-poisoning cases. *Qualitative Health Research* 23, 1481-1494.

Serafini G, Pompili M, Hansen KF, Obrietan K, Dwivedi Y, Amore M, Shomron N, Girardi P (2013). MicroRNAs: Fundamental regulators of gene expression in major affective disorders and suicidal behavior? *Frontiers in Cellular Neuroscience.* Published online: 15 November 2013. doi: 10.3389/fncel.2013.00208.

Serafini G, Pompili M, Seretti ME, Stefani H, Palermo M, Coryell W, Girardi P (2013). The role of inflammatory cytokines in suicidal behavior: A systematic review. *European Neuropsychopharmacology* 23, 1672-1686.

Shahtahmasebi S (2013). Examining the claim that 80-90% of suicide cases had depression. *Frontiers in Public Health* 1, 62.

Shaikh MA (2014). Prevalence and correlates of suicidal expression among school attending adolescents in Pakistan. *Journal of the Pakistan Medical Association* 64, 99-100.

Shaikh MMM, Chotaliya HJ, Modi AD, Parmar AP, Kalele SD (2013). A study of gross postmortem findings in cases of hanging and ligature strangulation. *Journal of Indian Academy of Forensic Medicine* 35, 63-65.

Shaw J, Dillard D (2013). Community perspectives on protective and contributing factors in Alaska native/American Indian suicide. *International Journal of Circumpolar Health* 72, 262-262.

Sheldon T (2013). Gp's suicide after suspension for administering an overdose provokes a storm in the Netherlands. *British Medical Journal* 347, F6673.

Sheppard K (2013). Deaf adults and health care: Giving voice to their stories. *Journal of the American Association of Nurse Practioners.* Published online: 21 November 2013. doi: 10.1002/2327-6942.12087.

Sher L (2014). Alcohol, testosterone and suicide. *Australian and New Zealand Journal of Psychiatry.* Published online: 24 February 2014. doi: 10.1177/0004867414525845.

Sher L, Braquehais MD (2013). Suicidal behavior in military veterans and health care professionals. *Australian and New Zealand Journal of Psychiatry.* Published online: 23 Decmber 2013. doi: 10.1177/0004867413517761.

Shireen F, Janapana H, Rehmatullah S, Temuri H, Azim F (2013). Trauma experience of youngsters and teens: A key issue in suicidal behavior among victims of bullying? *Pakistan Journal of Medical Sciences* 30, 206-210.

Shorter E, Wachtel LE (2013). Self-injurious behaviour in children: A treatable catatonic syndrome. *Australian and New Zealand Journal of Psychiatry* 47, 113-115.

Shultz E, Pandya M, Mehta N (2013). Technology and teaching: Suicide risk assessment. *Medical Education* 47, 1132-1133.

Silverman MM, Berman AL (2014). Suicide risk assessment and risk formulation part I: A focus on suicide ideation in assessing suicide risk. *Suicide and Life-Threatening Behavior*. Published online : 9 January 2014. doi: 10.1111/sltb.12065.

Sinclair RD (2014). Alopecia areata and suicide of children. *Medical Journal of Australia* 200, 145.

Singh D, Vohra V (2013). Histopathological study of lymph nodes in hanging and strangulation deaths. *Journal of Indian Academy of Forensic Medicine* 35, 137-139.

Siqueira Drake A (2013). The use of core competencies in suicide risk assessment and management in supervision: A feminist-narrative approach. *Journal of Feminist Family Therapy* 25, 183-199.

Slade K, Edelman R (2013). Can theory predict the process of suicide on entry to prison? *Crisis* 52, 82-89.

Slavich GM, Zimbardo PG (2013). Out of mind, out of sight: Unexpected scene elements frequently go unnoticed until primed. *Current Psychology* 32, 301-317.

Smalheiser NR, Lugli G, Zhang H, Rizavi H, Cook EH, Dwivedi Y (2014). Expression of microRNAs and other small RNAs in prefrontal cortex in schizophrenia, bipolar disorder and depressed subjects. *PLoS ONE* 9, e86469.

Sommerville DM (2013). "A burden too heavy to bear": War trauma, suicide, and confederate soldiers. *Civil War History* 59, 453-491.

Song TM, Song J, An JY, Hayman LL, Woo JM (2014). Psychological and social factors affecting internet searches on suicide in Korea: A big data analysis of google search trends. *Yonsei Medical Journal* 55, 254-263.

Sowa-Ku ma M, Szewczyk B, Sadlik K, Piekoszewski W, Trela F, Opoka W, Poleszak E, Pilc A, Nowak G (2013). Zinc, magnesium and nmda receptor alterations in the hippocampus of suicide victims. *Journal of Affective Disorders* 151, 924-931.

Spehr S, Dixon J (2013). Protest suicide: A systematic model with heuristic archetypes. *Journal for the Theory of Social Behaviour*. Published online: 1 December 2013. doi: 10.1111/jtsb.12047.

Squassina A, Manchia M, Chillotti C, Deiana V, Congiu D, Paribello F, Roncada P, Soggiu A, Piras C, Urbani A, Robertson GS, Keddy P, Turecki G, Rouleau GA, Alda M, Del Zompo M (2013). Differential effect of lithium on spermidine/spermine N1-acetyltransferase expression in suicidal behaviour. *The International Journal of Neuropsychopharmacology*, 2209-2218.

Stange JP, Sylvia LG, da Silva Magalhães PV, Miklowitz DJ, Otto MW, Frank E, Berk M, Hansen NS, Dougherty DD, Nierenberg AA, Deckersbach T (2014). Extreme attributions predict suicidal ideation and suicide attempts in bipolar disorder: Prospective data from STEP-BD. *World Psychiatry* 13, 95-96.

Sternudd HT (2014). 'I like to see blood': Visuality and self-cutting. *Visual Studies* 29, 14-29.

Stone MB, Hammad TA (2013). Fluoxetine and suicidal ideation in minor depression. *Journal of Psychiatric Research* 48, 131-132.

Sutherland O, Breen AV, Lewis SP (2013). Discursive narrative analysis: A study of online autobiographical accounts of self-injury. *Qualitative Report* 18, 1.

Swanson SA, Colman I (2013). Aboriginal populations and youth suicide response. *Canadian Medical Association Journal* 185, 1347.

Szabo A, Milfont TL, Merry SN, Robinson EM, Crengle S, Ameratunga SN, Denny SJ (2013). Equivalence of the short form of the Reynolds adolescent depression scale across groups. *Journal of Clinical Child and Adolescent Psychology*. Published online: 18 November 2013. doi: 10.1080/15374416.2013.848770.

Szentes B, Thomas CD (2013). An evolutionary theory of suicide. *Games* 4, 426-436.

Taastrom A, Klahn J, Staal N, Thomsen PH, Johansen A (2013). Children and adolescents in the psychiatric emergency department: A 10-year survey in Copenhagen county. *Nordic Journal of Psychiatry*. Published online: 28 October 2013. doi: 10.3109/08039488.2013.846410.

Tam P (2013). Commentary on 'the association between problematic internet use and depression, suicidal ideation and bipolar disorder in Korean adolescents'. *Australian and New Zealand Journal of Psychiatry* 47, 185-186.

Tanik FA (2014). Health-care reform in Turkey: Far from perfect. *The Lancet* 383, 28.

Tarbah F, Barguil Y, Müller C, Rickert A, Weinmann W, Nour M, Kintz P, Daldrup T (2013). Chromatographic hair analysis for natural kavalactones and their metabolites. A preliminary study. *Annales de Toxicologie Analytique* 25, 109-119.

Telisinghe PU, Colombage SM (2014). Patterns of suicide in Brunei Darussalam and comparison with neighbouring countries in South East Asia. *Journal of Forensic and Legal Medicine* 22, 16-19.

Thollon L, Llari M, André L, Adalian P, Leonetti G, Piercecchi-Marti MD (2013). Biomechanical analysis of skull fractures after uncontrolled hanging release. *Forensic Science International* 233, 220-229.

Tighe J, McKay K, Maple M (2013). 'I'm going to kill myself if you don't...': Contextual aspects of suicide in Australian Aboriginal communities. *International Journal of Culture and Mental Health*. Published online: 19 December 2013. doi: 10.1080/17542863.2013.861499.

Too LS, Milner A, Bugeja L, McClure R (2014). The socio-environmental determinants of railway suicide: A systematic review. *BMC Public Health* 14, 20.

Tran T, Luo W, Phung D, Harvey R, Berk M, Kennedy RL, Venkatesh S (2014). Risk stratification using data from electronic medical records better predicts suicide risks than clinician assessments. *BMC Psychiatry* 14, 76.

Tran T, Phung D, Luo W, Venkatesh S (2014). Stabilized sparse ordinal regression for medical risk stratification. *Knowledge and Information Systems*. Published online: 17 March 2014. doi: 10.1007/s10115-014-0740-4.

Trygged S, Hedlund E, Kareholt I (2014). Living in danger: Previous violence, socioeconomic position, and mortality risk among women over a 10-year period. *Social Work in Public Health* 29, 114-120.

Tully PJ, Wittert G, Selkow T, Baumeister H (2014). The real world mental health needs of heart failure patients are not reflected by the depression randomized controlled trial evidence. *PLoS ONE* 9, e85928.

Tumram NK, Ambade VN, Bardale RV, Dixit PG (2014). Injuries over neck in hanging deaths and its relation with ligature material: Is it vital? *Journal of Forensic and Legal Medicine* 22, 80-83.

Turecki G (2013). Polyamines and suicide risk. *Molecular Psychiatry* 18, 1242-1243.

Turkmen Z, Mercan S, Bavunoglu I, Cengiz S (2013). Development and validation of a densitometric-high-performance thin-layer chromatographic method for quantitative analysis of amitriptyline in gastric lavage. *Journal of Planar Chromatography-Modern Tlc* 26, 496-501.

Turner BJ, Chapman AL, Gratz KL (2013). Why stop self-injuring? Development of the reasons to stop self-injury questionnaire. *Behavior Modification*. Published online: 3 December 2013. doi: 10.1177/0145445513508977.

Umhau JC, George DT, Heaney RP, Lewis MD, Ursano RJ, Heilig M, Hibbeln JR, Schwandt ML (2013). Correction: Low vitamin d status and suicide: A case-control study of active duty military service members. *PLoS ONE*. Published online: 19 September 2013. doi: 10.1371/annotation/9af84cbe-5576-4c4b-871c-f7ab0c64b9fd.

Uys H (2013). Agents used and profiles of non-fatal suicidal behaviour in east London. *South African Journal of Psychiatry* 19, 109-110.

van Dulmen MHM, Goossens L (2013). Loneliness trajectories. *Journal of Adolescence* 36, 1247-1249.

van Heeringen K (2014). Brain imaging: Healthy networks for suicide prevention. *Crisis* 35, 1-4.

Van Orden K, Wiktorsson S, Berg A, Fassberg MM, Duberstein P, Waern M (2013). Attempted suicide in later life: An examination of the interpersonal theory of suicide. *Gerontologist* 53, 359.

Venta A, Sharp C (2013). Extending the concurrent validity of the self-injurious thoughts and behaviors interview to inpatient adolescents. *Journal of Psychopathology and Behavioral Assessment.* Published online: 13 December 2013. doi: 10.1007/s10862-013-9402-1.

Ventorp F (2013). The neurobiological basis of suicide. *Acta Psychiatrica Scandinavica* 128, 495.

Voelker R (2013). Firearm homicides decline while suicides involving guns increase. *JAMA* 310, 1219.

Wakefield JC, Schmitz MF (2014). Uncomplicated depression, suicide attempt, and the DSM-5 bereavement exclusion debate: An empirical evaluation. *Research on Social Work Practice* 24, 37-49.

Walter G, Pridmore S (2013). Understanding the causes of suicide: Psychological autopsies should not be our only resource. *Turk Psikiyatri Dergisi* 24, 285-286.

Wang CP, Jo B, Hendricks Brown C (2014). Causal inference in longitudinal comparative effectiveness studies with repeated measures of a continuous intermediate variable. *Statistics in Medicine.* Published online: 27 February 2014. doi: 10.1002/sim.6120.

Wang H, Xue Y, Chen Y, Zhang R, Wang H, Zhang Y, Gan J, Zhang L, Tan Q (2013). Efficacy of repetitive transcranial magnetic stimulation in the prevention of relapse of depression: Study protocol for a randomized controlled trial. *Trials* 14, 338.

Waniek K (2014). Reversed "betrayal funnel." A case of a children's home inmate who suffers from being disloyal to her alcoholic family. *Qualitative Sociology Review* 10, 60-78.

Webster LR (2014). Pain and suicide: The other side of the opioid story. *Pain Medicine* 15, 345-346.

Wee JH, Park JH, Choi SP, Park KN (2013). Outcomes of patients admitted for hanging injuries with decreased consciousness but without cardiac arrest. *American Journal of Emergency Medicine* 31, 1666-1670.

West E, Newton VL, Barton-Breck A (2013). Time frames and self-hurting: That was then, this is now. *Health, Risk & Society* 15, 580.

Westerlund M (2013). Talking suicide: Online conversations about a taboo subject. *Nordicom Review* 34, 35-46.

Wharff EA, Ross AM, Lambert S (2014). Field note - developing suicide risk assessment training for hospital social workers: An academic-community partnership. *Journal of Social Work Education* 50, 184-190.

Whitlock J, Wyman PA, Moore SR (2014). Connectedness and suicide prevention in adolescents: Pathways and implications. *Suicide and Life-Threatening Behavior.* Published online: 20 January 2014. doi: 10.1111/sltb.12071.

Wickens CM, Smart RG, Mann RE (2014). The impact of depression on driver performance. *International Journal of Mental Health and Addiction.* Published online: 8 March 2014. doi: 10.1007/s11469-014-9487-0.

Wiebe ER (2013). Invited commentary: How can we reconcile the findings of Keyes et al.'s study with the experience of our patients in clinical practice? *American Journal of Epidemiology* 178, 1389-1391.

Wilsnack SC, Wilsnack RW, Kantor LW (2013). Focus on: Women and the costs of alcohol use. *Alcohol Research-Current Reviews* 35, 219-228.

Wilson H (2013). Potential biomarkers of suicide risk identified. *Biomarkers in Medicine* 7, 686-686.

Wodarski JS (2013). Understanding suicide: Why we don't and how we might. *Journal of Evidence-Based Social Work* 10, 533-534.

Wolford-Clevenger C, Smith PN (2014). A theory-based approach to understanding suicide risk in shelter-seeking women. *Trauma Violence and Abuse*. Published online: 10 January 2014. doi: 10.1177/1524838013517562.

Wongpakaran T, Wongpakaran N (2013). Detection of suicide among the elderly in a long term care facility. *Clinical Interventions in Aging* 8, 1553-1559.

Wortzel HS, Shura RD, Brenner LA (2013). Chronic traumatic encephalopathy and suicide: A systematic review. *BioMed Research International* 2013, 424280.

Wu CY, Huang HC, Wu S, Sun FJ, Huang CR, Liu SI (2014). Validation of the Chinese SAD PERSONS scale to predict repeated self-harm in emergency attendees in Taiwan. *Acta Veterinaria Scandinavica* 14, 44.

Xerfan J (2013). Suicide movies: Social patterns 1900-2009. *International Journal of Social Psychiatry* 59, 304-305.

Xu Y, Phillips MR, Wang L, Chen Q, Li C, Wu X (2013). Retrospective identification of episodes of deliberate self-harm from emergency room registers in general hospitals: An example from Shanghai. *Archives of Suicide Research* 17, 345-359.

Yang K, Su J, Hu Z, Lang R, Sun X, Li X, Wang D, Wei M, Yin J (2013). Serotonin transporter (5-HTT) gene polymorphisms and susceptibility to epilepsy: A meta-analysis and meta-regression. *Genetic Testing and Molecular Biomarkers* 17, 890-897.

Yaseen ZS, Kopeykina I, Gutkovich Z, Bassirnia A, Cohen LJ, Galynker II (2014). Predictive validity of the suicide trigger scale (STS-3) for post-discharge suicide attempt in high-risk psychiatric inpatients. *PLoS ONE* 9, e86768.

Youngblut JM, Brooten D, Cantwell GP, del Moral T, Totapally B (2013). Parent health and functioning 13 months after infant or child NICU/PICU death. *Pediatrics* 132, E1295-E1301.

Yousuf S, Beh PS, Wong PW (2013). Attitudes towards suicide following an undergraduate suicide prevention module: Experience of medical students in Hong Kong. *Hong Kong Medical Journal* 19, 377-385.

Zanchin G, Bellamio M, Maggioni F (2014). Does suicide cause suicide headache? *Headache* 54, 745-746.

Zerbib P, Vinet A, Rogosnitzky M, Truant S, Chambon JP, Pruvot FR (2013). Gastrocele complicates the course of non-operated severe caustic injuries: Operative strategies. *World Journal of Surgery* 38, 1233-1237.

Zhang H, Chen Z, Jia Z, Gong Q (2014). Dysfunction of neural circuitry in depressive patients with suicidal behaviors: A review of structural and functional neuroimaging studies. *Progress in Neuro-Psychopharmacology and Biological Psychiatry* 53C, 61-66.

Zhang Y, Yip PS, Fu KW (2014). Validation of the Chinese version of the Reynolds' suicidal ideation questionnaire: Psychometric properties and its short version. *Health and Quality of Life Outcomes* 12, 33.

Zhao LX, Li HZ, Guo RY, Ma T, Hou RY, Ma XW, Du YF (2013). MiR-137, a new target for post-stroke depression? *Neural Regeneration Research* 8, 2441-2448.

Zupanc T, Pregelj P, Paska AV (2013). Tryptophan hydroxylase 2 (TPH 2) single nucleotide polymorphisms, suicide, and alcohol-related suicide. *Psychiatria Danubina* 25, 332-336.

www.ingramcontent.com/pod-product-compliance
Lightning Source LLC
Chambersburg PA
CBHW082353270326
41935CB00013B/1612